THE ENEMIES OF ROME

Also by Stephen P. Kershaw

The Search for Atlantis

THE ENEMIES OF
ROME

The Barbarian Rebellion
Against the Roman Empire

STEPHEN P. KERSHAW

PEGASUS BOOKS
NEW YORK LONDON

THE ENEMIES OF ROME

Pegasus Books, Ltd.
West 37th Street, 13th Floor
New York, NY 10018

Copyright © 2019 by Stephen P. Kershaw

First Pegasus Books hardcover edition January 2020

ISBN: 978-1-64313-310-2

10 9 8 7 6 5 4 3 2 1

Printed in the United States of America
Distributed by W. W. Norton & Company

In memoriam Dorothy Kershaw, AUC 2681–2771

Contents

CONTENTS

Acknowledgements

I owe a tremendous debt of gratitude to a great many individuals, groups and institutions without whose help, expertise and inspiration this book could never have been written. In no particular order, I would like to express my deepest thanks to many of my fellow ex-students and the brilliant teachers from Salterhebble County Primary School, Heath Grammar School ('Heathens' rather than barbarians) and Bristol University, without whose enthusiasm, dedication and know-how I would never have been able to engage with the ancient Romans, Greeks and barbarians, and their languages and culture. Among the many are Richard Sanderson, Alan 'Froggy' Guy, Frank Haigh and 'Big Jimmy Feesh', who ignited and sustained my interest in Roman history, and J. G. McQueen, Richard Jenkyns, Brian Warmington, Thomas Weidemann, Niall Rudd, Jim Tester, John Betts and Richard Buxton, who generously gave of their enormous knowledge. Also important to the process are my colleagues and students (both 'real' and 'virtual') at Oxford University Department for Continuing Education, European Studies, and the Victoria and Albert Museum, who, in their different ways, have facilitated my professional development in our explorations of the ancient world together. Credit must also go to all the fine people at Swan Hellenic, Cox & Kings, Learn Italy and Noble Caledonia, whose cultural itineraries have allowed me to explore the physical world of the Romans and barbarians in so much style. On the publishing side I give my heartfelt thanks to Duncan Proudfoot, Rebecca Sheppard, Howard Watson, Oliver Cotton and David Andrassy for their professional excellence in putting this book together. Underlying all this is the rock-solid support that my late parents, Philip and Dorothy Kershaw, gave me throughout my career, the love and understanding of my wife Lal, and Hero's faithful, and occasionally barbaric, canine companionship.

Maps

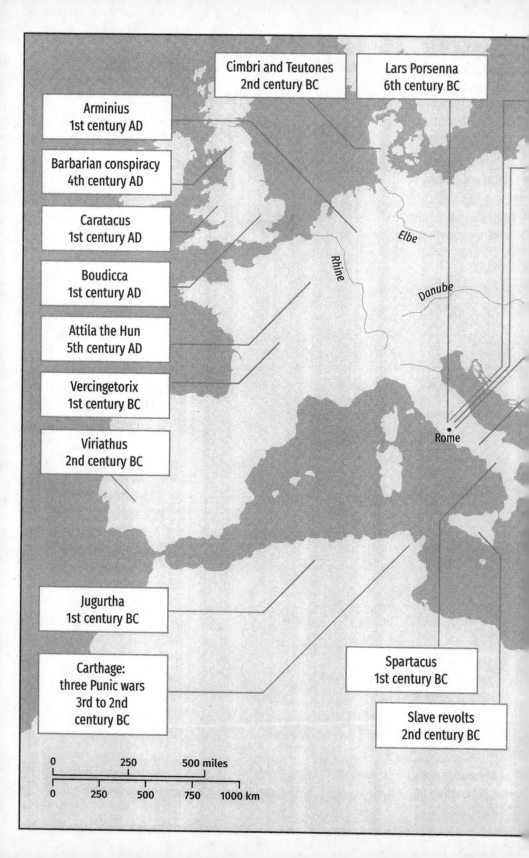

Cimbri and Teutones
2nd century BC

Lars Porsenna
6th century BC

Arminius
1st century AD

Barbarian conspiracy
4th century AD

Caratacus
1st century AD

Boudicca
1st century AD

Attila the Hun
5th century AD

Vercingetorix
1st century BC

Viriathus
2nd century BC

Jugurtha
1st century BC

Carthage:
three Punic wars
3rd to 2nd
century BC

Spartacus
1st century BC

Slave revolts
2nd century BC

Elbe

Rhine

Danube

Rome

0   250   500 miles
0   250   500   750   1000 km

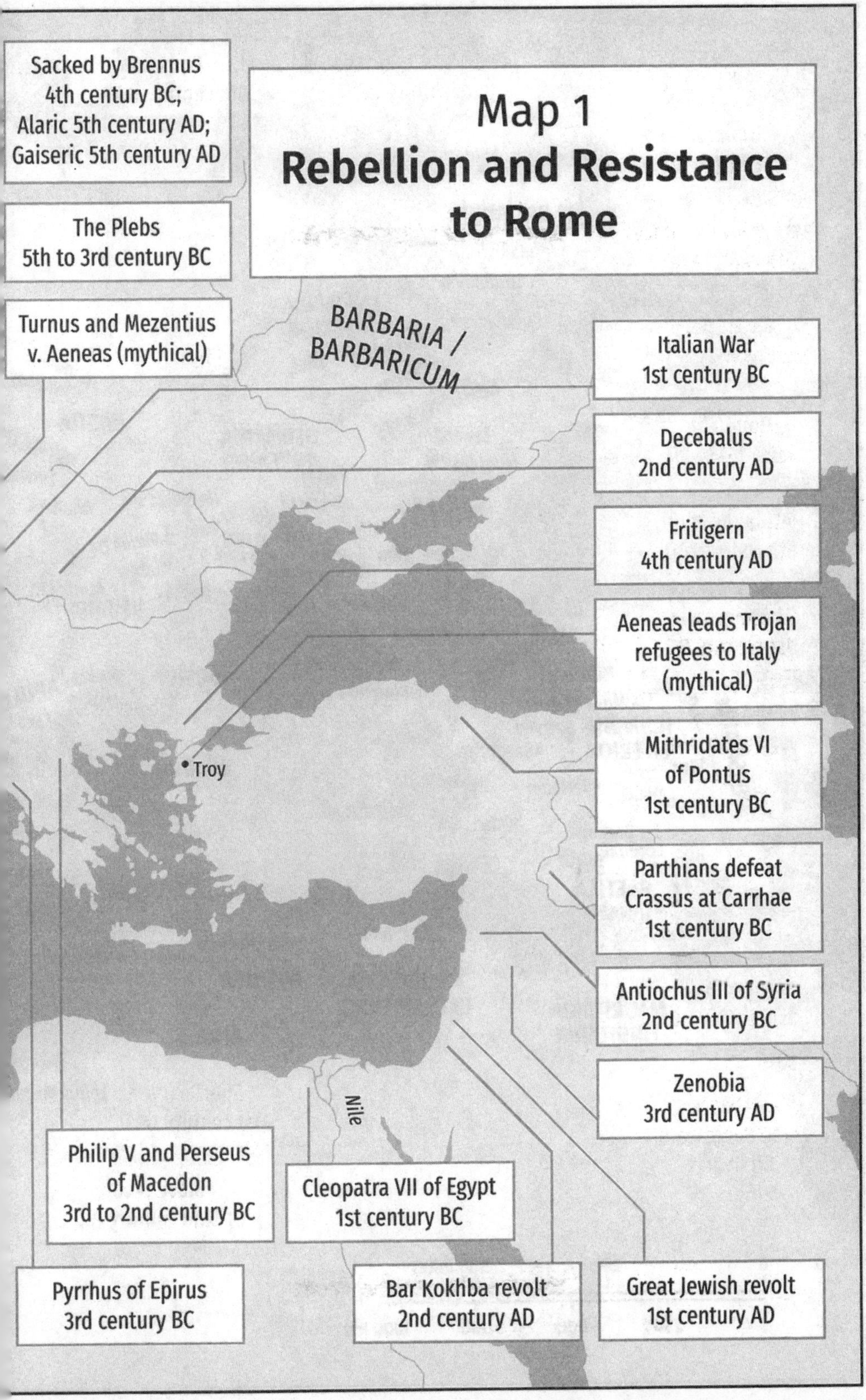

Map 1
Rebellion and Resistance to Rome

Sacked by Brennus
4th century BC;
Alaric 5th century AD;
Gaiseric 5th century AD

The Plebs
5th to 3rd century BC

Turnus and Mezentius
v. Aeneas (mythical)

BARBARIA /
BARBARICUM

Italian War
1st century BC

Decebalus
2nd century AD

Fritigern
4th century AD

Aeneas leads Trojan
refugees to Italy
(mythical)

Mithridates VI
of Pontus
1st century BC

Parthians defeat
Crassus at Carrhae
1st century BC

Antiochus III of Syria
2nd century BC

Zenobia
3rd century AD

• Troy

Nile

Philip V and Perseus
of Macedon
3rd to 2nd century BC

Cleopatra VII of Egypt
1st century BC

Pyrrhus of Epirus
3rd century BC

Bar Kokhba revolt
2nd century AD

Great Jewish revolt
1st century AD

Eboracum

BRITANNIA

Verulamium • Camulodunum
Londinium

**GERMANIA
INFERIOR**
BELGICA
Sequana (Seine) Trier
LUGDENENSIS
Rhenus (Rhine)
Cenabum
Liger (Loire)
Noviodunum • • Alesia
AQUITANIA • Bibracte
Lugdunum •
Garumna (Garonne) Avaricum
NARBONENSIS
**ALPES
COTTIAE**
Arelate
Nemausus **ALPES
MARITIMAE**
Iberus (Ebro) • Tolosa
Massilia
Numantia Narbo Martius
• Mons Veneris Emporiae
HISPANIA Segovia
Douro **CITERIOR** • Segobriga Tarraco
Tagus
Guadiana • Toletum • Saguntum
Sucro
Baecula *Balearic Is.*
Ilipa Corduba *Baetis*
Italica • **BAETICA** Carthago Nova /
Gades • • Tribola Cartagena

Caesarea

**MAURITANIA
TINGITANIA**

**MAURITANIA
CAESARIENSIS**

**GERMANIA
SUPERIOR**
RAETIA
Danuvius (Danube)
NORICU
Dravus
Mediolanum Aquileia
Mantua *Padus (Po)*
Mutina
Genua Ariminum
UMBRIA
Tiberis
CORSICA
Roma **APULI**
Ostia •
Cuma
SARDINIA Neapolis
Herculaneu
Pom
Rhegium
Syracuse

Utica Carthago **SICILIA**
Cirta • • Bulla Regia Agrigentum
Great Plains • Zama • Hadrumentum
NUMIDIA • Thapsus
• Capsa
AFRICA

Leptis Magna

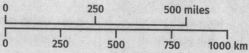

0   250   500 miles

0   250   500   750   1000 km

Map 2
The Roman
and Barbarian World

BARBARIA /
BARBARICUM

Borysthenes (Dneiper)

rnuntum •Aquincum
ANNONIA
SUPERIOR
PANNONIA
avus **INFERIOR**
•Sirmium   **DACIA**
                    Danuvius (Danube)
LYRICUM **MOESIA**   **MOESIA**
ALMATIA **SUPERIOR** **INFERIOR**
              THRACE
Dyrrhachium   Hebrus
rundisium   Amphipolis •Philippi Byzantium• •Libyssa
  •Apollonia Aegae•Thessalonica   •Nicomedia
rentum   •Pydna   Troy• Cyzicus• •Nicaea
Corcyra• Pharsalus Mytilene •Prusa
  Actium•   •Orchomenus •Pergamum
Leucas• **ACHAEA** Athens •Smyrna **ASIA**
  Corinth•   Ephesus• •Magnesia **LYCIA**
  Olympia• •Argos •Aphrodisias
              Sparta Delos   **PAMPHYLIA**
Peloponnese   Cybria
              Cos   Oenoanda Coracaesium
          Cnossos Rhodes
        CRETE

Panticapaeum

Pontus Euxinus
(Black Sea)

                Sinope
Amastris •   •
          BITHYNIA   **PONTUS** •Nicopolis
          Halys   Zela   Cabeira **ARMENIA**
          Ancyra• **GALATIA**
                          CAPPADOCIA
                  •Tyana
                CILICIA   Carrhae
                  •Tarsus   Euphrates
                  •Antiochia
                SYRIA •Palmyra
                  •Apamea

CYPRUS   •Damascus

        Tyre •
        Caesarea •
Canopus •Pelusium Jerusalem• **SYRIA**
  Alexandria Masada• **PALAESTINA**
Cyrene•   Petra •
CYRENE   **ARABIA**

        AEGYPTUS

Map 3
Rome's domination
of Italy to
the 1st century BC

First Samnite War 343–341 BC
Second Samnite War 326–304 BC
Third Samnite War 298–290 BC
Invasion by Pyrrhus 280–275 BC
First Punic War 264–241 BC
Second Punic War 218–201 BC
Slave Revolt in Sicily 135–132 and 104–100 BC
Italian / 'Social' War 91–88 BC
Spartacus' Revolt 73–71 BC

ALPS

Mediolanum
Verona
Ticinum • Trebia
Placentia
River Po
• Mutina

LIGURIA

Ariminum
River Metaurus
Sena Gallica
• Ancona

ILLYRICUM

Pisae •
Arretium
Lake Trasimene
Perusia
Volterrae •

PICENUM
SABINES
• Asculum

ETRURIA

Reate
• Corfinium
Alba Longa

CORSICA

MARSI/PAELIGNI

Tarquinii •
Fidenae • Veii
Antemnae • Capena
Rome • Tusculum
Lavinium • RUTULI
Ardea • Aricia

SAMNITES

• Arpi
• Cannae
• Asculum (in Apulia)
• Venusia

• Aquinum
Capua •
Cumae • Maleventum/Beneventum
Neapolis • Mt. Vesuvius
Pompeii

APULIA
• Brundisium

SARDINIA

• Forum Annii
LUCANIA

• Tarentum
• Metapontum
• Heraclea

• Thurii

BRUTII

Straits of Messina
• Locri

Eryx
• Panormus
Segesta
Aegates Islands
• Halycae
Lilybaeum • Selinus
SICILIA

Messana • Rhegium
Tauromenium
• Enna
• Catana
Leontini

Heraclea • Agrigentum
• Syracuse

Roman, Latin and Allied Territory 298–263 BC

Annexations 241–218 BC

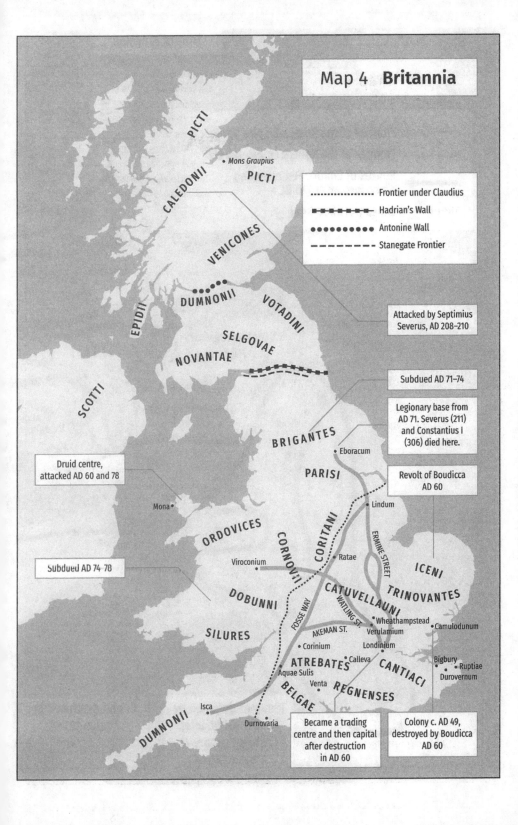

Map 4 **Britannia**

Frontier under Claudius
Hadrian's Wall
Antonine Wall
Stanegate Frontier

PICTI

CALEDONII

• Mons Graupius

PICTI

VENICONES

EPIDII

DUMNONII

VOTADINI

SELGOVAE

NOVANTAE

Attacked by Septimius
Severus, AD 208–210

SCOTTI

BRIGANTES

Subdued AD 71–74

• Eboracum

Legionary base from
AD 71. Severus (211)
and Constantius I
(306) died here.

Druid centre,
attacked AD 60 and 78

PARISI

Revolt of Boudicca
AD 60

Mona •

• Lindum

ORDOVICES

CORNOVII

CORITANI

Subdued AD 74–78

Viroconium •

• Ratae

ICENI

DOBUNNI

CATUVELLAUNI

TRINOVANTES

ERMINE STREET

SILURES

FOSSE WAY

WATLING ST.

• Wheathampstead
Verulamium •

• Camulodunum

AKEMAN ST.

• Corinium

Londinium •

Bigbury
• • Ruptiae
Durovernum

ATREBATES

Calleva •

CANTIACI

Aquae Sulis •

Venta •

BELGAE

REGNENSES

DUMNONII

Isca •

Durnovaria •

Became a trading
centre and then capital
after destruction
in AD 60

Colony c. AD 49,
destroyed by Boudicca
AD 60

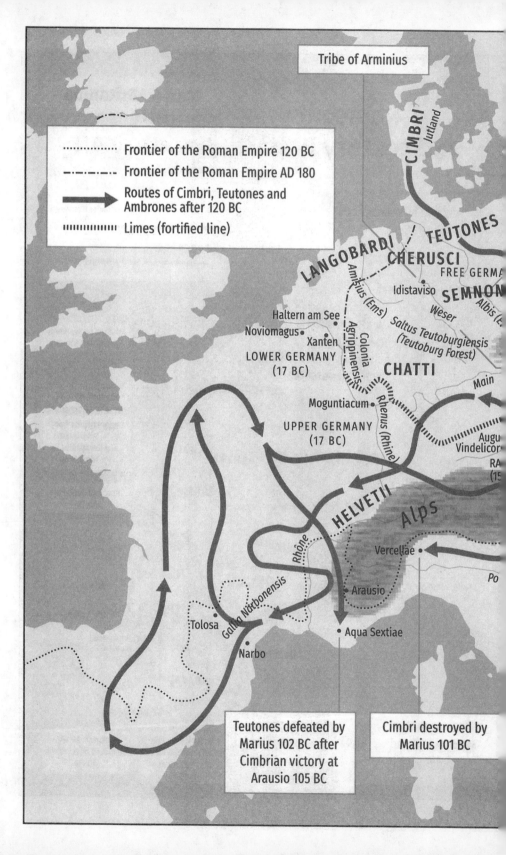

Tribe of Arminius

.... Frontier of the Roman Empire 120 BC
—··—··—·· Frontier of the Roman Empire AD 180
━━▶ Routes of Cimbri, Teutones and
Ambrones after 120 BC
▥▥▥▥▥ Limes (fortified line)

CIMBRI

Jutland

TEUTONES

LANGOBARDI

CHERUSCI

FREE GERMA

Idistaviso   SEMNON

Amisius (Ems)
Weser
Albis (E

Haltern am See
Noviomagus
Xanten
LOWER GERMANY
(17 BC)

Colonia
Agrippinensis

Saltus Teutoburgiensis
(Teutoburg Forest)

CHATTI

Main

Moguntiacum

UPPER GERMANY
(17 BC)

Rhenus (Rhine)

Augu
Vindelicor
RA
(1

HELVETII

Alps

Rhône

Vercellae

Po

Gallia Narbonensis

Arausio

Tolosa

Aqua Sextiae

Narbo

Teutones defeated by
Marius 102 BC after
Cimbrian victory at
Arausio 105 BC

Cimbri destroyed by
Marius 101 BC

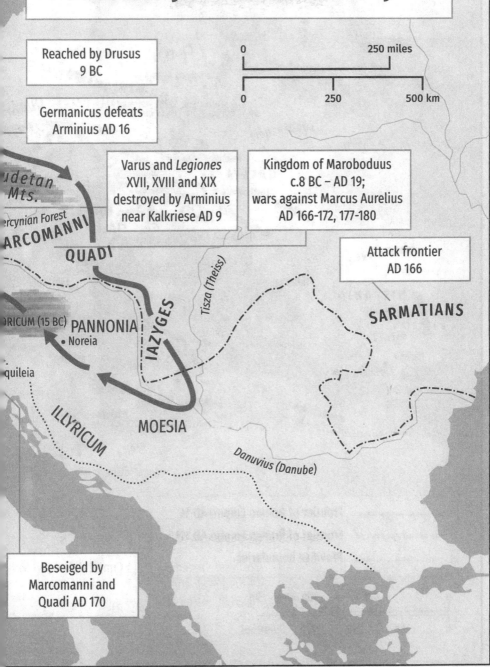

Map 5
Rome and the Germani
2nd century BC to 2nd century AD

Reached by Drusus
9 BC

0 ————————————— 250 miles

Germanicus defeats
Arminius AD 16

0 ———— 250 ———— 500 km

Varus and *Legiones*
XVII, XVIII and XIX
destroyed by Arminius
near Kalkriese AD 9

Kingdom of Maroboduus
c.8 BC – AD 19;
wars against Marcus Aurelius
AD 166-172, 177-180

udetan
Mts.

Attack frontier
AD 166

ercynian Forest

ARCOMANNI

QUADI

Tisza (Theiss)

SARMATIANS

RICUM (15 BC) PANNONIA

IAZYGES

• Noreia

quileia

ILLYRICUM

MOESIA

Danuvius (Danube)

Beseiged by
Marcomanni and
Quadi AD 170

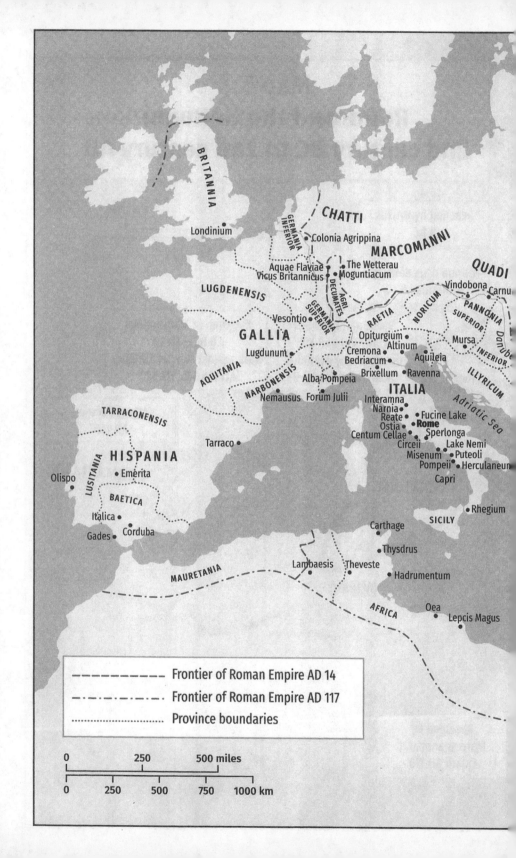

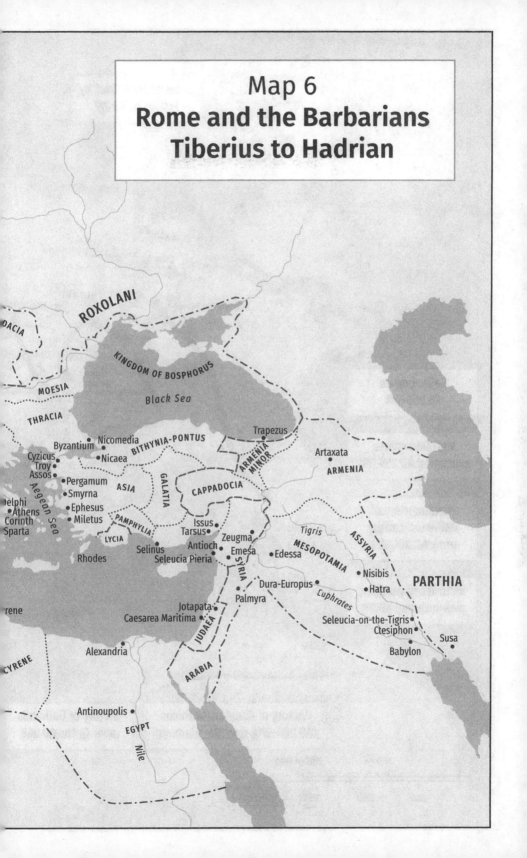

Map 6
Rome and the Barbarians
Tiberius to Hadrian

ROXOLANI

DACIA

KINGDOM OF BOSPHORUS

MOESIA

Black Sea

THRACIA

Byzantium • Nicomedia
Cyzicus • • Nicaea
Troy • • Pergamum
Assos • • Smyrna
Delphi • • Ephesus
Athens • • Miletus
Corinth
Sparta

Aegean Sea

BITHYNIA-PONTUS

Trapezus

ARMENIA MINOR

Artaxata

ARMENIA

ASIA
GALATIA
CAPPADOCIA

PAMPHYLIA
LYCIA
Rhodes

Selinus

Issus
Tarsus •
Antioch •
Seleucia Pieria •

Zeugma
Emesa

Tigris

Edessa

MESOPOTAMIA

ASSYRIA

Nisibis
Hatra

PARTHIA

SYRIA

Dura-Europus

Euphrates

Palmyra

Jotapata
Caesarea Maritima •

JUDAEA

Seleucia-on-the-Tigris •
Ctesiphon

Susa

Babylon

rene

CYRENE

Alexandria

Antinoupolis •

ARABIA

EGYPT

Nile

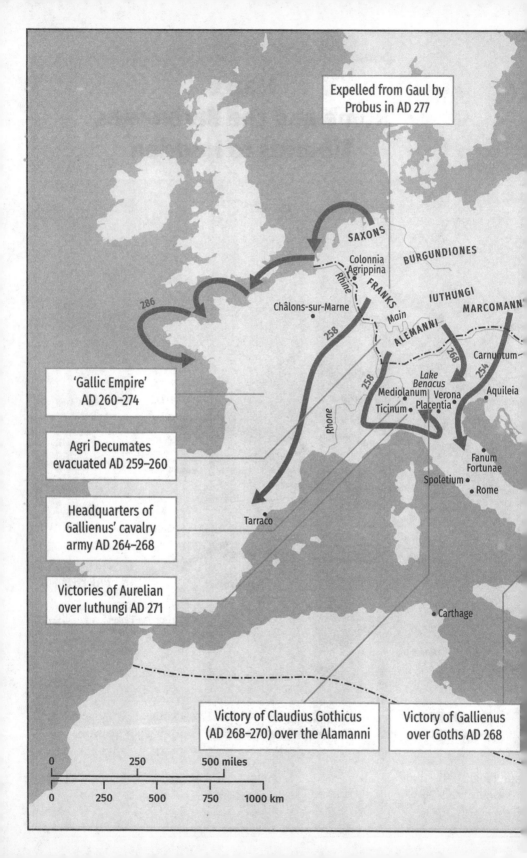

Expelled from Gaul by
Probus in AD 277

SAXONS

BURGUNDIONES

Colonnia
Agrippina

Rhine

FRANKS

IUTHUNGI

MARCOMANN

Châlons-sur-Marne

Main

ALEMANNI

286

258

268

254

Carnuntum

*Lake
Benacus*

Mediolanum

Verona

Aquileia

258

Ticinum

Placentia

Rhone

'Gallic Empire'
AD 260–274

Agri Decumates
evacuated AD 259–260

Fanum
Fortunae

Headquarters of
Gallienus' cavalry
army AD 264–268

Spoletium

Rome

Victories of Aurelian
over Iuthungi AD 271

Tarraco

Carthage

Victory of Claudius Gothicus
(AD 268–270) over the Alamanni

Victory of Gallienus
over Goths AD 268

| 0 | 250 | 500 miles |

| 0 | 250 | 500 | 750 | 1000 km |

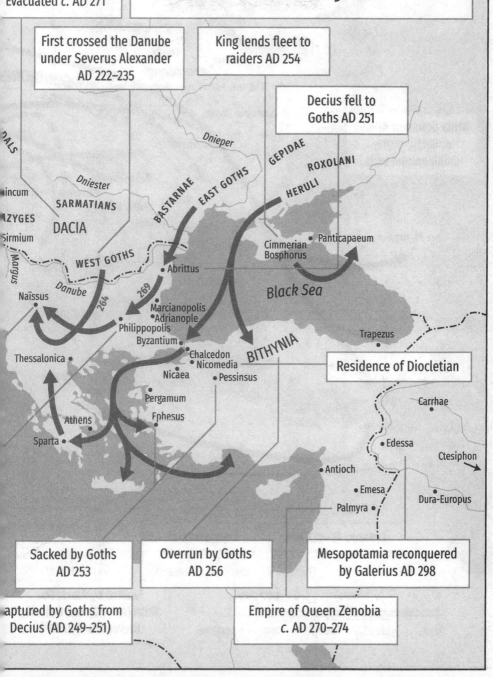

Map 7
The Omnishambles
3rd century AD

Evacuated c. AD 271

First crossed the Danube under Severus Alexander AD 222–235

King lends fleet to raiders AD 254

Decius fell to Goths AD 251

Dnieper

GEPIDAE

ROXOLANI

Dniester

BASTARNAE

EAST GOTHS

HERULI

SARMATIANS

incum

ZYGES

DACIA

Sirmium

Cimmerian Bosphorus

Panticapaeum

Magus

WEST GOTHS

Danube

269

264

Abrittus

Black Sea

Naïssus

Marcianopolis

Adrianople

Philippopolis

Byzantium

Trapezus

Thessalonica

Chalcedon

Nicomedia

BITHYNIA

Residence of Diocletian

Nicaea

Pessinsus

Carrhae

Pergamum

Athens

Ephesus

Edessa

Ctesiphon

Sparta

Antioch

Emesa

Dura-Europus

Palmyra

Sacked by Goths AD 253

Overrun by Goths AD 256

Mesopotamia reconquered by Galerius AD 298

aptured by Goths from Decius (AD 249–251)

Empire of Queen Zenobia c. AD 270–274

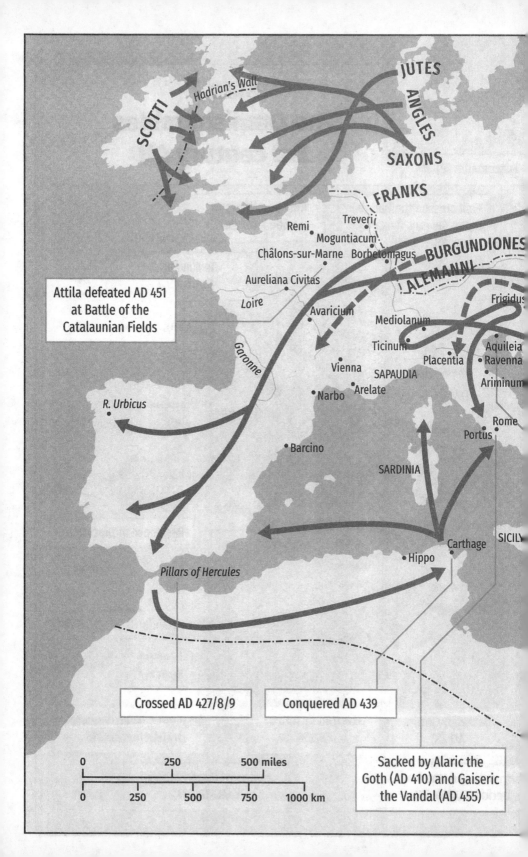

SCOTTI

JUTES

ANGLES

SAXONS

Hadrian's Wall

FRANKS

Remi

Treveri

Moguntiacum

Châlons-sur-Marne   Borbetomagus

BURGUNDIONES

ALEMANNI

Aureliana Civitas

Frigidus

Attila defeated AD 451 at Battle of the Catalaunian Fields

Loire

Avaricium

Mediolanum

Garonne

Ticinum

Aquileia

Placentia

Ravenna

R. Urbicus

Vienna

SAPAUDIA

Ariminum

Narbo

Arelate

Rome

Barcino

Portus

SARDINIA

Pillars of Hercules

Carthage

SICILY

Hippo

Crossed AD 427/8/9   **Conquered AD 439**

0	250	500 miles

0	250	500	750	1000 km

Sacked by Alaric the Goth (AD 410) and Gaiseric the Vandal (AD 455)

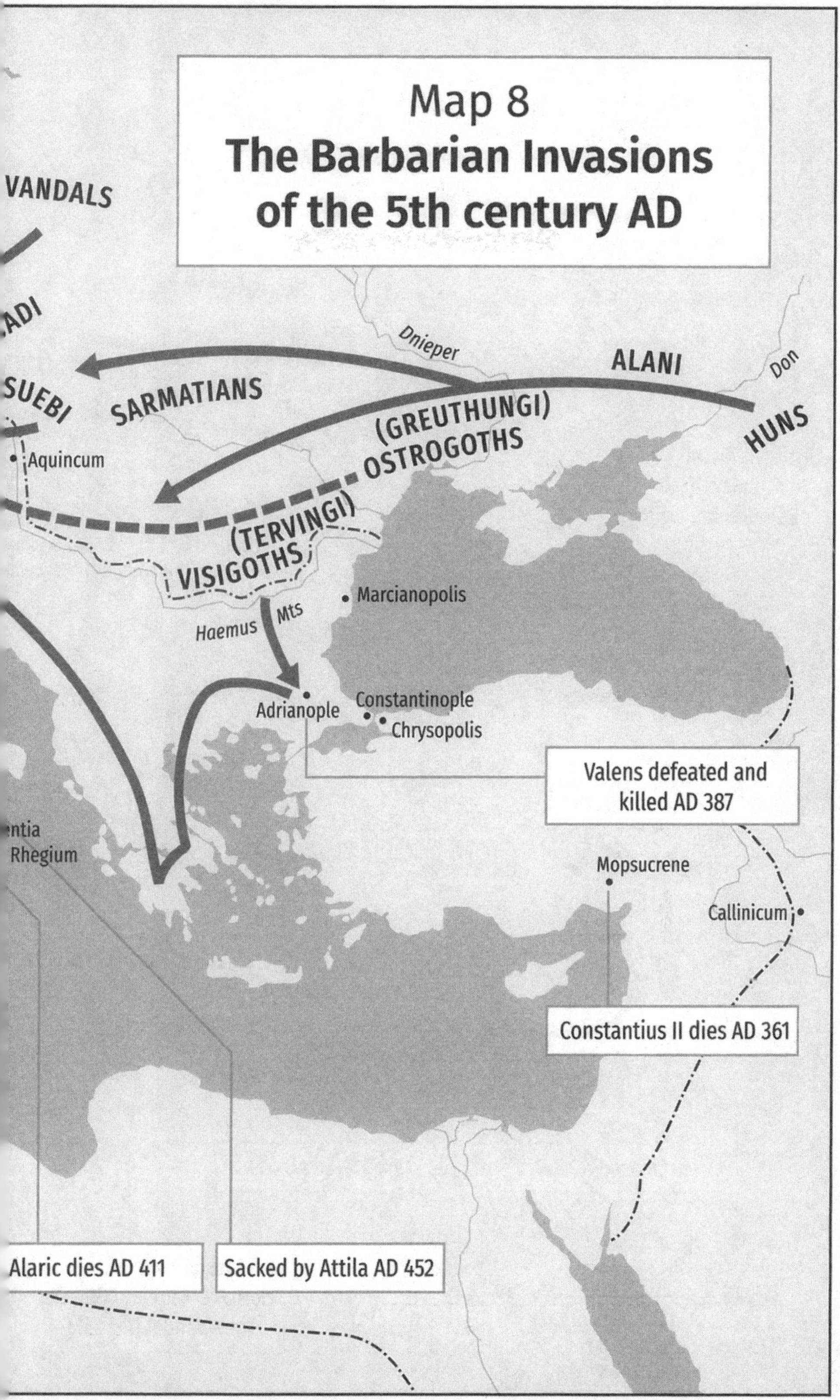

Map 8
The Barbarian Invasions of the 5th century AD

VANDALS

ADI

SUEBI

Aquincum

SARMATIANS

Dnieper

ALANI

Don

HUNS

(GREUTHUNGI)
OSTROGOTHS

(TERVINGI)
VISIGOTHS

Marcianopolis

Haemus Mts

Adrianople

Constantinople

Chrysopolis

Valens defeated and
killed AD 387

Mopsucrene

Callinicum

Constantius II dies AD 361

ntia
Rhegium

Alaric dies AD 411

Sacked by Attila AD 452

Introduction: What is a Barbarian?

On the north wall of the Basilica in Pompeii there is a piece of graffiti that reads:

> *L. ISTACIDI AT QVEM NON*
> *CENO BARBARVS ILLE MIHI EST*
> Lucius Istacidius: he, at whose place
> I do not eat, is a barbarian to me.[1]

Also at Pompeii, in house V.2.1, there is a metrical, but pretty well meaningless, scribbling that was probably used to teach someone how to write hexameter poetry:

> *BARBARA BARBARIBVS BARBABANT BARBARA BARBIS*
> Barbaric things bearded barbarically with barbaric beards.[2]

But what makes Lucius Istacidius seem barbarian, and what makes things and people barbaric in Roman eyes? Are all barbarians barbaric, in the modern sense of being primitive, wild, uncivilised, uncultured, and/or violent? Can barbarians be heroic? Can highly civilised people be barbarians? Should we be drawing clear-cut binary distinctions between Romans and barbarians, and between Romanness and barbarity? Did Romans and barbarians need those distinctions to define themselves?[3] Can a barbarian become a Roman, or vice versa? If a person's identity is 'cognitive [a state of mind], multi-layered, performative, situational, and dynamic',[4] what differentiates the Roman from the barbarian? Is it race, tribe, language, culture, psychology, moral values, symbols of identity, clothing, beards, religion, law, where you live, where you were born, skin colour,[5] patterns of behaviour, self-identification and the identification by others, or a combination of some or all or none of these? It has been cogently argued that 'Roman depictions of barbarians are not part of a dialogue between "us" and "them" ("we are like this whereas *you* are like that") but between "us" and "us", between Romans ("*we* are [or, more often, ought to be] like this because *they* are like that".'[6]

Further questions then arise: Were barbarians hostile to Rome by default? How unified were the barbarians? Was there a 'pan-barbarian' identity? What might the import or imitation of Roman products that we find in Barbaricum or Barbaria (the area outside the Roman Empire) tell us about barbarian attitudes to Rome? Did the Romans have 'barbarians on their mind', and were they obsessed with 'barbarophobia' to the extent that is often imagined?[7] Overall, barbarity is complex, and Roman responses to it are equally so.

The Romans inherited the word *barbarus*, which can be a noun (a barbarian) and an adjective (barbarous), from the Greek *barbaros*. This may have been in use as far back as the Bronze Age, where the word *pa-pa-ro* is used to signify a 'barbarian' outsider, in this case someone not from Pylos where the document was written.[8] The original meaning of *barbaros* relates to language: it is an onomatopoeic word signifying unintelligible speech by someone who just goes 'bar-bar-bar' when they talk. Homer does not use the term *barbaros*, but he does use *barbarophonos* ('of unintelligible speech') to describe Troy's Carian allies, who either don't speak Greek or speak it very badly. Certain Greek dialects were sometimes dubbed 'barbarian' if they were hard for others to understand. The comic poet Aristophanes may have suggested that Gorgias was a barbarian because he had a strong Sicilian dialect,[9] and Prodicus described Pittacus' Lesbian accent as 'barbarian',[10] not because the people of Lesbos didn't speak Greek or because the island was felt to be outside the boundaries of the Greek world, but because it was hard to understand.

Other ancient languages have similar words: Babylonian-Sumerian uses *barbaru* for 'foreigner', and there are several Indo-European words for incomprehensible speech, including *balbutio* in Latin (= I stammer, stutter, babble, lisp, speak obscurely/indistinctly), *blblati* ('to stammer') in Czech, and possibly *baby* in English. So, originally, it was speech that defined the barbarian as against the Greek: 'no other ancient people privileged language to such an extent in defining its own ethnicity'.[11] The fifth-century BC Greek historian Thucydides felt that Homer didn't use the term 'barbarians' because in his day Greeks 'hadn't yet been divided off so as to have a single common name by way of contrast':[12] in other words, the barbarian is defined by the Greek, and vice versa.

The Greek attitude changed as a result of the Persian invasions by Darius I and Xerxes I in 490 and 480–479 BC. The Greeks 'invented' the idea of the barbarian[13] as they came together in a way that they had never done before, emerged victorious, and started to distinguish themselves from the anti-Greek barbarians.

One notable turning point was when the great Athenian tragic playwright Aeschylus staged his *Persians* in 472 BC: from then on, the notion of barbarians as 'everyone who isn't Greek', be they Persians, Phoenicians, Phrygians, Thracians or anyone else, really started to take hold. These 'barbarians' also readily accepted monarchy, which the newly democratic Athenians regarded as tantamount to slavery. Freedom was what made people truly human; forced labour made them little better than animals. Freedom allowed people to develop reason, self-control, courage, generosity and high-mindedness; barbarians and slaves possessed no mental or spiritual faculties at all, and so were childlike, effeminate, irrational, undisciplined, cruel, cowardly, selfish, greedy, luxurious, oversexed and pusillanimous. This then led to two conclusions: (a) barbarians were naturally fitted to slavery; and (b) given that the Greeks felt it was morally right to help your friends and harm your enemies, it was the duty of the Greeks to enslave them: 'Hence, as the poets say, "It is right that Greeks should rule barbarians",[14] implying that the barbarian and the slave are identical by nature.'[15]

In due course, the Romans adapted the term in order to refer to anything that was non-Roman. There is irony here, in that, as far as the Greeks were concerned, the Romans themselves were technically barbarians.[16] But the Romans chose to focus more on the behavioural than the racial implications of the word, at least when it suited them, and made a wholesale cultural appropriation of the Greek idea. To be truly civilised, you had to live not in the 'savagery' of the natural environment on the fringes of the world, but at its centre:

It is beyond question that the Ethiopians are burned by the heat of the heavenly body near them, and are born with a scorched appearance, with curly beard and hair, and that in the opposite region of the world the races have white frosty skins, with yellow hair that hangs straight; while the latter are fierce owing to the rigidity of their climate but the former wise because of the mobility of theirs ... whereas in the middle of the earth [i.e. the Mediterranean region inhabited by the Romans], owing to a healthy blending of [fire and water], there are tracts that are fertile for all sorts of produce, and men are of medium bodily stature, with a marked blending even in the matter of complexion; customs are gentle, senses clear, intellects fertile and able to grasp the whole of nature; and they also have governments, which the outer races never have possessed.[17]

Barbarians came to be everyone who lived outside the limits of Rome's power, or who resisted or rebelled against it.

As far as many Greeks and Romans were concerned, the further you went from their culture, the wilder, weirder and more monstrous people became: the physical environment beyond the borders of Rome's empire (wherever those happened to be at any point in her history) meant that people who lived in Barbaria simply could not become civilised. And yet these people would interact with the Romans in ways that would determine the nature and course of Rome's long history, from the founding of the city in 753 BC, to the demise of the Western Empire in AD 476.

Mythical and Semi-Mythical Resistance: Aeneas to Tarquin the Proud

Aeneas: From Barbarian to Trojan-Italian

History is often said to be written by the victors, and in the case of Rome the authors were extremely eloquent. The story they tell follows a remarkable trajectory from Rome's origins as a tiny village of refugees from a conflict zone, to a dominant superpower, before being transformed into the medieval and Byzantine worlds. Yet it is deliciously ironic that the story of the Romans, who so often defined themselves against the barbarians, starts with Aeneas, one of the Trojans, a people who represented everything that the Greeks came to think of as barbarian and barbaric.

In myth, Aeneas was the product of an affair between the Trojan Anchises and the goddess Venus/Aphrodite. In the Greek traditions Aeneas was never one of Troy's finest warriors, and Achilles was quick to taunt him about it when they met in combat:

Do you not remember when, apart from your cattle, I
    caught you

alone, and chased you in the speed of your feet down the
hills of Ida
headlong, and that time as you ran you did not turn to
look back?[1]

On two occasions Aeneas fought the awesome Greek warrior
Diomedes[2] and had to be rescued, first by Aphrodite and then
by Apollo. He withdrew from the battle when he was menaced
by Menelaus and Antilochus, but he did have the courage to
challenge Achilles to single combat, even though he had to be
saved by Poseidon, who hurled him to the edge of the battlefield and ordered him to cease fighting Achilles, because he was
destined for greater things.

Aeneas' military prowess was overshadowed by the very
Roman quality of *pietas*: a sense of duty to your gods, state and
family. This manifested itself amid the carnage of the destruction of Troy after the Greeks infiltrated the city using the
Wooden Horse. Aeneas carried the aged Anchises through the
flames and escaped, along with his young son Ascanius/Iulus
and a small group of survivors, although not with his wife
Creusa, who he lost in the chaos. These barbarian refugees
headed for a new life in Italy, where they prepared the ground
for Rome ultimately to become the ruler of the world.

The Aeneas myth took its definitive form in Virgil's epic poem,
the *Aeneid* (started in 30 BC, but unfinished at his death in 19 BC):

I tell about war and the hero who first from Troy's frontier,
Displaced by destiny, came to the Lavinian shores,
To Italy – a man much travailed on sea and land
By the powers above, because of the brooding anger of
Juno,

Suffering much in war until he could found a city
And march his gods into Latium, whence rose the Latin
   race,
The royal line of Alba and the high walls of Rome.[3]

Virgil provided the poetic, mythological version of the tale, whereas his contemporary, the historian Livy,[4] narrated Rome's early history in the first book of his monumental *Ab Urbe Condita*: 'Aeneas was . . . destined to lay the foundations of a greater future . . . Once on [the Italian] shore, they set about scouring the countryside for what they could find, and while thus engaged they were met by a force of armed natives who, under their king Latinus [the ruler of Laurentum], came hurrying up . . . to protect themselves from the invaders.'[5]

Mythical traditions are always fluid, and there were two versions of what happened next. In one, there was a fight, Latinus was beaten, and then he came to terms with Aeneas and gave him his daughter Lavinia in marriage. The alternative version brings the two sides together in negotiations before the battle, in which Aeneas told Latinus who his men were, where they had come from, why they had left their homes, and what their objective in landing in Latinus' territory was. Latinus was so impressed by 'the noble bearing of the strangers and by their leader's high courage either for peace or war'[6] that he gave Aeneas his hand in friendship, a treaty, hospitality and his daughter Lavinia in marriage.

The Trojans had now found a permanent home, and the ancestry of the Romans had now grown to encompass the Latins – equally barbarian, at least to Greek sensibilities. The Trojans started to build a settlement, called Lavinium after Aeneas' new wife, and a child was soon born: Ascanius.[7]

Not everyone was happy with these arrangements, however. Turnus, prince of the Rutuli, had been engaged to Lavinia before Aeneas arrived. Dishonoured and enraged, he went on the offensive, but was defeated, although Latinus was also killed in the fighting. Turnus then sought the help of the formidable King Mezentius of the Etruscans, who was understandably worried by, and hostile to, the Trojan–Laurentian alliance. Virgil presents Mezentius as cruel and barbarous:

> Why, he would even have live men bound to dead bodies,
> Clamping them hand to hand and face to face – a horrible
> Method of torture – so that they died a lingering death
> Infected with putrefaction in that most vile embrace.[8]

In this dangerous situation Aeneas conferred the native name of Latins onto his Trojans, intending to strengthen the bond with his allies. And with the Trojans and Latins rapidly becoming one people, Aeneas felt confident to attack the Etruscans. In the battle the Latins were victorious: Aeneas drove his spear through the temples of Mezentius' horse, causing it to fall on top of the Etruscan, pinning him to the ground, and when the warrior offered his throat to Aeneas' sword, he cut it.

It just remained for Aeneas and Turnus to settle their differences man-to-man, or as Virgil put it, like bulls fighting for mastery of the herd: Turnus' sword shattered into fragments when he struck at Aeneas – in his excitement he had grabbed an ordinary man-made sword, not his usual Vulcan-made one; he fled, but Aeneas couldn't catch him because he had earlier been wounded in the leg; Turnus' sister Juturna gave Turnus his magic sword back; Venus retrieved Aeneas' spear for him; and so the two warriors stood with their spirits and weapons restored.

At this point Virgil inserts an absolutely crucial divine interlude, in which a key aspect of Roman identity is resolved. Juno had been implacably opposed to the Trojans ever since their prince Paris had judged her less beautiful than Aeneas' mother Venus in the 'Judgement of Paris',[9] but now Jupiter forbids her to harass the Trojans any more. She accepts, but only if this means the end of Troy and that the Italians are the dominant partners in the alliance from which the Roman people will spring; when the two nations unite they must be called 'Latins' or 'Italians', not 'Trojans'; and the Italians must not change their native dress or their language (the Romans always spoke Latin, not 'Roman'). During the fighting Turnus' brother-in-law Numanus Remulus had delivered an impassioned harangue: we Italians, he said, are hardy sons of toil, brought up as hunters, farmers and warriors; you Trojans, with your clothes dyed yellow and purple, delight in dancing and idleness – you are Phrygian women, not Phrygian men![10] In essence, the Romans must break with their effete barbarian past. Jupiter accepts.

Aeneas and Turnus can now engage for the last time. When Aeneas' spear roars louder than a thunderbolt and sticks in Turnus' thigh, bringing him to his knees, Turnus foregoes his claim to Lavinia and pleads for his life. Aeneas dithers until he sees the sword-belt that Turnus captured from his friend Pallas, at which point the red mist descends and he buries his sword in Turnus' chest, bringing Virgil's *Aeneid* to an unexpectedly shocking end. Livy says that the battle was the last of Aeneas' earthly labours in this world: 'He lies buried on the banks of the river Numicus, whatever it is lawful and right to call him – man or god.[11]

Alba Longa

Ascanius was too young to take over his father's power, but Lavinia was a formidable woman, and acted as regent until he came of age. Even Livy is baffled by the conflicting traditions about Ascanius' identity: 'Was it the one I have been discussing, or was it an elder brother, the son of Creusa, who was born before the sack of Troy and was with Aeneas in his escape from the burning city – the Iulus, in fact, whom the Julian family claim as their eponym? It is at any rate certain that Aeneas was his father.'[12]

Livy explains that whoever his mother might have been, it can be taken as a fact that Ascanius ultimately left Lavinium in charge of his (step)mother and went off to found a new settlement on the Alban hills: Alba Longa. The River Albula (now the Tiber) became the boundary between the Latins and Etruscans.

Virgil provides deep insights into the Roman self-image in his *Aeneid*, where, in Book 6, Aeneas goes down to the Underworld to visit the ghost of Anchises, just before he makes his first landfall in Italy. His father shows him a gathering of souls waiting to be born, each of whom reveals, in his own way, the type of quality that the Romans admired, principally moral rectitude and courage on the battlefield. His list starts with Silvius – an Alban name meaning 'Born in the Woods' – who was Aeneas' last child, born to Lavinia when Aeneas was an old man.[13] However, in Livy's account of the kings of Alba Longa, this Silvius is the son of Ascanius, succeeded by Aeneas Silvius, whose heir was Latinus Silvius.[14] All the kings of Alba kept the cognomen Silvius. The line then ran through Alba, Atys, Capys, Capetus and Tiberinus, who was drowned in the River Albula, giving his name to the River Tiber, which still runs through Rome. After Tiberinus came Agrippa, Romulus Silvius, who was struck by lightning, and Aventinus, who was buried on the hill now known as the Aventine. The next king was Proca(s). He had two sons, Numitor and Amulius, and bequeathed the realm of the Silvian family to Numitor, the elder: 'That, at least, was his intention, but respect for seniority was flouted . . . and Amulius drove out his brother and seized the throne. One act of violence led to another; he proceeded to murder his brother's male children, and made his niece, Rhea Silvia, a Vestal Virgin, ostensibly to do her honour, but actually by condemning her to perpetual virginity to preclude the possibility of issue.'[15]

Romulus and Remus

The Roman narrative, still firmly in the realm of myth and legend, now arrives at the story of Romulus and Remus, which is traditionally set in the middle of the eighth century BC. Our twenty-first-century knowledge of early Rome comes primarily from archaeology, and recent excavations of the black stone shrine known as Lapis Niger in the Roman Forum, led by Patrizia Fortuni, have found the remains of a wall, along with fragments of ceramics and grains, dating to the late ninth/early eighth century BC, therefore conflicting with the traditional foundation date of 753 BC.[16] But the Romans could not be expected to know this. They only started writing their own history relatively late. The first proper Roman historian was the Roman Senator Quintus Fabius Pictor, an annalist who wrote in Greek at the end of the third century BC, and recorded events for reference purposes rather than giving his own analysis. His work described the development of Rome from the earliest times, and although it is now lost, it was an important source for other historians such as Polybius,[17] Dionysius of Halicarnassus[18] and Livy.

However, despite not having accurate information, the Romans still had to explain their origins, and Livy's version became the definitive one:

> But (I suppose) it was predestined that this great city should be founded, and with it the beginning of the mightiest of empires, apart from that of the gods. The Vestal Virgin [Rhea Silvia] was raped, and after she gave birth to twin sons, she named Mars as their father – either because she believed it, or perhaps it seemed more respectable if a god was the cause of her guilt. But neither gods nor men protected her and her infants from the cruelty of the king. He ordered the priestess to be put in chains and thrown into prison, and the boys to be drowned in the river [Tiber].[19]

But destiny intervened. The Tiber had burst its banks, making it impossible to access the proper river, so the men tasked with drowning the children left them in a basket on the edge of the floodwater, where the Ruminal fig tree – said to have once been known as the fig tree of Romulus – stood in Livy's day in the Roman Forum. When the waters receded, the basket was left high and dry. A she-wolf came down from the neighbouring hills to drink, heard the children's cries, suckled them, and behaved so gently with them that the king's shepherd Faustulus found her licking them with her tongue. Faustulus gave them to his wife Larentia to nurse. Livy comments that some people rationalise the tale by saying that Larentia was actually a prostitute who was called 'Wolf-girl' by the shepherds[20] – in Latin *lupa*, 'she-wolf', was slang for 'prostitute'.[21]

The motifs in this story are interesting, focusing on surprisingly negative themes that emphasise violence and wildness:

Romulus and Remus' father Mars was the god of the fury of war; they were deliberately exposed to the brutality of nature, and rescued by a beast that was a byword for savagery; and shepherds were typically regarded as uncivilised outsiders. Barbarity lies at the heart of Rome's foundation myth.

Romulus and Remus' grandfather Numitor eventually acknowledged them, and they helped him to secure his position as King of Alba in his struggle with Amulius, after which they decided to found a new settlement on the site where they had been left to drown. There were population pressures on Alba, which was struggling to accommodate the Albans, the Latins and a large number of herdsmen. But the twins' plans foundered on jealousy and ambition. They quarrelled over which of them should rule the new settlement and give his name to it. So Romulus went to the Palatine Hill and Remus to the Aventine, from where they could scan the sky for omens: 'Remus, the story goes, was the first to receive a sign – six vultures; and no sooner was this made known to the people than double the number of birds appeared to Romulus. The followers of each promptly saluted their master as king, one side basing its claim upon priority, the other upon number. Angry words ensued, followed all too soon by blows, and in the course of the affray Remus was killed.'[22]

Livy also mentions a version in which Remus jeered at his brother and leaped over the half-built walls of the new city, prompting Romulus to kill him and to add the famous threat, 'And so will die anyone else who shall leap over my walls!'[23] So Romulus obtained sole power, and the city was named Roma after him.

Later Romans would wonder about Romulus' potential barbarism, and there is an illuminating exchange in Cicero's *De Re Publica* on this question:

Scipio. Now tell me: was Romulus a king of barbarians?
Laelius. If, as the Greeks say, all men are either Greeks or barbarians, I am afraid he was; but if that name ought to be applied on the basis of men's manners rather than their language, I do not consider the Greeks less barbarous than the Romans.
Scipio. Yet for the purposes of our present subject we consider only character, not race.[24]

So Roman behaviour meant that they were not barbarians, and in later years the Romans attributed their astonishing success to Rome's geographical position and its effects on their character: 'The peoples of Italy have the optimum constitution . . . both in physique and in the mental intelligence that is a match for their valour . . . It was, therefore, a divine intelligence that placed the city of the Roman people in an excellent and temperate country, so that she might acquire the right to rule over the whole world.'[25]

Actually, Rome was very inconveniently sited for the centre for a large empire, and a thousand years after Romulus it would become something of a backwater where some emperors never even went. Cities such as Nicomedia (modern İzmit, Turkey), Treveri (Trier, Germany), Mediolanum (Milan, Italy), Sirmium (Sremska Mitrovica, Serbia), Antioch (Antakya, Turkey), Serdica (Sofia, Bulgaria) and Thessalonica (Thessaloniki, Greece) eventually became far more significant, and in the end all roads did not lead to (or from) Rome. However, Rome's location did contribute to its early success in Italy. Of Rome's famous Seven Hills, the Palatine and Capitoline provided good defensive sites, overlooking a convenient crossing point over the Tiber, and the city itself, located about halfway down the western side of Italy, was on the intersection of some important lines of communication: north to Etruria, whose civilisation had a major influence on Rome's customs, religious procedures, symbols of power and architecture; south into the valley of the Trerus (modern Sacco) or round the base of the Alban Hills, and on to the culturally advanced Greek city-states of Magna Graecia ('Great Greece') in southern Italy. More local routes led down to the mouth of the Tiber, giving access the sea, and upriver into Sabine territory, past important Etruscan settlements and into the interior of Umbria. Rome had the potential to develop into an important hub.

The Reign of Romulus (Traditionally 753–715 BC)

Romulus doesn't only figure in historical works: he has his place in poetry too. In the catalogue of soon-to-be-born heroes in the *Aeneid*, Aeneas' father points him out:

> Further, a child of Mars shall go to join his grandsire –
> Romulus, born of the stock of Assaracus by his mother,
> Ilia. Look at the twin plumes upon his helmet's crest,
> Mars' cognisance, which marks him out for the world of
>   earth!
> His are the auguries, my son, whereby great Rome
> Shall rule to the ends of the earth, shall aspire to the high-
>   est achievement,
> Shall ring the seven hills with a wall to make one city,
> Blessed in her breed of men.[26]

Romulus fortified the Palatine Hill, established a number of important religious ceremonies, summoned his subjects, and gave them laws: 'In his view the rabble[27] over whom he ruled could be induced to respect the law only if he himself adopted certain visible signs of power; he proceeded, therefore, to increase the dignity and impressiveness of his position by various devices, of which the most important was the creation of the twelve lictors[28] to attend his person.'[29]

Rome continued to grow, and Romulus encouraged asylum seekers to go there: 'Hither fled for refuge all the rag-tag-and-bobtail from the neighbouring peoples: some free, some slaves, and all of them wanting nothing but a fresh start. That mob was the first real addition to the City's strength, the first step to her future greatness.'[30]

Again, the emphasis falls on outsiders, aliens and exiles. Romulus needed to exert a measure of social control over this rootless, diverse and somewhat barbaric population. So he created 100 senators, or 'Fathers', as they were called, whose descendants were called 'Patricians'.[31]

In local terms, Rome was powerful. But she had a serious long-term problem: there were not enough women. The Romans were going to die out, and the neighbouring communities refused to grant rights of intermarriage to such barbarous people: 'More often than not [Romulus'] envoys were dismissed with the question of whether Rome had thrown open her doors to female, as well as to male, runaways and vagabonds, as that would evidently be the most suitable way for Romans to get wives.'[32]

The young Romans hated being disrespected in this way, so Romulus prepared for the inevitable violence by making lavish preparations to celebrate the Consualia Festival,[33] and sent out invitations to the neighbouring communities. Prominent among the crowds who flocked to Rome were the Sabines, with their wives and children. They were welcomed hospitably, shown around the town, and then the festivities commenced. 'The preconcerted attack began. At a given signal the young Romans darted this way and that, to seize and carry off the maidens. In most cases these were taken by the men in whose path they chanced to be. Some, of exceptional beauty, had been marked out for the chief senators, and were carried off to their houses by plebeians to whom the office had been entrusted.'[34]

The fun of the fair turned to panic, tears and recriminations. The girls were terrified. Romulus tried to reassure them:

> He declared that their own parents were really to blame, in that they had been too proud to allow intermarriage with their neighbours; nevertheless, they need not fear; as married women they would share all the fortunes of Rome, all the privileges of the community, and they would be bound to their husbands by the dearest bond of all, their children . . . The men, too, played their part: they spoke honeyed words and vowed that it was passionate love which had prompted their offence. No plea can better touch a woman's heart.[35]

Needless to say, there was a backlash. But when the men of Caenina took up arms on the Sabines' behalf, the Romans defeated them. Tradition had it that Romulus himself killed their chieftain, Acron, and dedicated the armour which he had stripped from the corpse to Jupiter Feretrius. These came to be known as the 'Fat Spoils' (*Spolia Opima*),[36] and the distinction of winning them was incredibly rare.

Following further unsuccessful assaults upon Rome by the men of Crustumium and Antemnae, the Sabines took to the field themselves, using carefully designed treachery. Spurius Tarpeius, the commander of the Roman citadel, had a young daughter called Tarpeia, who was bribed by the Sabine king Titus Tatius to let a detachment of his soldiers into the fortress. But once inside, they crushed her to death under their shields. Livy relates a story that Tarpeia's price had been 'What the Sabines had on their shield-arms', in reference to gold bracelets and jewelled rings that they wore on their left arms, but they repaid her literally with the shields. There was also a version in which she actually demanded their shields, and got precisely what she had asked for.[37]

The Sabines were now in possession of the citadel of Rome. The battle then see-sawed until the Sabine women intervened. They forced their way between the flying spears, and appealed to their fathers and husbands: ' "We are mothers now," they cried; "our children are your sons – your grandsons: do not put on them the stain of parricide. If our marriage – if the relationship between you – is hateful to you, turn your anger against us. We are the cause of strife; on our account our husbands and fathers lie wounded or dead, and we would rather die ourselves than live on either widowed or orphaned." '[38]

The appeal worked. Peace broke out and the sides united under a single government, with Rome as the seat of power, but as a gesture to the Sabines, the Romans called themselves Quirites, after the Sabine town of Cures.[39] Once again, in early Rome we are in a world of homelessness and transience, of pillage and abduction. The Romans revered aspects of their history that their Greek counterparts would have seen as typically barbarian.

Roman tradition differs from that of other ancient societies in that women very often play crucial roles at key moments in history. Attitudes towards them in early Roman society become clear through a set of *Leges Regiae* ('Royal Laws') put forward by Romulus, designed to make them behave with modesty and decorum. A woman joined to her husband by *confarreatio* (formal marriage) shared in all his possessions and sacred rites, and nothing could annul these marriages apart from adultery, or if she poisoned his children or cloned his key. Quite how much authority the husband had over his wife is debatable: Cato tells us that husbands had the right to kill their wives for adultery or drinking (because drinking leads to adultery), but Dionysius of Halicarnassus states that the husband had at least to confer with the woman's relatives first. For her part, she had to conform entirely to her husband's wishes, but, if she was virtuous and obedient, she was the mistress of the house to the same degree as he was master of it. We are told that the wisdom of this legislation meant that no marriage was dissolved at Rome over a period of 500 years.

Further conflicts broke out with the neighbouring towns of Fidenae and Veii, and again the Romans were victorious. Livy then concludes his account of Romulus with an evaluation of his reign. Romulus scores highly for his military and political achievements, his vigour and wisdom, for founding Rome, and for making her strong by the arts of both war and peace, but he gets less credit for being better loved by the Plebeians and the army than by the Senate. A bizarre event then occurs: 'One day while he was holding a muster of his troops on the Campus Martius near the swamp of Capra, in order to review the army, a storm sprang up, with violent claps of thunder, and enveloped him in a cloud, so thick that it hid him from the sight of the assembled people; and from that moment Romulus was never seen on earth again.'[40]

The Kings of Rome

In a narrative where the dates are traditional, vague and subject to dispute, the historians of Rome had the city ruled for around 250 years by Romulus and six further kings. Numa Pompilius (traditionally 715–672 BC) succeeded Romulus, and is regarded as the founder of the Roman legal system. By the end of his reign Rome was as eminent for self-mastery as for military power. According to Virgil, Rome's third king, Tullus Hostilius ('The Hostile'), who traditionally ruled from 672 to 641 BC, was destined

To shake our land out of its indolence, stirring men up to
fight
Who have grown unadventurous and lost the habit of
victory.[41]

During his reign he came into conflict with Mettius Fufetius, the dictator of Alba Longa. Their method of conflict resolution was to organise a fight between three triplet brothers on each side: the Alban Curiatii versus the Roman Horatii. The sole survivor was the Roman Horatius. After peace terms were agreed, Horatius killed his sister for mourning her fiancé, who had been one of the Curiatii, on the grounds that she was being unpatriotic.[42]

The peace soon broke down. The Albans criticised Mettius for entrusting their nation's welfare to just three soldiers, convincing him to resort to 'evil measures' to regain their favour. He persuaded the men of Fidenae, a Roman colony, and of Veii, to declare war on Rome, while he played the part of the traitor under the guise of friendship.[43] Tullus Hostilius invoked the treaty with Mettius, and the Romano-Alban forces took to the field, with Mettius' Albans drawn up against the men of Fidenae, and Tullus confronting the Veientes. But Mettius simply retreated to some higher ground and watched the battle unfold. The Romans won; Mettius congratulated them; but Tullus saw through the deception, and devised a punishment that would serve as a warning to all mankind:[44] 'Mettius Fufetius [he said], just as a little while ago your heart was divided between the states of Fidenae and Rome, so now you shall give up your body to be torn two ways.'[45] His limbs were attached to two four-horse chariots that then ran in opposite directions, with horrifying results. The Romans loved *exempla* ('examples') to follow for their moral well-being, and the episode was depicted on the shield of Aeneas in Virgil's *Aeneid*:

> Near this was the scene where chariots, driven apart, had
>> torn
> Mettius to pieces (but you should have kept to your word,
>> Alban!) –
> Tullus is dragging away the remains of that false-tongued
>> man
> Through a wood, and the brambles there are drenched with
>> a bloody dew.[46]

Livy found the incident less edifying, however: 'Such was the first and last punishment among the Romans of a kind that disregards the laws of humanity. In other cases we may boast that with no nation have milder punishments found favour.'[47]

In the end Jupiter struck Tullus Hostilius with a thunderbolt for conducting a religious ritual incorrectly. He was succeeded by Ancus Marcius (r. 641–616 BC), famed as both a soldier and as an administrator, although Virgil regarded him as rather too much of a populist. Between 616 and 578 BC Tarquinius Priscus, a man of Etruscan origin, fought successfully against the Sabines and the Latins, before turning to significant infrastructure projects at Rome, handing the realm on to Servius Tullius (conventionally r. 578–534 BC), after whom, we are told, no Roman king would ever again rule with humanity and justice, although there would only be one more monarch, the notorious Tarquinius Superbus ('The Proud': traditional dates r. 534–510 BC). Egged on by Servius Tullius' daughter Tullia, he usurped the throne and embarked on a reign of terror, although the tradition does acknowledge his success on the battlefield, along with some major civil engineering schemes, which included the Cloaca Maxima (the Great Sewer).

With Tarquinius Superbus we again see the involvement of a remarkable woman – Lucretia. Her story starts with some Roman commanders drinking and boasting about their wives. Her husband Collatinus suggests that they should make unannounced visits to them, then and there. Everyone else's wife is partying like crazy, but not Lucretia. She is a paragon of womanly virtue, working by lamplight on her spinning. However, her beauty and proven chastity simply ignited the lust of Tarquinius Superbus' son Sextus Tarquinius. He went back to the house at night with his sword and made his way to Lucretia's room. She was asleep:

> Laying his left hand on her breast, 'Lucretia,' he whispered, 'not a sound! I am Sextus Tarquinius. I am armed – if you utter a word, I will kill you.' He used every weapon that might conquer a woman's heart. But all in vain; not even the

fear of death could make her submit. 'If death will not move you,' Sextus cried, 'dishonour shall. I will kill you first, then cut the throat of a slave and lay his naked body by your side. Will they not believe that you have been caught in adultery with a servant – and paid the price?' Even the most resolute chastity could not have stood against this dreadful threat. Lucretia yielded. Sextus enjoyed her, and rode away.[48]

She wrote to her father and husband, who both tried to comfort her: she was innocent; without intention there could never be guilt, but she was intransigent: ' "Never in the future will any unchaste woman live through the example of Lucretia!" Then she drew a knife that she had concealed under her robe, and plunged it into her heart.'[49]

This sordid tragedy prompted Lucius Iunius Brutus to rally the people of Rome against Tarquinius, who went into exile at Caere in 510 BC. Sextus Tarquinius fled to Gabii where he was assassinated. At Rome, the monarchy was replaced by two annually elected consuls, one of whom was Brutus, and from this point on kingship was anathema at Rome. Barbarians were ruled by kings; Rome had now become a republic.

Lars Porsenna versus the Early Heroes of Rome

Tarquinius Superbus did not surrender his kingship easily. Aided by Veii and Tarquinii he fought indecisively with the Romans at Silva Arsia, and then received help from Lars Porsenna (or Porsena) of Clusium, who marched on Rome in 508 BC. Back in the realm of legend, the incident was depicted on Aeneas' shield:

Again, you could see Porsenna telling the Romans to take back
The banished Tarquin, and laying strenuous siege to Rome,
While the sons of Aeneas took up the sword for freedom's sake:
He was pictured there to the life, pouring out threats and
   wild with
Chagrin, seeing that [Horatius] Cocles dared to break
   down the bridge
And Cloelia had slipped her fetters and was swimming
   across the river.[50]

Horatius Cocles is traditionally portrayed as the ideal
Roman: a farmer-soldier, stern, sedulous, serious and self-
sufficient, and showing dogged determination and an unflinch-
ing devotion to duty.

When the enemy approached, everyone withdrew from their
fields [straight away we see the ideal farmer-soldiers spring
into action] and made for the city, which they surrounded
with guards. However, the pile bridge [over the Tiber] nearly
provided the enemy with entry to the city, had there not
been one man, Horatius Cocles . . . He happened to have
been stationed as a guard at the bridge, [saw] the enemy
running . . . towards it, [and] ordered the Romans . . . to
break it down . . . He . . . then strode to the entrance of the
bridge . . . and astonished the enemy with his incredible
audacity. A sense of shame held two other men alongside
him. These were Spurius Larcius and Titus Herminius.[51]

The three men stood firm against the first assault and, when
the bridge was about to collapse, Horatius ordered the other
two to retreat to safety. He stayed until two sounds shattered

the air: the crash of the falling bridge and the cheer of the Romans. Then he jumped fully armed into the Tiber and swam across to safety, 'having dared a deed that was destined to win more celebrity than credence with posterity'.[52] He received a typically early Roman reward: 'His statue was erected in the open-air meeting place, and he was given as much farmland as he could plough around in one day.'[53]

But Porsenna's siege continued, prompting another legendary act of heroism by Gaius Mucius. He sought the Senate's permission to make his way into the enemy lines with a concealed dagger. He got close to Porsenna, but stabbed his secretary by mistake and was immediately apprehended. He told Porsenna that there would be a constant stream of Romans seeking to do what he had failed to achieve, and when Porsenna ordered him to be burned alive unless he revealed the details of this plot, Mucius plunged his right hand into the sacrificial fire and let it burn. Porsenna was so astonished by this superhuman endurance, and the fact that Mucius was a worse enemy to himself than to him, that he released him. Mucius was henceforth knowns as Scaevola, 'the Left-Handed Man', because of the loss of his right hand, and Porsenna opened negotiations. Peace was agreed, but not at a price that included the restoration of the Tarquins.[54]

Scaevola inspired the Roman women to emulate him, notably Cloelia. She was being held hostage by the Etruscans, but was able to elude her captors and swim back across the Tiber through a hail of missiles. Porsenna was so impressed with her 'more than masculine courage', beyond even that shown by Horatius and Mucius, that he said that while he would regard the treaty as broken if she were not returned, he would personally restore her to her family if the Romans surrendered her. Both sides did the honourable thing: Cloelia went to Porsenna and immediately back to Rome, and friendly relations were restored.[55]

In fact, this famous story has an alternative version in which the Romans capitulated to Porsenna, who took Rome and banned the use of iron weapons.[56] This has led scholars to wonder whether Porsenna was not trying to restore the Tarquin dynasty, but to overthrow it. But the Etruscan didn't stay long in Rome, and soon faced resistance from other Latin communities who, like the Romans, were seeking freedom from Etruscan domination. With the assistance of the culturally Greek tyrant Aristodemus Malakos ('the Effeminate') of Cumae, they defeated Porsenna's son Arruns at the Battle of Aricia in *c.*506 BC.[57] Given that Tarquinius Superbus had close links with both the Latins and Aristodemus, it is possible that it was actually Porsenna who abolished the monarchy at Rome, and that the Republic only emerged after he withdrew. Tarquinius initially took refuge with Mamilius Octavius of Tusculum, his son-in-law. Then, after his legendary defeat leading a league of Latin states at the Battle of Lake Regillus, where the deities Castor and Pollux allegedly fought on the Roman side, he joined Aristodemus at Cumae, where he died in 496 BC. Relations between the Latins and Rome were regularised in a treaty: 'Let them neither make war upon one another themselves nor call in foreign enemies, nor grant safe passage to those who shall make war upon either, but let them assist one another with all their might when warred upon and let each have an equal share of the spoils and booty taken in their common wars.'[58]

This would be a crucial factor in Rome's dealings with the tribes of Italy, and with barbarians from outside.

2

Brennus: The Gaul Who Sacked Rome

The treaty that Rome signed with the Latin League in 493 BC provided strength and stability for both sides, especially since they continually had to defend themselves against attacks from central Italian hill tribes such as the Aequi, Volsci and Sabines. These peoples were driven by a lack of land and resources to attempt to establish new homes in the more attractive territory around Latium. There was some sort of warfare almost every year, and Rome played, or claimed to have played, a leading role. However, the relatively localised nature of the conflicts changed with the arrival of a Gallic chieftain called Brennus (Brennos in the Greek sources). He stands as the first, and in many ways one of the most successful, of Rome's external barbarian opponents. Typically, there are quite full, albeit sometimes conflicting accounts of the events by both Roman and Greek sources, but nothing from the Gallic barbarian side: we have to look to the archaeology to provide a more neutral perspective, even if Brennus is given one of the most memorable soundbites in the whole of Roman history.

Invasion

Brennus was a chieftain of a Gallic tribe that our sources called the Senones or Sennones. Originally from central Gaul (modern Sens in Bourgogne-Franche-Comté in France still carries their name), these people had in the past made their way across the Alps into Italy. Plutarch tells his readers that the Gauls were of Celtic stock, and that tens of thousands of young warriors, plus a still greater number of women and children, had set out in search of new lands because their own country couldn't sustain their growing numbers.[1]

To the Romans the Gauls were always barbarous. Pliny the Elder tells us about the orator Crassus famously ridiculing an irritating and uncouth witness in court: '[The witness] kept asking him: "Now tell me, Crassus, what sort of a person do you take me to be?" "That sort of a person," said Crassus, pointing to a picture of a Gaul putting out his tongue in a very unbecoming fashion.'[2]

Both Plutarch and Dionysius of Halicarnassus[3] tell us that the reason the Gauls came into Italy was down to sex and wine. A Tyrrhenian chieftain called Lucumo had entrusted his son[4] to a loyal man named Arruns (or Arron) as guardian. Arruns took his responsibilities seriously, looked after the boy, and when Lucumo died he turned over his estate as agreed. However, the young man was less honourable: he fell in love with Arruns' beautiful young wife and 'corrupted her mind as well as her body'.[5] Arruns was unable to secure justice or exact vengeance on the lovers, so he decided to go abroad, ostensibly on a trade mission to Gaul. His young rival was delighted and gave him everything he needed, including wine, olive oil and figs. At this time, we are told, 'The Gauls . . . had no knowledge either of wine made from grapes, or of oils . . . produced by our olive trees. For wine they used a foul-smelling liquor made from barley rotted in water [i.e. beer], and for oil, stale lard, disgusting both in smell and taste.'[6]

The pleasure the Gauls got from tasting these things for the first time was so intense that they gathered their weapons and families, and set off in quest of the land that produced them, 'considering the rest of the world barren and wild'.[7] It helped that they had also been told that the area where they were produced was large, fertile and sparsely populated by people who were no better than women when it came to warfare. So there was no need to buy these products any more, since they could just seize the land instead. And they did, taking possession of an area from the Alps down to both the Adriatic and Tuscan seas.[8] The Senones settled on the Adriatic coast in what came to be called the Ager Gallicus, where they founded Sena Gallica[9] (modern Senigallia in the Marche region).

They conducted what to Roman and Greek eyes was a typically barbarian lifestyle: unurbanised, itinerant and uncultured:

They lived in unwalled villages, without any superfluous furniture; for as they slept on beds of leaves and fed on meat and were exclusively occupied with war and agriculture, their lives were very simple, and they had no knowledge whatever of any art or science. Their possessions consisted of cattle and gold, because these were the only things they could carry about with them everywhere according to circumstances and shift where they chose.[10]

Wine and Barbarity

The connection between wine and barbarism/civilisation is an important one in Greek and Roman antiquity. Humanity's relationship with the cultivated grape vine, *vitis vinifera sativa*, goes back into the Neolithic period, and viticulture had become established in the Greek world by Minoan and Mycenaean times – around the second millennium BC. For instance, one tripod cooking pot has been proven to have contained wine flavoured with pine resin and with toasted oak: essentially retsina. Viticulture represented an important cultural and social choice: in a sense, drinking wine differentiates humanity from the beasts – it's something that defines us as human beings. It makes us civilised.

Vine growing was closely associated with the dissemination of classical culture: so, for instance, the Greek settlers of Massilia (modern Marseilles) are represented by Justin as teaching the Gauls not just the pleasures of urban life and constitutional government, but also viticulture. Essentially that's how you de-barbarise people – you make them drink wine, rather than beer:

> The nations of the west also have their own intoxicant, made from grain soaked in water; there are a number of ways of making it in the various provinces of Gaul and Spain and under different names, although the principle.is the same . . . By Hercules, it used to be thought that the product of the earth in that country was corn. Alas, what wonderful ingenuity vice possesses! A method has actually been discovered for making even water intoxicated![11]

Wine was the everyday drink of all classes in Rome. It was also a key component in one of the central social institutions of the elite, the *convivium* (dinner and drinking party). Substantial quantities of wine were often drunk at *convivia*, although it was invariably heavily diluted with water. It was considered a mark of uncivilised peoples to drink wine neat, which had supposedly catastrophic effects on their mental and physical health.

So drinking unmixed wine = barbarity. And the Roman historian Ammianus Marcellinus says of the Gauls that:

> As a race they are given to drink, and are fond of a number of liquors that resemble wine; some of the baser sort wander about aimlessly in a fuddled state of perpetual intoxication, a condition which Cato described as a kind of self-induced madness. There seems then to be some truth in what Cicero said in his defence of Fonteius, that 'henceforth the Gauls will take their drink with water, a practice which they used to think equivalent to taking poison'.[12]

An index of how much the Romans had civilised the Gauls seems to be how much water they had got them to put into their alcohol.

Clusium

Hopes that wine consumption might have civilised the Gauls in Italy seem to have been dashed when 30,000 Sennones invaded Etruria and besieged Clusium in 391 BC. The city's inhabitants asked the Romans to send ambassadors to the barbarians (Plutarch specifically uses the Greek word *barbaroi*[13]) on their behalf. Three eminent men of the Fabian *gens* were duly despatched, and the Gauls stopped their assault and agreed to talks. When Brennus was asked what his people had suffered at the hands of the Clusians, he just laughed:

> The Clusians wrong us in that, being able to till only a small parcel of earth, they yet are bent on holding a large one, and will not share it with us, who are strangers, many in number and poor. This is the wrong which you too suffered, O Romans, formerly at the hands of the Albans, Fidenates, and Ardeates, and now lately at the hands of the Veientines, Capenates, and many of the Faliscans and Volscians. You march against these peoples, and if they will not share their goods with you, you enslave them, despoil them, and raze their cities to the ground; not that in so doing you are in any wise cruel or unjust, no, you are but obeying that most ancient of laws which gives to the stronger the goods of his weaker neighbours, the world over, beginning with God himself and ending with the beasts that perish ... Cease, therefore, to pity the Clusians when we besiege them, that you may not teach the Gauls to be kind and full of pity towards those who are wronged by the Romans.[14]

The Roman envoys saw that there was no chance of coming to terms with Brennus, so they slipped into Clusium and persuaded its citizens to attack the Gauls with them. According to Plutarch, in the fighting that followed, Quintus Ambustus, one of the Fabii, attacked and killed a particularly handsome Gaul. But as Ambustus was stripping his armour from the corpse, Brennus recognised him. In Brennus' eyes Ambustus had come as an ambassador, but had instigated an unjust war. So he called off the assault on Clusium, and headed for Rome instead, demanding that Ambustus should be handed over for punishment.

A lively debate ensued at Rome. Diodorus says that the Senate initially tried to buy the Celts off, but when their offer was rejected they voted to surrender the accused.[15] Plutarch adds that the Fetiales, the Roman priests who acted as the guardians of peace and also as arbiters of the grounds on which war could justly be made, pressured the Senate 'to turn the curse of what had been done upon the one guilty man, and so to make expiation for the rest'.[16] In the end the matter was referred to the *provocatio ad populum*, 'appeal to the people', who 'so scorned and mocked at religion'[17] that they overturned the decision of the Senate and the Fetiales. Inevitably, the Gauls bore down on Rome with an army said to number more than 70,000 men,[18] instigating widespread terror by their numbers, splendid equipment and furious violence.

It should be said that the entire story of the events at Clusium could well be 'alternative facts' and Roman propaganda. There was no valid reason for Clusium to seek Rome's help, and the Gauls didn't need any pretext to attack Rome, so it is possible that the story just serves to explain an otherwise unmotivated attack on Rome, but more importantly to cast Rome as a champion of Italy against the Gauls.[19] A variant theory has Brennus working in conceit with the Greek tyrant Dionysius I of Syracuse in his attempt to dominate Sicily. At this period Rome had close links with the city of Messana (modern Messina), which Dionysius wanted to capture, so if Brennus could tie up Rome's forces for a while, Dionysius would be freer to achieve his goals. But, if the Clusium affair is historically accurate, Rome's illegal intervention resulted in war, and a catastrophic defeat much closer to home.

Battle of the Allia

As the Gauls marched towards Rome, the Romans armed all the men of military age – over 40,000 of them, according to Plutarch, but generally untrained and inexperienced in combat – and headed out to meet them.[20] They marched for around ten miles along the River Tiber and encamped close to its confluence with the river Allia. When the barbarians attacked, the Romans deployed their 24,000 better fighters in a line from the river as far as the hills, while their weaker warriors took up a position on the highest hills. The barbarian troops also deployed in a long line, but with their elite troops on the hills. In 'a disorderly and shameful struggle'[21] these Gallic warriors easily drove the Romans off the high ground, causing further confusion to the troops on the plain as they fled. The ancient narratives[22] differ slightly in detail, but not in the end result: it became a bloodbath, and many Romans were massacred along the riverbanks and in the water.

Plutarch regards the Romans' defeat as their own fault: they had too many commanders, neglected to sacrifice with good omens, and failed to consult the prophets prior to giving battle.[23] Furthermore, although he is sceptical about the effect of this, he says, they fought on an 'unlucky day' (*dies nefastus*), just after the summer solstice when the moon was almost full,[24] on the anniversary of a disaster in which 300 men of the Fabian *gens* had been cut to pieces by the Tuscans. The extent of the defeat by the Gauls was so appalling that the day came to be called *dies Alliensis* (the Day of the Allia) after the river, and was regarded by the Romans as one of the unluckiest of all, 'since in the presence of calamity, timidity and superstition often overflow all bounds'.[25]

Many of the Roman survivors took to the city of Veii, which they had recently razed, and fortified it as best they could, while others made it to Rome and reported the disaster. Those at Veii thought that Rome had been utterly devastated. They were mistaken in this, although quite a few Roman families did flee to neighbouring cities. In fact, the Roman magistrates coordinated resistance efforts by ordering the populace to bring supplies of food, along with silver, gold, their most expensive clothing and their sacred things to the Capitoline Hill, which they fenced with ramparts and stocked with missiles. The Vestal Virgins put most of their sacred treasures into two jars, and hid them underground in the temple of Quirinus, but took the most important objects with them as they fled along the river. The Romans had time to do this because the barbarians failed to realise the magnitude of their victory, and in the euphoria after the battle they turned to revelry and the distribution of spoils taken from the Roman camp. They spent the first day severing the heads of the dead, and the next two thinking that the Romans were preparing a trap. But on the fourth day, once they learned the reality of the situation, they broke into the city via the Colline Gate.

Brennus' Sack of Rome

There is a fabulous (in all the senses of the word) story of how Rome's priests and senators followed the lead of Fabius, the Pontifex Maximus, and stoically put on their finest ceremonial garb and seated themselves in the courtyards of their houses on ivory-inlaid chairs, offering themselves as a sacrifice on behalf of Rome and the Roman people. When the Gauls entered Rome, they didn't know what to make of the eerie calm throughout the city. In the Forum, they found the humbler houses locked and barred but the mansions of the nobility open; the former they were ready enough to break into, but it was a long time before they could bring themselves to enter the latter: something akin to awe held them back at what met their gaze – those figures seated in the open courtyards, the robes and decorations august beyond reckoning, the majesty expressed in those grave, calm eyes like the majesty of gods. They might have been statues in some holy place, and for a while the Gallic warriors stood entranced; then, on an impulse, one of them touched the beard of a certain Marcus Papirius – it was long, as was the fashion of those days[26] – and the Roman struck him on the head with his ivory staff. That was the beginning: the barbarian flamed into anger and killed him, and the others were butchered where they sat. From that moment no mercy was shown; houses were ransacked and the empty shells set on fire.[27]

The Romans on the Capitol looked down with horror as if they were watching a theatrical performance of stereotypical barbarism, which went on for days. They became desensitised to the suffering, but resolved to defend the small enclave of freedom that they occupied. 'Their shields and swords in their right hands were their only remaining hope,' said Livy.[28]

Brennus' troops surrounded the Capitol, but the Romans managed to repel them for some time. Brennus remains a relatively anonymous presence in the Roman narrative, whereas Marcus Furius Camillus now assumes a significant role on the Roman side.[29] The Gauls started to run short of food, and sent out parties to plunder the surrounding territory. One of these made its way to Ardea, where Camillus had been staying after having been exiled from Rome by his political opponents on a charge of embezzling the booty from a previous local conflict: 'Seeing that the Ardeans were of sufficient numbers, but lacked courage, through the inexperience and effeminacy of their generals, he began to reason with the young men first, to the effect that the mishap of the Romans ought not to be laid to the valour of the Gauls, nor the sufferings of that infatuated people to the prowess of men who did not deserve their victory, but rather to the dictates of Fortune.'[30]

He played on the conventional image of the Gauls as 'alien and barbarous folk, whose only end in getting the mastery was, as in the work of fire, the utter destruction of what it conquered',[31] but also as people who could be defeated, given the right attitude. This won the Ardeans over, and Camillus led them in a surprise night attack on the Gauls, who were rendered defenceless by a classic barbarian combination of drunkenness and sleep.[32]

When news of Camillus' success reached the Romans at Veii, they asked him to assume command of the war. He was amenable to this, despite his past difficulties with Rome: 'I never would have prayed that my country should come into such misfortunes as these, so as to need me; a thousand times over I should have preferred that my life henceforth should be unenvied and without honour rather than that I should see Rome subjected to the cruelty of barbarians and placing her remaining hopes of safety in me alone.'[33]

However, he would not take up the command unless the citizens on the Capitoline Hill had legally elected him – something of a catch-22, given that it seemed practically impossible to get a messenger through to them. However, a young man called Pontius Cominius volunteered. He evaded the Gallic guards on the bridge by wrapping pieces of cork around his body and swimming across the Tiber by night, picked his way through the Celtic campfires, made his way to the Porta Carmentalis (Carmental Gate) at the south-west corner of the Capitoline, where there was a huge, jagged cliff, climbed up, hailed the sentries, told them who he was, got pulled up over the wall and delivered his message. After due consideration, the Senate appointed Camillus dictator. Pontius retraced his perilous steps and relayed the Senate's decision to the Romans outside the city. There were already 20,000 men ready for action, augmented by more from the allies, and the new dictator proceeded to Veii, put himself at the head of the soldiers there, and prepared his attack.[34]

Unfortunately for the Romans, Pontius' ascent and descent had left traces on the cliff. So Brennus sought out the nimblest mountain-climbers among his men and offered lavish rewards to anyone who could scale the heights. A large number of volunteers silently clambered up the cliff in the dead of night. They were right on the point of ambushing the sleeping watchmen when the sacred geese near the temple of Juno became aware of their approach. The birds were sharp of hearing, nervous and particularly wakeful because they had not been fed properly during the siege. They dashed at the Gauls, honking loudly; the garrison woke up; the barbarians took this as their cue to attack; and battle was joined. Roman tradition made Marcus Manlius, 'a man of consular dignity, mighty in body and exceeding stout of heart',[35] the hero of the hour. He confronted two onrushing Gauls, cut the right hand off one of them, and smashed his shield into the face of the other, knocking him backwards over the cliff. Manlius drove on with his counter-attack, killing some of the Gauls and pushing others off the precipice. For repelling the Gauls his comrades honoured him with a man's daily ration of wine and spelt (for Manlius' fate after the sack of Rome, see p. 50); for his dereliction of duty, the garrison commander was hurled down the cliff with his hands tied behind his back, in full view of the barbarians.[36]

Brennus' Defeat and Death

The Senones, it seems, now abandoned hope of taking the Capitoline by force, subterfuge or surprise, and began to think about a ransom settlement instead. Some sources talk of them suffering illness caused by the rotting corpses, the ash from the burning buildings and their unfamiliarity with the hot Italian climate, and also facing food shortages because fear of Camillus made them reluctant to forage far afield. Polybius also mentions an invasion of their own country by the Veneti, which made them keen to do a deal and return home.[37]

The Romans were also prepared to negotiate, partly because they had no idea what, if anything, Camillus was doing to help them, while Brennus behaved with characteristic barbarian duplicity:

The Senate . . . instructed the Military Tribunes to arrange the terms. The deal was then negotiated at a conference between the Tribune Quintus Sulpicius and Brennus, the petty King of the Gauls.[38] One thousand pounds of gold was agreed upon as the price of a people that was destined soon to rule the world. Insult was added to what was already in itself a disgusting disgrace: the weights brought by the Gauls were dishonest, and when the tribune objected, the arrogant

Gaul added his sword to the weight, and an expression unbearable to Roman ears was heard, '*Vae victis!*' [Woe to the conquered!][39]

Historians of Rome often give the barbarians some of the best lines, and although it is highly unlikely that Brennus actually used this beautifully elegant Latin phrase, which appears far less effectively in the Greek sources as *tois nenikemenois odune*,[40] it became a proverbial expression.

The Romans were overcome with anger and shame, but they had no choice other than to comply with Brennus' demands. But 1,000 pounds of gold were ultimately a small price for this 'people destined soon to rule the world', and ironically the arguments and delays caused by trying to raise the extra money were what brought about Brennus' downfall. Camillus used the time to march his army into Rome, where his fellow countrymen acknowledged him as dictator. Then he confronted the Gauls, denied the validity of the agreement, and told his own men to win back their country with iron rather than gold.[41] Brennus' objections led to inconclusive skirmishing, but in the night he broke camp and abandoned the city. By dawn the Gauls were about eight miles down the Gabinian Way, where Camillus fell upon them in full battle array. It was total carnage. The barbarian camp was taken, the gold was recovered, and Livy says that not one Gaul survived to tell of the disaster.[42]

Camillus himself returned to Rome in triumph amid a combination of ribald jesting from his soldiers and praise for him as a Romulus, Father of His Country, and a second Founder of the City. Brennus was ever to be remembered as 'The Gaul Who Sacked Rome'.

When Was Rome Sacked?

Establishing the chronology of these events causes the historians some tricky problems. As Plutarch comments, the Brennus
affair 'was a little more than three hundred and sixty years from
Rome's foundation, if one can believe that any accurate chronology has been preserved in this matter, when that of even later
events is disputed, owing to the confusion caused by this very
disaster'.[43]

However, Plutarch does say that the barbarians occupied
Rome for a total of seven months, entering the city a few days
after the ides (fifteenth) of July, and being expelled around the
ides (thirteenth) of February.[44] But we have no information
from the barbarian side, and the Roman and Greek sources
struggle to establish specific dates for this period. Our difficulties are compounded by the fact that neither the Greek nor the
Roman year started on 1 January – the Roman year started on
1 September in the fifth century BC and on 1 July in the fourth,
which is why we frequently find dates expressed in a form such
as 387/6 BC. The first attempts made to establish the absolute[45]
dates of Roman history were made by Greek historians who
tried to synchronise them with events elsewhere in the world.
And one of the key events was the Sack of Rome by the Gauls.
This is how Polybius links things together:

It was . . . the nineteenth year after the battle of Aegospotami
[fought in late summer 405 BC] and the sixteenth before
that of Leuctra [July 371 BC], the year in which the Spartans
ratified the so-called Peace of Antalcidas with the King of
Persia [signed in the spring of 386 BC], that in which also
Dionysius I of Syracuse . . . was besieging Rhegium [387

BC], and that in which the Gauls, after taking Rome itself by force, took possession of the whole of the city except the Capitol.[46]

A quick check on the arithmetic puts the sack of Rome in either 387 or 386 BC, or 387/6 BC.[47]

However, Roman history in the early Republic has another dating system, known as the Varronian chronology, which gives a different year. Originally the Romans used a relative chronology system, calling the years after the two annual consuls. So, for example, there is a piece of graffiti on the north wall of the Basilica in Pompeii, which says, 'C. Pumpidius Dip[h]ilus woz 'ere, five days before the *nones* of October when M. Lepidus and Q. Catulus were consuls'.[48] You simply have to know that Lepidus and Catulus held the consulship in 72 BC, and calculate that five days before the Nones is 3 October.

This works nicely as long as you have a complete list of the consuls, but for various reasons the Romans didn't: four pairs of consuls are missing. So to correct the anomaly the Romans proposed either a period of anarchy in the 360s, when no magistrates were elected, or one year of anarchy followed by three invented pairs of consuls,[49] or Marcus Terentius Varro's third way. This 'Varronian chronology'[50] also uses consulships, but has Rome ruled by dictators rather than consuls in 333, 324, 309 and 301 BC. This would have been a neat solution had Varro not effectively over-corrected the system by also including four years of anarchy, thereby invalidating all his dates prior to 300 BC. Despite this, the Varronian chronology became the definitive one, and was inscribed on the Arch of Augustus in Rome.[51] It starts from the foundation of the city by Romulus, *Ab Urbe Condita* ('From the Foundation of the

City', abbreviated to AUC), in AUC 1. This works out at 753 BC; the foundation of the Republic is 'The Year of the Consulship of Brutus and Collatinus', and AUC 245 or 509 BC; and crucially, Brennus' sack of Rome is placed at AUC 364, or 390 BC.

So 390 BC became the traditional, definitive date, but, as the analysis of Polybius' account shows, this cannot be correct. Nevertheless, Romans, Renaissance scholars and Wikipedia[52] all regularly reproduce the error. Rome was sacked in 387/6 BC.

Whenever they think it happened, the ancient commentators were struck by the strangeness of Brennus' sack of Rome: 'So weirdly was Rome taken, and saved more weirdly still.'[53]

The whole affair, particularly the defence of the Capitol,[54] became the stuff of legend, although the extent of the damage to Rome was probably exaggerated.[55] Had things been as serious as the sources imply, Roman history could have been snuffed out at this point, with the adult males killed and the women and children sold into slavery. Yet there is no archaeological evidence for a destruction level at this date, suggesting that the damage inflicted by the Gauls could have been fairly superficial. Nevertheless, the story had a far-reaching psychological impact, which manifested itself in the *metus Gallicus* ('Terror of the Gauls'),[56] a horror of being invaded by northern barbarians that lasted for centuries.

3

The Plebs: Barbarous Insiders
and Internal Resistors

The Romans, after making a truce on conditions satisfactory to the Gauls and being thus contrary to their expectation reinstated in their home now started on the road of aggrandizement, and continued in the following years to wage war on their neighbours.[1]

It would be around another 800 years from the time that the Romans had rid themselves of Brennus before the Eternal City would again be occupied by hostile barbarians. The Romans repaired their city and fortified it with the so-called Servian Wall, 4 metres thick, 8 metres high and 10 kilometres long, the remains of which still form an impressive part of the Roman cityscape. The ancient sources associated it with King Servius Tullius (traditionally r. 578–534 BC), but it must have been constructed in the early fourth century, because it uses tufa acquired from Veii, which was captured in 396 BC (Varronian chronology). The Romans were consolidating their position as a significant presence in central Italy. They probably had control over about 7,500 square kilometres, and maybe one million people, and the confederacy under which the Latins shared common interests with Rome became a further source of strength and stability. For their part, the Gauls made several other desultory incursions during the fourth century BC, but their increasing understanding of how vigorously the power of the Romans was growing led them to make a formal peace deal, which lasted from 344 to 331 BC.[2]

One of the fundamental internal social divisions in the Roman state was that between the Patricians and the Plebeians. The Patricians were a small group of hereditary landowning aristocrats who traced their origins back to the days of Romulus, and who could be identified by their names: Claudius and Julius are Patrician family names; Clodius and Licinius are not (see p. 45). The Patricians jealously guarded their own power, monopolised Rome's legal, political and religious offices, and established strict limitations on the social and political movements of everyone else. The non-Patricians, who were the vast majority of the Romans, were known as Plebeians or Plebs (Latin *plebs* = multitude). The word *plebs* comes from the root *ple-* meaning 'fill up', which indicates that the Plebs were seen as 'filler', a mere supplement to the 'true' Roman population, who were the Patricians.[3] Like the barbarians, the Plebs at this point were outsiders.

Struggling for Plebeian Equality in the Fifth Century BC

The Plebs had suffered considerable economic distress because of the Gallic invasion, and they now started to make quite insistent demands for reform. In fact, there had been a degree of class struggle at Rome at least since the establishment of the Republic. Nevertheless, a small percentage of the Plebeians were still able to acquire quite considerable wealth, and with it a certain degree of status, but because they were not from the right background, they could not exchange this wealth for a voice in the leadership of the state. At the same time, poorer Plebeians wanted something to be done about their legal and economic disabilities.

In the class struggle that now occurred, the Plebs were acutely aware that the security of the state essentially depended on them, and with that in mind they had one very powerful weapon at their disposal: *secessio* ('secession'), separating themselves en masse, walking out and founding a new city of their own. This was a very viable proposition, and they did indeed walk out: five secessions are listed, although not all are necessarily historical. In addition to the threat of forming a separate state, the Plebeians were able to articulate their demands by forming a state within a state.

Both aspects of his process can be seen taking place in the first secession of the Plebs, which took place around 494 BC.[4] This happened when, without orders from the consuls, a man named Lucius Sicinius Vellutus suggested that they should take themselves off in a body to Mons Sacer (the Sacred Mount),[5] some three miles from the city. There they made themselves a camp, properly fortified in the usual Roman way, and stayed for a number of days. They made no aggressive moves against Rome, and no hostile moves were made against them.

But there was panic in Rome. The senatorial party knew that something, anything, had to be done to restore internal harmony and reconcile the conflicting interests. So they despatched Menenius Agrippa, who was both an eloquent speaker and liked by the Plebeians because he was one of their own. He was allowed onto Mons Sacer where, 'in the primitive and uncouth style of those days',[6] he told a story:

> Long ago when the members of the human body did not, as now they do, agree together, but had each its own thoughts and the words to express them in, the other parts resented the fact that they should have the worry and trouble of providing everything for the belly, which remained idle, surrounded by its ministers, with nothing to do but enjoy the pleasant things they gave it. So the discontented members plotted together that the hand should carry no food to the mouth, that the mouth should take nothing that was offered it, and that the teeth should accept nothing to chew. But alas! while they sought in their resentment to subdue the belly by starvation, they themselves and the whole body wasted away to nothing. By this it was apparent that the belly, too, has no mean service to perform: it receives food, indeed; but it also nourishes in its turn the other members, giving back to all parts of the body, through all its veins, the blood it has made by the process of digestion; and upon this blood our life and our health depend.[7]

To make the point of the fable completely transparent, Menenius mansplained how it applied to the current anger of the people against their rulers, and was so successful that their resentment was completely mollified. Negotiations began under which it was agreed that special magistrates called *tribuni plebis* (tribunes of the Plebs) would be selected to represent the common people. Initially the office was unofficial, but the Plebs signalled their continuing willingness to revolt by taking a sacred oath to kill anyone who harmed their tribunes: 'The tribunes are sacrosanct by virtue of an ancient oath sworn by the people at the time of the original creation of this magistracy.'[8]

The Patricians eventually conceded that the tribunes should become organs of the state and, armed with their crucial powers to propose or veto legislation plus their personal inviolability, they represented a way in which the Senate could be bypassed, thwarted or overridden. Only Plebeians were allowed to hold the office. The first two tribunes were Gaius Licinius and Lucius Albinus, who in turn appointed three colleagues, including the Sicinius who had led the revolt.[9]

The next phase in the construction of the state-within-a-state came with the establishment of the Concilium Plebis Tributum (the Tribal Assembly of the Plebs), from which Patricians were excluded, and which was much more democratic than the Comitia Centuriata (Centuriate Assembly). The Comitia Centuriata met in the Campus Martius, and was arranged into centuries ('constituencies'), but organised in such a way that the richer ones dominated. It could pass *leges* (laws), and it elected magistrates (the consuls and later the praetors) who had *imperium*, the right to command an army, interpret and carry out the law, issue orders and expect them to be obeyed, and be attended by *lictors*, who carried the *fasces*, a bundle of rods, to which an axe was added whenever they left the city precincts, symbolising the right to inflict corporal and capital punishment that *imperium* conferred. The new Concilium Plebis Tributum was based on some twenty tribal groups instead of the rather cumbersome 193 centuries, and it represented the vast majority of the people. In its early days it lacked constitutional authority, but the Patricians were gradually forced to take notice of it, and in 471 BC the *lex Publilia* recognised its constitutional existence. The Plebeians now had the right to meet in the Forum and to elect their tribunes without interference from Rome's political elite. At least in theory.

The moment when any state receives a written code of laws is a crucial time in its development, and in the consulship of L. Valerius and M. Horatius (*c.*449 BC) the Plebeians received part of such code – the *lex Duodecim Tabularum* (the Law of the Twelve Tables), inscribed on a dozen tablets that were erected in the Forum. Tables I and II were all about trials, whereas Table III dealt with debt and the rights of creditors in an incredibly harsh way. People who were judged liable for an acknowledged and unpaid debt were granted thirty days in which to find the money. After that period, if the debt had still not been settled, the debtor was summoned to court and bound in stocks or fetters. If he couldn't satisfy the judgement after a further thirty days, and no one offered themselves as security on his behalf, the creditor could take possession of him, and the law said that 'he may bind him either in stocks or in fetters; he may bind him with weight not less[10] than 15 pounds, or with more if he shall desire to do so'.[11] Compromise solutions were still available to the debtor at this stage, but if agreement was not reached the debtor was held in bonds for sixty days, by which time the situation was becoming desperate:

> During that time they were brought before the court . . . on three successive market-days, and the amount for which they were judged liable was announced; and on the third market-day they suffered capital punishment or were delivered up for sale abroad [as a slave], across the Tiber. But it was in order to make good faith sacred . . . that they made

that capital punishment dreadful by a display of cruelty and fearful by unheard of terrors. For in cases where there were several creditors to whom the debtor had been adjudged, the Board allowed them the privilege of cutting up in pieces and sharing out the body – the body of a man – of him who had been made over to them; and listen, I will quote the actual words of the Law, lest you believe that maybe I shrink from their odium –

On third market-day creditors shall cut pieces. Should they have cut more or less than their due, it shall be with impunity.[12]

These extremely harsh laws, however, were subsequently abolished.

Table IV dealt with the rights of fathers over their children and wives. These included the destruction of disabled infants: 'The Twelve Tables ordain that a dreadfully deformed child shall be killed.'[13]

They also dealt with the emancipation of children from their father's *potestas* (power/control), since originally a father could sell his son into slavery, and if the buyer freed the son, the son came back into his father's *potestas*:

Descendants are freed from the authority of ascendants by 'emancipation', that is, if after they have been '*mancipati*' ('transferred as property') they have been manumitted. But a son stands in his own right only when he has been thrice transferred and thrice manumitted. For that is what the Law of the Twelve Tables ordains in the following terms –

If father thrice surrender son for sale, son shall be free from father.[14]

The repudiation of one's wife was also dealt with under these laws: '[Mark Antony] has ordered that mime-actress of his to "keep her own property," and, in accordance with the Twelve Tables, he has taken away her keys. He's turned her out! What an excellent and upright person he is in men's eyes from now on! The most honourable thing he did in his entire life was to divorce a female mime-artist!'[15]

Table V covered guardianship, and issues such as the status of women and their property, which shed very illuminating light on early Roman social attitudes: 'Our ancestors have seen fit that females, by reason of levity in disposition, should remain in guardianship even when they have attained their majority . . . We except the Vestal Virgins; even our ancestors saw fit, out of respect for the Virgins' priesthood, that these should be free from control.'[16]

In respect of the other laws, Table VI dealt with acquisition and possession; VII with land rights; VIII with torts (*iniuriae*); IX with public law; X with sacred law; and XI and XII with supplementary laws.

It was clear from the publication of the Twelve Tables where the real power in Rome lay, although at least those interests were now defined in writing for anyone who was able to read. But more comprehensive measures were needed to rectify Rome's inequalities, and most Plebeians of the mid-fifth century BC were still suffering economic hardship, while their representatives, regardless of how wealthy they might have become, were still subject to political and social discrimination. So we hear of a second secession, after which the Plebeians extracted further concessions that were secured in laws passed by the consuls of 449 BC, but although the Romans clearly regarded them as a watershed in the struggle for Plebeian equality, the exact details remain controversial. As Livy explains,

[the consuls of 449 BC, Valerius and Horatius] put through a bill, at the Comitia Centuriata, to the effect that any resolution [*plebiscitum*] passed by the commons at their Concilium Plebis Tributum should be binding upon the whole people, thereby giving a cutting edge to all measures brought forward by the Tribunes. As to the right of appeal [*provocatio*] – the one real safeguard of liberty – they . . . strengthened the whole basis on which it stood by the solemn enactment of a new measure, which provided that no one should declare the election of any magistrate without the right of appeal, and that anyone who did so could be killed without offence to law or religion. Then . . . they revived, in the interest of the Tribunes themselves the almost forgotten principle of their *sacrosanctitas* ['sacrosanctity']; this they did by reintroducing certain religious sanctions long fallen into disuse, and then proceeded to make the principle of inviolability legal as well as religious by a further enactment that an assault upon a Tribune . . . should carry a penalty of death or exile.[17]

Livy also informs us that a new form of assembly also came into being about this time, if not earlier: the Comitia Populi Tributa (aka Comitia Tributa), which should not to be confused with the Concilium Plebis Tributum (aka Concilium Plebis). So for more everyday business the whole people (*populus*) decided to meet by tribes, although they continued to meet by centuries for major decisions such as the election of consuls. The Roman constitution was developing a unique system in which the Comitia Centuriata and the Comitia Tributa comprised the same people meeting in differently organised groups, while the Concilium Plebis Tributum consisted of the Plebeians alone.

At this stage, Rome's social stratification was extremely rigid. But in *c.*445 BC the Tribune Gaius Canuleius forced through the *lex Canuleia*, which legalised intermarriage between Patricians and Plebeians, contrary to the Laws of the Twelve Tables. This was particularly important in the long term because Roman children were enrolled in their father's *gens* (clan), so the sons of Plebeian women could now also become Patrician. Intermarriage was not normal at this stage but, nevertheless, a crucial principle had been established.

Struggling for Plebeian Equality after Brennus' Sack of Rome

The events that followed the Sack of Rome by Brennus' barbarians showed that, despite the progress that had been made, it was hazardous for a Patrician to ally himself with the Plebs, even if he was one of Rome's greatest heroes. In AUC 369 (385 BC by the Varronian system), Rome was faced with a serious external war against the Volsci, Hernici and Latins, plus an even more serious internal rift which centred on the celebrated Patrician saviour of Rome, Marcus Manlius Capitolinus (see p. 34). In Livy's dramatic account,[18] Manlius was motivated by a combination of personal pride and envy directed at Camillus. In Manlius' mind, Camillus had attacked Brennus' Gauls when they were preoccupied with gold and were thinking about peace, whereas he himself had driven them from the Capitol, sword in hand, while they were assaulting the very heart of

Rome. Yet Camillus got all the glory; Manlius was left feeling angry and rejected. Livy says that this led Manlius to become the first Patrician *Popularis* (demagogue).[19] The term is generally used to describe a person who felt that he (they are always male in Roman history) could get what he wanted by whipping up popular feeling and sidestepping the Senate in order to gain personal advancement. Some *Populares* were undoubtedly genuine champions of valid causes, but they were not necessarily instinctive 'democrats'; many were merely demagogues. Political idealism was minimal at Rome, and Livy certainly doesn't ascribe lofty motives to Manlius: 'Being unfortunately a man of headstrong and passionate nature . . . he abused the Senate and courted the populace and, impelled by the breeze of popular favour more than by conviction or judgment, preferred notoriety to respectability.'[20]

Manlius focused on the emotive issue of debt. The rebuilding of Rome had forced many Plebeians into unsustainable borrowing, and now they were threatened with poverty, shame, shackles and imprisonment. The Senate's response was to name Aulus Cornelius Cossus as dictator, with Titus Quinctius Capitolinus as his *Magister Equitum*,[21] partly to deal with the Volscian War, which he did easily and ruthlessly, but primarily to handle the 'revolutionary schemes' of Manlius.[22]

The flashpoint came when Manlius saw a centurion being arrested for debt. Shouting about the arrogance of the Patricians, the callousness of the moneylenders, the sufferings of the Plebs and the misfortunes of the centurion who, he said, looked more like a prisoner of the Gauls than a Roman war hero, Manlius paid off the creditors in full view of everyone. The Plebs loved this, and became even more excited when Manlius sold one of his own farms to raise funds to protect any other

Roman citizens from being sold into slavery. According to Livy, 'their minds were so fired-up that they would follow the champion of their liberty through everything, right or wrong'.[23]

Manlius also railed against the Patricians, accusing them of concealing hoards of Gallic gold and diverting public money for their own use, which could easily be used to pay off all the Plebeian debt. Conspiracy theories circulated, and the Plebs demanded to be told where this 'stolen money' was.

The Dictator Cossus sent for Manlius and called his bluff: 'I challenge M. Manlius to take off from their hidden hoards those who, like sitting hens, are brooding over treasures which belong to the state. If you fail to do this, either because you yourself have your part in the spoils or because your charge is unfounded, I shall order you to be thrown into prison and will not suffer the people to be excited by the false hopes which you have raised.'[24]

Manlius made counter-accusations against Cossus: the Volscian War was just a smokescreen; he had really been appointed to challenge Manlius; he was the champion of the moneylenders against the Plebs; he and the senators should use their own wealth to alleviate the debt crisis; he was making twisted demands: 'The more you bid us expose your sleight of hand, the more I fear you may have robbed us even of our eyes, while we were watching you. And so it is not I that must be forced to tell of your plunder, but you that must be compelled to give it up.'[25]

The Dictator simply reiterated that Manlius should make his accusations stick or admit that they were false, and when Manlius refused to speak, he had him arrested. The Plebs were outraged, but they also had a deeply ingrained submissiveness to regular authority. No one challenged Cossus, although their sense of injustice was exacerbated when he held a triumph for his victory over the Volsci – it was really a triumph over Manlius, not over a foreign enemy, they said. As Cossus duly abdicated from the dictatorship, Manlius languished in prison until the crowds outside the jail became so menacing that the Senate voted to release him.

With no external wars to fight there was a brief hiatus, which both sides regarded as beneficial to their cause. Manlius tried to rouse the Plebs by inspirational oratory, which sheds interesting light on Roman attitudes towards them:

'How long will you remain ignorant of your own strength,' he asked, 'which Nature has willed that even the wild beasts know? . . . Count up your numbers and the numbers of your adversaries . . . Make show of war, and you will have peace . . . The gods gave me, in war and in peace, the inspiration to defend you from the barbarity of your enemies and the arrogance of your fellow citizens . . . The only reason you are so high and mighty with foreigners is that you have had to fight with them for supremacy, but you have no experience in defending your liberty against the Patricians . . . Violence works . . . I will be your leader.'

Manlius had overstepped the mark: 'It is said that this was the first step in his attempt to secure kingly power, but there is no clear tradition as to his fellow-conspirators or the extent to which his plans were developed.'[26]

The Senate felt that it was acceptable to sacrifice a single citizen to end a domestic war, and made a proposal that 'the magistrates should see to it that the Republic should come to no harm by the pernicious schemes of Marcus Manlius'.[27] Only bloodshed would resolve the situation, and they exploited class prejudice to turn the Plebs against him and achieve their aims:

> It is our intention to fix a day for his trial. Nothing is less desired by the people than kingly power. As soon as that body of Plebeians become aware that the quarrel is not with them, and find that from being his supporters they have become his judges; as soon as they see a Patrician on his trial, and learn that the charge before them is one of aiming at monarchy, they will not show favour to any man more than to their own liberty.[28]

Aspiring to be king of Rome was the ultimate act of treason. Initially the Plebs felt that there was a conspiracy to destroy their champion because he had abandoned the Patricians for them, and no facts seem to have been brought forward at his trial that had any relevance to the specific accusation. In his defence, Manlius deployed the evidence of 400 men that he had saved from enslavement for debt; his military distinctions; the spoils from thirty enemies that he had killed; two mural crowns for being the first to scale an enemy's walls; and eight civic crowns awarded for saving a fellow citizen's life. He bared his battle-scarred torso and diverted everyone's gaze to the Capitol that he had saved, which was in full view of the Campus Martius, where the indictment was taking place. His accusers realised that this emotional appeal would lead to his acquittal, so they adjourned the trial and shifted the venue to the Peletine Grove from which the Capitol was not visible. He was condemned, and hurled from the Tarpeian Rock. But if the Patricians thought that his death would defuse the discontent, they were badly mistaken: he simply became a martyr to the cause of social reform.

While Manlius had been championing the poor Plebeians in their struggle not only against the dangers of debt and enslavement, which remained a very real challenge, but also land shortage – we hear that he put forward unspecified agrarian proposals, which Livy says had always served the tribunes in stirring up rebellion[29] – the richer Plebs, who still had no access to any meaningful political power, began to demand access to all magistracies, the consulship included. After the demise of Manlius, it took a generation of struggle for the Plebeians to turn their situation from one of 'abject surrender'[30] to one where the Patricians had been forced to admit them to the consulship, although the Patrician riposte was to divert some of the functions of the consul to a new, exclusively Patrician, magistracy called the praetorship.

The process began, it was said, in 376/5 BC, when two tribunes, Gaius Licinius Stolo ('a man of mark, albeit a Plebeian'[31]) and Lucius Sextius ('a strenuous youth, whose aspirations were thwarted only by his lack of Patrician blood'[32]), made three radical proposals designed solely to curtail the influence of the Patricians and enhance that of the Plebs: one aiming to make the repayment of debts easier; another limiting the amount of public land that anyone could hold to 500 *iugera* (about 120 hectares) in the hope that large numbers of poorer peasants could be accommodated on the land;[33] and a third, which did away with the election of military tribunes, and prescribed that at least one of the consuls should be a Plebeian.[34]

The Patricians reacted to this threat to their money, lands and position by vetoing the proposals; Licinius and Sextius responded in kind, preventing any meaningful elections for five years, while themselves holding the office of tribune of the Plebs year after year, and continuing to expose the unfairness and inequality. There could be no equal rights, they said, while one side simply issued commands and the other could only protest ineffectually:

> And yet the Patricians – as they proceeded to assert – would never check their greed for land, nor cease murdering the Plebs with usury, until the commons should elect one of the two Consuls from their own number, to guard their liberties ... The Consulship remained for the commons to achieve; this was the citadel of liberty, this its pillar. If they attained to this, then would the Roman People hold that the kings had been really driven from the City, and their freedom firmly based; for the commons would thenceforward be partakers in all that made the Patricians now surpass them, – authority and honour, martial renown, birth and nobility, – great things for themselves to enjoy, but even greater to bequeath to their children.[35]

During the unrest, which allegedly involved irregular elections and the election of Camillus to two dictatorships, the Patricians conceded to an increase in the number of officials responsible for religious ceremonies from two to ten (from *Duumviri* to *Decemviri Sacris Faciundis*) and allowed half of them to be Plebeians. This was felt to set a precedent for the consulship, but matters were interrupted by a Gallic incursion and the appointment of Camillus to his fifth dictatorship.

The Roman sources are at variance over the events of this invasion: the annalist Quintus Claudius Quadrigarius said that the battle with the Gauls took place in 368 BC near the River Anio, and that Titus Manlius, a descendent of the Gaul-repelling Marcus Manlius, fought a duel on a bridge. Livy says that the exploits took place 'no less than ten years later', and then proceeds to make it happen six years later. But regardless of its date, it was a classic Roman versus barbarian clash:

> Armed and accoutred, [the Romans] led [Titus Manlius] forth to the Gaul, who in his stupid glee ... thrust his tongue out in derision ... The Gaul, whose huge bulk towered above the other, advanced his shield with the left arm, to parry the attack of his oncoming enemy, and delivered a slashing stroke with his sword, that made a mighty clatter but did no harm. The Roman, with the point of his weapon raised, struck up his adversary's shield with a blow from his own against its lower edge; and slipping in between the man's sword and his body, so close that no part of his own person was exposed, he gave one thrust and then immediately another, and gashing the groin and belly of his enemy brought him headlong to the ground, where he lay stretched out over a monstrous space. To the body of his fallen foe he offered no other indignity than to despoil it of one thing – a chain which, spattered with blood, he cast round his own neck.[36]

The 'Gallic terror' of the invasion was duly repulsed by Camillus' Roman army, thousands of barbarians fell in battle, and the survivors dispersed.

Camillus was awarded a triumph, but he found that defeating barbarians outside Rome was easier than subduing Plebeians inside the city. The tribunes of the Plebs gained the upper hand and, at the elections of 367 BC, against the wishes of the nobles, Lucius Sextius was elected as Rome's first ever Plebeian consul. It took the threat of another secession of the

Plebs to make the Patricians accept the result, although as a concession to the election of the Plebeian consul, the Patricians were allowed to elect a praetor to administer justice within the city of Rome. The praetorship was, however, opened to the Plebs thirty years later.[37]

The admission of the Plebeians to the consulship was ultimately recognised as being a major step forward: at last there was *concordia* (harmony), rather than *ira* (wrath), between the orders;[38] the Great Games were celebrated and expanded; and although the aged Camillus, hailed as next after Romulus as 'the Second Founder of Rome', died of plague shortly afterwards, he still had time to vow a temple to Concord, to commemorate the Harmony of the Orders (*Concordia Ordinum*).

Securing access to the consulship was not the last phase of the process, and the Plebeians continued to make further advances in both the political arena and among the major 'colleges' (*collegia*) of priests. They gained access to the newly created curule aedileship the year after it was set up to administer the Great Games.[39] When the tribunes Quintus and Gnaeus Ogulnius passed a measure (the *lex Ogulnia* of 300 BC) that raised the numbers of *Pontifices*, who controlled the religious calendar and looked after the cults of individual gods, and *Augures*, the official diviners who interpreted whether or not the gods approved of various proposed actions, from four to nine each, they stipulated that the new members who were co-opted must be Plebeians.

Perhaps the crowning victory in the Plebeian struggle for equality came in 287 BC, just after the end of the three so-called 'Samnite Wars', fought versus the Samnites alone, and in coalition with Etruscans, Umbrians and Gauls between 343 and

290 BC. The Samnites were a warlike Italic people from Samnium, an Oscan-speaking district of the central southern Apennines, who formed a confederacy of four tribal states, each administered by a *meddix* (= 'one who cares for'). Technically there was a treaty that fixed the boundary at the River Liris (now the Garigliano) in central Italy, but the two peoples were constantly at war. The Samnites were experts in mountain fighting, and the awkward conflicts did not always go Rome's way, but the Romans emerged victorious, stronger and dominant. The Samnites became allies (*socii*) of Rome, and when Rome defeated yet another coalition of Etruscans and Gauls in 284 BC she became the mistress of the entire Italian peninsula, apart from the Greek cities of the south, who still saw Romans as *barbaroi*.

As ever, the Romans seemed to have greater difficulty in resolving their internal conflicts than they did in subduing barbarous Italians, and the persistent issues with debt provoked one final secession of the Plebs in 287 BC. On this occasion they crossed the River Tiber to the Janiculum Hill, and Quintus Hortensius was elected Dictator. But Hortensius was a Plebeian, and he pushed through a measure, the *lex Hortensia*, decreeing that resolutions (*plebiscita*) made by the Concilium Plebis, even though they had only been voted on by Plebeians, should have the same force as the laws (*leges*) passed in the Comitia Centuriata, and that they should be binding on the entire population, Patricians included. So now both *plebiscita* and *leges* from the rival institutions carried equal weight, the Roman state had become as democratic as it ever would, and the Struggle of the Orders effectively came to an end. However, Roman society remained rigidly stratified, and rather than seeing it opening out into an egalitarian society, we simply witness the development of a new Patricio-Plebeian elite. Significant numbers of Plebeians became wealthy, and many of them began to have the same interests as the Patrician aristocrats. So, with new access to political power for influential Plebeians, new political families came into being, and given that the Roman voters had deeply entrenched and traditional voting habits, they tended to elect people from the leading families year after year. Effectively an open oligarchy was created, and new terms came into being, such as *nobiles*, which meant not 'Patricians', but all men whose families had achieved the consulship: it was a nobility not of birth, but of political office. Yet the rough and ex-barbarous Plebs were no longer outsiders to the Roman political system. A more cohesive Rome could now face up to external enemies in a more unified way.

4

Pyrrhus of Epirus: Cadmean and Pyrrhic Victories

The Greek historian Polybius, writing in the mid-second century BC to explain Rome's rise to power to a Greek audience, said that,

> Those who desire a complete and comprehensive account of the development of Rome's present supremacy . . . must acquaint themselves with the period and with the process whereby the Romans began to advance towards better fortunes after the defeat they had suffered on their own soil,[1] and with the details of how and when, after becoming the masters of Italy, they applied themselves to the conquest of countries further afield.[2]

Italy and Epirus

Like Rome, the long-established culturally Greek cities of Magna Graecia in the south of Italy were subject to persistent attacks by various barbarian Italian tribes. At the same time as Rome had been fending off Brennus' Gauls, Thourioi (Thurii or

Thurium in Latin, near modern Sibari) on the Gulf of Tarentum had been assailed by the formidable Lucanians of southern Italy, who, like their neighbours the Samnites, spoke a variety of the Umbrian-Oscan language. The Greeks had formed a defensive league to resist them, but sometimes they needed outside help, and in 334 BC Tarentum (Taras to its Greek inhabitants, modern Taranto) asked Alexander the Great's uncle, Alexander I of Epirus[3] (aka Alexander of Molossis, r. 350–331 BC), to help them fight off the Lucanians and their neighbours the Bruttii, who were another ancient Italic people inhabiting the toe of Italy (roughly modern Calabria). Alexander I obliged. He crossed into Italy, defeated the Samnites and Lucanians near Paestum in 332 BC, made a treaty with the Romans,[4] and won further victories over the Lucanians and Bruttii, until he himself was defeated at the Battle of Pandosia in 331 BC, and was killed by a treacherous Lucanian javelin-thrower.[5]

Issues of 'barbarian' identity become quite convoluted in the events involving Rome and Epirus/Molossis, and remain so in twenty-first-century discussions pertaining to Balkan politics, becoming particularly vitriolic in numerous internet forums. Thucydides unequivocally includes the Molossians in a list of northern *barbaroi*, although it is not clear whether their barbarity is down to their primitive level of civilisation or their language, or both: '[The Spartan admiral Cnemus] had with him [various] Hellenic troops [and] of barbarians [*barbaroi*], a thousand Chaonians . . . also some Thesprotians [plus] a force of Molossians.'[6]

On the other hand, the fifth-century BC tragedian Euripides may also have tried to manipulate the mythical tradition and make the Molossians Greek, as a compliment to the Molossian royal family. In his *Andromache*, King Menelaus is worried that

Molossus, the son of the Trojan/barbarian Andromache by Achilles' son Neoptolemus, might become a barbarian ruling Greeks: 'Yet come now (it is no shame to touch on this point): if . . . this woman has children, will you set them up as kings over the land of Phthia, and will they, barbarians by birth, rule over Greeks?'[7]

But the goddess Thetis explains that fate has other plans for him: 'Andromache . . . must migrate to the land of the Molossians and be married to Helenus,[8] and with her must go her son [Molossus], the last of the line of Aeacus.[9] It is fated that his descendants in unbroken succession will rule over Molossia in blessedness.'[10]

So in this version, Molossus, with his Greek family ties to Achilles, will rule the northern Molossian tribe that Thucydides had classified as a 'barbarian people'. Alexander I of Molossis/ Epirus certainly claimed this peerless Greek mythological pedigree for himself, although Plutarch still regarded his people as barbarian: their ancestry might have been illustrious, but their behaviour gave them away: 'The kings who followed in this line soon lapsed into barbarism [ekbarbarothenton] and became quite obscure.'[11]

The 'obscurity' is the clue to the attitude of the Greeks here: what little interest they showed in the Molossians/Epirotes is full of contradiction and confusion, especially when it comes to ethnic identity, and the situation is not helped by the lack of writings from the 'barbarians' themselves.

Pyrrhus' Rise to Prominence

Alexander I's incursion into Italy was an abnormal event, because Tarentum had traditionally acted as the protector of the Greek cities, but in 285 BC some of the smaller Greek states, led by Thourioi, started to see Rome as a better bet. Rome was happy enough to flex her muscles in this area and, when she did, Tarentum attacked ten Roman ships when they sailed into the Gulf of Tarentum in 282 BC, and also the city of Thouroi itself, which had been a long-standing rival.

When the Romans demanded reparations, the Tarentines started to worry about their independence. So again they turned to Epirus, this time to Alexander I's nephew King Pyrrhus. The son of Aeacides and Phthia, Pyrrhus was born in 319 BC, and lived during the generation of rulers known as the Successors (*Diadokhoi*), who sought to forge their own kingdoms out of what had been Alexander III the Great's empire (Alexander III died in 323 BC). Pyrrhus was the great-great-grandson of Tharrhypas, who 'historians say, first introduced Greek customs and letters and regulated his cities by humane laws':[12] he may have been regarded as a bit of a barbarian by most Greeks, but he saw himself as thoroughly Hellenised, and regarded the Italians as the barbarians.

Pyrrhus had an eventful childhood. While he was still a babe in arms his father was expelled from his kingdom, and after a dramatic escape over a swollen river, Pyrrhus was taken to Glaucias, the King of the Illyrians, where he won the ruler's heart:

> Pyrrhus . . . crept across the floor, clutched the king's robe, and pulled himself on to his feet at the knees of Glaucias, who was moved at first to laughter, then to pity, as he saw the child clinging to his knees and weeping like a formal suppliant. Some say, however, that the child did not suppli- cate Glaucias, but caught hold of an altar of the gods and

stood there with his arms thrown round it, and that Glaucias thought this a sign from Heaven.[13]

He grew up at Glaucias' court until, at the age of twelve, he was taken back to Epirus and installed on the throne by armed force. He ruled as a minor from 307/6 to 303/2 BC, when he was expelled again and replaced by his cousin, the 'stern and arbitrary ruler'[14] Neoptolemus II.

Pyrrhus turned to Demetrius Poliorcetes ('the Besieger' – a nickname ironically given to him because of his failure to conquer Rhodes in a massive siege operation in 305 BC, after which the Rhodians erected the Colossus of Rhodes), who was the husband of his sister Deidamia. Pyrrhus fought heroically, but in a losing cause, alongside Demetrius and his father Antigonus I Monophthalmus (the 'One-Eyed') in their defeat to three other Successors of Alexander the Great, Cassander of Macedon, Lysimachus of Thrace and Seleucus I Nicator (the 'Conqueror') of Syria, at the enormous Battle of Ipsus in Phrygia in 301 BC. Demetrius and Pyrrhus ultimately ended up at the court of another of Alexander's Successors, Ptolemy I Soter ('Saviour') of Egypt, where Pyrrhus' athleticism and prowess in hunting impressed both Ptolemy and his wife Berenice, whose daughter Antigone he duly married.[15]

With military and financial backing from Ptolemy I, Pyrrhus was able to reinstate himself as King of Epirus, albeit initially as joint ruler with Neoptolemus II. In 297 BC, when Pyrrhus got wind of a plot to murder him by poison, he got his retaliation in first and killed Neoptolemus II at a banquet. He then set about consolidating his position and expanding his realm, and the early years of his reign saw him annex southern Illyria and, by some judicious interventions in the dynastic quarrels that were afflicting Macedon, he secured possession of some key border areas, along with Ambracia, Acarnania and Amphilochia. Pyrrhus' relations with Demetrius Poliorcetes became somewhat strained when Demetrius became King of Macedon in 294 BC: 'greed for power, the natural disease of dynasties, made them formidable and suspicious neighbours',[16] and their relations were not helped by the death of Deidamia. There was warfare from 291 BC onwards, in which we are told Pyrrhus yielded to none of his adversaries in daring and prowess, because he wanted the glory of Achilles to belong to him by right of valour rather than of blood alone,[17] and he certainly achieved substantial territorial gains in Thessaly and Macedonia, although these were largely lost within a decade to Lysimachus, another of the mighty Hellenistic warlords.

Territorial gains were also achieved by more pacific means, and when his wife Antigone died, having given birth to a son named Ptolemy, Pyrrhus married several women: the daughter of the Paeonian king Audoleon; Bircenna, the daughter of the Dardanian chief Bardyllis; and Lanassa, the daughter of Agathocles of Syracuse, who brought Leucas and Corcyra with her as part of her dowry. Polygamy was the normal practice among the kings of these regions, but the mixture of barbarian and Greek within Pyrrhus' household caused problems. The culturally Greek Lanassa was offended because Pyrrhus seemed to like his barbarian wives more than her, so she retired to Corcyra, from where she invited Demetrius to marry her. This he did, taking Corcyra from Pyrrhus as well as his wife.

Despite this setback, by the mid-280s BC Pyrrhus' kingdom was strong, stable and largely Hellenised. Symbolic of this is the development of the oracular site of Dodona. Archaeological evidence suggests that the area had been occupied since the

Bronze Age, with the earliest cult probably dedicated to the Earth Goddess or another female fertility deity. This was superseded by the cult of Zeus, introduced by the Selloi tribe from Thesprotia. It was referred to by Homer, and in Apollonius Rhodius' *Argonautica* Jason's vessel, the *Argo*, had the power of prophecy because it had an oak beam from Dodona built into it. Herodotus told a tale that he learned from the sanctuary's priests in which two black pigeons, the *peleiades*, flew from Egypt; one of them landed in Libya, where the temple of Zeus Ammon was subsequently erected; the other alighted in Dodona, on Zeus' sacred oak tree, where it spoke in a human voice to show where the oracle should be established.[18] The god's will was ascertained from the rustling of the oak's leaves and observing the flight of the birds nesting in it. There is evidence of offerings of bronze tripods, statuettes, jewellery and weapons from southern Greece dating from as early as the eighth century BC, but the sanctuary did not achieve true architectural monumentality until the reign of Pyrrhus, and most of the sanctuary's significant buildings, including the magnificent theatre, the impressively rebuilt temple of Zeus, the bouleuterion, the prytaneum and the stadium, date from this period.

Plutarch tells us that at this stage of Pyrrhus' career, Fortune gave him the option of enjoying what he had achieved without any further hassle, living in peace and reigning over his own people.[19] But he was not that kind of man: it made him sick with boredom not to be either inflicting or suffering mischief. But his 'people skills' were effective: although he tended to look down on his inferiors, he was nevertheless orderly and restrained in his everyday living habits, and adept at turning the favour of his superiors to his own advantage. He was alleged to have healing powers, and his physical appearance was striking: 'Pyrrhus had more of the terror than of the majesty of kingly power. He had not many teeth, but his upper jaw was one continuous bone, on which the usual intervals between the teeth were indicated by slight depressions . . . It is said, further, that the great toe of his right foot had a divine virtue, so that after the rest of his body had been consumed, this was found to be untouched and unharmed by the fire.'[20]

Italy Turns to Pyrrhus; Pyrrhus Turns to Italy

Like Achilles, Pyrrhus simply couldn't tolerate idleness, 'but ate his heart away . . . and pined for war-cry and battle'.[21] So, in the summer of 281 BC, when the invitation to intervene in Italy came from Tarentum and various other Italian Greek cities, it was a very tempting prospect. The Tarentines told Pyrrhus that they wanted him to lead them, and that he would find 20,000 cavalry and 350,000 infantry when he arrived. The offer was too good for Pyrrhus to turn down. He accepted, and crossed over to Italy with around 20,000 seasoned infantry-men, 3,000 cavalry, about 20 elephants, and ambitions that went beyond the conquest of Rome and into Italy, Sicily, Libya, Carthage, Macedonia and Greece. Plutarch tells a moral fable that when Pyrrhus' wise advisor Cineas asked him, 'What will we do then?' Pyrrhus replied, 'Drink huge cups of wine every day, and delight our hearts with enjoyable talk.' 'Why don't we just do that now?' was Cineas' reply. 'That way we can save ourselves and everyone else a good deal of danger, bloodshed, and suffering.'[22] But Cineas' point was lost on Pyrrhus, who couldn't give up his hopes of conquest, and Cineas was sent to Tarentum with the first 3,000 troops. Pyrrhus followed with the main contingent, enduring losses in a heavy storm at sea, and assumed the command of the combined forces at Tarentum. The Roman army, commanded by the Consul Laevinus, moved south against him.

Pyrrhus and his Greek allies represented the most severe military threat that Rome had yet faced, but Laevinus still rejected Pyrrhus' offer of arbitration, telling him that the Romans neither chose him as a mediator nor feared him as an enemy.[23] Pyrrhus pitched camp between the cities of Pandosia and Heraclea, and when the Romans approached he was impressed by their organisation: 'The military organisation of barbarians [*barbaron*] is not barbarous [*barbaros*].'[24] The man who was regarded by many Greeks as a barbarian still saw the Romans as the barbarians.

The Romans struck first, crossing the River Siris and drawing themselves up in good order. For his part, Pyrrhus was an intelligent and inspiring presence in the fight:

He was conspicuous at once for the beauty and splendour of his richly ornamented armour, and showed by his deeds that his valour did not belie his fame; and this most of all because, while actively participating in the fight and vigorously repelling his assailants, he did not become confused in his calculations nor lose his presence of mind, but directed the battle as if he were surveying it from a distance, darting hither and thither himself and bringing aid to those whom he thought to be overwhelmed.[25]

He had a narrow escape when a 'barbarian' Roman killed his horse, after which he fought for a while on foot in the phalanx. The combat was a finely balanced one – Plutarch says that there were seven twists of fortune – but ultimately the Romans were pushed back by Pyrrhus' elephants. This was the first time elephants had been used in battle on Italian soil, and the Roman horses were so terrified by the strange beasts that they ran away before they even got close, which allowed Pyrrhus to unleash his Thessalian cavalry and rout them.

Trying to establish accurate casualty figures for any ancient military engagement is extremely difficult, and the ancient sources vary between 7,000 and 15,000 Roman dead as against 4,000 and 13,000 on Pyrrhus' side. But these seem to have been his best troops, and he also lost many of his most trusted friends and generals. The Battle of Heraclea was the first of the so-called 'Pyrrhic victories', won at such a cost that they were not worthwhile. What we call a Pyrrhic victory was known to the Greeks and Romans as a Cadmean victory (*kadmeios nike*[26]). In myth, Cadmus was the founder of Thebes in Greece. When he had found the right location for the city, he sent his companions to fetch water from the nearby Spring of Ares, not realising that a horrendous dragon lived there. It stung them, crushed them in its coils or blasted them with its poisonous breath, and so although the mighty Cadmus then slew the monster, his victory had been achieved at a terrible cost. Alternatively, the phrase might have originated from the myth of Cadmus' descendants Eteocles and Polynices, who fought for the possession of Thebes and killed each other in the process.[27]

Nevertheless, despite his losses, Pyrrhus was proud of his achievements. After the battle many of the Lucanians and Samnites joined him, but the Romans were not inclined to capitulate. Laevinus retained his office; the depleted legions were restored to full strength; new ones were recruited; and the rhetoric was uncompromising. Pyrrhus was happy to negotiate

– capturing Rome was probably beyond him, and he was satisfied with the enhanced reputation that the victory had given him – and he sent Cineas to deliver gifts and make generous and alluring proposals to the Senate. But as the senators dithered, the venerable blind old hardliner Appius Claudius Caecus convinced them to fight on. Cineas was politely sent back to tell Pyrrhus to leave Italy. He delivered the message, along with observations about how the Senate impressed him as a 'Council of many kings' and how he feared the Roman people would turn out to be a Lernaean Hydra (a Greek mythological monster with many heads, which grew two new ones whenever one was chopped off[28]) because the Consul Laevinus already had twice as many soldiers as he had before the defeat, and there were many more where they came from.[29]

The Romans sent Gaius Fabricius Luscinus to negotiate the release of the prisoners. Fabricius was not impressed by Pyrrhus' gold and elephants, or by Cineas' Epicurean philosophy, but Pyrrhus was impressed with Fabricius. He allowed him to take the prisoners, but on condition that, if the Senate didn't vote for the peace, they should be sent back again, although they would be allowed a reunion with their relatives and to celebrate the festival of Saturn. The Senate maintained its pro-war position, and so the prisoners were duly returned after the festival, with the Senate reinforcing the honourable nature of the agreement by decreeing the death penalty for any prisoner who stayed behind. The theme of Roman honour was also reinforced by an anecdote that one of Pyrrhus' doctors wrote to Fabricius, offering to poison the king if they rewarded him for putting an end to the war.[30] This offended the Roman's sense of fair play, so he wrote to Pyrrhus to tell him. Pyrrhus punished the doctor and offered to return the prisoners again as a token of his goodwill. The Romans, though, refused to take them back for nothing: they did not want a favour from their enemy or a reward for not perpetrating a crime against him. So they released an equal number of Tarentine and Samnite prisoners that they had taken. Despite all the honourable gestures on either side, the Romans refused to discuss peace and friendship while Pyrrhus was still in Italy, and Pyrrhus refused to leave.

In 279 BC Pyrrhus marched his army to Asculum and engaged the Romans again, but this time the terrain was unsuitable for his cavalry and elephants, and night put a stop to the fighting after a full day's attritional combat. It is relatively unusual for an ancient pitched battle to last into a second day,[31] which gives an indication of the evenness of the engagement, but on the following morning Pyrrhus was able to redeploy his troops and force the Romans to fight on level ground. His massed attacked was fiercely resisted, but the Romans finally buckled under the sheer weight of the onslaught: 'The factor which did most to enable the Greeks to prevail was the weight and fury of the elephants' charge. Against this even the Romans' courage was of little avail: they felt as they might have done before the rush of a tidal wave or the shock of an earthquake, and it was better to give way than to stand their ground to no purpose, and suffer a terrible fate without gaining the least advantage.'[32]

Again, casualties were high on both sides: Hieronymus, who claims he had access to Pyrrhus' own commentaries, says he lost 3,500 men to the Romans' 6,000; Dionysius put the total body count on both sides at 15,000. Dionysius also says that Pyrrhus took a wound in the arm from a javelin. Plutarch preserves a conversation that shows that Pyrrhus knew that the real damage had been done to his army: 'The story goes that when one of Pyrrhus' friends congratulated him on his victory, he replied, "One more victory like that over the Romans will destroy us completely!" He had lost a great part of the force he had brought with him, with a few exceptions almost all his friends and commanders had been killed, and there were no reinforcements that he could summon from home.'[33]

Despite their losses, the Romans again didn't make peace with Pyrrhus, but formed a mutually defensive alliance with Carthage. The two powers had not always been implacable enemies, and this treaty retained the terms of previous agreements between them (for Rome's treaty relations with Carthage before this point, see p. 90), while adding some clauses:

If the Romans or the Carthaginians make a written alliance against Pyrrhus they shall both conclude it in such a way that they may help each other in the land of the party on whom he is making war.

Whichever party may need help, the Carthaginians shall provide the ships both for transport and for operations, but each shall provide the pay for its own men.

The Carthaginians shall also give help to the Romans by sea if need arises, but no one shall compel the crews to disembark against their will.[34]

The reason the Carthaginians signed is probably that they were afraid that the Romans might be tempted to make peace with Pyrrhus after Ausculum.[35] They would have liked the conflict in Italy to keep going, especially if Pyrrhus had genuine ambitions to invade Africa. The Carthaginians also made a deal with the warlike Sicilian people known as the Mamertini, whose name means 'Sons of Mars', aka Mamers, the war god.[36]

Sicily

As Pyrrhus pondered his next move, Fortune threw him two new options. Emissaries came from Greece to tell him that Ptolemy Ceraunus ('Thunderbolt'), the son of Ptolemy I of Egypt, who had rather deviously made himself King of Macedonia, had been killed in battle fighting a Gallic invasion led by a warlord called Belgius. So there was an opportunity for Pyrrhus to step into Ceraunus' shoes. But an alternative opportunity came his way from Sicily, where he was offered control of the cities of Agrigentum, Syracuse and Leontini in return for expelling the Carthaginians from the island. Sicily proved to be the more attractive choice, so Pyrrhus installed a garrison in Tarentum and sent Cineas to hold preliminary discussions, to the deep annoyance of the Tarentines, who felt that he should either help them against Rome or get out of their territory. Pyrrhus did neither. He set sail for Sicily, probably towards the end of the summer of 278 BC.

Pyrrhus' Sicilian campaign started well. He had an easy landing at Tauromenium (modern Taormina); we hear of a deep affection towards him from the Sicilian people; the cities went over to him as promised; and he routed the Carthaginians (or the Phoenicians, as some sources call them – Carthage had been founded by the Phoenicians), capturing city after city, often without a fight. Our sources for Pyrrhus' campaigns in Sicily are very poor – the relevant passages of Diodorus have been lost, Plutarch is very sketchy and the Byzantine historian Justin is of questionable quality – and putting accurate dates on the events is almost impossible. But Pyrrhus is credited with some glorious exploits, including being the first to scale the wall of the precipitously located Elymian city of Eryx (modern

Erice): 'Many were the foes against whom he strove; some of them he pushed from the wall on either side and hurled them to the ground, but most he laid dead in heaps about him with the strokes of his sword. He himself suffered no harm, but was a terrible sight for his enemies to look upon.'[37]

This was a feat on a par with the hero Hercules, who was reputed to have killed the King of the Elymians in a wrestling bout during his Labours, and it went one better than Alexander the Great's famous capture of the Rock of Aornus, which he only achieved after its defenders had abandoned it.

By the winter of 277 BC, Tauromenium, Catana, Syracuse, Leontini, Agrigentum, Enna, Heraclea, Azones, Selinus, Halicyae, Segesta, Eryx, Iaetia, Panormus and Hectae were all his, and if he could capture Carthage's main base on the island at Lilybaeum, he would have total control of Sicily. When he laid siege to it, the Carthaginians sought peace. Pyrrhus rejected their proposals, but he failed to take the city and abandoned the assault.

Significantly in the context of who should be considered barbarian in this conflict, the Greek author Plutarch calls the Carthaginians 'barbarians',[38] a term that he also applies to the Mamertini, who were antagonising their Greek neighbours in the vicinity of Messana. After leaving Lilybaeum, Pyrrhus put the Mamertini firmly in their place, executing the tax-gatherers who were collecting tribute. But Pyrrhus now seems to have expanded his objectives to include conquests in Africa, and to act incredibly arrogantly towards the Greeks. Plutarch regarded this as a major turning point in his career: 'He had not behaved in this way at the very beginning, but had even gone beyond others in trying to win men's hearts by gracious intercourse with them, by trusting everybody, and by doing nobody any harm. But now he ceased to be a popular leader and became a tyrant, and added to his name for severity a name for ingratitude and faithlessness.'[39]

Pyrrhus succeeded in alienating his erstwhile allies. At Syracuse, Sosistratus and the garrison commander Thoenon, who had been instrumental in persuading him to come to Sicily in the first place, and who had helped him enormously in his activities on the island, now fell under his suspicion. Sosistratus defected, but Thoenon was put to death.[40] Discontent spread throughout the Sicilian Greeks, some of whom joined the Carthaginians, while others even looked to the Mamertini. Carthaginian reinforcements sailed over from Africa, and with the situation threatening to spiral out of control, Pyrrhus used the fact that the Samnites and Tarentines were doing badly in their struggle with Rome as a pretext for returning to Italy, although not before he had allegedly uttered the prophetic words, 'What a wrestling school for Carthaginians and Romans we are leaving behind us, my friends!'[41]

Pyrrhus had to fight the Carthaginians in the Strait of Messina to extricate his fleet from Sicily, and once he had landed in Italy he was intercepted by 10,000 Mamertini. In a hard-fought engagement he lost two of his elephants, incurred a headwound and retired from the field, prompting one of the 'barbarians' to challenge him to come out if he were still alive. He did, seething with anger, covered in blood and terrifying to look at: 'and before the barbarian could strike [Pyrrhus] dealt him such a blow on his head with his sword that, what with the might of his arm and the excellent temper of his steel, it cleaved its way down through, so that at one instant the parts of the sundered body fell to either side. This checked the barbarians from any further advance, for they were amazed and confounded at Pyrrhus, and thought him some superior being.'[42]

He completed the journey without further significant problems, and in the autumn of 276 BC he arrived back in Tarentum with 20,000 infantry and 3,000 cavalry, who he supplemented with the best of the Tarentine troops. But Pyrrhus needed money to pay these fighters, many of whom were undoubtedly mercenaries, and he was short of cash. So, 'observing that Pyrrhus was embarrassed and was seeking funds from every possible source, the worst and most depraved of his friends, Euegorus ... Balacrus ... and Deinarchus ... , followers of godless and accursed doctrines, suggested an impious source for the raising of funds, namely, to open up the sacred treasures of Persephone.'[43]

This refers to a temple at Locris, where there was 'an unfathomed quantity of gold, buried in the earth out of sight of the multitude. Pyrrhus, misled by these flatterers and because of his necessity that was stronger than any scruples, employed as his agents in the sacrilege the men who had made the proposal; and placing the gold plundered from the temple in ships, he sent it along with his other funds to Taras, having now become filled with great cheer.'[44]

However, the ships carrying the plunder were wrecked in a storm, evidence, as Dionysius of Halicarnassus sees it, of the just power of the gods. He describes how Pyrrhus was terrified by this, and returned all the loot to the goddess, in the hope of appeasing her wrath. But to no avail: 'It was for this reason that Pyrrhus was defeated by the Romans ... in a battle to the finish.'[45]

Maleventum/Beneventum and Home

The Romans' resilience was now tested to the full. War-weariness was setting in, and their citizen population was considerably depleted from the fighting: in 280 BC, when the Plebeian censor Cnaius Domitius Calvinus Maximus held the *Lustrum* ceremony, 287,222 citizens were registered; in 275 BC the censors celebrated the *Lustrum* after 271,224 citizens had been registered, a total loss of 15,998.[46] Draft-dodging became an issue. When Manius Curius Dentatus, 'Toothy' (who, according to Pliny the Elder, acquired his cognomen because he was born with teeth;[47] consul in 275 BC), was recruiting an army to face Pyrrhus, many refused to enlist, and only the threat of being sold into slavery persuaded them to join up (with one exception, who had all his possessions sold).[48]

The incorruptible and frugal Dentatus moved his forces into Samnite territory, while his colleague Lucius Cornelius Lentulus Caudinus headed into Lucania. The Italians appealed to Pyrrhus, who immediately took the field, dividing his forces into two, despatching one contingent to Lucania and leading the other in person to confront Dentatus, who was encamped near the city of Maleventum (modern Benevento).

Pyrrhus seems to have had the numerical advantage, even if our sources exaggerate this quite seriously. Dionysius of Halicarnassus makes it three to one in his favour, although the likelihood is that he deployed between 30,000 to 50,000 against 20,000 to 25,000.[49] But he needed to make this tell before the Romans could unite their forces, while Dentatus, who was an experienced commander with three triumphs to his name already, naturally sought to delay. Pyrrhus decided to lead a surprise night attack on the Roman camp, using a detachment of his elite soldiers and the most warlike elephants. Because this involved moving through some densely wooded mountainous country at night, it was a risky undertaking: 'hoplites burdened with helmets, breastplates and shields and advancing against hilly positions by long trails that were not even used by people but were mere goat-paths through woods and crags, would keep no order and, even before the enemy came in sight, would be weakened in body by thirst and fatigue.'[50]

The journey took longer than expected, and when dawn broke Pyrrhus and his men appeared in full view of the Romans. Dentatus responded quickly and effectively, putting Pyrrhus' force to flight and capturing some of their elephants.[51] Pyrrhus himself escaped and managed to rejoin the main body of his troops, while Dentatus led his troops forward in full battle array: 'Manius Curius [Dentatus], observing that the phalanx of King Pyrrhus could not be resisted when in extended order, took pains to fight in confined quarters, where the phalanx, being massed together, would embarrass itself.'[52]

He succeeded in this, even though the ancient sources focus more on the elephants:

Manius . . . routed the enemy at some points, but at one was overwhelmed by the elephants and driven back upon his camp, where he was obliged to call upon the guards, who were standing on the parapets in great numbers, all in arms, and full of fresh vigour. Down they came from their strong places, and hurling their javelins at the elephants compelled them to wheel about and run back through the ranks of their own men, thus causing disorder and confusion there.[53]

In Orosius' account, the Roman weaponry is rather more colourful. In his account they 'prepared fire-darts, which they wound with tow, smeared with pitch, and capped with barbed spurs. They hurled these flaming missiles at the backs of the elephants and at the towers on their backs, and thus without difficulty turned back the raging and burning beasts to bring destruction upon the army of which they were part of the reserve.'[54]

Aelian takes things one stage further with the Romans' use of fire against the beasts, and has them using burning pigs:

> The elephant has a terror of . . . the squealing of a pig. It was by these means, they say, that the Romans turned the elephants of Pyrrhus of Epirus to flight, and that the Romans won a glorious victory . . . they smeared some pigs with liquid pitch, set a light to them, and let them loose against the enemy. Goaded with pain and shrieking because of their burns, the pigs fell upon the troops of elephants, driving them mad and throwing them into terrible confusion. So the elephants broke ranks and were no longer tractable in spite of having been trained since they were small, either because elephants by some instinct hate and loathe pigs, or because they dread the shrill and discordant sound of their voices.[55]

Whatever the precise details of the engagement, Roman propaganda turned it into an overwhelming defeat for Pyrrhus, with tens of thousands of casualties and the capture of the surviving elephants, who appeared in Dentatus' triumph. The Byzantine author Justin, however, claims that the Romans never defeated Pyrrhus on the battlefield, so it may have been more of a 'Pyrrhic victory' for Rome this time. But it was *seen* as a victory by the Romans, and Maleventum (literally, 'Ill Wind', 'Badly Come' or 'Bad Result'[56]) had its negative-sounding *Male-* changed to *Bene-* ('Well'), to turn it into its more favourably omened opposite, Beneventum.

Dentatus' colleague Caudinus had, in the meantime, defeated the Lucanians, and he was also awarded a triumph. Pyrrhus had by now run too short of manpower and money, and although he left a garrison behind in Tarentum in the expectation that he might one day return, he never did. In autumn 275 BC or spring 274 BC, he sailed back to Epirus with less than 30 per cent of his original force, leaving Plutarch to reflect on his failures:

> Thus Pyrrhus was excluded from his hopes of Italy and Sicily, after squandering six years' time in his wars there, and after being worsted in his undertakings, but he kept his brave spirit unconquered in the midst of his defeats; and men believed that in military experience, personal prowess, and daring, he was by far the first of the kings of his time, but that what he won by his exploits he lost by indulging in vain hopes, since through passionate desire for what he had not he always failed to establish securely what he had. For this reason Antigonus used to liken him to a player with dice who makes many fine throws but does not understand how to use them when they are made.[57]

Pyrrhus had no further direct impact on Rome. He shifted his attentions to Macedon, which had been suffering Gallic invasions while he was in Italy and Sicily. Antigonus II Gonatas had inflicted a crushing defeat on the barbarians in 278 BC, but had also enlisted large numbers of them in his forces as mercenaries (they were good warriors and they were cheap), and used them to expand his territory. Pyrrhus picked a fight with him in 274 BC, and won a significant victory, which, because of the presence of Gallic warriors in Antigonus' army, allowed him to pose as a Greek champion over barbarians. He dedicated the most splendid of his spoils in the temple of Athena Itonis in Thessaly with an inscription in elegiac couplets:

These shields, now suspended here as a gift to Athena Itonis, Pyrrhus the Molossian took from valiant Gauls, after defeating the entire army of Antigonus; which is no great wonder; for now, as well as in olden time, the Aeacidae are brave spearmen.[58]

Further battlefield success saw Pyrrhus reign briefly as King of Macedon in 274 BC, but as it had done before in his career, unpopularity quickly followed success. Having taken control of Aegae, the burial centre of the Macedonian kings, he left it garrisoned by some of the Gauls who were fighting as mercenaries on his side. They behaved, in Plutarch's eyes, like typical barbarians: 'The Gauls, a race insatiable of wealth, set themselves to digging up the tombs of the kings who had been buried there; the treasure they plundered, the bones they insolently cast to the four winds.'[59]

Pyrrhus may simply have been afraid to punish the barbarians, but he appeared altogether too laidback about this for the Macedonians' liking. As his approval ratings fell, he characteristically set his sights on new adventures, this time in Greece. Cleonymus of Sparta, whose designs on becoming king there had been thwarted by Areus, a much younger rival who also attracted the amorous interests of Cleonymus' lovely wife Chilonis,[60] invited Pyrrhus to Sparta while Areus was away on Crete. Pyrrhus accepted the invitation, and brought 25,000 infantry, 2,000 cavalry and 24 elephants along too. But after some very intense fighting he was unable to secure possession of Sparta, and shifted his focus to Argos.

Amid typically confused and confusing fighting at Argos, which was supported by Antigonus II Gonatas of Macedon, Pyrrhus managed to infiltrate the city, but not fully to gain control of it. He found himself hemmed in by the Argives, so he mounted his horse and plunged into his pursuers. When he received a light spear-wound he turned against the man who had inflicted it. He was the son of a poor old woman who was watching the combat from her house, and when she saw her son in danger, she hurled a rooftile at Pyrrhus. It hit him on the head and crushed the vertebrae at the base of his neck, making him dizzy and impairing his vision. He fell off his horse. Just as Pyrrhus was starting to recover, a man called Zopyrus, who was serving under Antigonus, saw who he was and dragged him into a doorway, where he made a terribly botched job of decapitating him. Antigonus' son Alcyoneus took the severed head to his father, prompting the king to accuse him of being 'impious and barbarous', before granting Pyrrhus an honourable funeral.[61]

5

Hannibal at the Gates

The conflict that I am going to write about was the most
memorable war that has ever been waged – the war, that is,
that the people of Carthage fought under the leadership of
Hannibal against the Roman people.[1]

The conflict with Pyrrhus, and its aftermath, had left Rome in
control of the Italian peninsula, which she organised into a
confederacy of Roman citizens, and Latin and Italian allies. In
the western Mediterranean, Carthage, on the coast of modern
Tunisia, was the dominant power. Carthage was a prosperous,
cultured, mercantile state, far removed from the modern
concept of barbarians, but one of the biggest difficulties facing
historians is that they have to rely largely on information
provided by Carthage's enemies, since hardly anything of the
Carthaginians' own literature now survives. Essentially, we get
our picture of the Carthaginians from Greeks – against whom
they fought over Sicily – and Romans – with whom they were
involved in a life and death struggle – so it's not surprising that
the picture is an extremely hostile one. To both the Romans
and the Greeks, the Carthaginians were both barbarian, at least

in the linguistic sense, and barbaric. Yet this didn't apply to Hannibal, or at least not completely, since our sources often overstated his talents, in order to excuse the defeats Rome suffered at his hands and to glorify their own victories. As Oscar Wilde rightly said, 'The truth is rarely pure and never simple.'[2]

Rome and Carthage Before the Wars

Carthage's origins go back to Phoenicia in the eastern Mediterranean. The Phoenicians were a great trading people, famous for dealing in the purple dye extracted from murex shellfish. Our name Phoenicians comes from the usual Greek name for them, *Phoinikes*, which is also linked to the noun *phoinix*, meaning 'the colour purple-red'. Since the Carthaginians came originally from Phoenicia, and the Latin word for Phoenician was *Poenicus* or *Punicus*, derived from the Greek *phoinix*, the wars between Rome and Carthage are called the Punic Wars.

The Phoenician colonies in the west were founded from the city of Tyre. The date universally accepted in antiquity for the foundation of Carthage was 814 BC. Carthage meant 'new city' (*Qart-hadasht* in Phoenician). The most popular foundation myth about Carthage told of a dynastic quarrel at Tyre, in which Elissa, sister of King Pygmalion, was forced to leave her native land, and arrived in Africa, where she made a deal with the inhabitants to purchase as much land as could be covered by an ox hide; she then cut the hide into thin strips and laid them around the whole hill of the promontory of Carthage. The citadel was subsequently called *Byrsa*, a Punic word that means ox hide in Greek.

Elissa's city became very prosperous, and the local king Iarbas asked to marry her. She asked for three months to give her answer, during which time she constructed a funeral pyre in honour of her late husband Acherbas, before climbing onto it and stabbing herself to death, claiming that in this way she would be rejoining her husband. The story of Elissa, or Dido as she is also known, existed in several different versions until the poet Virgil effectively took ownership of it with his tale of her love affair with Aeneas. It's interesting that Virgil set his story several centuries earlier than the accepted foundation date so that he could weave it into his epic about Aeneas' escape from the sack of Troy, and create a stupendous tragic romance between the founders of the two cities who were now to dispute the mastery of the western Mediterranean. When Aeneas departed from Carthage and broke Dido's heart, she prayed for war between their respective peoples:

> This is my prayer; I pour out this last utterance with my blood. You, Tyrians, persecute his stock and all the race to come with hatred, and perform these duties to my ashes! Let there be no love and no treaty between our peoples! Rise up from my bones, unknown avenger, to harass the Trojan colonists with fire and sword – now, in the future, at what-ever time you have the strength! I pray that shores will fight against shores, waves against waves, weapons against weap-ons, themselves and all their descendants![3]

Her prayers were answered. The 'unknown avenger' would be Hannibal.

In the sixth and early fifth centuries BC, the Carthaginians controlled a large part of North Africa, areas of Sicily, Sardinia and Corsica, and part of southern Spain. They needed an effect-ive military to maintain this empire, but because their population was relatively small, they preferred hiring mercenaries using state revenues to diverting large numbers of citizens from the mercantile activities that generated Carthage's prosperity in the first place. The army itself, which fought under Carthaginian generals, was a diverse barbarian coalition that included: excellent Libyan light infantry who were adept at ambushes and hit-and-run raids; North African cavalry from Numidia and Mauretania, who were unquestionably among the finest equestrian fighters in the western Mediterranean; Spanish mercenaries, many of whom wielded a unique type of short sword that came to be adopted by the Romans as their weapon of choice – the *gladius*; particularly savage slingers from the Balearic Islands who had to be paid in women rather than money; and Gauls, with their reputation for impetuosity and unreliability. Non-barbarian contingents were also recruited from the Italians of Campania, whose lack of numbers and bad reputation for treachery and barbaric behaviour was offset by their effectiveness in battle, and from the Greeks, whose fighting capabilities were greatly admired. The Roman comedian Plautus,[4] who lived through Hannibal's invasion of Italy, provided a wonderful parody of the mercenary soldiers of his time in his play *The Swaggering Soldier* (*Miles Gloriosus*), where the central character Pyrgopolynices ('Tower-Many-Victories') is a stupid, conceited, lustful soldier who boasts constantly about prowess on the battlefield and in the bedroom.[5]

Controlling such an ethnically diverse army presented considerable challenges for its commanders, but overall Carthage was not a particularly bellicose state. Its merchants did not typically regard warfare as cost-effective. Trade mattered most, and we have a humorous exchange in a Plautus comedy *Poenulus* or *The Little Carthaginian*, which stereotypes the

Carthaginians and their barbarian speech patterns, but also pokes fun at Roman attitudes. In the last act of the play, a slave called Milphio addresses a man from Carthage called Hanno: 'Avo!' he says, attempting to speak Punic, but instantly reverting to Latin, 'Where are you from? What town?' Hanno replies in nonsense Punic:[6] 'Annobynmytthymballebechaedreannech.' The slave's master Agorastocles asks, 'What's he saying?' Milphio has hardly any idea, but he responds, 'He says that he's Hanno of Carthage, a Carthaginian, son of Mytthymbal.' 'Muphursa,' says Hanno, 'Miuulechianna', and Agorastocles keeps asking, 'What's he saying? Why has he come?' Milphio bluffs: 'Don't you hear? He's stating that he wants to give African mice to the magistrates for the procession at the games.' Hanno continues, 'Lech lachanna nilimniichto.' Agorastocles asks, 'What's he saying now?' Milphio tells him, 'He says he's brought shoe-laces, water-channels, and nuts; now he's begging that you'll help him get them sold.' The conversation then continues until Milphio admits, 'Actually, now I really don't know *what* he's on about,' at which point Hanno delivers the punchline by saying, 'OK. So that you'll understand, I'll speak Latin from now on,' in perfect Latin.[7]

Cicero suggests that it was the fact that the Carthaginians were traders like Hanno that made them so untrustworthy: 'The Carthaginians were given to fraud and lying, not so much by race as by the nature of their position, because owing to their harbours, which brought them into communication with merchants and strangers speaking many different languages, they were inspired by the love of gain with the love of cheating.'[8]

Yet despite these xenophobic jokes and comments, diplomatic relations between Rome and Carthage had been pretty civil since the first year of the Republic. Polybius records two early treaties inscribed on bronze tablets held in the treasury of the aediles, which indicated that Carthage's focus was on protecting her commercial interests in the western Mediterranean, and that Rome had very little interest in overseas trade at this stage. In the treaty dating to 509/8 BC Carthage wanted trade regulations and the banning of all foreign shipping from the coast of North Africa and the western end of the Mediterranean, while Rome wanted recognition of her rights in Latium.[9] A second treaty, probably drafted by the Carthaginians and signed in 348 BC,[10] defined where Romans were not allowed to raid, trade or found a city; specified what happened if the Carthaginians captured a city in Latium that was not subject to Rome; regulated where prisoners taken from allies of Rome or Carthage could not be disembarked; disallowed both sides from abusing the right of obtaining water and provisions from the allies of the other; and dealt with special conditions of interaction between Romans in Sardinia, Africa, Sicily and Carthage, and Carthaginians in Rome.[11] There is also a possibility that the two states renewed their agreement around 306 BC, and Polybius also discusses 'a third and final treaty [which] was made with Carthage by the Romans at the time of Pyrrhus' invasion . . . and before the Carthaginians embarked on the war for the possession of Sicily'.[12]

The First Punic War

Neither side represented an existential threat to the other, until a curious concatenation of events brought them into conflict in 264 BC. The Mamertini had seized Messana in Sicily, but then found themselves comprehensively defeated by Hiero II of Syracuse. Some of the Mamertini appealed to Carthage for help, others to Rome, and both factions offered to deliver Messana up to whoever helped them.[13] Initially the Romans expressed worry that the Carthaginians might secure total control of Sicily, and then use it as a bridgehead for the invasion of Italy. There is no evidence that they were intending to do this, but the Mamertini played on Rome's fears, especially in the light of the experiences with Pyrrhus, that they might. However, set against this was the morally dubious issue of giving support to the piratical Mamertini and the need for rehabilitation after the Pyrrhic war. The Senate voted against sending help, but the consuls Marcus Fulvius Flaccus[14] and Appius Claudius Caudex ('Tree Trunk' or 'Blockhead') played upon the people's greed for war booty, and the Comitia sanctioned the mission, with Caudex as general.[15]

When Caudex arrived to help the Mamertini, it was 'the first crossing that the Romans had made out of Italy with an armed force'.[16] He found that Carthage had joined forces with Syracuse and had put the Mamertini under siege. But when Hiero of Syracuse decided to make peace with the Romans, it left Rome and Carthage in a conflict that neither side had directly intended: the First Punic War (264–241 BC).

The Carthaginian commander in the First Punic War was Hamilcar Barca ('Thunderbolt'). The Barca (or Barcas) family claimed descent from a brother of the mythical Dido,[17] and by his first wife, whose name has not come down to us, Hamilcar had three equally anonymous daughters, plus three sons, Hasdrubal, Mago and Hannibal (*Hnb'l* in Punic, 'He who Finds Favour with Baal'), who was born in 247 BC. The Latin historian Valerius Maximus preserves a famous anecdote that as

Hamilcar watched his three sons playing, he boasted that he was rearing so many lion cubs for the ruin of the Roman empire.[18] But his dreams would have to wait.

Rome's forces got the upper hand, and after they captured the Carthaginian base at Agrigentum, mission-creep set in, and they began to hope that they could drive the Carthaginians out of Sicily altogether.[19] To do this, though, they would need a fleet. So, with characteristic Roman single-mindedness, they built one, using a captured Carthaginian warship as a template. To compensate for their inexperience at sea they recruited some 33,000 rowers, trained them on land before drilling them at sea, and offset their initial lack of seamanship by developing a device known as the *corvus* ('raven'), a gangplank with an iron spike at the end, which could be dropped onto the deck of an enemy ship and allow their marines to make a sea battle resemble one on land.[20]

The First Punic War was a long-drawn-out, fluctuating conflict, but when the Romans under Gaius Lutatius Catulus finally achieved an overwhelming naval victory at the Aegates Islands in 241 BC, Hamilcar, like any self-respecting Carthaginian businessman would, conducted a cost-benefit analysis of the war, and negotiated peace.[21] This entailed the evacuation of Sicily and all the islands between there and Italy; the release of prisoners without ransom; and a hefty indemnity.[22] This left the Carthaginian treasury seriously depleted, and when the outstanding payments to their Numidian and Libyan mercenaries were not paid on time, the soldiers rebelled: '[The mutineers] passed a resolution . . . to torture and kill every Carthaginian and send back to the capital, with his hands cut off, every ally of Carthage. [Hamilcar] continued to put to the sword those of the enemy who were conquered in the field, while those brought to him as captive prisoners he threw to the elephants to be trampled to death.'²³ This nasty, violent confrontation fed into the traditional Roman picture of the Carthaginians as cruel, duplicitous and barbarous.

The Romans, meanwhile, exploited Carthage's preoccupations, and grabbed Sardinia and Corsica in a barefaced act of imperialism. These islands, along with Sicily, were rich in corn, and from 227 BC onwards the Romans appointed two additional annual praetors with Sicily and Sardinia–Corsica as their *provinciae* ('spheres of duty assigned to a magistrate'). A *provincia* was often a geographical area, although it could also be a specific job, such as overseeing the corn-supply or fighting pirates. But these islands became the first of Rome's overseas provinces, and represented a significant step on Rome's path to world domination.

Hannibal Takes Control

Despite the Romans' victory in the First Punic War they never quite shook off their mistrust of a people that they still saw as powerful and dishonest. The Carthaginians, on the other hand, resented the takeover of Sardinia and Corsica, and on the personal level Hamilcar Barca himself had not been defeated – it had been other commanders who had lost the war. Self-esteem and economic necessity now prompted the Carthaginian government to task Hamilcar with securing their control over Spain and conquering new territory. It was said that when he sailed for Cadiz in 237 BC he was accompanied by the nine-year-old Hannibal, who had begged to be allowed to go with him: 'Hamilcar . . . led him up to the altar and made him swear, touching the sacred offerings, that as soon as he was able he would be the enemy of the Roman people.'²⁴

Hamilcar himself does not seem to have made any aggressive moves against Rome, and in the winter of 229/8 BC he died in battle, either going down heroically against warlike Celtiberians,[25] or drowning in an unnamed river while fighting and looking after his family's safety during a siege.[26] His son-in-law Hasdrubal the Fair was appointed as his successor, and he too favoured diplomatic over military solutions. He refounded the city of Mastia as *Qart-hadasht* ('New City', the same name as Carthage itself; modern Cartagena), which became the Carthaginian headquarters in Spain. His administration is regarded as judicious and effective, but the Romans remained uneasy, and in 226 BC they sent an embassy which made an agreement with him that included the important clause: 'The Carthaginians shall not cross the River Ebro in arms.'[27]

Hasdrubal the Fair's command came to an end when he was assassinated in 221 BC by a Celtic mercenary in *Qart-hadasht*. There was no question about who would be his successor: both the army and the people wanted Hannibal Barca.[28]

In many ways it is Livy's work that has defined Hannibal's image as a historical character, but it also sheds a good deal of light on the way the Romans responded to him. He was adaptable, bold and inspiring:

Incredibly daring in grabbing hold of dangers, he showed superb judgement when he was faced with them. No exertion could exhaust his body or overcome his spirit; he was equally resilient to heat and cold; his desire for food and drink was defined by natural appetites, not by pleasure; neither his time for wakefulness, nor time for sleep, was ever determined by day or night – only the time that remained when his work was done was given over to rest . . . He was far and away the finest horseman and footsoldier; he was always the first into the action, and the last to withdraw from the hand-to-hand combat. But the man's virtues were equalled by prodigious vices: inhuman cruelty; beyond Punic perfidy; no truthfulness; no sanctity; no fear of the gods; no respect for an oath; no sense of right and wrong.[29]

The image of 'abominable' (*dirus*) or 'treacherous' (*perfidus*) Hannibal and his Punic perfidy was deeply embedded in Rome,[30] and *Punica fides* ('Punic faith') became a byword for the most extreme form of treachery. However, Polybius is a little more circumspect, commenting that even though he stands accused of excessive cruelty and avarice, it is very difficult to assess his real nature. Polybius doesn't discuss whether the accusations are 'fake news', but he does note that some people attributed Hannibal's acts of cruelty to his friend Hannibal Monomachus ('Gladiator'), before simply recording that 'at any rate among the Carthaginians he was notorious for his love of money and among the Romans for his cruelty'.[31]

Livy tells us that Hannibal had a lively expression and a powerful gaze, and that he looked like his father,[32] but beyond this his physical appearance is elusive. Carthaginian coinage is unhelpful, because the currency minted at Carthage during the Second Punic War tended to show either a wreathed head of the goddess Tanit on the obverse ('heads') with an unbridled horse on the reverse ('tails'), or the god Melqart (the 'Carthaginian Hercules') on the obverse with an elephant on the reverse.[33] Because these coins are stylistically distinct from issues before and after the Second Punic War, it has sometimes been postulated that we can see Hannibal's features in Melqart, but this is pure speculation. Further speculation is rife, particularly in internet discussions, where the level of vitriol is frequently inversely proportional to the level of understanding, about whether or not Hannibal, given that he was African, was black. To assert that he was, as do Joel A. Rogers, Ivan Van Sertima and others,[34] fundamentally misunderstands the nature of North Africans in general and Carthaginians in particular. Roman sources would undoubtedly have commented on it; coins with portraits of members of his family show no evidence of it; and not one Greek or Roman source describes Carthaginians as 'Ethiopians', which was their default term for black-skinned people. As the inclusion of the Semitic deity Baal in his name shows, Hannibal's ancestry went back to Phoenicia (broadly modern Lebanon): his roots were Semitic, not sub-Saharan African.

Once in control of the Carthaginian forces, Hannibal managed to bring most of the Iberian peninsula south of the River Ebro under his control – except for the city of Saguntum, which, some years before Hannibal's time,[35] had placed itself under the protection of Rome. It was effectively an ally of Rome within Carthage's sphere of influence, and when Hannibal captured it in December 219 BC, war with Rome was pretty much inevitable. The Roman Senate despatched representatives to Carthage demanding Hannibal's surrender, and in theatrical fashion Fabius Buteo 'pointed to the bosom of his toga and declared . . . that in its folds he carried both peace and war, and that he would let fall from it whichever they instructed him to leave. The Carthaginian Suffete [senator] answered that he should bring out whichever he thought best, and when the envoy replied that it would be war, many of the Suffetes shouted at once, "We accept it!" '[36]

It is impossible to overestimate the significance of the Second Punic War in Rome's history, and the Romans knew it:

> A number of things contributed to give this war its unique character: in the first place, it was fought between peoples unrivalled throughout previous history in material resources, and themselves at the peak of their prosperity and power; secondly, it was a struggle between old antagonists, each of whom had learned, in the first Punic War, to appreciate the military capabilities of the other; thirdly, the final issue hung so much in doubt that the eventual victors came nearer to destruction than their adversaries. Moreover, high passions were at work throughout, and mutual hatred was hardly less sharp a weapon than the sword; on the Roman side there was rage at the unprovoked attack by a previously beaten enemy; on the Carthaginian, bitter resentment at what was felt to be the grasping and tyrannical attitude of their conquerors.[37]

The Second Punic War

In June 218 BC Hannibal crossed the River Ebro and marched out of Spain with a force that Polybius says probably numbered 50,000 infantry, 9,000 cavalry and 37 elephants (Livy gives him 90,000 foot and 12,000 horse). By now his multicultural barbarian coalition had become a unified army of experienced and expert warriors, and he had their unstinting loyalty. Wherever he led, they would follow.

Hannibal certainly stole a march on the Romans at the outset. The Roman Consul Publius Cornelius Scipio[38] set out to intercept him at the mouth of the River Rhône, but when he stopped to take on supplies at Massalia (modern Marseille) he discovered that he was three days behind schedule. Hannibal was already crossing the river. Getting thirty-seven elephants across was a major challenge: 'Their Indian mahouts . . . led the elephants [onto rafts] along [an] earthen causeway with two females in front, whom the rest obediently followed. [But when] the rafts were pulled away from the causeway, the animals panicked [and] some became so terror-stricken that they leaped into the river when they were half-way across.'[39]

They were saved, though, 'because through the power and the length of their trunks they were able to keep these above the surface and breathe through them, and also spout out any water which had entered their mouths. In this way most of them survived and crossed the river on their feet.'[40]

Only at this stage did it become apparent to the Romans what Hannibal's real objective was.

Hannibal's men moved from the Rhône to the foothills of the Alps, where just the sight of the mountains filled them with dread: 'The height of the mountains, with their snows almost merging with the sky . . . the shapeless huts perched on the rocks, flocks and beasts of burden shrivelled by the frost, the humans with their shaggy, unkempt hair, all animals and inanimate objects stiff with cold.'[41]

They were assailed by Gallic tribesmen who knew the terrain intimately, and in the melee many of Hannibal's men fell from the cliffs to their deaths thousands of feet below, and the beasts of burden were sent tumbling over the edge like falling masonry.[42] Yet Hannibal was able to win through, and his men reached the summit sometime in the autumn.

Hannibal's route over the Alps remains disputed, although most scholars favour the Col du Clapier, the Little St Bernard

Pass or the Col de la Traversette. Recent research from the Col de la Traversette has found a layer of churned-up soil containing DNA evidence for the bacteria Clostridia, which are often found in faeces. The research team called this MAD ('mass animal deposition' – a euphemism for horse dung), and suggested that it might have been produced by the movement of thousands of defecating animals and humans, and that it could fit the time of Hannibal's invasion.[43] Their suggestions, however, are not universally accepted. Nevertheless, as Hannibal reached the summit, in one of history's great dramatic moments, he told his men, 'that they were not just walking over the walls of Italy, but of the city of Rome itself'.[44]

The next phase of the journey should have been 'downhill all the way' but Hannibal lost nearly as many men as he had done on the ascent. He had completed an astonishing feat of military daring, but at a horribly high price. The survivors of the march from Cartagena looked more like beasts than men, and he had only 26,000 soldiers left. Yet with these he overran northern Italy in about two months. A skirmish at Ticinus in which Scipio was wounded underlined the superiority of Hannibal's Numidian cavalry, and in a major set-piece engagement near the River Trebia[45] the Romans under Tiberius Sempronius Longus saved less than 10,000 men out of a force of around 40,000.

Hannibal's success at Trebia forced the Romans to withdraw from northern Italy and encouraged the local Gauls to join him. The following year, 217 BC, Hannibal, who was supposedly riding the last surviving elephant Surus ('the Syrian'), contracted ophthalmia and lost the sight of one eye, but that did not prevent him luring the Consul Gaius Flaminius,[46] a commander who, according to Polybius, 'possessed a rare talent for the arts of demagogy and playing to the gallery, but very little for the practical conduct of the war',[47] into an ambush on 21 June. It took place close to Lake Trasimene in the early morning mist: Flaminius was killed, and according to Polybius the Roman losses were 15,000 dead (10,000 in Livy). There was now no army between Hannibal and Rome, but he didn't have the capabilities to take the city by storm, and he couldn't lay siege to it because he didn't have a convenient supply base. It is a credit to the solidity of Rome's alliances within Italy that, despite Hannibal's amazing successes, charisma and impetus, not one central Italian town went over to him.

Rome responded to the death of the consul by electing Quintus Fabius Maximus Verrucosus ('Warty')[48] as dictator. He adopted an attritional 'Fabian' strategy of non-engagement in major battles, choosing to grind Hannibal down by harassing him from hard-to-get-at places. This controversial approach earned him the nickname *Cunctator* ('Delayer'), and a watching-and-waiting game followed, which was typified by an incident that occurred in Campania in the summer of 217 BC. Fabius managed to shut Hannibal into a valley near Callicula, whose only exit was an easily defendable narrow pass. Hannibal made his men tie torches onto the horns of some 2,000 captured cattle, and in the middle of the night they lit them and drove the beasts into full view of the Romans. The Romans thought this was Hannibal's army on the march, and went to intercept it, only for Hannibal's main force to slip through the now vacant pass and escape practically scot-free.[49]

Fabius' dictatorship expired in 216 BC, and factional politics between the Fabii and the Aemilii/Cornelii led the Romans to gift Hannibal the advantage once again. The two new consuls, Lucius Aemilius Paullus and Gaius Terentius Varro, were anti-Fabian, and when they took command of the war, they abandoned the delaying tactics and decided to overwhelm Hannibal in one massive onslaught. How many of the Romans actually took to the field is not known exactly, but Polybius puts their overall number at 86,000, all but 10,000 of whom took part in the battle, against which Hannibal deployed around 50,000, and all the sources agree that he was vastly outnumbered. Yet he offered battle on flat open ground beside the River Aufidus near the town of Cannae.[50]

Hannibal planned to turn the strength of the Roman infantry into its greatest weakness. By coordinating a perfectly handled retreat by his forces in the centre with successful attacks by his cavalry on the wings, he drew the Roman legions into a killing field, surrounded them and practically annihilated them. This extraordinary example of how to completely encircle a numerically stronger army with a smaller one is still taught in military academies worldwide. Hannibal's losses, mainly Gauls, were in the low thousands, and Livy gives a vivid picture of the carnage on the battlefield the following day: 'Most strange of all was a Numidian soldier, still living, and lying, with nose and ears horribly lacerated, underneath the body of a Roman who, when his useless hands had been no longer able to grasp his sword, had died in the act of tearing his enemy, in bestial fury, with his teeth.'[51] That Roman was one of probably around 50,000 men killed.

By all the established protocols of ancient warfare, the Romans should have surrendered at that point. But the same dogged determination that had defeated Pyrrhus now kicked in: the prisoners of war were not ransomed, to stop the possibility of peace negotiations; wealthy families contributed loans towards the war effort; the *tributum* (tax paid by Roman citizens) went up by 100 per cent; the currency was debased; the allies increased their quota of troops; criminals and debtors were freed from prison; even slaves volunteered for the army, and were bought off their owners at public expense; the survivors of Cannae were sent to do service in Sicily for twelve years without a break, under humiliating conditions; and Aemilian aggression was replaced by a return to Fabian delaying. The effectiveness of the approach was acknowledged by the ghost of Anchises in Virgil's *Aeneid*:

Fabii, where do you lead my lagging steps? O Fabius,
The greatest, you the preserver of Rome by delaying
    tactics![52]

Very slowly the war swung in Rome's favour. Cannae should have been one of the world's most decisive battles, but it turned out to be one of the least. It was Hannibal's Cadmean victory (see p. 70), and by 215 BC he was desperately in need of fresh troops, but he couldn't acquire a seaport to give himself any easy links with Carthage, and even had he been able to achieve that, he also faced factional political difficulties – there were plenty of anti-Barcid Carthaginians at home who were happy to see him fail. He did make a surprise march on Rome in 212 BC, which took him to within five miles of the city, but although this created panic he was unable to take it. Further setbacks in the south of Italy meant that only help from abroad could give Hannibal a realistic chance of victory.

An alliance in 215 BC with Philip V of Macedon might have turned the conflict in Hannibal's favour, but the Romans apprehended the envoys negotiating the alliance, and nothing came of it. Syracuse defected to Carthage, but a two-and-a-half-year Roman blockade followed. Central to the Syracusan defensive strategy was Archimedes, who designed machines that could discharge stones heavy enough to drive back the marines from the bows of the ships, and which could lift attacking vessels bodily out if the water. But not even his ingenuity could keep the Romans at bay forever. In 211 BC Syracuse was smitten by plague, and the Roman commander Marcus Claudius Marcellus captured the city thanks to the treachery of a Spanish mercenary. As Livy described it: 'Many brutalities were committed in hot blood and the greed of gain, and it is on record that Archimedes, while intent upon figures which he had traced in the dust, and regardless of the hideous uproar of an army let loose to ravage and despoil a captured city, was killed by a soldier who did not know who he was.'[53]

Although Archimedes' murder was an ignorant and barbaric act, the sack of Syracuse became an important watershed in the Hellenisation and 'debarbarisation' of Rome. Marcellus took the city's 'most beautiful public monuments', consisting of both statues and paintings, to Rome:[54] 'before this time, Rome . . . neither had nor knew about these elegant and exquisite things . . . but was filled with barbaric weapons and blood-stained spoils, [and] there was no sight which was pleasurable, or even unfearful, to unwarlike and refined spectators'.[55]

A couple of years later Fabius Maximus 'Cunctator' would also take a lot of statues and paintings from Tarentum,[56] including a colossal bronze of Heracles that he dedicated on the Capitoline Hill.[57] We now start to see a split between the 'sensible old-school Roman' and a new cultured philhellene attitude that first crystallised around Fabius Maximus and Marcellus. Trumpeting the superiority of Greek achievements was deeply annoying to Roman conservatives, but Marcellus was unapologetic: '[He] spoke of this with pride even to the Greeks, declaring that [by bringing the spoils of Syracuse to Rome] he had taught the ignorant Romans to admire and honour the wonderful and beautiful productions of Greece.'[58]

Marcellus' actions raised a number of issues surrounding the ethics of the ownership of art: why do we value it? Who should own it? Where does it belong? What should happen to it in wartime? For the next half a century Rome was inundated with Greek statues and paintings, many of them famous masterpieces, and because they were displayed publicly and prominently, they interacted with the character and taste of ordinary Romans to create a unique cultural atmosphere.

Culturally Rome was slowly becoming more Greek, and therefore less barbarian. Yet voices were raised in dissent, and there were those, like Livy, who saw the arrival of Greek art in Rome as initiating a moral decline of Roman society: '[The statues and paintings from Syracuse] were . . . undoubtedly legitimate spoils of war; but on the other hand it was from these that you can see the very beginning of the craze for Greek works of art and, consequently the licentiousness with which all kinds of buildings, sacred or profane, were despoiled.'[59]

Plutarch says that after the sack of Syracuse, 'Marcellus made [the Roman people] idle and full of pretentious waffle about art and artists, even to the point of wasting the greater part of the day in this kind of dilettantism.'[60]

The loss of Sicily left Hannibal without his crucial stepping stone to Carthage, while in Spain Gnaeus Cornelius Scipio Calvus (consul 222 BC) and his brother Publius Cornelius Scipio (consul 218 BC) managed to prevent Hannibal's brother Hasdrubal from sending reinforcements to Italy. But in

211 BC both Scipios were killed. So Rome now sent a new general, another Publius Cornelius Scipio (see p. 488, n. 38). He was just twenty-four years old and had never held any high office, but the two dead Scipios had been his father and uncle, and when he had put himself forward for the command in Spain he was elected by popular vote. He would repay the people's confidence in spectacular fashion.

Scipio wanted to make a direct strike on Carthage. His first move in 209 BC was to capture Cartagena in a combined land–sea operation; the following year he used a modified version of Hannibal's tactics at Cannae to defeat Hasdrubal Barca at Baecula, and in 206 BC Scipio comprehensively hammered Hasdrubal's successor, Hasdrubal Gisgo, at Ilipa. Although the tide looked like it was turning in the Romans' favour, they didn't have everything their own way. In Italy in 208 BC they lost both consuls, one of whom was Marcellus, in an encounter with Hannibal: 'Hannibal . . . immediately hurried to the spot and stood for a long time by the dead body, admiring its strength and beauty. He uttered not a single boastful word, nor did he show any sign of exultation, such as might be expected of a man who had just rid himself of a formidable enemy . . . he gave orders that his body should be treated with honour.'[61]

The only truly concerted attempt to reinforce Hannibal in Italy ended when, after his defeat by Scipio, Hasdrubal gambled Spain in order to win Italy. He crossed the Alps himself, but tragically for him his envoys were intercepted, and so disclosed the rendezvous point to the Romans. The two sides came together at the River Metaurus in Umbria in 207 BC:

More of the [Carthaginian] elephants were killed by their own riders than by the enemy. The riders used to carry a mallet and a carpenter's chisel and when one of the creatures began to run amuck and attack its own people, the keeper would put the chisel between its ears at the junction between head and neck and drive it in with a heavy blow . . . When at last no doubt remained that the day was lost, Hasdrubal . . . galloped straight into the midst of a Roman cohort. There, still fighting, he found a death worthy of his father Hamilcar and his brother Hannibal.[62]

The victorious Roman Consul Gaius Claudius Nero informed Hannibal of his brother's fate by throwing his severed head into the Carthaginian camp; the poet Horace was later to celebrate his victory and see it as a key moment in the war:

What you, Rome, owe to the Neros is attested by the river Metaurus, by the overthrow of Hasdrubal, and by that glorious day which, driving the dark clouds away from Latium, was the first to smile with heartening victory since the dreaded African [Hannibal] galloped through the towns of Italy like a fire through pine trees or the East Wind through Sicilian waves. After that the young men of Rome grew strong through struggles that were always successful; and shrines wrecked by the impious depredations of the Carthaginians once more housed gods that stood upright. ['Treacherous Hannibal' then laments his brother's death, and Rome's resilience:] 'We are like stags, which are by nature the prey of savage wolves; yet we actually pursue men whom it is a glorious triumph to trick and evade. That people . . . is like an oak buffeted by a hard two-headed axe on Mt Algidus where dark leaves grow thick; in spite of losses, in spite of bloody deaths, it draws strength and

courage from the steel itself. Not more persistently did the
Hydra grow stronger, the more its body was hacked . . .
Plunge it in the deep, it emerges all the finer; wrestle with it,
amid loud applause it will throw a previously unbeaten
champion, and then go on to fight battles for its wives to tell
of. No more will I be sending proud tidings to Carthage.
Fallen, fallen is every hope and the success that has attended
our name, now that Hasdrubal has been killed.'[63]

There then seems to have been a lull in the fighting in Italy.
The triumphant Scipio returned from Spain and received the
province of Sicily, with permission to invade Africa if it was in
the public interest, which he did in 204 BC. His tactical brilliance enabled him to almost totally annihilate two African
armies on the same night,[64] and follow this up at the Battle of
the Great Plains with a brilliant Hannibalesque encircling
movement.[65]

At Carthage the 'peace party' now sought terms. Scipio made
his demands – harsh, but probably fair – and the Carthaginians
agreed to them. The Roman Senate still had to ratify the deal,
so an interim truce was called, which gave the Carthaginians
the opportunity to recall an emotional Hannibal: 'They say
that rarely has any other man leaving his country to go into
exile departed so sorrowfully as Hannibal on withdrawing from
the enemy's land.'[66]

The truce only lasted a few months. In early spring 202 BC,
a large Roman convoy was driven ashore in a storm directly
opposite Carthage. The shipwrecks took place with the whole
town looking on, and the damaged vessels were towed into
Carthage's port. This, combined with Hannibal's return,
prompted Carthage to break off the armistice, and so to set the

stage for a trial of strength between Hannibal and Scipio to decide 'whether Rome or Carthage should give laws to the nations ... For not Africa, they said, or Italy but the whole world would be the reward of victory.'[67]

Hannibal took up a position near Zama to the west of Carthage, and let Scipio know that he wanted to meet before they finally engaged in battle. Some historians think that Livy's reference to an interpreter proves the story to be false, since both men spoke Greek, and Hannibal perhaps Latin too; but in these circumstances protocol would have dictated that Scipio would have used Latin, and Hannibal Punic, whatever other alternatives were available.

If their meeting was historical, it failed to find a compromise. They returned to their armies, and battle commenced the next day, on a fine morning in the summer or autumn of 202 BC. The ancient accounts dramatise the engagement beautifully: 'It would be impossible to find more warlike soldiers, or generals who had been more successful or were more thoroughly versed in the art of war, nor had Fortune ever offered the opposing armies a greater prize than this.'[68]

The armies were roughly equal in number, but Scipio's had the edge in quality, and although Hannibal had around eighty elephants he was at a serious disadvantage when it came to cavalry. It was to be his only defeat: at the end of the day 20,000 of his warriors lay dead, and as many were taken prisoner. Hannibal himself escaped with a small band of horsemen, and advised the Carthaginian government to accept Roman peace terms. They did, and although Carthage survived, it was no longer allowed to be an international power. The conquering Scipio returned to Rome, where he was given his immortal cognomen of Africanus.

Post-war Hannibal

Hannibal lived for around twenty more years after Zama, although he never served again as a Carthaginian general. Obviously, post-war Carthage needed to rebuild, restore its finances and improve its administration, but the government had simply too many competing vested interests. Factionalism was stronger than nationalism, and when Hannibal turned whistleblower on a number of eminent officials who were embezzling public funds, they tried to bring in the Romans against him. At the forefront of the Romans who were particularly hostile to Hannibal was the ultra-conservative Marcus Porcius Cato (consul 195 BC), aka Cato the Elder, Cato Censor, Cato the Wise and Cato the Ancient. He later became famous for allegedly concluding every speech he made with the words, *'Ceterum censeo Carthaginem esse delendam'* ('Furthermore, I consider that Carthage must be destroyed'), better known by its direct speech version *'Carthago delenda est'* ('Carthage must be destroyed').[69]

Cato had his suspicions that Hannibal was forging links with Rome's enemy Antiochus III, the culturally Greek King of Syria (the dynasty there were called the 'Seleucids', see pp. 123–126), and he despatched an embassy to impeach Hannibal and have him deported to Rome. Hannibal realised what the likely outcome of this would be, so he fled to Tyre, where he found a warm welcome.[70] He would never again see Carthage.

When Hannibal met up with Antiochus III at Ephesus in the autumn of 195 BC,[71] the Syrian was dithering about whether to engage in a war with Rome, and now he dithered about whether to welcome Hannibal. In the end, Antiochus hedged his bets, making preparations to fight Rome, but remaining highly circumspect about the Carthaginian. Livy narrates a remarkable conversation that took place between Hannibal and his old nemesis Scipio Africanus, who was part of an embassy to Ephesus at the time. Scipio asked Hannibal who he thought was the greatest general of all time. ' "Alexander the Great," replied Hannibal ... "To whom would you give second place?" asked Scipio. Hannibal reflected for a moment and then said: "Pyrrhus." ' Scipio, whose ego was becoming a little nettled by this time, asked Hannibal who he thought was the third greatest. Hannibal unhesitatingly chose himself:

> Scipio burst into laughter at this, and asked, 'What would you be saying if you had conquered me?' 'In that case,' Hannibal replied, 'I would definitely have put myself not only before Alexander and Pyrrhus, but before all other generals.'
> This answer, full of Carthaginian cunning [*Punico astu*], and with its unexpected kind of flattery, says Claudius, was very gratifying to Scipio, because Hannibal had set him apart from the general run of commanders, as one whose excellence was beyond compare.[72]

When Antiochus III finally did go to war with Rome in 192 BC, he spurned Hannibal's strategic advice, and unsurprisingly found himself quickly on the back foot (see pp. 123–126). Hannibal was sent to Tyre to recruit reinforcements, but the Rhodians intercepted him and blockaded him at Coracesium (modern Alanya in Turkey), and when Antiochus III was finally defeated, a key clause in the terms imposed on him was that he had to hand over Hannibal: 'There will never be any real certainty in our minds that the Roman people has peace in any place where Hannibal is; we demand his surrender before all else.'[73]

Hannibal escaped, and his fugitive wanderings took him to the court of Prusias I ('the Lame') of Bithynia (r. 228–182 BC), on the Black Sea coast of modern Turkey. Prusias found himself embroiled in a conflict with King Eumenes II of Pergamum (Pergamon) in 186 BC, in which Hannibal invented a deliciously cunning tactic for assaulting enemy ships – hurling pots full of poisonous serpents onto their decks.[74]

In the end, Hannibal couldn't elude the long arm of the Romans and the tenacity of their hatred, and in 183 BC they witnessed the passing both of Scipio Africanus, who died from natural causes, and his great rival. Plutarch says that everyone at Rome knew where Hannibal was, but they turned a blind eye because of his weakness and old age – Hannibal was then sixty-three. But Titus Quinctius Flamininus, sent on a diplomatic mission to Prusias, who had misjudged the international situation by staying neutral during Rome's war with Antiochus III, again demanded the surrender of Hannibal.[75] Prusias resented being made to violate the laws of hospitality, but dared not refuse.

Hannibal knew that the Romans wanted to destroy him at all costs, and was under no illusions about the spineless Prusias. He had a refuge just outside Libyssa on the south coast of the Bithynian peninsula, which had seven underground exits from his bedroom. But Prusias surrounded the entire area with guards. The game was up. Hannibal broached the poison that he had prepared for just this eventuality:

'Let us', he said, 'free the Roman people from their long-standing anxiety, seeing that they find it tedious to wait for an old man's death. It is no magnificent or memorable victory that Flamininus will win over a man unarmed and betrayed. This day will surely prove how far the moral standards of the Romans have changed. The fathers of these Romans sent a warning to King Pyrrhus, bidding him beware of poison – and he was an enemy in arms, with an army in Italy: these Romans themselves have sent an envoy of consular rank to suggest to Prusias the crime of murdering his guest.' Then . . . he drained the cup. So Hannibal's life came to its end.[76]

So in the end Prusias and Flamininus, not Hannibal, were the perpetrators of Punic-style treachery. The Romans had behaved as barbarians. The story has to be fictitious, but, as so many of Rome's enemies do in their histories, Hannibal gets the most memorable words. Plutarch adds that these events destroyed Flamininus' reputation: 'Many of the Senate thought the conduct of Titus odious, officious, and cruel; for he had killed Hannibal when he was like a bird permitted to live a tame and harmless life because too old to fly and without a tail, and there had been no necessity for his doing this, but he did it to win fame, that his name might be associated with the death of Hannibal.'[77]

This looked bad in comparison to the generous conduct of Scipio Africanus who neither drove Hannibal out of Africa, demanded his surrender from his fellow citizens nor treated him with any disrespect.

Responses to Hannibal veered from hatred to admiration. Centuries later, the satirist Juvenal reflected on his death:

Alas, alas for glory,
What an end was here: the defeat, the ignominious
Flight into exile, everyone crowding to see
The once-mighty Hannibal turned humble hanger-on,
Sitting outside the door of a petty Eastern despot
Till His Majesty deign to awake. No sword, no spear,
No battle-flung stone was to snuff the fiery spirit
That once had wrecked a world: those crushing defeats,
Those rivers of spilt blood were all wiped out by a
Ring, a poisoned ring.

He had become a classroom cliché:

On, on, you madman, drive
Over your savage Alps, to thrill young schoolboys
And supply a theme for speech-day recitations![78]

In life and death Hannibal imprinted himself indelibly on the Roman consciousness, and for hundreds of years afterwards, when Roman mothers wanted to calm their naughty children, they would shout, '*Hannibal ante portas!*' (Hannibal is at the gates!)

6

Graecia Capta: Resistance in the Greek East – Philip V, Antiochus III and Perseus of Macedon

At the start of his work, Polybius asked his readers a serious question: 'Who is so worthless or indolent as not to wish to know by what means and under what system of polity the Romans in less than fifty-three years have succeeded in subjecting nearly the whole inhabited world to their sole government – a thing unique in history?'[1]

Polybius' fifty-three years run from the 104th Olympiad (220–216 BC), and include the Hannibalic War alongside various other conflicts involving the culturally Greek Hellenistic kingdoms that had been carved out of Alexander the Great's empire, and which were ruled by the Antigonids of Macedon, Seleucids of Syria, Attalids of Pergamun and Ptolemies of Egypt, as well as several minor powers situated in Greece itself. Polybius' time frame ends in 167 BC, when Lucius Aemilius Paullus (who would be awarded the nickname Macedonicus by the Senate) held an astonishing triumph, in which he displayed mind-boggling quantities of plunder pillaged from Macedon and Epirus, together with King Perseus of Macedon himself. It was an amazing and lightning-fast process of conquest, but it had an ironic, reciprocal effect on Rome. As the poet Horace put it:

Graecia capta ferum uictorem cepit
Captured Greece captured her savage conqueror[2]

If the military dominance was Roman, the cultural backlash was Greek. Now it was the Romans who were the barbarians.

Barbarism in the Greek and Macedonian World

There had been sporadic interaction between Rome and the Greeks living beyond Magna Graecia for centuries, but Rome's victories over Pyrrhus and Hannibal astounded the Hellenistic world, which now recognised Rome as a significant player on the international stage.

The attritional conflicts with Epirus, Carthage, and within Italy, had left Rome's people weary of war, her treasury short of funds, Italy devastated and her state with more land than it knew what to do with, plus several recently acquired provinces to deal with. But the Republican Romans were nothing if not energetic when it came to military matters. The dust had hardly settled on the battlefield of Zama when Rome got ready to engage in a new conflict that would entwine her inextricably with the Hellenistic Greek kingdoms, and produce cultural changes that would transform her in the most radical way: these hitherto barbarian Romans began to assimilate a Greekness that changed their outlook forever.

However, it is also interesting that Rome's Macedonian opponents had issues with barbarism. The Greeks continually struggled to make up their minds about the Macedonians, who lived in the transitional area between Greece and barbarian Thrace: were they barbarians or not? To Greek ears their speech was weird, and therefore bar-bar-baric: it was parodied by comic poets such as Strattis in his *Macedonians* or *Pausanias*,[3] and Plutarch noted that it was different to Greek, commenting on Alexander the Great jumping up and shouting 'in his native Macedonian' (*Makedonisti*).[4] It is debatable as to whether this 'Macedonian' was a non-Greek tongue, or (more likely) some combination of the Doric or Aeolic Greek dialects with a heavy sprinkling of Thracian and Illyrian patois.[5] People had also been arguing about the Greekness or otherwise of the Macedonian royal family since at least as far back as the fifth century BC:

> Now that these [Macedonians] are Greeks, as they themselves say, I myself chance to know and will prove it . . .; and further, the Hellenodicae [Greeks who presided at the Olympic Games] determined that it is so. For when Alexander I chose to contend and entered the lists for that purpose, the Greeks who were to run against him were for barring him from the race, saying that the contest should be for Greeks and not for foreigners; but Alexander proving himself to be an Argive, he was judged to be a Greek; so he contended in the 200 metres race.[6]

In mythology, the ethnicity of the Macedonians is hazy, and their eponymous ancestor Macedon stands outside the mainstream Greek family trees. Hesiod made the Macedonians akin to the Greeks, but not on a level with them, by stating that Macedon was only the son of a *sister* of the Greek ancestor Hellen;[7] Hellanicus, on the other hand, made Macedon a grandson of Hellen;[8] Pindar and Bacchylides wrote encomia for

Alexander I, which would imply that at least the royal family was thought of as Greek,[9] but the fifth-century BC sophist Thrasymachus strongly disagreed.[10] The tragic playwright Euripides ended his days at the court of the Macedonian king Archelaus, and was at pains to manipulate the mythical genealogies of Archelaus' ancestors in order to make him Greek, and his kingdom Hellenic. Clearly it mattered to the Macedonians that they should not be thought of as barbarians.

Philip V and the First Two Macedonian Wars

Prior to the Hannibalic War, Rome had made a couple of military interventions into Illyria in north-west Greece, one in 229 BC (the First Illyrian War), another in 219–218 BC (the Second Illyrian War, under the command of the Consul Lucius Aemilius Paullus). These were significant enough to make King Philip V of Macedon apprehensive about Rome's wider intentions, and after Aemilius Paullus lost his life leading the Romans to their catastrophic defeat at Cannae, Philip V sensed Roman weakness and sought to ally himself with the likely victor, Carthage. The Romans discovered Philip's intentions by capturing his envoys, but already had more than enough to contend with at the time with Hannibal still on the loose in Italy, so they essentially got the Aetolian League in central Greece to fight Philip V for them by proxy in a war that began in 214 BC. This support eventually drifted away, and in 205 BC the Peace of Phoenice, in Epirus, was signed with Philip.

The Epirote spokesman asked Philip V and the Roman commander Publius Sempronius[11] to bring this so-called First Macedonian War[12] to an end, and to grant the Epirotes their pardon. Negotiations over territory went satisfactorily, and spheres of alliance were agreed upon: 'The king included in the treaty King Prusias of Bithynia, the Achaeans, Boeotians, Thessalians, Acarnanians and Epirotes; and the Romans included[13] Ilium [Troy], King Attalus [I of Pergamum], Pleuratus, Nabis tyrant of Sparta, the Eleans, Messenians and Athenians.'[14]

The terms[15] were ratified by all the Roman tribes, primarily because they wanted to focus exclusively on the Hannibalic War. But Livy suggests that they were also rather cynically postponing the conflict until they were free of the Punic threat, and the wording of the Peace of Phoenice made it easy for the Romans to concoct any flimsy pretext they wanted to support their Greek 'friends' who were being 'oppressed' by Philip.

For the meantime, though, the Greek world was merely a sideshow, and although the Romans kept an eye on Philip V's activities, they had no immediate interest in involving themselves in Hellenistic power politics. But things changed in 202 BC when Philip V and Antiochus III of Syria made a clandestine pact to carve up the European and Asian territories of Egypt, which was currently being ruled by a child, Ptolemy V Epiphanes. He had inherited the throne at the age of five, and the country effectively ground to a halt under a series of unscrupulous and ineffective regents. The famous Rosetta Stone, which provided the key to the decipherment of Egyptian hieroglyphs, was produced later in his reign, on 27 March 196 BC. It makes him sound considerably more powerful than he was:

> In the reign of the young one,[16] who has received royalty from his father, the lord of crowns, whose glory is great, who established Egypt and is pious towards the gods, the conqueror of his enemies, who restored the life of men, the lord of the Thirty-Year festivals, like Hephaistos [i.e. Ptah]

the Great, a king like the Sun [= Ra], the great king of the upper and lower regions,[17] son of the Father-Loving Gods, approved by Hephaistos, to whom the Sun granted victory, the living image of Zeus [= Amun] son of the Sun, Ptolemy the everliving, beloved of Ptah . . .[18]

But his weakness, and Philip and Antiochus' opportunism, was upsetting the Hellenistic balance of power.

Rome got dragged into the conflict when Pergamum, Rhodes and Athens appealed to her for help after Philip committed various war crimes and attacked Athenian territory. This was awkward for the Romans because they had strict legislation, the *ius fetiale*, which only allowed them to engage in war if they or their allies (*socii*) were the injured party. Technically, *all* Rome's wars had to be defensive. Neither Pergamum, Rhodes nor Athens were *socii* of Rome, and Philip had done nothing directly against the Romans, but the three powers played on the possibility that Antiochus III and Philip V might attack Italy from Greece. Also, Philip's alliance with Hannibal was never far from Roman minds, but they could still not engage in an illegal war. So the Fetiales (see p. 29), who were Rome's arbiters of war and peace, simply decided to widen the scope of *socii* to include *amici* – 'friends'. Rome could now fight its 'defensive' war.

Rome gave Philip V an ultimatum: stop interfering in Greece, and compensate Rhodes and Pergamum for their losses. Philip, of course, refused. So the Second Macedonian War was declared in 200 BC, and once again the Romans were initially regarded as the barbarians, despite the philhellenism of their young general Titus Quinctius Flamininus (consul 198 BC):

Now, we are told that Pyrrhus, when for the first time he beheld . . . the army of the Romans in full array, had said that he saw nothing barbaric in the barbarians' line of battle;[19] and so those who for the first time met Titus were compelled to speak in a similar strain. For they had heard the Macedonians say that a commander of a barbarian host was coming against them, who subdued and enslaved everywhere by force of arms; and then, when they met a man who was young in years, humane in aspect, a Greek in voice and language, and a lover of genuine honour, they were wonderfully charmed.[20]

The Roman legionaries got the better of the Macedonian phalanx at the Battle of Cynoscephalae ('Dogs' Heads') in Thessaly in the summer of 197 BC.

Flamininus proved his pro-Greek, unbarbarian credentials by making a proclamation at the Isthmian Games, held at Corinth in 196 BC: 'The Senate of Rome and their general Titus Quinctius, having defeated King Philip and the Macedonians, order that the following states [incorporating the Corinthians, Locrians, Phocians, Euboeans, Achaeans of Phthiotis, Magnesians, Thessalians and Perrhaebians] shall be free, exempt from taxes, and ruled by their own laws.'[21]

The response was ecstatic: 'When the herald . . . had recited the proclamation, a shout of joy arose, so incredibly loud that it reached the sea. The whole audience rose to their feet, and no heed was paid to the contending athletes, but all were eager to spring forward and greet and hail the Saviour and champion of Greece.'[22]

He had 'liberated' Greece, and he was accorded honours verging on the divine. He received statues, an annual festival, sacrifices, and a hymn of praise that contained expressions of reverence to great Zeus, Rome, Titus and the Good Faith of the

Roman faith, and ended 'Hail, Paean Apollo! Hail, O Titus our Saviour!'[23]

The use of 'Saviour' (*Soter* in Greek) places him right on the divide between humans and gods, and he was still being worshipped at Chalcis in Plutarch's day, centuries later.

Yet the Greeks' freedom was conditional, and clearly depended on the 'protection' of Rome, and when Flamininus withdrew his troops from their territory in 194 BC, he told them to

> cultivate harmony between themselves; and that all should direct their views to the general interest of the whole . . . He then exhorted them, as the arms of others had procured their liberty, and the good faith of foreigners had restored it to them, to apply now their own diligent care to the watching and guarding of it; that the Roman people might perceive that those on whom they had bestowed liberty were deserving of it, and that their kindness had not been ill placed.[24]

It is clear that the Romans felt the Greeks owed them a debt of gratitude, as the Praetor Marcus Valerius Messalla made explicit to the city of Teos in 193 BC: 'As for the honours to the god and privileges to you, we will try to help to increase them, while you carefully maintain in the future your goodwill towards us.'[25]

And if there was the slightest doubt in the Greek mind about their obligations to Rome, the treaty that the Romans imposed on the Aetolian League made it crystal clear: 'The people of Aetolia [are obliged to uphold] the *imperium* and majesty of the Roman people.'[26]

Flamininus returned to Rome and in 194 BC he displayed the fabulous wealth of the Hellenistic world to the Romans in a triumph that lasted for three days, and featured an array of bronze and marble statues plundered from the Greek states and from Philip's private collection.[27] The influx of Greek art and ideas, which followed Marcus Claudius Marcellus' capture of Syracuse in the Second Punic War, had deeply affected the ways in which many Romans thought (see pp. 103–4), but wealth such as this, from the Greek mainland, now also started to transform the way Rome looked. The fabric of the city started to fill up with triumphal monuments; Romans wanted to emulate the impressive architecture of the Hellenistic kingdoms; and Rome's Seven Hills provided the perfect setting for the buildings and ceremonies that demonstrated the power and efficiency of Rome's government.

Antiochus III 'the Great' of Syria

As the ruler of the once mighty Seleucid kingdom based in Syria that had evolved after Alexander the Great's empire, Antiochus III the Great was keen to resurrect the grandeur of his realm, and pursued an expansionist policy both in Asia Minor and, in 196 BC, across the Hellespont and into Thrace. Rome was uneasy about this, especially when Hannibal joined up with him following his exile from Carthage (see pp. 109 ff.):

> For Hannibal the African, a most inveterate enemy of Rome and an exile from his native country, had already at that time come to the court of King Antiochus, and was trying to incite him to further achievements while Fortune gave his power successful course. Antiochus himself also, in consequence of the magnitude of his achievements, by which he had won the title of Great, was already fixing his eyes on universal dominion, and had a particular hostility to the Romans.[28]

However, the Romans were unwilling or unable to find or concoct a pretext for war at this stage, and when Flamininus withdrew the Roman army from Greece in 194 BC, Antiochus took this as an implicit acknowledgement of the status quo. But the next year, when he sent ambassadors to Rome to confirm what he thought was a friendly relationship, he was presented with a demand to withdraw from Europe and a threat to 'liberate' the Greek cities of Asia Minor from him, just like Rome had freed the mainland cities from Philip V.

Liberation and freedom became the buzzwords of the moment. The members of the Aetolian League were extremely dissatisfied with the way the Romans had treated them, especially in the light of the help they had provided in the struggles against Philip V, and so they invited Antiochus to liberate them: 'The Aetolians ... had long been most inimically disposed towards the Romans, and they suggested to him, as a pretext that would account for the war, that he should offer the Greeks their freedom.'[29]

Plutarch comments that the Greeks didn't want to be set free, because they were free already, and accuses the Aetolians of cynically teaching Antiochus 'to make use of that fairest of all names' for his own purposes.[30] Antiochus certainly cast himself as the liberator when he landed around 10,000 soldiers at Demetrias in Greece in late autumn 192 BC, and was elected commander-in-chief of the Aetolian League.

The Romans responded by despatching the Consul Manius Acilius Glabrio (consul 191 BC) with an army that also included Flamininus, to keep the Greeks onside. Glabrio routed Antiochus' forces at the Battle of Thermopylae in 191 BC, and drove him back to Asia Minor, before turning on the Aetolian League, which he would have annihilated had it not been for Flamininus' intervention.[31] Rome took the offensive to Antiochus by invading Asia Minor, and in late 190/early 189 BC Scipio Africanus the Elder's brother Lucius Cornelius Scipio Asiaticus comprehensively defeated him at the Battle of Magnesia. The Romans demanded the surrender of Hannibal,[32] and under the terms of the Treaty of Apamea of 188 BC Antiochus had to pay an indemnity of 15,000 talents, surrender his elephants and fleet, provide hostages, including his son Antiochus IV, and give up his holdings to the north and west of the Taurus Mountains.[33] Rome reallocated the surrendered territories to her allies Rhodes and Eumenes II of Pergamum, and then pulled her forces out; Antiochus III turned his focus to the east, but was murdered the following year while extorting tribute in a temple of Baal near Susa.

The defeat of Antiochus III further cemented Rome's place among the major players in the Mediterranean, and the more powerful Rome appeared to be, the more the Hellenistic states looked towards her to settle its internal disputes. This in turn drew the Romans deeper into the Greek world and accelerated the process of the Hellenisation/debarbarisation of Rome. The triumph celebrated in 187 BC by Marcus Fulvius Nobilior for his victory over the Aetolians in Greece displayed 285 bronze and 230 marble statues,[34] and Scipio Asiaticus' the year after contained almost 650 kilograms of engraved silver vases. This massive influx of Greek art presented challenges to Roman attitudes that they simply couldn't ignore, and they expended a great deal of energy praising, criticising and assessing it, as they struggled to find a proper role for it and adapt it to their own purposes.[35] There was an instant anti-Hellenic backlash in the Senate, with the philhellenic faction that was closely linked to the Scipios starting to lose ground to the conservative, anti-Hellenic Cato the Elder and his supporters, who felt Greece and the east were having a negative effect on the Roman character. For them, Roman 'barbarism' was preferable to effete Hellenism. Indicative of this was their suppression of the worship of the Greek god Bacchus. This had been widespread in Italy for some time, but in 186 BC the Senate banned the Bacchic mysteries (*orgia* in Greek) because they were felt to be too subversive.[36]

Perseus of Macedon: Third Macedonian War

Philip V died at Amphipolis in 179 BC, to be succeeded by his eldest and very charismatic son, Perseus. He renewed Philip's treaty with Rome, and set about making Macedonia great again. He was popular on the domestic front, and cemented his position in the wider world by marrying the Seleucid princess Laodice, the daughter of Seleucus IV Philopator, and giving his sister in marriage to Prusias II Cynegus ('the Hunter') of Bithynia. In the Greek sphere, he supported those with anti-Roman leanings, which won him considerable support: having a friendly and powerful presence who was much more local meant the Greeks had a viable alternative to distant, semi-barbarian Rome.

There was no way that Perseus' policies would be tolerated at Rome, particularly as the pro-Roman Eumenes II of Pergamum was one of his major competitors. Eumenes II's reign (197–160/59 BC) saw Pergamum reach the height of its power and splendour, as he developed the city into 'the Athens of the East', a grand showpiece city, where a library containing some 200,000 volumes stood at the heart of some gloriously theatrical architectural ensembles that were adorned with works of sculpture of the highest quality, such as the Great Altar of Zeus: 'He built up the city . . . and . . . from love of splendour, added sacred buildings and libraries and raised the settlement of Pergamon to what it now is.'[37]

Eumenes also pursued a vigorous policy of forming relationships with the states of the Greek mainland, and he bestowed lavish gifts on Athens and Delphi, which were warmly reciprocated by the honours he received.

But Greece was not big enough for Eumenes II and Perseus, and the Pergamene king was instrumental in getting Rome to fabricate a case against Perseus to justify a war that the Macedonian was not seeking to provoke. But neutrality was no longer an option: anyone who was not with Rome was seen to be against her. The Greek historian Appian saw the situation for what it was: Rome was determined to destroy a 'virtuous, wise and popular king'.[38] This Third Macedonian War was declared in 171 BC, and ended on the north-east coast of Greece on 22 June 168 BC, when the Roman legionaries of Lucius Aemilius Paullus Macedonicus effectively killed off the Macedonian phalanx as a fighting force, and destroyed the Antigonid dynasty with it, at the Battle of Pydna.[39] Perseus became the star attraction in Aemilius Paullus' extraordinary triumphal procession 167 BC, and died in captivity a few years later.

Roman policy in the aftermath of the Third Macedonian War was very hardline: anti-Romans in Aetolia were executed; Epirus was plundered in a frenzied free-for-all, and 150,000 of its inhabitants were sold into slavery. Polybius was among 1,000 Achaeans deported to Italy, although he became the educator of Aemilius Paullus' sons Fabius and Scipio Aemilianus (who had been adopted by his first cousin Publius Cornelius

Scipio, the eldest son of Scipio Africanus the Elder), and so provided another channel by which Greek culture insinuated itself into Rome's aristocracy.

Plunder on this scale obviously benefitted the plunderers, generating so much money that the Roman people could stop paying direct taxes. Never before had such riches been exhibited at Rome as when Lucius Aemilius Paullus Macedonicus held his triumph:

The triumph lasted three days. On the first, which was scarcely long enough for the sight, were to be seen the statues, pictures, and colossal images which were taken from the enemy, drawn upon two hundred and fifty chariots. [These spoils also featured an Athena by Pheidias, the greatest of all Greek sculptors, that was duly erected on the Palatine Hill.⁴⁰] On the second, was carried in a great many wagons, the finest and richest armour of the Macedonians, both of brass and steel, all newly polished and gleaming; . . . after these wagons loaded with armour there followed three thousand men who carried the silver that was coined, in seven hundred and fifty vessels, each of which weighed three talents, and was carried by four men. Others brought silver bowls and drinking horns and flat bowls and wine cups . . . all extraordinary as well for the size as for the thickness of their embossed work. On the third day [there was a sacrificial procession, followed by the exhibition of staggering amounts of gold and silver, followed by] the consecrated bowl which Aemilius had caused to be made of ten talents of gold set with precious stones. [Then came the gold plate from Perseus' table.] Next to these came Perseus' chariot, and, and lying on that this diadem. [Perseus, his family, friends and attendants followed, and] after these were carried four hundred golden crowns, sent from the cities by embassies to Aemilius in honour of his victory. [Finally came Aemilius himself] magnificently adorned [and his army].[41]

After triumphal processions such as this, some of the artworks found their way into private collections, but others were dedicated and displayed in public sanctuaries. Rome was becoming a kind of museum of Greek art, and the quantity and quality of its collections was remarkable.

Macedon was plundered again in 148 BC, this time by Quintus Caecilius Metellus Macedonicus, who brought back the 'Granicus Monument' of Lysippos, a group of twenty-five bronze equestrian statues of Alexander the Great and his companions, which Alexander himself had erected. With every Greek artefact that arrived at Rome, the Romans became more Hellenised, but ultimately they felt the only way that they could truly Romanise Macedon was to annex it as a *provincia* under a Roman magistrate, and to include Illyria and Epirus as part of its territory, which is what they did in 147 BC.

146 BC: Carthage (and Corinth) Must Be Destroyed!

The year 146 BC was a crucial one in Rome's expansion, marked by the destruction of two major cities. In Greece, Rome finally terminated Greek independence when Lucius Mummius Achaicus defeated the Achaean League and took possession of 'Wealthy Corinth', as Homer had called it: 'He proceeded to storm Corinth and set it on fire. The majority of those in it were put to the sword by the Romans, but the women and children Mummius sold into slavery. He also sold all the slaves who had been set free and had fought on the side of the Achaeans but had not fallen at once on the field of battle. Mummius carried off the most admired votive offerings and works of art.'[42]

Mummius' act of plunder was said to have 'filled the whole of Italy' with statues and paintings,[43] and 150 years later Strabo commented that these spoils still provided 'the greatest number and the best of the public monuments of Rome'.[44] Greece itself now came under the control of the governor of Macedon, and later Romans celebrated the conquests as though they were justified acts of vengeance for the Greek conquest of their Trojan ancestors:

That one[45] shall ride in triumph to the lofty Capitol,
The conqueror of Corinth, renowned for the Greeks he has
    slain.
That one[46] shall wipe out Argos and Agamemnon's
    Mycenae,
Destroying an heir of Aeacus,[47] the seed of warrior Achilles,
Avenging his Trojan sires and the sacrilege done to
    Minerva.[48]

A similar act of vengeance that invited comparisons with Troy occurred when Rome turned against Carthage again. Cato the Elder had seen Carthage's prosperity for himself when he had been on an embassy there in 153 BC, and as soon as he got back, he became obsessed with destroying the city (see p. 109). It took him four years, but in 149 BC he secured the declaration of the Third Punic War. Pliny the Elder describes a theatrical moment in the Senate when Cato exhibited a very fresh, early ripened fig, which had been picked less than three days before in Carthage.[49] The realisation that their old enemy was so close to Rome apparently convinced them to eradicate Carthage permanently.

The Carthaginians managed to keep the Romans at bay until the spring of 146 BC, when Publius Cornelius Scipio Aemilianus (aka Scipio Aemilianus or Scipio Africanus the Younger[50]) captured the city. In a brutal demonstration of Roman power 50,000 Carthaginians were sold into slavery; the city was burned for seventeen days; the city walls were completely destroyed; Carthage's territory was annexed and became the Roman province of Africa; but the famous story that the Romans ploughed the city with salt to prevent anything ever growing there again is more nineteenth-century AD myth than second-century BC history.[51]

As Scipio Aemilianus watched Carthage burn, he wept, and quoted Homer's *Iliad*: 'A day will come when sacred Troy shall perish, and Priam and his people shall be slain.'[52]

Given that the Romans traced their ancestry back to Troy, he was fully aware of the irony of this, as he acknowledged when he turned to his tutor Polybius, grasped his hand and said: 'A glorious moment, Polybius; but I have a terrible fear and foreboding that some day someone else will pronounce the same fate for my own country.'[53]

Captured Greece and the 'De-barbarisation' and Corruption of Rome

Rome's great poet Horace realised the importance of this period for Roman civilisation:

It was late when the Roman applied his brains to Greek
writing.
In the peace which followed the Punic wars he began to
wonder
if Aeschylus, Thespis and Sophocles had anything useful to
offer,
and if he himself could produce an adequate version.[54]

Greece's highly sophisticated culture mesmerised some
Romans, and repelled others, who preferred old-school 'barbarism'. The reaction to it is often crudely characterised as
polarising into a clash between the pro-Greek-culture-in-Rome
'Scipionic Circle', centred on Scipio Aemilianus, and the anti-
Hellenic Roman traditionalists, whose figurehead was Cato the
Elder. Livy reproduces a speech by Cato where he rages against
the 'diverse vices, avarice, and luxury [and] every sort of libid-
inous temptation' coming into Rome from the Greek world,
and particularly its art: 'Believe me, those statues from Syracuse
were enemy standards brought against the city of Rome.
Already I am hearing far too many people praising and wonder-
ing at the artworks of Corinth and Athens, and laughing at the
terracotta antefixes of the Roman gods.'[55]
These 'terracotta antefixes' were architectural features that
adorned the older, Etruscan-influenced temples in Rome, and
it's easy both to see the cutting-edge, arty Roman hipsters
who loved the on-trend developments in Greek art having a
bit of a laugh at them, and to see just how annoying that
would have been to Roman traditionalists such as Cato.
Indeed, Pliny the Elder, some 250 years later, felt that the
plunder from Corinth and Carthage was a significant factor
in the destruction of Roman morals, because it created a

climate in which there was a taste for vices and the opportunity for indulging in them.[56]

Juvenal, writing a generation after Pliny, expressed similar sentiments in his *Satires*, albeit in searing xenophobic terms: 'And now let me speak at once of the race which is most dear to our rich men, and which I avoid above all others; no shyness shall stand in my way. I cannot abide, Quirites, a Rome of Greeks!'[57]

One thing that really annoyed the traditionalists was what they felt was the 'hipper than thou' attitude, allied to a dismissiveness of Roman traditions (such as terracotta antefixes) in favour of Greek ones. Even Rome's greatest general Scipio Africanus the Elder was accused of 'going Greek' in Syracuse, because he behaved in a way that was 'un-soldierly, not to mention un-Roman; he strolled about the gymnasium wearing a Greek cloak and sandals, focussing his attention on books and physical exercise'.[58]

Reading, particularly Greek texts, was obviously not what a manly Roman general should be doing, and wearing a Greek cloak and sandals 'for the sake of luxury and pleasure' was just as bad, at least if Cicero's comments about the adverse reaction provoked by a statue of Lucius Scipio, erected after he defeated Antiochus III and which depicted him wearing these same items, are anything to go by.[59]

Greek ideas also began to filter through into Roman education. Aemilius Paullus brought his sons up using Greek-style learning resources, training them in sculpture and drawing, as well as in literature.[60] Scipio Aemilianus became the patron of the comic poet Terence, whose play *The Brothers* was first performed at the funeral games of Aemilius Paullus in 160 BC, and dramatises a vaguely Catonian versus Scipionic clash in relation to education policies. The play itself is based on two Greek originals, *The Brothers* by Menander, with a scene from *Joined in Death* by Diphilus, and explores the issue of how best to educate young men, through a conflict between Demea, a 'harsh old man' (*senex durus*)/'angry old man' (*senex iratus*) type, and his liberal-minded brother Micio who is a 'lenient old man' (*senex lenis*). Cato is very much aligned with Demea, and for him, as he wrote to his son in a real-life example of these educational disagreements, these Scipios were not just making fashion statements and reading effete literature, they were attacking the very heart of Roman morality: 'I will show you the results of my own experience at Athens: that it is a good idea to dip into their literature but not to learn it thoroughly. I shall convince you that they are a most iniquitous and intractable people, and you may take my word as the word of a prophet: if that people shall ever bestow its literature upon us, it will corrupt everything.'[61]

But Greek literature came to embed itself very deeply in Roman culture, and although arguments about whether this was a civilising or a corrupting force raged for centuries, every Greek word, image and idea that the Romans assimilated made them less 'barbarian', and Horace, at any rate, knew it:

When Greece surrendered she took control of her rough
    invader,
and brought the arts to rustic Latium. Then the primitive
metre of Saturn dried up; and the fetid smell gave way
to cleaner air; nevertheless for many years
there remained, and still remain today, signs of the
    farmyard.[62]

7

Viriathus: Iberian Shepherd, Hunter and Warrior

The Romans in Hispania

Around 150 years after Rome had created her first *provinciae*, Cicero reminded the Senate of an uncomfortable fact: 'Words cannot express how bitterly we are hated among foreign nations owing to the wanton and outrageous conduct of the men whom we have sent to govern them.'[1]

Those actions and emotions are vividly illustrated by events in the Iberian peninsula (modern Spain and Portugal, known to the Romans as Hispania) in the middle of the second century BC. The victories over Carthage in the first two Punic Wars had initiated the process of bringing Hispania under Roman control, and it is interesting to observe that (with the exception of Basque) the indigenous languages spoken in modern Portugal and Spain all derive from Latin, and none of them (again, with the exception of Basque) have any significant links to the languages spoken there before the Romans moved in. It is frequently said that modern Spain is a Roman creation.

In 197 BC the Senate divided their possessions in Spain into two *provinciae* – Hispania Citerior ('Nearer Spain', closer to Rome) and Hispania Ulterior ('Further Spain'), with the border at Cartago Nova (modern Cartagena). Over the following years these *provinciae* were gradually extended inland, turning the peninsula into an almost perpetual war zone for around 175 years. In 179 BC the Praetor Tiberius Sempronius Gracchus the Elder[2] had quashed various uprisings, and imposed a treaty in which the towns involved had to pay tribute, provide soldiers for Rome and could not rebuild their walls. Central Hispania had been overcome, pacified and controlled, and Gracchus was awarded a triumph for his efforts.

Roman misgovernment was endemic in the *provinciae*, to the point where governors were being brought to trial in Rome for extortion and the inhabitants of Hispania were up in arms. The Lusitanian War(s), named after the tribespeople of Hispania Ulterior, broke out in 155 BC and ran intermittently down to 139 BC,[3] and the parallel Numantine War (154–133 BC) was waged in Hispania Citerior.

The ancient geography writer Strabo gives us a concise characterisation of the Lusitanians, who to his eyes were classic barbarians – clever at laying ambushes, sharp, swift of foot, somewhat volatile, but easy to train as soldiers. They fought with a small shield about 60 centimetres across, with a concave outer surface, and suspended by leather thongs. They carried a dagger and wore linen body armour, although a few of them had chainmail jackets, and triple-crested helmets, or helmets made out of sinews. Their infantrymen wore greaves (armour protecting the lower leg) and carried a number of javelins, although some of them also wielded bronze-tipped spears. The Lusitanians who lived near the River Douro were said to live a lifestyle modelled on that of the Spartans: they anointed their bodies with oil, used hot-air baths made of heated stones, bathed in cold water and just ate one frugal meal a day. They were scrupulous in their religious rituals, not only making animal sacrifices, but also practising divination using the entrails of captive enemies. The priest would cover the victim with a military cloak, stab him, and then interpret the auguries from the way he fell. They also cut off the right hands of their prisoners, and consecrated them to the gods.[4]

The Lusitanian War became known as the 'Fiery War' (*Pyrinos Polemos* in Greek):

> The war between the Romans and the Celtiberians[5] was called the 'fiery war,' so remarkable was the uninterrupted character of the engagements. For while wars in Greece and Asia are as a rule decided by one battle, or more rarely by two, and while the battles themselves are decided in a brief space of time by the result of the first attack and encounter, in this war it was just the opposite. The engagements as a rule were only stopped by darkness, the combatants refusing either to let their courage flag or to yield to bodily fatigue, and ever rallying, recovering confidence and beginning afresh. Winter indeed alone put a certain check on the progress of the whole war and on the continuous character of the regular battles, so that on the whole if we can conceive a war to be fiery it would be this and no other one.[6]

One of the triggers for the outbreak of hostilities was when the settlement of Segeda in Hispania Citerior refused to pay tribute or provide soldiers, and started rebuilding its walls. Quintus Fulvius Nobilior (consul 153 BC) took the offensive, only to suffer extensive losses, particularly when some elephants that he was using became excited and started killing his own men. The historian Polybius was in Hispania during the Lusitanian War, and watched the conflict ebb and flow until the spring of 150 BC, when the governors Lucius Licinius Lucullus (Citerior) and Servius Sulpicius Galba (Ulterior) invaded Lusitania and forced its inhabitants to seek a truce. They then perpetrated a cynical and infamous act of treachery which ancient writers regarded as typical of barbarians, not Romans. Galba promised them forgiveness and good land, and they came to meet him. But then

> he divided them into three parts, and showing to each division a certain plain, he commanded them to remain in this open country, until he should come and assign them their places. When he came to the first division, he told them as friends to lay down their arms. When they had done so he surrounded them with a ditch and sent in soldiers with swords who slew them all ... In like manner he hastened to the second and third divisions and destroyed them while they were still ignorant of the fate of the first. Thus he avenged treachery with treachery, imitating barbarians in a way unworthy of a Roman.[7]

Eight thousand Lusitanians were killed or sold into slavery; Lucullus and Galba were both acquitted in a subsequent 'war crimes' trial in Rome.

Viriathus

Among those who escaped from Galba's Hispanic atrocity was a man who the Romans called Viriathus, transcribed by the

Greeks as Ouriatthos or Hyriatthos. The name may mean 'Adorned with Bracelets' in Celtic, although the Latin *vir-* has links to 'man' (*vir*) and 'rod' (*virga*).[8] Conventional thinking places his birthdate around 180 BC, and his place of birth is equally hard to pinpoint. Speculation about this is often clouded by modern Portuguese and/or Spanish nationalism, although we can at least say that he came from Lusitania, lived on the Atlantic coast, and did most of his fighting in southern Lusitania.[9] Neither do we know the names of his parents. Diodorus presents the trajectory of his early career as ascending from a shepherd who was well known for hunting and fighting bandits, to being chosen as the leader of his people. Numerous bandits then joined him, and his success in various battles won him respect as a general. By 147 BC he had 'established himself as a chieftain, rather than a thief and a robber'.[10]

There is much in this narrative that is conventional in Roman views of eminent barbarians: his rise from obscure beginnings to stellar leadership due to the excellence of his personal values and morals is a cliché that is repeated time and again in the 'barbarian history' of Roman affairs. Diodorus Siculus speaks highly of his engaging and admirable personality:

This Viriathus . . . was [a shepherd and] a practised mountaineer; to this mode of life, indeed, his physical endowment well suited him, since in strength of arm, in speed of foot, and in agility and nimbleness generally he was far superior to the other Iberians. Having accustomed himself to a regime of little food, much exercise, and a bare minimum of sleep, and in short by living at all times under arms and in constant conflict with beasts of the wild and with brigands, he had made his name a byword with the populace . . . He not only won acclaim as a warrior but gained besides a reputation for exceptional qualities of leadership. He was, moreover, scrupulous in the division of spoils and according to their deserts honoured with gifts those of his men who distinguished themselves for bravery.[11]

This is a picture thoroughly endorsed by Dio Cassius:

He trained himself to be very swift both in pursuit and in flight, and of powerful endurance in a hand-to-hand conflict. He was glad enough to get any food that came to hand and whatever drink fell to his lot; most of his life he lived under the open sky and was satisfied with nature's bedding. Consequently he was superior to any heat or cold, and was never either troubled by hunger or annoyed by any other privation; for he found full satisfaction for all his needs in whatever he had at hand, as if it were the very best. And yet, possessed of such a physique, as the result both of nature and training, he excelled still more in his mental powers. He was swift to plan and accomplish whatever was needful, for he not only knew what must be done, but also understood the proper occasion for it; and he was equally clever at feigning ignorance of the most obvious facts and knowledge of the most hidden secrets. Furthermore, he was . . . seen to be neither humble nor overbearing; indeed, in him obscurity of family and reputation for strength were so combined that he seemed to be neither inferior nor superior to any one. And, in fine, he carried on the war not for the sake of personal gain or power nor through anger, but for the sake of warlike deeds in themselves; hence he was accounted at once a lover of war and a master of war.[12]

Because Roman historians so often write with a transparent moral purpose, it can be hard to judge the veracity of assessments such as these, but he certainly had the charisma to bring the chieftains of other tribes, who regularly fought among one another, along to his cause, and to keep them onside with relatively few desertions and defections.

The Fiery War (Second Lusitanian War)
Part 1: Viriathus on the Offensive

Our prime ancient source for Viriathus' war against Rome is found in Book 6 of Appian's *Roman History*, which is itself based on Polybius, supplemented by material in Livy, Appian and Diodorus Siculus. These authors all stress how the conflicts in Spain were difficult and unpleasant, as Rome not only had to fight a hostile people, but also in a hostile environment for which their military was not especially well-equipped. After the atrocities perpetrated by Lucullus and Galba, the Romans pressed their offensive into Turdetania, and forced the Hispanic tribes to send olive branches and ask for land in return for total submission to Rome. But when the new Praetor of Hispania Ulterior, Gaius Vetilius, was on the verge of concluding the deal, Viriathus stepped in and reminded the Lusitanians of the serial perfidy of the Romans. He offered them an alternative solution, inspired them with his oratory and was chosen as their leader.

The ruse that Viriathus used to extricate the Lusitanians was to have them deploy in full battle array, but then scatter in all directions and regroup at the city of Tribola.[13] To give them time to do this Viriathus stayed behind with a thousand chosen fighters, harassing the Romans by continually attacking and retreating with his swift cavalry for two days, before departing under the cover of night to rejoin the main force. The plan worked perfectly.[14]

Throughout their campaigns in Hispania the Romans were hampered by the weight of their armour, their ignorance of the local geography and the inferiority of their horses, but Vetilius still pursued Viriathus to Tribola. The Lusitanians exploited all the Romans' shortcomings by laying in ambush in some dense thickets and catching the Romans at the perfect moment: 'On both sides they began killing the Romans, driving them over the cliffs and taking them prisoners. Vetilius himself was taken prisoner; and the man who captured him, not knowing who he was, but seeing that he was old and fat, and considering him worthless, killed him.'[15]

A mere 6,000 badly demoralised survivors of the 10,000-strong Roman army escaped to the seaside city of Carpessus, where they were stationed on the walls of the town. Their commander then sent 5,000 allied warriors from the Hispanic Belli and Titthi tribes to attack Viriathus, but not one of them survived to tell the tale. The Romans waited quietly in the town for help from home, although given Rome's preoccupations with the Third Punic War and the fighting in Greece, sending a relief force to Hispania was not the Senate's number one priority.

In 146 BC, while Rome was destroying Carthage and sacking Corinth, Viriathus was plundering the fertile country of Carpetania towards Toletum (modern Toledo), and continued to do so until the arrival of Gaius Plautius Hypsaeus with an army of 10,000 infantry and 1,300 cavalry. Once again Viriathus exploited the sluggishness of the Roman legions with his guerrilla tactics, feigning flight and luring Plautius into pursuing him with about 4,000 men, before turning on them and inflicting very severe casualties. Nevertheless, Plautius doggedly followed the elusive Viriathus as he crossed the River Tagus and encamped on some tree-covered high ground, which the Romans called Mons Veneris ('Venus' Mountain').[16] Plautius caught up with him, and in his eagerness to overturn his previous defeat, he engaged with Viriathus' army, only to find himself once again on the wrong end of a humiliating defeat. Having fled in disorder he went into winter quarters, even though it was still midsummer, which gave Viriathus total freedom to ravage the province, forcing the farmers either to pay him the value of their crops or have them destroyed.

After Plautius returned to Rome he was condemned by the people because he had dishonoured his government, and was forced into exile.[17] Viriathus used Mons Veneris as his strategic base, and continued to exploit his hit-and-run tactics in ways that subsequently found their way into Roman military manuals. The Roman sources are often vague about the precise chronology of the fighting, but Frontinus tells how on one occasion Viriathus laid an ambush, sent a few fighters to drive off the flocks of the Segobrigenses,[18] and then, when the townspeople rushed out to protect their livestock, his men pretended to flee and lured them into the trap, where they were cut to pieces.[19] Frontinus gives another example of 'false flight', also in relation to the Segobrigenses, where Viriathus retreated for three days, but then quickly turned round and covered the same distance in just one day, catching the Segobrigenses off guard when they were sacrificing, to murderous effect.[20] At some stage the governor of Hispania Citerior, Claudius Unimanus, sent troops to help out, but we are told that Viriathus almost totally exterminated his army, and then set up trophies in the mountains that were adorned with the official Roman robes and *fasces* that he had captured.[21] Yet despite Viriathus' successes, the ferocity of the resistance to him was exemplified by Rome's allies, the Segovienses:[22] Viriathus had captured their wives and children, but when he proposed to send them back they chose to witness the execution of their loved ones rather than to fail the Romans.[23]

The severity of the situation was now starting to dawn on Rome. Viriathus' tactical nous was clear for all to see, and his victories were starting to bring him wider support in the Iberian peninsula, but by 145 BC Carthage and Corinth were smouldering ruins, and the Romans could look westwards again. Quintus Fabius Maximus Aemilianus (consul 145 BC), the eldest son of Lucius Aemilius Paullus and the elder brother of Scipio Africanus the Younger, was sent out to Hispania and given the power to levy troops. To spare the exhausted veterans of the Punic and Macedonian wars, he recruited two legions of young men who had never been involved in a war before, and requested additional forces from the allies. When he arrived at Urso (modern Osuna), he could deploy 15,000 infantry and about 2,000 cavalry, but was reluctant to commit them to combat until they were properly trained. Maximus himself went to sacrifice to Hercules at the temple of Melqart at Gades (modern Cadiz). Viriathus, meanwhile, surprised and killed a number of Maximus' wood-cutters, and followed up by defeating the forces who came to relieve them. Viriathus gained plentiful plunder; the Romans lost confidence.

As his name shows, Quintus Fabius Maximus Aemilianus was, by adoption, a member of the *gens Fabia*, whose most famous son Quintus Fabius Maximus 'Cunctator' had done so much to defeat Hannibal (see pp. 100 ff.). The younger

Maximus learned the lessons of history, and used his first-hand knowledge of the tactics used by his blood father, Paullus, in the Macedonian War, to spend around a year (mid-145 to mid-144 BC) training his men, and gradually blooding them in small-scale engagements. Whereas Viriathus' advantage lay in his mobility and local knowledge, he was still leading a war-band of temporary warriors, and constantly had to face the logistical challenges of supplying them and keeping them in the field. The Romans, on the other hand, struggled to engage him on their own terms, but they had the advantage of a well-organised, logistically sophisticated military system, and they could take as long as they needed. When Maximus did strike, he did so effectively. Appian says that he was the second Roman general to put Viriathus to flight (although the Lusitanian fought valiantly), and that Maximus captured and plundered one of his cities, and burned another.[24] Viriathus retreated to Baecula (modern Bailén), where the Romans again inflicted significant losses on his warriors. The tide was starting to turn slightly in Rome's favour, but the impending end of the campaigning season meant that Maximius wintered at Corduba, before returning to Rome and being replaced by Quintus Pompeius Aulus.

Viriathus was beginning to have more respect for the Romans, and from 143 BC he managed to initiate another conflict in Hispania by detaching the warlike Celtiberian tribes of the Titthi, Belli and Arevaci from their alliances with Rome, thereby reigniting a dormant conflict known as the Numantine War (aka the Third Celtiberian War), which tied up Rome's troops and some of her finest generals in other parts of the peninsula for a decade, even though Viriathus himself had no direct involvement. Yet there was never a real sense of overarching Hispanic identity that would enable Viriathus to mobilise all the various tribes in one major onslaught against Rome, so he persisted with the strategy that had served him so well thus far. After an initial setback against Quintus, Viriathus returned to his·stronghold on Mons Veneris from where he launched an attack in which he slaughtered around a thousand of Quintus' men, captured some standards and drove them back to their camp. He also drove out the garrison of Itucca[25] and ravaged the country of the Bastitani in the south-east of the peninsula. Rather than coming to their aid, the spineless, inexperienced Quintus went into winter quarters at Corduba in the middle of autumn, and entrusted the defence of the region to a Spaniard from the city of Italica called Gaius Marcius.

The Hispanic situation was creating ever-increasing concern at Rome. In 142 BC the consulship was held by Quintus Fabius Maximus Servilianus, the adoptive son of Q. Fabius Maximus Aemilianus (consul 145 BC) and brother of Scipio Africanus the Younger. Servilianus was sent to Hispania to succeed Quintus, taking two legions from Rome plus some allies, bringing his forces up to about 18,000 foot and 1,600 horse. He also wrote to King Micipsa of Numidia in North Africa, asking for war elephants. Viriathus could not let Servilianus gain the initiative, so he attacked him as he was making for Itucca. Appian's description of the ensuing engagement is classic wild-barbarism-versus-ordered-Romanness: Viriathus' warriors attacked 'with loud shouts and barbaric clamour,[26] his men wearing the long hair which in battles they are accustomed to shake in order to terrify their enemies, but [Servilianus] was not dismayed. He stood his ground bravely, and the enemy was driven off without accomplishing anything.'[27]

Once his elephants had arrived, Servilianus set up a large base camp, from which he took the attack to Viriathus. Initially the Romans got the upper hand, but then 'the pursuit became disorderly, and when Viriathus observed this as he fled, he rallied, slew about 3,000 of the Romans, and drove the rest to their camp. He attacked the camp also, where only a few made a stand about the gates, the greater part hiding under their tents from fear, and being with difficulty brought back to their duty by the general and the tribunes.'[28]

The Romans were saved by the approach of darkness, but Viriathus persisted with his guerrilla activities, attacking at unexpected times of day and night with his light-armed infantry and fast cavalry, and finally driving Servilianus back to Itucca.

Viriathus' relationship with the people of Itucca provided Diodorus with the opportunity to develop his picture of him as a plain-speaking, self-taught and unspoilt man. The people of Itucca vacillated between their loyalty to him and to the Romans, and he taunted them about this lack of consistency and good judgement by telling them a story: 'A middle-aged man took two wives, of which the younger, wanting her husband to be the same age as her, pulled out his grey hair, while the older one pulled out his black hair, and finally thanks to these two women pulling at it, his head became completely bald. A similar fate awaits the people of Itucca: the Romans kill their enemies, the Lusitanians kill theirs, so that your city will soon be deserted.'[29]

Diodorus uses this barbarian, who had no formal education but was tutored by common sense, as a moral example for his readers: 'A man who lives according to the principles of nature has concise speech, strengthened by the practice of virtue. By a brief and simple saying, this speaker can utter a maxim, which the hearer will readily recall.'[30]

Barbarian behaviour can teach Greeks and Romans a great deal.

The Fiery War Part 2: Viriathus on the Defensive

Rather like Pyrrhus and Hannibal in Italy, Viriathus had no effective means of dislodging Roman forces from fortified towns, and the longer the Fiery War went on, the more difficulty he faced in provisioning his warriors and replacing his casualties. As his army dwindled, he gave up trying to take Itucca, burned his camp in the night and headed back to Lusitania. By now Servilianus knew better than to try to overtake him, so he ravaged the territory of Baeturia[31] and plundered five unnamed towns that had collaborated with Viriathus, marched against the Cunei of what is now southern Portugal, and finally sought out his enemy in Lusitania. Again the fighting was brutal. Ten thousand bandits led by Curius and Apuleius assaulted the Romans, and although Curius was killed in the fight they still took a great deal of their booty. However, Servilianus quickly captured it back, and took the towns of Escadia, Gemella and Obolcola,[32] which had been garrisoned by Viriathus, while either plundering or sparing others. Servilianus' reprisals were severe: of the 10,000 prisoners he took, he beheaded 500 and sold the rest as slaves; and when the bandit chieftain Connoba surrendered, he spared him, but cut off the hands of all of his men.[33]

As ever, Viriathus fought back effectively. As Servilianus was besieging Erisana, whose location is unknown, Viriathus managed to infiltrate the town at night and make a dawn attack on the soldiers who were working in the trenches, forcing them to down tools and run. He followed up with an impressive attack on Servilianus' main force, which he drove against some cliffs, giving it no chance of escape.

By now Viriathus' desire for the Fiery War was cooling, and in his moment of triumph, rather than destroying Servilianus' army, he offered him a deal:

> Viriathus was not arrogant in the hour of victory, but considering this a favourable opportunity of bringing the war to an end by a conspicuous act of generosity, he made an agreement with [the Romans], which was ratified by the Roman people. Viriathus was declared to be a friend of the Roman nation, and it was decreed that all of his followers should have the land which they then occupied. Thus the Viriathic war, which had been so extremely tedious to the Romans, seemed to have been brought to an end by this act of generosity.[34]

In describing events in this way, Appian is very much playing on the stereotype of the 'noble savage' dealing with the 'corrupt Roman', but as Diodorus also says, Fabius had been forced to accept terms dishonourable to the Roman name.[35] Livy regarded the agreement in a negative light, commenting that Servilianus had spoilt his success by concluding a peace 'on equal terms',[36] and more significantly Servilianus' own brother Quintus Servilius Caepio (consul 140 BC) immediately denounced it as being completely unworthy of the dignity of the Roman people, and the Senate authorised the resumption of hostilities.

There remain serious question marks over why Viriathus chose this particular moment to seek peace, but one suggestion is that it was connected with his marital problems. In 141 BC he had married the daughter or sister of an aristocratic Lusitanian called Astolpas. History does not record her name, although legend has it that she was called Tongina, and was a young, pale-skinned, dark-haired beauty with a feisty attitude. But there was a source of tension in the fact that her rich and noble background was at odds with Viriathus' more down-to-earth origins, and this exposed various inequalities in Lusitanian society. In Diodorus' account of the wedding, a vast number of gold and silver cups along with some exquisite rich carpets were brought out to grace the ceremony. But Viriathus was far from impressed:

> Supporting himself on a lance, [Viriathus] regarded them not with admiration . . . but rather in scorn and contempt . . . He spoke many things with much wisdom and prudence, and concluded with many emphatic remarks, on the subject of ingratitude towards benefactors and of the folly [of] trusting in the gifts of fortune, which are so uncertain; especially, since it was apparent, that all those highly esteemed riches of his father-in-law were liable to be a prey to whoever could them take away upon his spear's point.[37]

Viriathus was telling Astolpas that although he was exceptionally wealthy, he was still in thrall to Rome, or indeed to Viriathus, and he went on to say that Astolpas should be thanking him, not the other way round: Astolpas hadn't needed to give Viriathus anything of his own because Viriathus was 'lord and owner of all'. Everyone asked Viriathus to sit down, but he refused, and although a splendid banquet had been laid out, he only distributed some bread and meat among the people who had come with him. He barely ate anything himself before he sacrificed 'after the manner of the Iberians', ordered his bride to be brought, put her on the back of a horse, and carried her off into the mountains.[38] Diodorus explains that he did this because 'he regarded sobriety and temperance the greatest riches; liberty as his homeland; and outstanding valour as the surest possession. In conversation he spoke plainly and sincerely what he thought; his own unblemished character led him (without any formal education) to express himself faultlessly.'[39]

This is very much part of Viriathus' characterisation as the intelligent, cultured, morally unimpeachable barbarian – a noble savage. And when Viriathus cast his eyes over all the wealth that was on show at the wedding, he had asked Astolpas, 'Why haven't the Romans taken all this wealth, even though they have the power to do so?' Astolpas replied that lots of Romans had seen it, but none of them had thought to take it or even ask for it. 'So why,' said Viriathus, 'have you abandoned the people who allow you to enjoy your property quietly, to join me, who am from a poor and humble background?' It was a politically astute point to make. Why indeed would the wealthy Astolpas ally himself with the rough, impoverished Viriathus, and walk a dangerous tightrope between him and Rome? Astolpas' reply is not recorded; what matters is Viriathus' question, and the fact that it shows that even a barbarian could become a moral exemplar for decadent Romans and Greeks.

Once the fighting had resumed on an official basis in 139 BC, Quintus Servilius Caepio took the offensive, while Viriathus fled and destroyed everything in his path. The armies finally came together in Carpetania, where Viriathus escaped by repeating the tactics he had used at Tribola: 'Viriathus . . .

ordered the greater part of it to retreat through a hidden defile, while he drew up the remainder on a hill as though he intended to fight. When he judged that those who had been sent before had reached a place of safety, he darted after them with such disregard of the enemy and such swiftness that his pursuers did not know whither he had gone.'[40]

Caepio took his frustration out on the Vettones and the Callaici, thereby extending Roman military activities north of the River Tagus and near to the coast of the Atlantic for the first time.

Yet despite his trailblazing activities, Caepio failed to win the respect of the ancient historians. Dio Cassius says that 'Caepio accomplished nothing worthy of mention . . . but visited many injuries upon his own men, so that he even came near being killed by them. For he treated them all, and especially the cavalry, with such harshness and cruelty that a great number of unseemly jokes and stories were told about him during the nights; and the more he grew vexed at it, the more they jested in the endeavour to infuriate him.'[41]

When he couldn't discover who was behind this, he decided to punish all the cavalry, and ordered them to cross a river and go foraging for wood on the mountain where Viriathus was camped. Despite the danger, they accomplished their mission, and then piled the wood all around Caepio's headquarters. They would have burned him to death had he not escaped in the nick of time.

In stark contrast to Roman ineptitude, we hear extraordinary stories of the power and resilience of the barbarian women. These also carry an element of moral stereotyping, but they are indicative of the ways ancient historians use idealised barbarism to highlight inadequate Roman maleness. Appian digresses to tell his readers about Lusitanian women warriors 'fighting and dying alongside the men, and not uttering a single cry in the midst of the slaughter',[42] and about the incredibly warlike Bracari, whose women bore arms alongside the men with a 'freedom or death' attitude, and who either killed themselves or slew their children with their own hands when they were captured.[43]

Betrayal and Death

Viriathus came to the realisation that he could win battles but never win the war. As a second Roman army under Marcus Popilius Laenas (consul 139 BC) moved into Lusitania, Viriathus saw that his situation was hopeless. He opened peace talks with Laenas without even resorting to arms, killed a number of leaders (including his own son-in-law) whose surrender had been demanded by the Romans and handed over the rest. They all had their hands cut off on Laenas' orders – a punishment that as Lusitanians they would have understood. Laenas still had so many conditions that he elected to state them individually, worrying that if he outlined them all at once, it would simply drive Viriathus to despair and all-out war.[44] Dio adds that the only sticking point came when Laenas demanded that the warriors should surrender their weapons, which for them was non-negotiable.[45]

So Viriathus ultimately sought a deal with Caepio, using his trusted Latin-speaking companions Audax, Ditalco and Minurus[46] to conduct the negotiations. Their names suggest that they were not Lusitanians, and they had already realised that Viriathus was the loser, so they allowed themselves to be bribed into assassinating him. He was said to have slept very little, and when he did, he kept his armour on, just in case of an emergency. This made him feel secure enough to allow his friends to visit him at night, so the assassins exploited this to enter his tent on the pretext of some business or other, just as he had fallen asleep. Appian says they stabbed him in the throat, which was the only unprotected part of his body; Diodorus speaks of some well-aimed blows of the sword; and both authors say the killers immediately escaped back to Caepio.[47]

When they asked for their money they were disappointed: Caepio told them that 'it was never pleasing to the Romans that generals should be killed by their own soldiers'.[48] We hear no more about the assassins, but history has judged the deed harshly. In his *Book of Memorable Doings and Sayings*, written around AD 30, Valerius Maximus comments that 'the murder of Viriathus too is open to a double charge of treachery, one involving his friends, because he was killed by their hands, the other Consul Quintus Servilius Caepio, in that he instigated the crime with a promise of immunity. He did not earn victory, he bought it.'[49]

Viriathus' men were surprised that he was not awake early in the morning, and when they discovered him lying dead in his armour they were smitten with grief for their leader, fear for themselves and frustration at not being able to find the perpetrators. They gave their leader a funeral appropriate for a high-status barbarian: his body was laid out in splendid garments and burned on a high pyre; sacrifices were offered for him; infantry and cavalry ran around him in their armour, singing his praises 'in barbarian style' (*barbarikos*); everyone stayed until the fire had gone out; and 200 pairs of gladiators fought duels at his tomb.

The Lusitanian resistance to Rome did not continue long after Viriathus' death. He was replaced by a man named Tautalus, but his leadership was ineffective, and Caepio quickly forced him to surrender on condition that the Lusitanians should be treated as subjects. He disarmed them, but granted them enough to stop them turning to banditry because of poverty.

Viriathus' defeat did not bring an immediate halt to the fighting in Hispania. Velleius Paterculus writes that 'on the death of Viriathus through the perfidy rather than the valour of Servilius Caepio, there broke out in Numantia a war that was more serious still.'[50]

History pretty much repeated itself when, in 137 BC, the Celtiberians allowed another defeated Roman army to get away unscathed, but the promise of independence for the Celtiberians was scuppered when the Roman Senate again refused to ratify the terms. So the fighting went on, and ultimately it took Scipio Aemilianus, the destroyer of Carthage, to bring it to an end, starving the inhabitants of Numantia into famine, cannibalism and capitulation after an eight-month blockade. The city was destroyed, the survivors were sold into slavery, and Scipio, now called Publius Cornelius Scipio Aemilianus Africanus Numantinus, celebrated a triumph. Overall, it was 'job done' again, in the most characteristic Roman manner.

There is no doubt that Viriathus won the (sometimes grudging and slightly patronising) respect of a great many Greeks and Romans, despite his barbarian background. Appian rounded off his account by describing him as 'a man who, for a barbarian, had the highest qualities of a commander, and was always foremost in facing danger',[51] and Florus characterised him as 'a man of extreme cunning, who from being a hunter became a brigand, and from a brigand suddenly became a leader and general, and, if Fortune had favoured him, would have become the Romulus of Spain'.[52]

He is still a national hero in Portugal.

8

Jugurtha: The Struggle to Free Africa from Rome

In the Beginning . . .

Big barbarian personalities were frequently used by Roman historians to make serious moral and political points. That, very often, is why they wrote history in the first place. And just as Viriathus, despite being a barbarian, was held up as an example of the Roman virtues of sobriety, liberty, courage, resilience, plain-speaking and moral excellence, so the historian and politician Sallust wrote a monograph, published around 41 BC, entitled *Bellum Jugurthinum* ('The Jugurthine War') about the North African prince Jugurtha, to highlight the decadence of Rome at the end of the second century BC. Given today's morality, he asks, 'Who in the world is there who does not vie with his ancestors in riches and extravagance rather than in uprightness and exertion?'[1]

He puts this down to an adverse 'peace dividend' following the destruction of Carthage: 'Fear of the enemy abroad kept the state within the bounds of good morals. But when that dread departed from the minds of the people, there arose, of course, those vices which tend to be fostered by prosperity: promiscuity and arrogance. Thus the peacetime for which they had longed in time of adversity, after they had gained it, proved to be more cruel and bitter than adversity itself.'[2]

Roman writers frequently moan about the debilitating effects of peace, and Sallust says that he wants to write about the war with Jugurtha, firstly because it was a serious, terrible and fluctuating conflict, but secondly because it was 'then for the first time resistance was put in the way of the arrogance of the nobility'.[3] Certainly the Jugurthine War was a conflict that exposed senatorial corruption, highlighted the incompetence of several senatorial commanders, caused a serious disconnect between the Senate and the Equites (the 'Knights', Rome's elite businessmen and financiers), and showed just how easily the Senate could be defied by a man of ability, be he Roman or barbarian.

Back in the Second Punic War (218–201 BC), King Masinissa of Numidia, which occupied modern Algeria and part of Tunisia, had been recognised as a friend by Scipio Africanus, and had fought effectively on the Roman side. After the war was over, the Romans had given Masinissa some quite extensive territories in North Africa, and he remained a loyal ally of the Romans until his death at the age of ninety or more in 148 BC. He was succeeded by his son Micipsa who had two sons of his own, Adherbal and Hiempsal, but who also brought up Jugurtha, who was the son of his late brother Mastanabal. Jugurtha was classed as a 'private citizen', with no claim to the throne, because he was the child of a concubine.

Jugurtha grew up to be a talented, vigorous, warlike, unscrupulous, popular young man, who was motivated by military glory. Micipsa became worried on behalf of himself and his two natural sons, but feared that if he simply removed him by violent means it might provoke a backlash. So he resorted to the tactic used by many kings to get rid of dangerous contenders, and sent him on a mission from which he hoped there would be no return. It was 134 BC, and Micipsa sent a contingent of cavalry and infantry to help the Romans in the Numantine War, and gave Jugurtha command of them, in the hope that he would die in action, be this due to his own impetuousness or the savagery of the enemy.

In Hispania Jugurtha joined up with Publius Scipio Aemilianus Africanus Numantinus, who brought the Numantine War to an end in 133 BC. To Micipsa's disappointment Jugurtha not only survived, but 'acquired (through hard work and studious application, and also by his strict obedience and by often courting dangers) such a glorious reputation that he was enormously popular with [the Roman] soldiers and a source of great dread to the Numantines. In fact, he was both vigorous in battle and wise in counsel, a thing most difficult to achieve.'⁴

This, along with his affable personality, made him extremely popular with both Scipio and many of the other Romans he met. Some of these, who Sallust says valued riches more than virtue and integrity, encouraged him to consider making a power-grab in Numidia when Micipsa died: '[Jugurtha] had the greatest masculinity, and at Rome everything was up for sale.'⁵

Knowing the price of the Romans was priceless to Jugurtha. Scipio, though, took him to one side and gave him some sage advice:

he advised the young man to cultivate the friendship of the Roman people through official channels rather than through powerbrokers, and not to form the habit of bribery. It was dangerous, he said, to buy from a few what belonged to the many, that if Jugurtha was willing to remain true to his character, then fame and royal power would come to him unsought; but if he proceeded too hastily, he would bring about his own ruin by means of his own money.[6]

Scipio then sent Jugurtha home with a letter, telling Micipsa what a splendid individual his nephew was, which seems to have changed Micipsa's attitude towards him. At some point, he added Jugurtha to his will, with the same status as his sons. Sallust dramatises a conversation Micipsa, nearing the end of his life, had with Jugurtha in what sounds rather like a rhetorical exercise on the theme of a dying father addressing his adoptive son. Micipsa hopes that there will be harmony in his realm after he is gone: 'I deliver to you and my two sons a realm that will be strong if you three are virtuous, but if evil, then weak.'[7] He encourages Jugurtha not to be aggressive, and exhorts Adherbal and Hiempsal to love, respect and emulate Jugurtha.

Micipsa died in 118 BC,[8] and the post-mortem harmony that he had hoped for never materialised. In a town known as Thirmida,[9] Hiempsal happened to be using a house that belonged to Jugurtha's very loyal chief attendant. Jugurtha got him to make a spurious inspection of the house and to have duplicate keys cut. Jugurtha's men duly arrived in the dead of night and burst in. They found Hiempsal cowering in a maid-servant's hut, killed him, and took his head back to Jugurtha.

The murder of Hiempsal terrorised Africa, and split the allegiances of the Numidians: Adherbal gained more supporters, but Jugurtha had the better warriors. Jugurtha started to take control of numerous cities and to prepare for total power over

Numidia; Adherbal sent envoys to Rome to seek help, but in the meantime he offered battle to Jugurtha. He was defeated and fled, via the Roman province of Africa, to Rome.

In the cold light of day, Jugurtha started to worry about the consequences of his takeover of Numidia. The only way he could think of to deflect the anticipated Roman backlash was to exploit the greed of the Roman nobles, and his own cash. So he sent envoys to Rome laden with gold and silver, and instructions to lavish presents on his old friends and to win new ones by bribery. The plan worked well, and in due course both Adherbal and Jugurtha were given the opportunity to address the Senate.[10] Adherbal made a long address, concluding with an emotional appeal: 'Members of the Senate – I implore you in your own name, by your children and parents, by the majesty of the Roman people – aid me in my distress, proceed against injustice; do not permit the kingdom of Numidia, which is yours, to waste away through crime and the shedding of our family's blood.'[11]

Jugurtha's envoys' response was brief, relied heavily on bribery, claimed that Hiempsal had been killed by the Numidians because of his ruthlessness, accused Adherbal of starting an unprovoked war, and concluded by asking the Senate to judge Jugurtha on the basis of his actions at Numantia.

After due discussion,[12] the Senate, many of whom 'valued money more than integrity',[13] decreed that a ten-man senatorial commission under Lucius Opimius (consul 121 BC) should divide Numidia between Jugurtha and Adherbal. Sallust portrays Jugurtha as being extremely pleased with the outcome of the commission's activities, and famously remarks that Jugurtha 'felt convinced of the truth of what he had heard from his friends at Numantia, that everything at Rome was for sale'.[14]

In reality, however, Adherbal probably got the better deal.

First Campaigns: Roman Failures

Jugurtha seems to have bided his time for a few years until he could make his move: 'He himself was fierce and aggressive, but his intended victim was quiet, nonaggressive, of a tranquil disposition, open to attack and more given to fear than inspiring it.'[15]

When Jugurtha's attack on his supposedly non-violent rival came, in the spring of 112 BC,[16] it was an unexpected hit-and-run raid, designed to get Adherbal to respond, and thereby furnish Jugurtha with a pretext for war. Initially Adherbal didn't rise to the bait, but Jugurtha's persistence ultimately forced him to put an army in the field.

Close to the well-fortified town of Cirta (modern Constantine in Algeria) in the interior of Numidia, Jugurtha made a dawn raid on Adherbal's camp, and routed his troops. Adherbal himself escaped into the town, where he was assisted by some Italian nationals living there. When Jugurtha put Cirta under siege, the Senate's response was again to send envoys to Africa. Their mission was 'to approach both kings and announce in the name of the Senate and the Roman People that it was their desire and decision that the combatants should lay down their arms and settle their disagreement by right rather than by war'.[17]

There was no chance that either Jugurtha or Adherbal would or could do this: Jugurtha laid the blame on Adherbal, but Adherbal could not put his case to the envoys because Jugurtha denied him access to them.

Once the Romans had departed, Jugurtha resumed his operations against Cirta. Adherbal managed to smuggle a letter out of the city and have it sent to Rome, where it was read in the

Senate. Again the senators were divided; again 'the public good was ... trumped by private influence';[18] and again commissioners were sent to Africa, this time including Marcus Aemilius Scaurus, the *princeps senatus* (against whom Sallust is extremely biased). They summoned Jugurtha to the province of Africa. He was torn between fear and greed, but greed won out in the end: he ignored the commission's threats, and pressed on with the siege.

The Italians in Cirta were confident that Rome would protect them, and they now advised Adherbal to hand himself and the town over to Jugurtha, in return for guarantees on his life. In the autumn of 112 BC, despite his mistrust of Jugurtha, Adherbal did as the Italians suggested, and his mistrust was well placed: Jugurtha tortured Adherbal to death, and massacred all the adult Numidians along with the Italian businessmen.

The massacre at Cirta changed the entire situation. The Senate could no longer dither and send ineffectual embassies. They had to act. Pressure was being put on them by various factions, led by Gaius Memmius, the tribune for 111 BC, who suspected bribery and was worried about the possible threat to Rome's grain supply, much of which came from Africa. Simultaneously the Equites were calling for protection of their business interests in Africa, and for vengeance. So one of the consuls for 111 BC, Lucius Calpurnius Bestia, was detailed to take an army and invade Numidia.

Bestia's initial incursion into Numidia was successful, but Jugurtha started to send ambassadors to him, who tempted him with money and pointed out how awkward the war was – just as with Viriathus, the Roman heavy infantry was useless against Jugurtha's highly mobile fighters. In this way, 'the consul's mind, diseased as it was by avarice, was easily turned from its purpose',[19] and peace negotiations took place. For the price of thirty elephants, some cattle and horses, plus a small amount of silver, Jugurtha remained King of Numidia.

Bestia returned to Rome, where Memmius strongly suspected bribery. The tribune had a deep hatred of the power of the nobles, and used his inspiring oratory to highlight their arrogant cruelty and inflame the desire for revenge:

> Slaves bought for cash do not put up with the unjust power of their masters; do you, Citizens, born to power, endure slavery with resignation? But who are these persons who have taken possession of our country? Wicked men, with gory hands, of monstrous greed, guilty, and at the same time arrogant, who have made good faith, reputation, a sense of duty, in short everything honorable and dishonorable, a source of gain.[20]

Memmius was able to secure safe conduct for Jugurtha so that he could travel to Rome and expose the bribed senators. Jugurtha made the journey, but bribed the Tribune Gaius Baebius, so that when Memmius started to question Jugurtha, he interposed his veto to prevent him answering, much to the anger and frustration of the people.

At this point Jugurtha went one transgression too far. Masinissa's grandson Massiva was living in Rome in exile, having fled Numidia after the capture of Cirta and the death of Adherbal. He was a potential threat to Jugurtha's kingship and had a degree of support at Rome, so Jugurtha detailed his close attendant Bomilcar to arrange for an assassin to murder Massiva, inevitably for a price. Jugurtha preferred that this should be done in secret, but if that was impossible, any method would do.

The deed was done, but in an amateurish way. The assassin was apprehended, and he turned informer. Bomilcar was put on trial, but Jugurtha managed to smuggle him out of the country. With Rome now despairing of a settlement, Jugurtha was made to leave Rome, and as he did so he looked back and delivered one of the great barbarian soundbites of Roman history: 'A city for sale, and soon to perish if it finds a buyer.'[21]

Rome's offensive in Numidia now continued under the consul for 110 BC, Spurius Postumius Albinus. He hoped to finish the job in time for the elections, which were typically held in November.[22] But Jugurtha was too elusive. He made the campaign drag on and just toyed with Albinus, inventing excuse after excuse for delay, retreating, attacking, offering surrender and then withdrawing the offer. At Rome people started to suspect that something more sinister was going on than Albinus' incompetence, and in the end he left Numidia towards the end of the year, leaving his brother Aulus in command.

Aulus, whom Sallust regarded as a conceited ignoramus,[23] wanted to conclude the war as speedily as he could. The arrival of a newly elected consul might deprive him of the glory of victory or some attractive bribe money from Jugurtha, so he raided Jugurtha's treasury at the strongly fortified town of Suthul.[24] Jugurtha withstood the attack without difficulty, and managed to lure Aulus away into the desert, bribing a number of Roman soldiers into collaborating with him. When the Numidians attacked the Roman camp in the dead of night, some Ligurian and Thracian auxiliaries deserted, and the

Primus Pilus[25] of one of the legions made it easy for Jugurtha's men to enter the camp. The terms of surrender that Aulus accepted were utterly humiliating: his men were allowed to depart on condition that they passed under a yoke of surrender, which was made by sticking two spears in the ground and tying another to them to form a crossbar,[26] and Aulus had to leave Numidia within ten days.

The reaction to Aulus' dishonourable capitulation was one of outrage. In 109 BC the Tribune Gaius Mamilius Limetanus passed a bill, the *lex Mamilia*, to establish the 'Mamilian Commission', which would investigate all aspects of the corruption scandal. Marcus Aemilius Scaurus was one of the three commissioners, but Sallust tells us that, 'nevertheless, the investigation was conducted with harshness and violence, on hearsay evidence and at the whim of the Plebs; for just as had often happened in the case of the nobles, so the Plebs had been made insolent at that time by success.'[27]

Among those condemned and exiled were L. Opimius (consul 121 BC), who had led the delegation that divided Numidia between Jugurtha and Adherbal in 116 BC, the generals Lucius Calpurnius Bestia (consul 111 BC) and Spurius Postumius Albinus (consul 110 BC), and Gaius Galba, whose speech in his own defence became one of the oratorical extracts that Roman schoolboys had to learn by heart.[28]

Metellus' Campaigns: Indecisive Roman Success

Making a nice wordplay in Latin, Sallust tells us that after the treaty (*foedus*) of Aulus and the foul (*foedam*) flight of the Roman army, Quintus Caecilius Metellus (consul 109 BC, later given the *agnomer* Numidicus), an energetic man with a sound and untarnished reputation who opposed the popular party and was impervious to the corrupting power of money, was put in command.[29] He had the backing of the whole community, and he proceeded to recruit new soldiers in Italy and restore discipline and morale among Spurius Albinus' troops in Africa. Jugurtha became dispirited by this. Yet again he sought terms, but Metellus had his measure. He knew his barbarians, and he played Jugurtha at his own game: 'The Numidians were a treacherous race, of fickle disposition, and eager for revolt. Accordingly, [Metellus] approached the envoys . . . and by gradually sounding them out . . . he tried to induce them by lavish promises to deliver Jugurtha into his hands, preferably alive, but if that proved unsuccessful, then dead.'[30]

Metellus' advance into Numidia was very circumspect, and Jugurtha realised that he was dealing with a man who was his equal in what would later be known as Machiavellian dealings. The Romans were clearly learning the lessons from fighting the likes of Viriathus, since Jugurtha's attempts to lure them into ambushes came to nothing, and it was he who blinked first. He chose a favourable place to deal the Romans a knockout blow on the plain by the River Muthul, but it was Metellus' persistence that won the day:

Two great men, struggle[d] with each other, equals as individuals but with unequal resources. For Metellus had valiant soldiers but an unfavorable position, while Jugurtha had favorable circumstances in all else except his soldiers. At last the Romans, realizing that they had no place of refuge and that the foe gave them no opportunity for fighting (and it was already evening), charged straight up the hill as they had been ordered. After losing that position, the Numidians gave way and fled. A few were killed; most were saved by their speed and by the fact that the region was unfamiliar to their enemies.[31]

Jugurtha still remained far from submissive, even though he had to recruit new warriors because of the barbarian habits of his people: 'Not a single Numidian follows his king in flight, but all disperse to wherever their inclination takes them; and this is not considered shameful when on military service. Such are their ways.'[32]

So Metellus changed tactics and began to lay waste to the countryside, burn the towns and massacre all the men of military age. This forced Jugurtha into becoming more aggressive: pursuit rather than flight became the order of the day.

Metellus' success went down very well at Rome. The Senate voted him a *Supplicatio*, a thanksgiving lasting several days, in which business activities stopped, temples were opened, sacrifices were made, and statues of the gods were displayed on sacred couches. This fired Metellus up to finish the war. Jugurtha started to harass Metellus by destroying fodder and fouling springs, which pushed him into a change of tactics: he laid siege to Jugurtha's main stronghold at Zama (probably Zama Regia – there were several Zamas). An incredibly ferocious battle raged around the town, but Metellus could not bring his assault to a successful conclusion.[33] Around October 109 BC, the Romans abandoned the attack and returned to their winter quarters, from where Metellus kept up the pressure by trying to get Bomilcar to betray Jugurtha. This almost worked. Jugurtha was on the point of surrendering when he 'considered how great a fall it was from kingship to slavery'[34] and decided to fight on.

Metellus' command was extended into 108 BC and the war became dirty. The town of Vaga (modern Bedja, about 95 kilometres south-west of Utica) was garrisoned by Metellus' troops, but 'the common throng, as usual – and especially so in the case of the Numidians – was of a fickle disposition, prone to rebellion and disorder, fond of revolution and opposed to peace and quiet.'[35]

Jugurtha talked their leaders into perpetrating a massacre on a public holiday, but they only enjoyed their success for a couple of days before Metellus responded and exacted brutal vengeance.

Around the same time Bomilcar was having serious worries about his own personal safety. So he decided to get his retaliation against Jugurtha in first. Unfortunately for him, he chose his co-conspirator badly. This was a man named Nabdalsa, but he got cold feet at the crucial moment and turned informer against Bomilcar to save his own skin. Bomilcar was duly executed, but the incident destroyed Jugurtha's trust in everyone around him. He could never rest easily in his bed from then on.

Metellus continued to stalk Jugurtha across the African desert, while the king made contact with the nomadic Gaetulians to the south and his father-in-law King Bocchus of Mauretania. Metellus played safe, taking up a position at the heavily fortified city of Cirta to await their arrival. But at this point he received some devastating news. His subordinate, Gaius Marius, had been elected to the consulship of 108 BC and had been given the command in Numidia for the same year.

Gaius Marius was a *novus homo*, a 'New Man' whose family had not been involved in high-level politics at Rome before.

He had been born at Arpinum in 155 BC; served with distinction as a military tribune under Scipio Aemilianus during the Numantine War in 133 BC; held the praetorship in 115 BC; made an astute marriage into the eminent but impoverished *gens Julia*; and joined Metellus' staff in 109 BC, with whom he had also fought very effectively. But when he expressed a wish to go to Rome to stand for consul, Metellus' response had been to refuse and insult him. Marius responded by trying to undermine Metellus: he won over the soldiers, and the Equites based in Africa; promised a pretender called Gauda that he could have Jugurtha's throne if he became consul; and garnered support from the Plebs at Rome. Eventually Metellus gave in. Marius went to Rome, accused Metellus of deliberately prolonging the war, promised to bring back Jugurtha dead or alive, and was elected. The Tribune Titus Manlius Mancinus then had the Jugurthan command transferred to Marius by special decree, thereby dealing a hammer blow to the Senate's monopoly over foreign and military appointments.

Metellus was livid – more than was appropriate, according to Sallust.[36] Amid his tears of rage and uncontrolled verbal outbursts, he abandoned any attempt to seek a military solution and so help his successor, and though he attempted to subvert Bocchus, the Mauretanian was not yet ready to betray Jugurtha. The war ground to a halt.

Marius versus Jugurtha: Victory for Rome at Last

The mood at Rome was optimistic. Marius was popular with army veterans, but he needed more troops. In order to do this he had to waive the normal rules concerning the property qualifications for military service. The Senate thought this would amount to political suicide, but they were completely wrong: after an emotive speech to the people,[37] in which he addressed them in their own manner of speaking, he enrolled a great many poor and/or unemployed people who wanted regular work, a popular leader, adventure and plunder. Far more people than expected flocked to his standard, and he trained them up to legionary level. It was a crucial moment in Rome's history: never before had the army had such a powerful position in Roman political life.

Marius landed and, much to Metellus' annoyance, started to win some successes in Numidia that gave his new recruits the easy plunder that they craved. Bocchus started to sense that Jugurtha was likely to lose, and opened a dialogue about peace, but at this stage Marius was more interested in victory on the battlefield than in diplomacy and betrayal. He marched through the desert to Capsa (modern Gafsa in Tunisia), an oasis town in the very south-east of Numidia, where his dawn raid took the citizens by complete surprise. Marius burned the town, killed the adult Numidians, sold the rest into slavery and distributed the booty among the soldiers. Sallust regarded this as tantamount to a war crime, but still justified it because of the 'fickleness and untrustworthiness' of Capsa's barbarian population.[38]

Despite the capture of Capsa, Marius was really no nearer defeating Jugurtha than any of his predecessors had been, but he still had the goodwill of the people on his side, and his command was extended into 106 BC. In that year he made the long western march to the River Muluccha (modern Moulouya) where, thanks to the initiative and courage of a Ligurian soldier, he captured Jugurtha's chief treasury. The ever-vacillating Bocchus now linked up with Jugurtha again and, in the vicinity of Cirta late one autumn evening, they came as close as they ever had to destroying the Roman army. The African forces attacked 'not in battle array or after the fashion of a proper battle but in swarms',[39] and forced Marius' men to take refuge for the night on two neighbouring hills. It was then that the innate barbarism of Jugurtha's warriors became their undoing: 'After kindling many fires, the barbarians, as is their usual habit, spent the greater part of the night in rejoicing, in exultation and in noisy chatter, while even their leaders, who were filled with confidence because the men had not taken to flight, acted as if they were victorious.'[40]

By daybreak the Africans were weak, sleep-deprived and helpless in the face of the inevitable Roman counter-attack. It was by far the worst defeat that Jugurtha had suffered to date, and it was compounded when he again attacked Marius' army as they were heading, in square formation, for their winter quarters. After the battle 'the whole landscape, wherever the eye could reach, was strewn with missiles, arms, and corpses, and the ground in the midst of this was soaked with blood'.[41] The blood was African.

Bocchus finally realised that he really was on the wrong side. He sent ambassadors to the Romans, and they received a civil welcome from Marius' second-in-command, Lucius Cornelius Sulla. Sulla was everything that Marius was not: Patrician, well-educated in Greek and Roman literature, fond of luxurious leisure, eloquent and lucky. Bocchus liked Sulla, and asked to negotiate exclusively with him. This was very risky for Sulla: 'He put faith in a Barbarian, and one who was faithless towards his own relations, and to secure his surrender of another.'[42] Yet he still made the long and dangerous journey to Bocchus' palace, where he politely, but forcibly,

told him that a deal was on the table, but only if Bocchus'
actions spoke louder than his words: he must give up Jugurtha.
After some incredibly complex machinations characterised by
a good deal of 'Punic faith' (*Punica fides*, see p. 95), the trap
was set.

> Bocchus (as if going to meet [Jugurtha] out of respect)
> proceeded with a few friends and our quaestor (i.e. Sulla,
> who was technically Proquaestor) to a mound in plain sight
> of those who were lying in ambush. The Numidian drew
> near to the same place with most of his close followers,
> unarmed, as had been agreed, and immediately upon a given
> signal a rush was made simultaneously on all sides from the
> ambush. His companions were cut to pieces; Jugurtha was
> delivered to Sulla in bonds and taken by him to Marius.[43]

As the commander-in-chief, the glory for this technically
belonged to Marius, who held the *imperium*, and this caused
enormous ill-feeling on Sulla's part. Sulla had a commemora-
tive signet ring made for himself: 'He was arrogant enough to
have a representation of his exploit engraved on a seal-ring
which he wore, and continued to use it ever after. The device
was, Bocchus delivering, and Sulla receiving, Jugurtha.'[44]

We can get a rough idea of the design from coins that Sulla's
son Faustus later minted, showing Sulla sitting on a tribunal in
a dominant position and labelled as 'Lucky' (*Felix*), with
Bocchus offering an olive branch, and Jugurtha with his arms
tied behind his back. But for the moment it was Marius who
receive the accolades.

Jugurtha was displayed to the Roman people bound in chains
and walking in front of Marius' chariot with his two sons at

Marius' triumph on the Kalends of January 104 BC.[45] The wealth of his kingdom was also exhibited, to general amazement:

> This was a sight which they had despaired of beholding, nor could any one have expected, while Jugurtha was alive, to conquer the enemy; so versatile was he in adapting himself to the turns of fortune, and so great craft did he combine with his courage. But we are told that when he had been led in triumph he lost his reason; and that when, after the triumph, he was cast into prison, where some tore his tunic from his body, and others were so eager to snatch away his golden ear-ring that they tore off with it the lobe of his ear, and when he had been thrust down naked into the dungeon pit,[46] in utter bewilderment and with a grin on his lips he said: 'Hercules! How cold this Roman bath is!' But the wretch, after struggling with hunger for six days and up to the last moment clinging to the desire of life, paid the penalty which his crimes deserved.[47]

Rome's struggle with Numidia was over. Bocchus was rewarded with the western part of Numidia (probably from the River Ampsaga in the east to the Muluccha in the west), while Jugurtha's half-brother Gauda became a client king with control over the western part.[48] But a new barbarian challenge was looming in the north, and the importance of Marius is made clear by the very last words of Sallust's *Bellum Jugurthinum*: 'At that time the hopes and welfare of the State were placed in him.'[49]

9

The Cimbri and the Teutones:
A Germanic Threat to Italy

The termination of Jugurtha made Marius the hero of the hour. But he would be called into action almost immediately. As he was dealing with Jugurtha in the south, attacks by some Germanic tribes in the north were causing considerable alarm. This was not an entirely new problem for Rome and the tribes in question were the Cimbri and the Teutones.

The Cimbri and the Teutones

The Cimbri originated from north Jutland, in modern Denmark. In his *Germania*, written around AD 98, the historian Tacitus tells his readers about them:

In [a] remote corner of Germany, bordering on the Ocean dwell the Cimbri, a now insignificant tribe, but of great renown. Of their ancient glory widespread traces yet remain; on both sides of the Rhenus (River Rhine) are encampments of vast extent, and by their circuit you may even now measure the warlike strength of the tribe, and find evidence of that mighty emigration. Rome was in her 640th year when we first heard of the Cimbrian invader in the consulship of Caecilius Metellus and Papirius Carbo [113 BC].[1]

Towards the end of the second century BC the Cimbri had problems with overpopulation that were exacerbated by encroachments by the sea. However, as Strabo (lived 64/63 BC–c.AD 24) was keen to point out, some of the ancient writers saw the environmental problems as more cataclysmic than they were, and the story sometimes gets dragged into speculation about Plato's Atlantis tale:[2]

> As for the Cimbri, some things that are told about them are incorrect and others are extremely improbable. For instance, one could not accept such a reason for their having become a wandering and piratical folk as this – that while they were dwelling on a Peninsula they were driven out of their habitations by a great flood-tide; for in fact they still hold the country which they held in earlier times . . . it is ridiculous to suppose that they departed from their homes because they were incensed on account of a phenomenon that is natural and eternal, occurring twice every day. And the assertion that an excessive flood-tide once occurred looks like a fabrication, for when the ocean is affected in this way it is subject to increases and diminutions, but these are regulated and periodical.[3]

Strabo also dismisses stories of the Cimbri going to war against the flood-tides, and of them allowing their homes to be destroyed by the water in order to train themselves to be fearless, but he is more accepting of tales of their widespread piratical wandering as far east as the Kerch Strait that joins the Black Sea and the Sea of Azov, which was known in antiquity as the Cimmerian Bosphorus, and thought to be named after the Cimbri.[4]

To the Greeks and Romans who wrote about them, the Cimbri had some fascinatingly barbaric customs. Their wives used to go with them on their raids, and they were accompanied by priestesses. These grey-haired women were seers, wore bronze belts and white garments with linen cloaks held on by clasps, and went barefoot. They would use prisoners of war to make their prophecies. The priestess would crown them with wreaths and lead them to a bronze vessel called a kettle, with a capacity of around 500 litres. She would then ascend to a raised platform, bend over the kettle and cut the throat of each prisoner after he had been lifted up. Some of the priestesses then used the blood that poured into the vessel to make their predictions, while others would open the body and inspect the entrails, which always resulted in a prophecy of victory. When the Cimbri went to war they would beat hides that had been stretched over the frames of their wagons to create an unworldly noise.[5]

The Cimbri migrated along with the Ambrones from Jutland and their other Germanic neighbours, the Teutones, although, strangely, Tacitus doesn't mention either of these tribes in this context. As far back as the fourth century BC the Greek explorer and geographer Pytheas of Massilia[6] had written about the Teutones, telling his readers that they bought amber off another neighbouring people called the Gutones (possibly the Goths) and used it for fuel.[7] Plutarch adds that the Romans of the day guessed that the invaders were German peoples from the Northern Ocean, because of their imposing physical stature, their light-blue eyes, and the fact that the Germans call robbers Cimbri.[8]

The Germanic Incursions

Once they had crossed the River Elbe, the Cimbri and Teutones made a rather circuitous journey to Noricum (roughly modern Austria and part of Slovenia), where Gnaeus Papirius Carbo, the consul of 113 BC, confronted them. We know very little about the battle. Strabo tells us that Carbo clashed with the Cimbri to no effect near Noreia (modern Neumarkt in Austria);[9] Livy says the Cimbri came in search of plunder, and that Carbo and his army were defeated;[10] Appian calls them Teutones, and in his narrative Carbo complained to them that the people of Noricum were foreign friends of Rome, and took the offensive against them. The Teutones apologised for their ignorance of this relationship, and promised to leave Noricum alone. Carbo claimed to accept their apology, but then treacherously ambushed them as they moved on:

> He suffered severely for his perfidy, and lost a large part of his army. He would probably have perished with his whole force had not darkness and a tremendous thunder-storm fallen upon them while the fight was in progress, separating the combatants and putting an end to the battle by sheer terror from heaven. Even as it was, the Romans only escaped in small bands into the woods and came together with difficulty three days later. The Teutones passed into Gaul.[11]

Some of them settled in the territory of the Helvetii, where some surviving inscriptions to the god Mercurius Cimbrianus found at Miltenberg and Heidelberg possibly indicate their presence.[12] The Helvetii were allegedly wealthy and peaceful, but when they saw that the Cimbri were much better off than them because of their plunder, they became much more belligerent, and joined them in their future expeditions.

The Cimbri and Teutones moved closer to Rome when they entered the Rhône valley in about 110 BC. They wanted land to settle in and the following year they opened negotiations with Rome, saying that 'the people of Mars should give them some land by way of pay and use their hands and weapons for any purpose it wished.'[13]

When the Senate spurned their offer, they tried to get what they wanted by military force, and defeated the Consul Marcus Junius Silanus. The dual defeats of Carbo and Silanus caused considerable trauma at Rome: 'After so many men had been killed, some were crying for sons or brothers; others, orphaned by the death of their fathers, lamented the loss of their parents and the desolation of Italy; and a very large number of women, deprived of their husbands, were turned into poor widows.'[14]

But the Senate, as they so often had done in the past, remained intransigent, and the barbarians did not follow up their victory.

In 107 BC, as the people of Rome were assigning the command in Numidia to Marius, in the west of Gallia Narbonensis the other consul, Lucius Cassius Longinus, was lured into an ambush by the Gallic Tigurini and killed. His legate, Gaius Popilius Laenas, made a deal with the barbarians that allowed the Roman survivors to leave in safety, in return for hostages and half of their possessions. His men were humiliated by being sent under the yoke of surrender, and he was subsequently put on trial for treason and went into exile.

The general unrest in the area is further indicated by the revolt of Tolosa (modern Toulouse). The city had turned from its alliance with the Romans, put the garrison in chains and placed its hopes in the Cimbri. In 106 BC the Consul Quintus Servilius Caepio recovered Tolosa easily enough in a night attack, but caused outrage and scandal by plundering the temples. These were said to have contained the gold that Brennus' Gauls had supposedly pillaged from Delphi in the third century BC.[15] But the gold disappeared: no treasure of any importance found its way to Rome, although the soldiers did very well for themselves.[16] Caepio fell under suspicion, and it was said that he received his just deserts in the end: not only was he exiled as a temple-robber, but he had only female children, who all became prostitutes.[17]

Before Nemesis caught up with Caepio, the Cimbri returned to attack Gallia Narbonensis again in 105 BC. The Consul Gnaeus Mallius Maximus was sent to reinforce him, but their unwillingness to cooperate brought disaster. In an initial skirmish, the cavalry commander, the ex-Consul Marcus Aemilius Scaurus, was knocked off his horse and captured by the Cimbri. When they called him into their council he refused their request to act as their leader, talked them out of crossing the Alps and invading Italy, and was killed by a 'savage young man' called Boiorix, whose name is a Celtic/Illyrian compound meaning 'King of the Boii'.[18] He died in a manner worthy of a true Roman, stoically accepting a painful death, some say by being burned alive in a wicker cage.[19]

Mallius now sent despatches begging Caepio to combine forces with him and confront the barbarians; but Caepio refused. He crossed the Rhône, bragging to his men that he would 'bring help to the frightened Consul', but he dismissed any possibility of discussing with him how to conduct the war, and he refused to listen to the envoys sent by the Senate, asking the generals to cooperate. Caepio was equally dismissive of the Cimbri's ambassadors, who again offered peace in return for land and seed corn. His attitude prompted them to attack immediately, and although his camp was very close to that of Mallius, still he couldn't be persuaded to link up with him.

The outcome of the battle, fought near Arausio (modern Orange) on the day before the Nones of October 105 BC, was the worst Roman defeat since Cannae: Rutilius Rufus says that at least 70,000 regular troops and light-armed troops lost their lives; according to Valerius Antias, the numbers were 80,000 soldiers and 40,000 servants and camp followers.[20] Again the Cimbri failed to exploit their victory. They had no real overarching strategic vision, and they just moved into Hispania, only to be expelled by the Celtiberians before heading back towards Italy. The Romans punished Caepio for his incompetence by confiscating his possessions (the first time this had happened since King Tarquinius Superbus) and abrogating his powers; the gods punished his moral transgressions (see p. 180).

Marius to the Rescue

Florus was of the opinion that this crisis would have caused the fall of Rome had she not had the good fortune to have Gaius Marius.[21] The war with Jugurtha was now over, and the people wanted their hero to save them from the Germanic menace. He was duly voted consul for the second time in absentia, both aspects of which were illegal, but the people wouldn't tolerate any opposition.[22] He held continuous consulships until the end of the war, and started preparing for war against a multitude that was said to number 300,000 armed fighting men accompanied by much larger hordes of women and children, whose courage and daring made them irresistible, and who came on with the swiftness and force of fire when they engaged in battle.[23]

Before Marius confronted the Northmen, he made an incredibly influential contribution to the future of Rome by reorganising the army into the finest fighting machine of its day. Recruitment now became voluntary; soldiering became a profession; warfare became a fine art; discipline got stricter; promotion was won by merit, not by social background; the equipment and comfort of the soldiers became paramount; the old, cumbersome chequerboard formation of *hastati*, *principes* and *triarii* was abandoned; the legion was established at (theoretically) 6,000 men in ten cohorts of 600, each comprising six centuries;[24] all ranks were now issued with entrenching tools, the *pilum* (a heavy, short-range throwing spear; see p. 184) and a *gladius* (a short thrusting sword), and were trained in gladiator-style, hand-to-hand fighting; Rome's allies supplied the cavalry; and the eagle became the legionary standard. The outdated system of annual commands, which had created so much difficulty in so many wars, was abolished, and now Rome's armies took the oath for the entire war rather than for a single campaign, and to the commander rather than the state.

These new arrangements meant that the army's allegiance was always to its general, opening the door for future commanders to defy their colleagues, the Senate and the Comitia, but for now Marius put the soldiers through an intensive training regime in the Rhône valley, which involved all kinds of running, long marches, carrying their own baggage and preparing their own food. Their resilience and love of hard work earned them the nickname 'Marius' Mules',[25] and by 102 BC they were ready.

The barbarians now moved towards Italy in a three-pronged assault: the Teutones and Ambrones moved down the west coast via Liguria; the Cimbri came round the Alps through Noricum; and the Tigurini came through on the east. Florus says that Marius bided his time and kept his soldiers in camp 'until the irresistible fury and rage, which in barbarians takes the place of courage, spent itself. The barbarians, therefore, made off, jeering at our men and – such was their confidence that they would capture Rome – advising them to give them any messages which they had for their wives.'[26]

Marius was unconcerned by this taunting, and allowed the Teutones to cross the Rhône before attacking them at Aquae Sextiae (modern Aix-en-Provence). 'Their numbers were limitless, they were hideous in their aspect, and their speech and cries were unlike those of other peoples',[27] but Marius had their measure, and when his Mules heard 'the threats and the intolerable boasting of the barbarians',[28] they could barely be restrained from attacking.

Marius held back until he had difficulty with his water supply. 'When the men demanded water, Marius replied, "If you are men, there it is yonder for you." With such ardour, then, did they fight and such was the slaughter of the enemy that the victorious Romans drank as much barbarian gore as water from the blood-stained stream.'[29]

It was a chaotic and violent battle in which the Germanic women 'met them, swords and axes in their hands, and with hideous shrieks of rage tried to drive back fugitives and pursuers alike, the fugitives as traitors, and the pursuers as foes; they mixed themselves up with the combatants, with bare hands tore away the shields of the Romans or grasped their swords, and endured wounds and mutilations, their fierce spirits unvanquished to the end.'[30] But their menfolk were vanquished. A hundred thousand were killed or captured, including their king, Teutobodus, whose towering physique amazed the Romans when he was displayed in Marius' triumphal procession.[31]

The following year (101 BC), Marius was again consul, and he linked up with his consular colleague of the previous year, Quintus Lutatius Catulus, in Cisalpine Gaul. Florus mocked the generic 'stupidity of barbarians', saying that the Cimbri tried to cross a river, not using a bridge or boats but by swimming, and when that failed by damming it by throwing trees into it.[32] But when the Romans engaged them near Vercellae (modern Vercelli near Turin), in the Po valley,[33] it was another brutal and hard-fought contest. The Cimbric cavalry were magnificent:

Their horsemen, 15,000 strong, rode out in splendid style, with helmets made to resemble the maws of frightful wild beasts or the heads of strange animals, which, with their towering crests of feathers, made their wearers appear taller than they really were; they were also equipped with breastplates of iron, and carried gleaming white shields. For hurling, each man had two lances; and at close quarters they used large, heavy swords.[34]

Against them the Romans deployed Marius' newly designed *pilum*:

Up to this time, it seems, that part of the shaft which was let into the iron head was fastened there by two iron nails; but now, leaving one of these as it was, Marius removed the other, and put in its place a wooden pin that could easily be broken. His design was that the javelin, after striking the enemy's shield, should not stand straight out, but that the wooden peg should break, thus allowing the shaft to bend in the iron head and trail along the ground, being held fast by the twist at the point of the weapon.[35]

This meant that if it stuck in an enemy's shield, it was difficult to extract and effectively made the shield unusable, and once it had bent the *pilum* could not be thrown back.

Once again, the barbarian women impressed the Roman historians, creating a barricade with the wagons and fighting from it with axes and pikes:

Their death was as honourable as their resistance; for when, after sending a delegation to Marius, they had failed to secure their liberty and to be made priestesses[36] – a request which could not lawfully be granted – they strangled all their infants or dashed them to pieces, and themselves either fell by wounds inflicted by one another, or else, making ropes of their own hair, hanged themselves on trees or the yokes of their wagons.[37]

King Boiorix fell fighting, along with 120,000 of his tribes-people; 60,000 prisoners were taken; Marius and Catulus celebrated a joint triumph;[38] and the Tigurini 'resorted to ignoble flight and depredations and finally vanished away'.[39]

The northern threat was over. The Romans instantly characterised the Cimbri and Teutones as archetypal barbarian wild-men, and in Latin literature 'Teuton' became the default synonym for 'German'.

10

The Italian War: Resistance and Rebellion in Italy

Unrest in Italy

While Rome had been engaged with barbarians to or from the north, south and west, there had been growing unrest at home among the Italian allies at what they regarded as unfair discrimination against them. Although originally the Italians had been *forced* to become part of the Roman state, ultimately the benefits this brought had turned it into a privilege. They profited just as much as the Romans from the spread of Roman power: hence their loyalty, without which Rome could never have emerged successful in her wars of defence and expansion in the third and second centuries BC. Indeed, the recent champion of Roman military success, Marius, himself came from a small Italian town. The Italians had proved their worth time and again, but their attempts to secure Roman citizenship had always come to nothing: they had helped to put Rome on the path to greatness, but they were not citizens of Rome.

The full Roman citizenry was made up of the citizens of Rome itself, along with those of the cities on which Rome had conferred full citizenship, the *Municipia*, the colonies, and members of various small rural communities. Beneath them, with restricted rights, came the Latin allies (*socii nominis Latini*), who possessed rights of *connubium* (marriage) and *commercium* (trade) with Romans and with each other, *Ius adipiscendi civitatem Romanam per magistratum* (citizenship by holding office in a Latin community[1]) and *Ius suffragii ferendi* (Latins in Rome could vote in a tribe which was chosen by lot in the Comitia Tributa). Furthermore, they were not subject to tax/tribute, and although they did have to supply troops to the army, they still had their own constitution, laws, magistrates, census and coinage. At the bottom of the pile were the other Italian allies, who again were not subject to tribute, but were very much subordinate to Rome: they were only allowed to trade indirectly with each other through Rome; in the military, they had to supply contingents to Rome's army, but the rich eastern campaigns always fell to the Romans, whereas the unpleasant frontier tasks in Spain and elsewhere fell to the allies; their chances of promotion were limited; they didn't get fair shares of the war booty; they found themselves in an increasingly deteriorating economic situation; they suffered from extortion, sometimes even brutality, from Roman officials, without any right of appeal; and although some of them were very wealthy, they resented the fact that they couldn't exchange their wealth for distinction.

There were also questions of identity. Later Roman historians could not characterise the Italians as out-and-out barbarians, since they ultimately became fully Romanised and were assimilated into the Roman state, but they still had an element of 'otherness': Latin wasn't necessarily their first language; the Romans often regarded their lifestyles as wild, uncivilised and quasi-barbarian at best; and, rightly or wrongly, the Italians often felt that the Romans really did put them on a par with other barbarians.

Overall, there were too many vested interests in Roman society that stacked up against the Italians being given the franchise: the Senate couldn't rely on being able to manipulate the newer voters; the Equites didn't want commercial competition; and the Plebs didn't want to share their doles and privileges with anyone. So, over the years, the attempts of the Italian allies to secure equal rights, and various attempts on their behalf, had come to nothing.

Champions and Opponents of the Italians

In 129 BC, when Scipio Aemilianus emerged as a champion of the Latins and Italians over proposals to redistribute land in Italy, he was found dead in mysterious circumstances – murder, suicide and natural causes were all suggested[2] – and his proposals were not carried through. Three years later the Tribune Marcus Iunius Pennus seems to have put forward a law expelling all non-Romans (except slaves) from the city, much to the disgust of Cicero: 'It is a wicked thing to prohibit non-citizens from entering a town that is not their own and physically to expel them from it, as Pennus did in our father's day.'[3]

This was followed in 125 BC by a much more generous proposal by Marcus Fulvius Flaccus that all Italian allies should receive the full franchise or the right of appeal against Roman magistrates, but his proposal was shelved by the Senate. The pressure was kept up in 122 BC by the reformer Gaius Gracchus with a scheme to promote allies of Latin status to full citizenship, raise the others to Latin status, and to establish some large overseas colonies that were open to Italians as well as Roman citizens. Again these efforts were defeated by the Senate with counter-proposals by the tribune Marcus Livius Drusus the Elder. Drusus cynically outbid Gaius Gracchus in a quest for popular support, suggesting simply that the Latin allies should not be mistreated by Roman commanders, and proposing the founding of twelve new colonies, each with 3,000 settlers taken from the poorer classes. The Roman Plebs had no desire to share these kinds of benefits with the Italians, and although Drusus' measures were never meant to be enacted, he was successful in gaining sufficient support to veto Gaius' proposals.

The issue seems to have gone cold for around twenty years, at least as a live political concern at Rome or in the minds of the historians. But in 100 BC, when Marius had returned to Rome after crushing the Cimbri and the Teutones, very much the man of the hour with Rome at his feet and hoping to fulfil a prophecy by becoming consul seven times, he left the passing of legislation to the Tribune Lucius Appuleius Saturninus and Praetor Gaius Servilius Glaucia, who had been elected amid violent rioting. Saturninus brought forward several measures on Marius' behalf,[4] including citizen colonies for the veterans in Sicily, Achaea and Macedon, funded from the gold of Tolosa (see p. 180). Latins and Italians were to be able to participate in all of these, and so get a chance of citizenship, in what was a half-fulfilment of a promise Marius had made at Vercellae: 'We are told that when he had bestowed citizenship upon as many as a thousand men of Camerinum for conspicuous bravery in the war, the act was held to be illegal and was impeached by some; to whom he replied that the clash of arms had prevented his hearing the voice of the law.'[5]

This pro-Italian clause led to further riots, and Rome's urban population, in jealousy, turned on Saturninus and the Italian veterans.

In order to head off senatorial opposition, Saturninus added a clause to his bill which demanded that every senator should swear to obey his laws, and, typically for the spineless Senate at this time, only one of them refused – Marius' old enemy Quintus Caecilius Metellus Numidicus (consul 109 BC), who went into exile on Rhodes. When the elections for 99 BC came around, Glaucia's rival for the consulship, Gaius Memmius, was openly murdered on the morning of the vote. This was a step too far: Marius, the citizens in general, the Equites and the Senate had all had enough. The Senate seized their opportunity and declared a *Senatus Consultum Ultimum* (SCU) and called on Marius to save the state; Saturninus and Glaucia opened the prison and seized the Capitol; street fighting broke out; the rioters were outnumbered and found themselves blockaded on the Capitol; they surrendered to Marius; he promised them that their lives would be spared, and took them to the Senate House; but while the Senate debated their fate, a mob broke in and pelted them to death with roof tiles.

So the Senate had regained control, and Marius had lost his influence. He could only look on while the Senate declared Saturninus' legislation invalid because it had been passed *per vim* (through violence). Ultimately, he left Italy and journeyed to the east, hoping to provoke Mithridates VI of Pontus into a war (for the conflict with Mithridates, see pp. 221 ff.). Meanwhile, Rome's Italian allies were back to square one.

Five years after this outbreak of bloody violence, a very ungenerous and reactionary measure, the *lex Licinia Mucia*, was passed. Named after Quintus Mucius Scaevola Pontifex and Lucius Licinius Crassus (consuls 95 BC), who proposed it, the law was intended to stop people who were not Roman citizens from claiming that they were, on pain of expulsion from Rome. Cicero was in two minds about it: he disapproved of the possibility of the expulsion of Italians from Rome, but liked some of the thinking behind it:

> It may not be right, of course, for one who is not a citizen to exercise the rights and privileges of citizenship; and the law on this point was secured by two of our wisest consuls, Crassus and Scaevola. Still, to debar foreigners from enjoying the advantages of the city is altogether contrary to the laws of humanity.[6]
>
> As to the *lex Licinia Mucia*, which dealt with the reduction of the number of citizens, I can see that it is universally agreed that, for all that it was carried by the two consuls who were of all those we have known the wisest, it was not only ineffective but positively badly damaging to Rome.[7]

The effect the law had on the allies was to alienate them still further from the Romans. Diodorus Siculus relates an illuminating anecdote about Quintus Pompaedius Silo, the head of the Marsi, an Italian tribe:

The Marsic leader Pompaedius[8] embarked on a grandiose and fantastic venture. Assembling ten thousand men drawn from the ranks of those who had occasion to fear judicial investigations, he led them on Rome, with swords concealed beneath their garb of peace. It was his intention to surround the senate with armed men and demand citizenship, or, if persuasion failed, to ravage the seat of empire with fire and sword. Encountering Gaius Domitius,[9] who asked him, 'Where are you going, Pompaedius, with so large a band?' he said, 'To Rome, to get citizenship, at the summons of the tribunes.'[10]

In the end, Domitius talked Pompaedius out of his plan, but the incident illustrates the strength of feeling, and the paranoia that was created by the legislation. The Roman historian Quintus Asconius Pedianus (c.9 BC–c.AD 76) says that Rome's allies 'were fired by an enormous appetite for Roman citizenship'[11] and regards the law as 'the chief cause of the Italian War which broke out three years later'.[12]

The Italian War broke out in 91 BC, when Marcus Livius Drusus the Younger, son of the Drusus who had thwarted Gaius Gracchus, was tribune. The Younger Drusus comes across as an honest and well-meaning member of the senatorial party, a rich and popular man who genuinely believed that he could not only help the Italian allies and defuse their dangerous discontent, but also that he could conciliate the Optimates (the traditionalist, pro-Patrician senators), Populares (senators who supported the interests of the Plebeians), Equites and Italians in the process. His feeling was that the enfranchisement of Rome's allies was necessary in order to avoid a major explosion in Italy, but also that once this had been achieved the new elements in the state would be a source of strength to the Senate's control. In reality, very few Italians would actually use their vote because of the distances involved in getting to Rome: at this time the Comitia Centuriata and the Concilium Plebis were only attended by around 10 per cent of those eligible to do so. In Drusus' opinion, the only Italians who could realistically make the trips to Rome to participate in politics would be those who could afford it, which would give them similar interests to the senatorial party and allow the Optimates to manipulate them quite easily.

Drusus the Younger realised that he would need a high level of popularity to achieve his controversial aims, and he tried to please all of the people all of the time: the Senate and Equites were to be sweetened by bringing 300 Equites into the Senate, and handing control of the jury courts to this new expanded body; the Plebs and Populares were to have fresh corn doles and more colonies, but this time in Italy and Sicily, not overseas; and the Italian allies would benefit from the repeal of the *lex Licinia Mucia* and the grant of full citizenship. Under this scheme the Senate would be broadened and strengthened, the Equites honoured, the People helped, and the Italians would get the vote in return for land.

And, at first, the proposals were carried; but the Consul Lucius Marcius Philippus strongly opposed them, and managed to get them declared null and void on the grounds that they had been lumped together into one bill. This was contrary to the *lex Caecilia Didia*, which specified that each individual element of a piece of legislation had to be voted on separately. Doubts now started to set in, which were magnified by the presence in Rome of a large number of Italians, who had crowded into the city in optimistic anticipation. The Senate was not confident that the new voters would definitely choose Optimate candidates, like the current ones did, and they also became jealous of admitting Equites into their midst; the Equites wanted to keep their monopoly of the courts; the so-called 'Urban mob' didn't want to share their doles with the Italians; and rumours began to circulate that the Italians were forming local committees and preparing to march on Rome.

Things had come to the point where Drusus felt he needed an armed escort. He went home to let passions cool, but was assassinated.[13] With the last friend of the Italians now gone, all the disparate elements in the Roman state rallied to meet the 'Italian threat'. In an attempt to forestall a future Drusus, the mixed-race Tribune Quintus Varius Severus (also called Hybrida because of his Spanish mother[14]) carried the *lex Varia*, a bill to try all supporters of the Italians for treason (*maiestas*). Several senators were exiled, including Julius Caesar's uncle Gaius Aurelius Cotta, but Varius could not convict Drusus' eminent conservative supporter Marcus Aemilius Scaurus (consul 115 BC), who successfully defended himself by asking the court whether they would choose to believe a provincial Spaniard rather than the *Princeps Senatus* (Leader of the Senate). Hybrida was later convicted and executed under the same law that he had introduced. In the meantime, the Italians went to war.

The Italian ('Social') War

The Italian War, or 'Social War' as it is often called in a rather anachronistic Anglicisation of the Latin *Bellum Sociale* (= 'the War of the Allies', although Florus said that this was a euphemism to lessen the odium of it, since it was really a war against citizens[15]), took place between 91 and 88 BC.[16] The Optimates probably blamed Drusus for the outbreak of the war because they needed a scapegoat: they completely failed to see that it was their attitudes that were pushing the Italians towards increasingly desperate measures.

The outbreak of the Italian War came at Asculum in Picenum. The Romans were becoming increasingly nervous about the possibility of a conflict, and had sent out agents throughout Italy. The people of Asculum started to fear that their plans had been revealed, and the Praetor Quintus Servilius, his legate Fonteius and all the Roman residents were murdered in 91 BC. The Piceni were joined by the Paeligni and Marsi, both warlike central Italian hill tribes, and by the Oscan-speaking people of Samnium and Lucania in the south. Overall, about two-thirds of Italy rebelled against Rome, although the northern areas generally kept out of the conflict and the Latins stayed loyal, including the key colonies scattered in rebel territory. Apulia in the east and Campania in the west were also loyal at first.

On the whole, the rebels came from the poor mountain districts of Italy, but they were of hardy stock, and were stiffened with some of Marius' veterans. They organised an Italian League, which was an independent state based at Corfinium, which they renamed Italica.[17] This became their capital, and had its own Assembly, Senate of 500, ten praetors and two consuls. They even minted coinage with Oscan inscriptions, and a vivid motif of the Italian bull goring the Roman wolf. It was an impressive achievement for them to finance a major war and control some 100,000 men, even for a few years, but in the end the League was too divided in its aims, and too short-lived, to be considered an important political experiment. Whereas the larger part of the rebel area, who spoke Latin, simply wanted the franchise, the Samnites and Lucanians wanted to be free of Rome altogether.

The threat to the Romans was extremely serious, since the Italians had inside knowledge of Roman strategy and tactics, but for once the Roman Senate acted energetically. They called in Gauls, Spaniards and Numidians, and brought the strength of their army up to around 150,000. Rome also had the advantage of the central position in Italy, as well as command of the sea to ensure food, but when it came to discipline and generalship there was little to choose between the two sides. In general, because the Italians were on the offensive, they had the better of the early exchanges, but at last the greater resources of Rome saw her through. Like so many civil wars, the conflict was extremely violent and very bloody: Diodorus Siculus, who was alive at the time, regarded it as 'greater than all previous wars', including the Trojan War and the Second Punic War.[18]

In the first campaign of 90 BC, the Senate deployed its armies under two militarily inexperienced consuls: Lucius Julius Caesar (with Sulla on his staff) in the south, and Publius Rutilius Lupus (with Marius on his staff) in central Italy. Gaius Papius Mutilus the Samnite was able to keep Caesar at bay, and he eventually overran Campania, which was the main Roman supply base, although the Romans did manage to hold on to Capua. In the north, the war was mainly fought among the Marsi, in the area about 50 kilometres east of Rome, where Rutilius was killed and several loyal cities fell; but the Romans were able to blockade Asculum, and Marius succeeded to the command, with Sulla detached to help him, and he was able to restore the situation, even if he seemed reluctant to attack his old allies.[19]

Rumours now started to circulate at Rome that the rebels were active in Etruria and Umbria, and with the treasury severely depleted and the chances of victory seeming remote, Rome made some significant concessions. Firstly, at the end of 90 BC, the Consul Caesar put through the *lex Julia de Civitate Latinis et Socii Danda*, which granted full citizenship to the Latins and to the loyal Italians who hadn't joined in the revolt; a *lex Calpurnia* gave authorisation to Roman commanders to grant citizenship on the battlefield; and in 89 BC the *lex Plautia Papiria* allowed any Italian who appeared before the Praetor Peregrinus at Rome within sixty days to become a citizen. Appian felt that this was what almost all of the Italians wanted,[20] although Cicero says that there were some exceptions: 'The Julian Law, which gave citizenship to allies and Latins, was such that any communities that did not themselves accept it as binding on them could not have the citizenship. In this connection, a serious dispute arose at Heraclia and at Naples; in those two cities a large proportion of the populations was in favour of keeping the independence of their treaty of alliance rather than accepting Roman citizenship.'[21]

The fact that these concessions split the Italians was of benefit to the Romans, and when Gnaeus Pompeius Strabo, the new consul of 89 BC, took Corfinium, as well as Asculum in a great and bloody fight, the war in the north was nearly over. In the south, Sulla took over, and in a brilliantly effective campaign recovered Campania and killed the rebel leader Mutilus, which left only Samnium and Lucania in the fight. Sulla stood for election, and was elected consul for 88 BC. The Marsi in the north now surrendered, and the last rebel general, Quintus Pompaedius Silo, was defeated and killed by Quintus Caecilius Metellus Pius in Apulia in the south. Apart from some sporadic guerrilla warfare that dragged on until 83 BC, this effectively terminated the Italian War.

Aftermath

Velleius Paterculus was of the opinion that 'by gradually granting Roman citizenship to those who had not taken up arms or had laid them down in good time, Rome's strength was repaired'.[22]

There were certainly many repairs that needed to be made. The Romans as well as the Italians – Appian says that the war carried off more than 300,000 of the youth of Italy[23] – had suffered some serious reverses in the conflict and they were lucky that Etruria did not join the revolt. In the end, although they did manage to crush the Italians on the battlefield, the Romans also had to give the allies what they had been fighting for. The result was a great step towards the unification of Italy, and the cultural differences in the Italian peninsula started to become less pronounced, even though there were further political battles to fight as the new citizens struggled for fairer integration into Rome's political system. There were numerous violent outbreaks, whose ramifications saw Roman armies marching on Rome, years where no consuls could be elected, the eclipse of Marius, and the emergence of Sulla as the dominant figure at Rome, ultimately as dictator. Rebellion and resistance to Rome did not come exclusively from those that might conventionally be regarded as barbarian, but once the Italian situation had settled down, all the inhabitants of the peninsula could develop an 'us-and-them' attitude to the peoples who lived beyond their borders.

11

Spartacus: The Gladiator
Who Challenged Rome

If the rebellion and resistance in Italy finally subsided after the Italian War, there still remained a degree of admiration in some quarters for those who challenged the authority of Rome from within. In the entrance to House I.7.7 at Pompeii there is a sketchy picture depicting two horsemen, a trumpeter and two men fighting on foot. An inscription above one of the mounted figures, written right to left in Oscan, is still legible, and it names the man who Karl Marx described as 'the most splendid fellow in the whole of ancient history . . . a great general . . . noble character . . . true representative of the ancient proletariat':[1] *skatraps*, i.e. Spartacus.[2]

Spartacus led the largest and best recorded slave revolt in antiquity. And yet it is still really difficult to assess because of the paucity and disparity of the ancient sources. The contemporary Sallust's *Histories* are fragmentary; Cicero also lived through the events, but only really mentions them in passing; for Livy's treatment of the revolt we have to rely on Florus' second-century AD *Epitome* of his great work, alongside the fourth-century AD excerpts known as the *Periochae*; Plutarch's *Life of Crassus* and

Appian's *Civil Wars* provide similar but differently nuanced narratives, and may go back to Sallust, but constructing a coherent narrative of these events, which created a powerful effect on Roman attitudes ever after, is fraught with difficulty.

He's Spartacus

As Rome expanded its dominions from the Second Punic War onwards, the long-term military commitments that were demanded from many Roman soldiers in Hispania, Greece, Macedonia and elsewhere led them to sell their small farms, which were financially impossible to run in absentia, and migrate to the city. The traditional ideal of the citizen farmer-soldier was ever harder to live up to, and the growth of the cities of Italy also engendered changes in the countryside. Small farms gradually metamorphosed into enormous plantations known as *latifundia* ('broad farms'), owned by absentee landlords and worked by slaves, who because of the extent of Rome's overseas conquests, and the prevalence of piracy, were becoming ever more numerous, and therefore very cheap: the slave market on the island of Delos could allegedly process 10,000 slaves on the same day.[3]

The rich ... employed slave hands and shepherds on these estates to avoid having free men dragged off the land to serve in the army,[4] and they derived great profit from this form of ownership too, as the slaves had many children and no liability to military service and their numbers increased freely. For these reasons the powerful were becoming extremely rich, and the number of slaves in the country was reaching large proportions, while the Italian people were suffering from depopulation and a shortage of men, worn down as they were by poverty and taxes and military service.[5]

The slave population in the Italian countryside became proportionately very high (2,000,000 slaves in an Italian population of 6,000,000 in some estimates), and the Romans often stereotyped the tasks of their slaves by nationality – Gauls or Spaniards would make good herdsmen, for instance – and physically strong captives were regularly sent to the gladiatorial schools for a career in the arena. Spartacus was one of the latter: 'Spartacus . . . was a Thracian from the nomadic tribes[6] and not only had a great spirit and great physical strength, but was, much more than one would expect from his condition, most intelligent and cultured[7] being more like a Greek than a Thracian.'[8]

Thrace lay on the northern fringes of the Greek and Roman world. Its boundaries shifted at different times, but in the Roman era it encompassed an area from the Haemus Mountains in the north, the Black Sea in the east, the Sea of Marmara, Hellespont and Aegean Sea in the south, and the River Nestus, which rises in the Rila Mountains of modern Bulgaria and issues into the Aegean Sea near the island of Thasos, in the west. Philip II of Macedon had conquered the area in the fourth century BC, and after the death of his son Alexander the Great, Thrace was ruled by the kings of Macedon, until the Romans defeated Perseus at Pydna in 168 BC (see p. 127) and incorporated parts of Thrace in the province of Macedonia.

The Thracians were an Indo-European people who were regarded by the Greeks and Romans as primitive, disunited, warlike and bloodthirsty,[9] although their burial tumuli have revealed large quantities of gold and silver artefacts, largely imported from 'non-barbarian' areas. Herodotus tells of how they would sell their children and allow their girls to have sex with as many men as they liked;[10] they were held responsible for some of the worst atrocities in the Peloponnesian War;[11] Plato characterised them as passionate, spirited and bellicose;[12] Polybius noted that Perseus' ally Cotys was completely unlike a Thracian because he was sober, gentle and steady;[13] Ephorus, Strabo and Polyaenus write about the Thracians using trickery to violate treaties, justifying one surprise night attack by claiming that the truce only specified the number of days and therefore didn't include the nights, thereby giving rise to the notion of 'Thracian pretence' (rather like *Punica fides*; see p. 95);[14] they brandished and struck their weapons against each other prior to battle;[15] Tacitus described them as being so bold and uncivilised that they would even disobey their own kings;[16] and they were in the habit of impaling the heads of Romans on their weapon of choice, which was called a *rumpia* in Latin (*rhompaia* in Greek).[17]

The Thracians were everything that a Roman expected from a barbarian, and Plutarch's 'more like a Greek than a Thracian' comment is a well-worn barbarophobic cliché: any non-Greek/Roman whose achievements were special was thought to be different from other run-of-the-mill barbarians, and the Romans felt deeply humiliated by what Spartacus achieved:

One can tolerate . . . even the disgrace of a war against slaves; for although, by force of circumstances, they are liable to any kind of treatment, yet they form as it were a class (though an inferior class) of human beings and can be admitted to the blessings of liberty which we enjoy. But I know not what name to give to the war which was stirred up at the instigation of Spartacus; for the common soldiers being slaves and their leaders being gladiators – the former men of the humblest, the latter men of the worst, class – added insult to the injury which they inflicted upon Rome.[18]

To explain the fact that some Italians took his side against the Romans, despite the fact that he was so disreputable,[19] Spartacus was often credited with qualities that the Romans grudgingly admired – immense bodily strength and spirit, and a certain nobility of action: 'Spartacus the barbarian, having been done a favour by someone, showed himself to be grateful to the man. For even among barbarians, human nature is self-taught to return an equal favour for those who bestow benefits on us.'[20]

It could be that Spartacus had once served as a Roman auxiliary soldier. Appian says that 'he once fought as a soldier *Rhomaiois*,[21] but the Greek here could mean either that he fought alongside the Romans or that he fought against them. However, Florus implies that he did fight for Rome: 'From being a Thracian mercenary [Spartacus] had become a soldier, and from a soldier a deserter, then a highwayman, and finally, thanks to his strength, a gladiator.'[22]

Following his capture, Spartacus' gladiatorial career began in the training school (*ludus*) run as a commercial enterprise by a private entrepreneur (*lanista*) called Lentulus Batiatus at Capua.[23] Batiatus acquired his gladiators by purchase or recruitment, trained them and then hired them out to the promoter (*editor*) of the shows. Gladiators were valuable commodities and were normally trained to high levels of fitness, and given a well-balanced diet and careful medical attention.

Florus tells us that Spartacus fought as a *Murmillo*.[24] As such he would have been equipped with a short-to-medium sword, worn a helmet with a brim and a distinctive fish ornament, carried a *scutum* (a tall, oblong, curved shield with a boss), had his right arm protected by a wrapping of heavily quilted linen known as a *manica*, and had a gaiter and short greave on his left leg, with just a gaiter on his right. Ironically, given Spartacus' origins, his usual opponent would have been the *Thraex/Thrax* ('Thracian'), wielding a curved short sword and protected by a brimmed helmet with a crescent-shaped crest and a griffin's head ornament, a small rectangular shield, a *manica*, and quilted wrappings with high greaves on each leg. Like most gladiators they would have worn a loincloth (*subligaculum*) and a wide metal belt (*balteus*), and gone barefoot. The Thracians were very popular in graffiti, and seem to have had a particular appeal to women. There are vases depicting Thracians on one side and erotic scenes on the other, and terracotta lamps sometimes carry erotic scenes with the female partner dressed up as a Thracian and dominating a submissive *Murmillo*.[25] In later years at Pompeii, the *Thraex* Celadus would boast that he 'makes the girls sigh'[26] as well as being 'the splendour of the girls'[27] and 'the master of the girls'.[28]

A graffito from Nero's reign gives us the results of some gladiatorial games held in Pompeii, in which 'Neronian' and 'Julian' gladiators from the imperial training school at Capua were involved in *Thraex* versus *Murmillo* combats:

Thraex versus *Murmillo*. Lucius Sempronius: reprieved; Platanus, Julian: won.
Thraex versus *Murmillo*. Pugnax, Neronian, fought 3: won; Murranus, Neronian, fought 3; died . . .
Thraex versus *Murmillo*. Herma, Julian, fought 4: won; Quintus Petillius . . . reprieved . . .

Thraex versus *Murmillo*. Nodu[. . .], Julian, fought 7: won;
  Lucius Petronius, fought 14; died.
Thraex versus *Murmillo*. Lucius Fabius, fought 9: died;
  Astus, Julian, fought 14; won.[29]

Spartacus' name might be significant. It appears that the
Thracian royal family used the name, and Sallust tells us that 'A
few of the slaves, who were prudent men and who had free and
noble minds . . . praised [Spartacus' advice?] and held that they
ought to do what Spartacus suggested.'[30]

The suggestion is that there were a few slaves of elite origins
among Spartacus' followers, who would perhaps only have
followed him if he had been of noble descent himself, but again
we see the tendency of the Romans only to admire a barbarian
who was noble.

Slave Revolts Against Rome

Slavery was, for the most part, taken completely for granted by
the Romans and by their barbarian neighbours and subjects.
The vast majority of slaves put up with their condition for the
vast majority of the time, gross inequalities and lack of individual freedom were facts of life that were generally accepted
and tolerated, and, like everywhere else at the time, Rome was
a slave-owning society for its entire history. Furthermore, slaves
were not even regarded as a social group. They were property.
But nevertheless they were an integral part of Rome's social
fabric, and fugitive slaves were always a headache for slave-
owners, who lived in a perpetual state of wariness or fear that is
neatly expressed in the proverbial phrase *tot servi quot hostes*
(loosely 'all slaves are our enemies'), and in the famous story of

the Senate rejecting a proposal to identify slaves by their dress: 'On one occasion a proposal was made by the Senate to distinguish slaves from freedmen by their dress; it then became apparent how great would be the impending danger if our slaves began to count our numbers.'[31]

In some ways this fear was entirely justified, and Spartacus was by no means the first slave to rebel against Rome. In 198 BC a number of African prisoners of war, who had been enslaved during the Second Punic War, rebelled at Setia in Italy. They struck when the Setians were celebrating some games, and captured the city amid slaughter and chaos. The Roman response under the Urban Praetor Lucius Cornelius Lentulus was swift: the ringleaders were arrested, the fugitives were hunted down and further executions followed.[32] A couple of years later the Praetor Manius Acilius Glabrio put down a slave insurrection that practically turned Etruria into a battlefield. Again, the reprisals were harsh: many of the rebels were killed or captured, and their leaders were flogged and crucified.[33] A similar zero-tolerance approach was applied by the Praetor Lucius Postumius to 7,000 people who had infested the roads and public pastures around Tarentum with robberies in 185 BC, but these events were minor compared to what happened in Sicily some fifty years later.

Sicily erupted into a major slave war that lasted from 135 to 132 BC. Our principal account comes from Diodorus Siculus, a native of Agyrion on the island. As so often is the case, the books that describe the events are lost, leaving us, in this case, with two somewhat contradictory summaries of his narrative by Photius, who was Patriarch of the Orthodox Church at Constantinople in the ninth century AD,[34] and Constantine Porphyrogenitus who ruled the Byzantine Empire from

AD 945 to 949.[35] But the big picture seems to be that as Sicily prospered in the post-Punic Wars era, vast numbers of slaves from very diverse origins were held and mistreated there. They were herded and branded like cattle; they were treated with complete disrespect, and not provided with their basic needs for food and clothing; they turned to crime to provide their basic necessities; murder and robbery became endemic; attempts by the governors to take the situation in hand were met with obstruction from the landowners; and eventually the slaves could endure the situation no longer.

The revolt was put in motion by a Syrian slave from Apamea, who belonged to Antigenes of Enna. The slave's name was Eunus, but he took on the name of 'King Antiochus' after the rulers of his homeland. He had a reputation for being a fire-breathing magician and conjuror who could foretell the future, and he led the slaves of eastern Sicily. They broke into Enna and were joined by further slaves.

> Then entering the houses, they made such a great slaughter, that they did not spare even the suckling children, but plucked them violently from their mother's breasts and dashed them against the ground. It cannot be expressed how vilely and filthily, for the satisfying of their lusts, they used men's wives in the very presence of their husbands. These villains were joined by a multitude of the slaves who were in the city. They first executed their rage and cruelty upon their own masters, and then fell to murdering others.[36]

Among their victims was Damophilus of Enna, a proud and wealthy man whose cruelty and inhumanity towards the slaves were only outshone by his wife, Megallis; he was stabbed and beheaded in the theatre in front of a baying crowd; she was whipped and thrown over a precipice; their kind, gentle daughter, who had always treated slaves with courtesy, was spared.

Eunus/Antiochus' followers deployed agricultural implements until they could get their hands on decent Roman weapons, and were joined by what Diodorus calls 'an infinite number of slaves'.[37] In the meantime, in the west of the island, a Cilician *vilicus* (slave manager) called Cleon, who was also credited with religious and mystical powers, gathered an army of slaves that swelled to 200,000 men. Copycat risings took place on a small scale at Rome, Athens and Delos, until the Roman Senate finally got round to sending out an effective army under Publius Rupilius, who captured Tauromenium (modern Taormina), Enna and Eunus himself, who died in prison in Morgantina, consumed by lice.

While Rome was still facing Eunus and Cleon in Sicily, the eastern end of the Mediterranean was thrown into short-lived chaos by the death of King Attalus III of Pergamum in 133 BC, who caused considerable surprise by bequeathing his kingdom to Rome. Among the ramifications of this was an attempt by a pretender called Aristonicus to claim Pergamum for himself, on the grounds that he was the illegitimate son of Attalus' father, King Eumenes II. He issued coins called *cistophori* ('basket-bearers') to underpin his claim, won a few early successes, but was defeated by the people of Ephesus. This led him to try to put together a coalition of the lower classes, slaves who were promised their freedom and non-Greeks of the region, calling them 'Citizens of the Sun' (*Heliopolitae*).[38] Aristonicus intended to found a state called 'Sun City' (Heliopolis), where everyone would be free. He is sometimes seen as a social revolutionary, but the fact that slaves were invited to join his war against Rome doesn't mean that this was a slave rebellion in any meaningful sense: Aristonicus was much more of an opportunistic contender for regal power, exploiting the (very real) resentment felt by slaves and others to suit his own dynastic aims. He overcame the first wave of Roman troops, and killed the Consul Publius Licinius Crassus in battle, but was ultimately captured by Marcus Perperna and taken to Rome, where he was executed in prison in 130 BC.

Diodorus Siculus gives us an account of a Second Sicilian Slave Revolt, again preserved in the writings of Photius and Constantine Porphyrogenitus, which broke out in 104 BC. As part of the recruitment process for Marius' campaigns against the Cimbri and Teutones (see pp. 181 ff.), the Senate had instructed the praetor governing Sicily, Publius Licinius Nerva, to conduct an investigation into free people who were being illegally kept in slavery on the island. By liberating about 800 slaves he kindled hopes of liberty in all the slaves on Sicily, but then immediately stopped the process. Some slaves started to assert their own liberty, kill their masters as they were asleep in their beds, and recruit new followers. After a stuttering start the rebels won some successes, captured some Roman military hardware and horses, and were soon numbered in the tens of thousands. Under the leadership of Salvius (nicknamed Tryphon) in the east of Sicily and Athenion in the west, the slaves created 'an *Iliad* of calamities' all over the island.[39] Free men, driven by lawlessness and/or poverty, also joined in the ravages, driving away whole herds of cattle, robbing barns, carrying away the crops and killing everyone they came across. It was total anarchy: 'They who a little before were pre-eminent amongst their fellow citizens for their wealth and distinction, by a sudden change of fortune were not only treated with the greatest contempt and scorn imaginable, and robbed of all they had by their slaves; but they were forced to bear insufferable abuse from their fellow freemen.'[40]

The unrest also spread across the Strait of Messina into southern Italy, and the Praetor Lucius Licinius Lucullus had to be given the command against some rebel slaves at Capua, from where, as Propraetor, he crossed to Sicily with 17,000 troops. Tryphon and Athenion never really exercised a united leadership, and although Lucullus defeated them in battle, he failed to follow up effectively, and was subsequently put on trial at Rome for not carrying out his duties properly.

Lucullus' successor, Gaius Servilius, was equally useless, partly because Lucullus disbanded his troops and demolished his fortifications so as not to allow Servilius to conduct the war properly. Lucullus was subsequently banished, but in the mean-time Tryphon died, leaving Athenion to take sole control and ravage Sicily unopposed. In 100 BC the Consul Manius Aquillius took over. He was a brave and effective leader who brought the slaves to battle, killed Athenion himself in hand-to-hand fighting, and mopped up the remaining resistance very efficiently. A thousand survivors under a new leader called Satyrus surrendered:

> when they were brought as prisoners to Rome, [Aquillius] consigned them to fight with wild beasts, where it is reported they ended their lives with great gallantry and nobleness of mind; for they scorned to fight with beasts, but slew each other at the public altars; and after all the others were dead, Satyrus being the last, with a heroic spirit killed himself. This was the tragic end of the slave war, after it had contin-ued for the space of almost four years.[41]

Spartacus Breaks Out

The themes of cruelty and desperation loom large in the story of Spartacus. Several sources emphasise the initial innocence of Spartacus and his followers on the one hand, and the unpleasantness of the conditions in which the Capuan *lanista* Batiatus kept them on the other.[42] In 73 BC their desolation led 200 of them to plan to break free, but their scheme was betrayed, and only about seventy of them overpowered their guards and made it out.[43] They armed themselves with kitchen utensils from a cookhouse, and three leaders are mentioned at first: Spartacus the Thracian, and the Gauls Crixus[44] and Oenomaus. It was a true barbarian uprising.

Out on the road the Thracians and Celts encountered and captured some wagons that were transporting weapons for gladiators in another city. Equipped with familiar weapons they took up a strong position on Mount Vesuvius, and after they had beaten off the militia sent against them from Capua, they 'got hold of proper arms and gladly took them in exchange for their own gladiatorial equipment which they threw away, as being barbarous and dishonourable weapons to use'.[45]

From the earliest stages of the breakout, Spartacus' band seems to have been joined not just by runaway slaves, but also by free shepherds, herdsmen and farmhands from the downtrodden local proletariat, many of whom would have been working on the *latifundia* of the region. As they plundered the nearby areas their numbers increased exponentially.[46]

Rome's central government had to act. They sent Gaius Clodius Glaber with a small and badly trained force of 3,000 hastily conscripted soldiers.[47] Clodius was able to confine the gladiators on a precipitous hilltop, but this was covered with wild vines, and Spartacus' men used these to make ropes and ladders. These enabled them to descend the cliffs and take the Romans completely by surprise. Clodius' men fled, allowing Spartacus to take his camp: more weapons now became available for distribution to the runaways that were joining his ranks.[48]

The Romans still regarded the situation as one of banditry rather than outright war. The surviving sources make it awkward to construct a clear narrative of the events of 73 BC, but the rebels continued to outwit the commanders who confronted them. The Praetor Publius Varinius[49] moved against them, but made the mistake of dividing his forces, which allowed the rebels to pick off his subordinates Lucius Furius and Lucius Cossinus. Furius was routed, and although Spartacus narrowly failed to capture Cossinus while he was bathing near Salinae, he did seize all his baggage and later capture his camp, killing him in the process. Flushed with success, the fugitives got the better of Varinius himself in a series of engagements. On one occasion, Spartacus extricated himself from a tight situation by putting stakes at short intervals before the gate of his camp, and then dressing up corpses and tying them to the stakes to make them look like sentries. He then lit all the campfires, before secretly sneaking away by night.[50]

By the end of the campaign Spartacus had captured Varinius' horse and his lictors with their *fasces*,[51] and the rebels were running amok throughout Campania, and laying waste to Nola, Nuceria, Thurii and Metapontum with terrible destruction.[52] At the farming community of Forum Annii at the northern end of the Campus Atinas (modern Vallo di Diano) on the borders with Lucania,

the fugitive slaves immediately began to rape young girls and married women while others cut down those who tried to resist them and who were trying to escape, inflicting wounds on them in a depraved manner, when their backs were turned, and left in their trail the torn bodies of half-dead persons. Others threw firebrands onto the roofs of houses. Many slaves in the town were by nature sympathetic allies and uncovered things that their masters had hidden away or dragged out the masters themselves from their hiding places. Nothing was either too sacred or too wicked to be spared the rage of these barbarians and their servile characters.[53]

The ex-gladiators exacted their vengeance in the most appropriate way they could imagine, taking on the roles of *lanistae* and *editores*, and giving gladiatorial shows themselves:

At the funeral rites of a woman whom they had taken prisoner and who had committed suicide because of her anguish over the violation of her sexual honour, they staged gladiatorial games [*munus gladiatorium*] using 400 prisoners they had taken. Those who had once been the spectacle were now to be spectators. It was as gladiatorial entrepreneurs [*lanistae gladiatorum*] rather than as military commanders that they staged [*ediderunt*] these games.[54]

The rebel army grew to a total of 70,000.[55] They had people with the skills to manufacture shields of wickerwork and animal skins, as well as swords by melting down the iron in the slave prisons,[56] and herds of horses were rounded up to create a cavalry force. They were looking more and more like a regular army.

72 BC: Rome Sends in the Consuls;
Rome Sends in Crassus

The seriousness of the situation finally dawned on Rome, and particularly the rich land- and slave-owners in the Senate. Both consuls, Lucius Gellius Publicola and Gnaeus Cornelius Lentulus Clodianus, were sent out with two legions to deal with Spartacus. Gellius was able to defeat and kill Crixus, who had marched off on his own with 30,000 warriors. The Thracian, meanwhile, had decided to try to lead his people out of Italy and towards the Alps, from where they could disperse to their various homelands, but he found himself hemmed in by the two Roman command-ers: '[Spartacus] turned upon them one after the other and beat them in detail. They retreated in confusion in different direc-tions. Spartacus sacrificed 300 Roman prisoners to the shade of Crixus, and marched on Rome with 120,000 foot, having burned all his useless material, killed all his prisoners, and butchered his pack-animals in order to expedite his movement.'[57]

The prospect of an attack on Rome caused panic in the city, but it never materialised. Spartacus did not have the right resources to take the city, and he quickly abandoned the idea. At some point, however, Spartacus won further engagements, including one near Mutina against the ex-Consul Gaius Cassius Longinus Varus, who was now the governor of Cisalpine Gaul and commanded an army of 10,000 men. Cassius only just managed to escape with his own life.[58] But if Spartacus rejected the idea of attacking Rome, his followers decided against leav-ing Italy. Plunder was more attractive, and their leader was powerless to stop them.

Plutarch remarks on the 'effeminacy and luxury' of the Romans who took part in these campaigns.[59] The consuls were told to return to civilian life, and the Senate now looked else-where for a commander. They chose the Praetor Marcus Licinius Crassus, 'a man distinguished among the Romans for birth and wealth',[60] who assumed the praetorship and marched against Spartacus with six new legions.[61] The first thing Crassus did was to restore discipline in the good old-fashioned Roman way. He decimated his own army:

> He took 500 of those who had been the first to fly and had shown themselves the greatest cowards, and, dividing them into fifty squads of ten men each, put to death one man, chosen by lot, from each squad. This was a traditional method of punishing soldiers, now revived by Crassus after having been out of use for many years. Those who are punished in this way not only lose their lives but are also disgraced, since the whole army are there as spectators, and the actual circumstances of the execution are very savage and repulsive.[62]

Having made the point to his soldiers that he was more dangerous than Spartacus, Crassus took the field: 'He overcame immediately 10,000 of the Spartacans, who were encamped somewhere in a detached position, and killed two-thirds of them. He then marched boldly against Spartacus himself, vanquished him in a brilliant engagement, and pursued his fleeing forces to the sea, where they tried to pass over to Sicily.'[63]

This posed the threat of yet another slave war on the island, and it is possible that the governor of Sicily, the later disgraced Gaius Verres, helped to prevent the crossing.[64] When their makeshift rafts proved useless, Spartacus tried to enlist the help of some Cilician pirates. They agreed, took his money and promptly sailed away. Crassus then confined them to the toe of Italy by building a 65-kilometre-long line of circumvallation consisting of ditch, wall and paling, from coast to coast across the peninsula.[65]

73 BC: Spartacus versus Crassus

Crassus' siegeworks restricted Spartacus' opportunities for plunder. An attempt to force his way out cost him 12,000 casualties against three dead and seven wounded Romans.[66] The situation started to become desperate: 'So he waited for a night when it was snowing and a wintry storm had got up, and then, after filling up a small section of the ditch with earth and timber and branches of trees [Frontinus says he used the bodies of prisoners and cattle that he had slaughtered[67]], managed to get a third of his army across.'[68]

Dissention now started to grow in the rebel camp.[69] Spartacus had to rescue a breakaway faction who were attacked by Crassus near a Lucanian lake. But, meanwhile, nervousness at Rome led to Gnaeus Pompeius ('Pompey') being summoned from Spain, where he had been dealing with an insurrection led by Sertorius, and Lucullus from Thrace, who had been fighting Mithridates VI of Pontus (see pp. 232 ff.). Whether this was on Crassus' initiative or not,[70] it meant that he needed to finish the war before someone else took the credit.

Spartacus took the opportunity to offer terms, but these were rejected, and Crassus bore down on a contingent of Gauls and Germans led by Castus and Cannicus, who had become separated from Spartacus' main army close to the head of the River Silarus. The details of the fight are hazy. Plutarch tells of a botched attempt by Crassus secretly to occupy some high ground that was discovered by two Gallic women who had climbed up into the mountains to spend their menstrual periods there. The discovery precipitated a battle in which Crassus's troops killed 12,300 men, of which only two were wounded in the back.[71] Frontinus, on the other hand, presents the engagement as a carefully managed ambush by Crassus in which 35,000 rebels were killed along with their commander, and five Roman eagles and twenty-six standards were recaptured, plus five sets of *fasces*.[72]

Spartacus himself had not been involved in the destruction of Castus and Cannicus' detachment. He fell back into the mountains of Petilia, where he was able to overpower a pursuing force under two of Crassus' subordinates. But this success brought Spartacus' downfall. His men became overconfident. Again they went against Spartacus' better judgement and sought a direct confrontation with Crassus, which simply played into the Roman's hands. Skirmishing escalated into a full-scale battle. As Plutarch tells it,

> when his horse was brought to him, [Spartacus] drew his sword and killed it, saying that the enemy had plenty of good horses which would be his if he won, and, if he lost, he would not need a horse at all. Then he made straight for Crassus himself, charging forward through the press of weapons and wounded men, and, though he did not reach Crassus, he cut down two centurions who fell on him together. Finally, when his own men had taken to flight, he himself, surrounded by enemies, still stood his ground and died fighting to the last.[73]

Appian's version has a different ending: 'The battle was long and bloody, as might have been expected with so many thousands of desperate men. Spartacus was wounded in the thigh with a spear and sank upon his knee, holding his shield in front of him and contending in this way against his assailants until he and the great mass of those with him were surrounded and slain . . . The body of Spartacus was not found.'[74]

Florus gives Spartacus a particularly appropriate end, fighting in the front rank *sine missione* ('to the death') – the technical term from the gladiatorial arena, as befitted a true gladiator.[75]

The rebel casualty figures were numbered in the tens of thousands. Although Spartacus' rebellion had been extraordinary in its extent and temporary success, there was to be no Hollywoodesque 'I'm Spartacus' moment. Six thousand of his surviving supporters were crucified, 30 metres apart along the entire length of the Appian Way from Capua to Rome.[76] Crassus' fears about who took the credit were realised when Pompey alighted 'like an idle carrion-bird',[77] and prevented 5,000 fugitives escaping to the north. Crassus had risked his life and done all the hard work but Pompey had technically concluded the war, so he got the triumph, while Crassus merely received an *ovatio*, even though he violated protocol by wearing a laurel wreath rather than the myrtle of Venus Victrix that was appropriate for adversaries of a low or unworthy character, such as slaves or pirates.[78] Florus was left to make the moral point that the slave uprisings, or Servile Wars as they are known, were caused by excessive expenditure that aimed at conciliating the Plebs by pandering to their love of 'bread and circuses',[79] while in the twentieth century, Soviet school textbooks made Spartacus a substitute for Christ on the cross, and elevated him to the status of Stalin.

12

Mithridates VI: The 'Poison King' of Pontus

While Rome was engaging external barbarian enemies to the north, west and south, as well as dealing with internal conflicts in Italy itself, one of the great unsung characters of ancient history was ruling the Kingdom of Pontus, on the Black Sea coast of what is now Turkey. Channelling Alexander the Great, he was extraordinarily ambitious, and for three decades he was undoubtedly the most effective enemy of the Romans in the east. He exploited Rome's preoccupations very effectively, and played on the ill-feeling towards corrupt Roman governors in its provinces. His name was Mithridates VI Eupator (also spelled Mithradates).

Mithridates Becomes King of Pontus

Pontus was a very ethnically diverse kingdom: twenty-two different languages were spoken there, but by the time Mithridates VI came to the throne it had also assimilated a small degree of Greek culture, initially from Greek colonists on the Black Sea, and subsequently from Alexander the Great and his successors. However, it remained proudly independent, and by the time of Mithridates' father, Mithridates V (ruled 150–120 BC), Pontus was a prosperous Hellenistic state, and also a formal 'ally and friend' of Rome, and Mithridates V sided with the Romans in the Third Punic War that led to the destruction of Carthage in 146 BC.

Mithridates VI was sometimes compared to Carthage's greatest son. Velleius Paterculus described him as: 'Ever eager for war, of exceptional bravery, always great in spirit and sometimes in achievement, in strategy a general, in bodily prowess a soldier, in hatred of the Romans, a Hannibal.'[1]

In 120 BC, at the age of eleven, his father's death left him heir to the throne but when his mother Laodice took power as regent, friends who feared for the boy's life took him to hide in the mountains. There, we are told, he became a man of toughness, ambition and resilience. Seven years later, having come of age, he returned, imprisoned his mother, killed his younger brother, took the throne that was rightfully his, and married his full sister, also called Laodice.

Mithridates developed a formidable reputation: he was courageous; his athletic prowess was legendary; his appetites for food and drink were Herculean;[2] he spoke twenty-two languages fluently;[3] he was a friend to Greek intellectuals; his generosity towards his friends was obvious; and he was clever, energetic and extremely resourceful.

He had a large frame, as his armour, which he sent to Nemea and to Delphi, shows, and was so strong that he rode horseback and hurled the javelin to the last, and could ride 180 km in one day, changing horses at intervals. He used to drive a chariot with sixteen horses at once. He cultivated

Greek learning . . . and was fond of music. He was abstemi-
ous and patient . . . for the most part, and yielded only to
pleasures with women.[4]

However, unfortunately for his ambitions to dominate Asia
Minor and beyond, in Greek and Roman eyes he was a barbarian. His philhellenism was offset by his lifestyle. At heart, he
was an oriental monarch: he was also suspicious, cruel and
murderous – at one point he had the 500 women of his harem
put to death so that they would not fall into enemy hands (see
p. 233) – and he ruled through fear, not loyalty. He was suspicious of his own bodyguards, and was guarded at night by a
bull, a horse and a stag, who would wake him at any sign of
danger by bellowing, neighing and bleating.[5] If he could have
thought of the phrase 'let them hate me so long as they fear
me', he would have used it.[6]

Mithridatic Imperialism

Once he was firmly ensconced on the throne, Mithridates set
out on a series of imperialistic ventures. He captured what is
now the Crimea on the north coast of the Black Sea. There
were several Greek cities in the area, and one of these,
Panticapaeum, was made the local capital and given over to one
of his sons to rule on his behalf. This northern conquest was
followed by that of Lesser Armenia to the east, and of Colchis
on the eastern coast of the Black Sea, which is the place associated with the myth of the Golden Fleece.[7] The Crimean and
Colchian expeditions were commanded by Mithridates' general
Diophantus, and they generated substantial amounts of revenue
and a good supply of native soldiers.

Meanwhile, Mithridates VI himself personally led several operations against neighbouring rulers, particularly to the south and west in central Asia Minor. In 104 BC, when Rome was dealing with the challenges posed by the Cimbri and Teutones, he occupied Galatia, Paphlagonia and Cappadocia. This was not a direct threat to Rome, but did bring him into conflict with rulers who, like him, were nominally allies and friends of Rome. When Roman senatorial envoys were sent out to order him to restore the conquered territories to their rightful owners, he simply treated them with contempt.

Once Gaius Marius had successfully eradicated the threat from the Cimbri and Teutones, he was eager for a trial of strength with Mithridates, and in 101 BC his henchman Saturninus tried to precipitate a conflict by deliberately insulting Mithridates' ambassadors, who had arrived in Rome with large sums of money for bribing the Senate. Nothing came of this, apart from scandal in Rome, although in 98 BC Marius went on a tour of inspection in Asia Minor (on the pretext of fulfilling a vow to Cybele at Pessinus in Phrygia), but unfortunately for his belligerent ambitions he had no special authority to engage with Mithridates, and had to be content with giving him a strict telling-off at a private interview.

Despite being to all intents and purposes a barbarian, Mithridates still tried to weaponise his philhellenism, posing as the champion of the Greeks against the barbarian (in their eyes) Romans. Epigraphical evidence gives an indication of his success in this regard. As far back as 115 BC, an official named Dionysus had erected a statue of Mithridates on the island of Delos, but Mithridates subsequently decided to improve his education by visiting Greece in person and making a 'Grand Tour' in the Greek world, where Delos was one of his ports of call, maybe in 102/1 BC. There is certainly a hero shrine on Delos, which was dedicated to him in that year by an Athenian priest called Helianax. This contained busts of several of Mithridates' courtiers, foreign allies and associates, as well as a fine statue of Mithridates himself, wearing the uniform of a Roman general. The choice of attire for the statue suggests that relations with Rome were reasonably amicable at this point. Further evidence of Mithridates' popularity at Delos and Athens can be seen in a dedication in the Delian Serapeum dating from about 94/3 BC, which Dicaeus, a priest of Serapis, made on behalf of the Athenian people, the Roman people, King Mithridates and his own parents.

In 96 BC Lucius Cornelius Sulla, the capturer of Jugurtha, was the proconsular governor of Cilicia. He installed a puppet ruler called Ariobarzanes I Philoromaios as King of Cappadocia on Mithridates' southern border, and also prevented Mithridates from linking up with his new ally, Tigranes, the King of Armenia. Then in 92 BC, Rome ordered Mithridates to relinquish his gains in Asia Minor entirely. He obeyed, promptly but resentfully. Mithridates was still allowed to keep his conquests in Colchis and the Crimea, which did not impinge on Rome's interests, but at this point it must have dawned on him that if he was going to fulfil his dreams, he would have to defeat Rome.

And the defeat of Rome did seem to be on his agenda: at the height of his career we are told that he could deploy an army of more than 125,000 infantry, several thousand cavalry and a great number of scythed chariots, while his fleet was said to total 400 warships. His first real chance came when the Italian/Social War broke out in Italy in 91 BC (see pp. 187–198). The fact that Rome was now totally preoccupied domestically gave

Mithridates and Tigranes (who was now his son-in-law) a window of opportunity in which they seized Bithynia to the west and Cappadocia to the south (again). The Romans sent out a commission under Manius Aquillius (consul 101 BC), which restored King Nicomedes VI to the throne of Bithynia. Mithridates withdrew without a fight, but the Romans also demanded an extortionate fee from Nicomedes for helping him. So, under financial pressure from Aquillius and his other Roman creditors, Nicomedes invaded Pontus. Mithridates played things cannily, and simply withdrew. Now armed with suitable pretexts for war whenever he chose to deploy them, he allowed Nicomedes to advance unopposed to the city of Amastris.

The First Mithridatic War

Feeling abundantly justified, and confident of success, Mithridates struck first and struck hard, precipitating what historians call the First Mithridatic War (88–84 BC). The king swept through Cappadocia and the Roman province of Asia, promising freedom to the Greek cities along with the cancellation of debts. With the help of the local citizens he perpetrated the so-called 'Asiatic Vespers', a massacre of the Roman and/or Italian residents of the region that some sources say accounted for the lives of 80,000 men, women and children in a single day. This provides compelling proof, if ever it were needed, of the intense ill-feeling towards Roman rule in the provinces at this time.

There was a terrible massacre in the Asclepieion at Pergamum, and Delos too fell victim. The island, which had taken its position in the war against Mithridates under the influence of an organised and flourishing Italian community there, had defected from Athens when the city took Mithridates' side against Rome. Athens sent an expedition to reclaim it, under the philosopher-politician Apellicon of Teos. Delos was a sacred island, the birthplace of the god Apollo and theoretically immune from war, but the only sanction against Mithridates' transgressions was the wrath of the gods, and in 88 BC that was not sufficient to save it: 'Mithridates' general Menophanes . . . sailed in with warships . . . and massacred the foreigners and the islanders together. He looted an enormous wealth from the merchants, and the entire mass of consecrated treasures, he sold the women and the children into slavery, and demolished Delos to its foundations.'[8]

Appian and Pausanias say that the dead numbered as many as 20,000[9] and Delos never recovered: the Italian marketplace, which as a monument to Roman capitalism was unique in Greece, naturally suffered badly, although it was rebuilt and reused until 69 BC, when the pirates of Athenodorus, an ally of Mithridates, destroyed what was left.

Mithridates also invaded the European mainland. He was 'invited' to liberate Greece by the Athenian democratic party, and his agent Aristion led a revolution against the unpopular oligarchy there and established himself as despot. Mithridates' general Archelaus gained control of most of the Aegean and occupied southern and central Greece. Eretria, Chalcis and Euboea all went over to Mithridates, and even the Spartans were defeated. Pretty well all the islands of the Aegean, with the notable exception of Rhodes, went over to Mithridates too. This again vividly illustrates the level of general hostility towards Roman policies in the region. Roman forces under Quintus Bruttius Sura confronted Mithridates' commander Archelaus near Chaeroneia in Boeotia, Greece, and although they stemmed his onslaught in an indecisive battle lasting some three days, they still withdrew.[10]

At this point (87 BC) Sulla himself crossed over into Epirus with five legions. Mithridates was powerless to prevent him moving across into Macedonia, or from gathering men and supplies en route, or from despoiling the temples at Olympia, Epidaurus and Delphi, and pillaging other treasures in order fund his army.[11] On 1 March 86 BC, the Roman forces took Athens by storm. Plutarch remarks that 'When Sulla was besieging Athens, he had very little time to waste in the operations, "Since other labour was pressing."'[12]

Sulla then forced Archelaus out of Athens' harbour at the Peiraieus after a fiercely contested siege that left the port in permanent ruins. Nevertheless, the Pontic army continued to move through Thrace and Macedonia, until the two sides eventually clashed in a pitched battle, again at Chaeroneia in Boeotia. Sulla managed to neutralise the impact of Archelaus' chariots by narrowing the distance between the battle lines, so that they could not get up to full speed:

The first of their chariots were driven along feebly and engaged sluggishly, so that the Romans, after repulsing them, clapped their hands and laughed and called for more, as they are wont to do at the races in the circus. Thereupon the infantry forces engaged, the Barbarians holding their spears before them at full length, and endeavouring, by locking their shields together, to keep their line of battle intact; while the Romans threw down their *pila*, drew their swords, and sought to dash the spears aside, that they might get at their enemies as soon as possible, in the fury that possessed them.[13]

The Roman intensity won out, and Archelaus' troops were routed: only 10,000 of them (less than 10 per cent of the total force) were still capable of fighting another day;[14] Livy puts the casualties at 100,000.[15]

Eighty thousand high-quality Pontic reinforcements now arrived in Greece by sea under Mithridates' military expert Dorylaus, and a second major battle was fought on the Boeotian plain near to Orchomenus. Sulla countered the Pontic cavalry and chariots by digging ditches and planting stakes in the ground to curtail their mobility, and once again prevailed: 'The marshes were filled with their blood, and the lake with their dead bodies, so that even to this day many bows, helmets, fragments of steel breastplates, and swords of barbarian make are found embedded in the mud, although almost two hundred years have passed since this battle.'[16]

Sulla stormed the Pontic camp but Archelaus escaped by hiding in a swamp. When Mithridates heard the news from Orchomenus, he started to reflect on the huge numbers of men he had deployed in Greece since the start of the war, and the alarming rate of attrition which they had suffered. He ordered Archelaus to make the best peace deal possible.[17]

These victories on the battlefield allowed Sulla to start to menace Mithridates by moving north-east through Macedonia to the Hellespont in 85 BC. He sent Lucius Licinius Lucullus – the Roman politician famous for his luxury, who once spent 50,000 *sestertii* on a banquet at a time when the annual pay of a soldier was 480 – to Egypt and Libya to recruit naval forces.

Rome, meanwhile, was undergoing great political upheavals. Sulla's opponents now sent out Lucius Valerius Flaccus and Gaius Flavius Fimbria to deal with Mithridates, but also with secret orders to turn against Sulla (that, anyway, was how Sulla saw things). However, Fimbria then organised a mutiny, killed Flaccus, and defeated Mithridates' reserve army, commanded by Mithridates' son, also called Mithridates, on the banks of the River Rhyndacus (the modern River Mustafakemalpaşa in north-western Turkey), and took control of Pergamum. Mithridates Senior managed to escape from Pergamum, where he had based himself, but by the summer of 85 BC he was prepared to negotiate terms. Fimbria, who had only two some-what dubiously loyal legions, was besieged at Pergamum by Sulla. When his army deserted him, Fimbria fell on his sword, but did it so badly that a slave had to complete the job.[18] Sulla took over his army.

Mithridates and Sulla now met at Dardanus in the Troad (close to Troy). Mithridates was escorted by 20,000 infantry and 6,000 cavalry, plus a large number of scythed chariots; Sulla only had four cohorts of infantry and a few hundred horsemen. After long and heated discussions, terms were agreed, which were remarkably lenient on Mithridates, but crushing to his holdings in the province of Asia. Mithridates agreed that all the territory he had conquered in Asia would be abandoned; he would evacu-ate Pergamum (his headquarters) and relinquish his gains in Bithynia, Paphlagonia and Cappadocia; seventy ships of his Aegean fleet, along with 500 bowmen, would be surrendered; and a modest indemnity of 2,000 talents would be paid. In return, Mithridates retained his position as King of Pontus and was recognised as an ally of Rome.[19]

Essentially, the Treaty of Dardanus allowed Mithridates to be a problem for Rome for quite some time to come. The prov-ince of Asia, on the other hand, was treated very harshly: cities that had supported Mithridates lost all their rights and inde-pendence; some had their walls dismantled; and an enormous indemnity of 20,000 talents was imposed on the province. Consequently the unfortunate provincials fell badly into debt, primarily because they were forced to borrow from ruthless Roman businessmen at extortionate rates of interest in order to pay back the indemnity. But this was not something that worried Sulla: these were problems for others to handle in future; he was anxious to return to Rome to take vengeance on his political enemies, which he did in the most savage way imaginable.[20]

The Second Mithridatic War

No sooner had Sulla gone back to Rome than Lucius Licinius Murena, who had been left behind with the two ex-Fimbrian legions to tidy things up in Asia, started to look for any excuse he could find for war: he wanted a triumph. Mithridates' general Archelaus now went over to Murena, and persuaded him to make the first move by making incursions into Pontus in what became the Second Mithridatic War (83–81 BC). When Mithridates complained that this was a violation of the treaty, Murena replied that he could not see one because Sulla had not written one down – he had left after making sure that what had been agreed verbally was carried out in practice. While Mithridates sent envoys to the Senate and Sulla in Rome, Murena overran 400 of Mithridates' villages. The king did not fight back at this point, but waited for his envoys to return. The Praetor Quintus Calidius was sent out from Rome, and publicly told Murena that the Senate ordered him not to aggravate the king. But Murena ignored him and invaded Mithridates' territory anyway. Mithridates now decided to face Murena in the field, and in 82 BC he inflicted a heavy defeat on him.[21] Sulla sent Aulus Gabinius to tell Murena not to fight Mithridates. Murena was recalled and peace was re-established in 81 BC, on the same terms as before. Cicero saw clearly that Mithridates had come out of this quite well: 'Lucius Sulla has triumphed, Lucius Murena has triumphed over Mithridates, two most gallant men, and most consummate generals; but yet they have triumphed in such a way that he, though routed and defeated, is still king.'[22]

The Third Mithridatic War

Events in Italy now served to take Mithridates off the Roman radar. Sulla succeeded in making himself dictator of Rome, and carried out a chilling series of 'proscriptions', cold-bloodedly calculated murders of his personal and political enemies that ran into the thousands. He also made controversial changes to Rome's constitution, which were contested from the moment he died in 78 BC: the Romans were soon fighting among themselves. The fact that they had taken their eye off the ball presented Mithridates with an open goal, and when Nicomedes IV Philopator of Bithynia died childless in 74 BC, bequeathing his kingdom to the Romans, he invaded Bithynia again to initiate the Third Mithridatic War (74–63 BC). Appian says his well-prepared, multi-ethnic army numbered about 140,000 foot and 16,000 horse,[23] and he defeated the scratch Roman forces of the Consul Marcus Aurelius Cotta at Chalcedon on the opposite side of the Bosphorus from Byzantium.[24]

The other consul, Lucius Licinius Lucullus, might have given the most extravagant banquets Rome had ever witnessed, but he also became a master tactician. Having secured his appointment by intrigue, he took over the war, studied strategy and tactics on the outward journey,[25] and re-established discipline in the army. He was able to prevent Mithridates taking Cyzicus on the southern coast of the Sea of Marmara, and defeat him in siege operations during the winter of 74/3 BC. At this point, the Roman focus on Mithridates was diverted somewhat by the outbreak, in Italy, of the slave revolt of Spartacus (see p. 213 ff.), but Lucullus was still able to drive Mithridates from his coastal acquisitions, before invading Pontus the following winter (73/2 BC). Plutarch makes an interesting aside in his account, when he says that 'Sallust says, to my amazement, that camels were then seen by the Romans for the first time. He must have thought that the soldiers of Scipio who conquered Antiochus before this, and those who had lately fought Archelaüs at Orchomenus and Chaeroneia, were unacquainted with the camel.'[26]

Lucullus failed to get to grips with the elusive Pontic king, and had to spend the winter under canvas. Guerrilla action then ensued, until, eventually, Lucullus defeated Mithridates very heavily at Cabeira in Pontus.[27]

> After he had suffered this manifest disaster, Mithridates ordered that the princesses of the royal house should be killed, and decided to escape from Cabeira, where he was staying, without the knowledge of his subjects. But he was pursued by some Gauls, who did not realise who he was, and he would have been captured, if they had not come across a mule which was carrying Mithridates' gold and silver, and they stopped to plunder this treasure. Mithridates himself reached Armenia.[28]

Throughout the next couple of years (71/70 BC), while Rome was dealing with Spartacus' slave revolt, Lucullus captured all manner of strongholds in Pontus, but not Mithridates himself. Once the elusive king arrived in Armenia, Tigranes refused to give him up. Lucullus was well aware that as long as Mithridates was still at large, the war wasn't over, and his dogged pursuit led him to cross the River Euphrates at Tomisa in 69 BC and invade Armenia with 12,000 infantry and 3,000 cavalry.[29] Unfortunately, he did this without the Senate's permission, which was tantamount to an act of treason, but he still brilliantly defeated Tigranes, despite being considerably outnumbered, at the fortress of Tigranocerta, which he captured.[30]

As Lucullus moved further east, he started to lose his hold over the territories he left behind, notably the province of Asia, and also Cilicia, to the point where he was left with control of only Bithynia and his field forces. But worse than this, in 68 BC, just as he was closing in on Tigranes' capital, Artaxata, his troops mutinied: they didn't like his strict discipline; they wanted easy campaigns and easy plunder; they had been in the east for far too long, and they responded badly to rumours that he was going to invade Parthia.[31] So he had no alternative but to retire to Mesopotamia for the winter.

This, of course, allowed Mithridates to hit back yet again. In 67 BC he invaded Pontus and conducted guerrilla operations against the Romans in Bithynia. Gaius Valerius Triarius, Lucullus' general, was defeated by Mithridates at Zela with 7,000 casualties,[32] and Lucullus' own forces continued to desert. And if this wasn't bad enough, the Equites, Rome's wealthy commercial class, were implacably opposed to Lucullus' financial arrangements for the province of Asia, where he had reduced the debt, which had risen from 20,000 talents under Sulla to 120,000 talents, back to 40,000; he had also fixed the interest rate at 12 per cent. Rome's hardcore ruling elite, the Optimates, were annoyed that he had attacked Tigranes without formal permission. And finally, the Plebs and the Populares didn't like him because he wasn't one of them, and they thought he was taking too long to end the war. So Lucullus was stripped of his command, which allowed Mithridates and Tigranes to regain their territories.

The burning question at Rome was who would replace Lucullus, and early in 66 BC the Tribune Gaius Manilius passed the *lex Manilia* to give Pompey the Great the command against Mithridates. This caused enormous controversy at Rome, but there were sound military reasons for doing this. Pompey had just finished an impressively successful campaign to eradicate the pirates from the Mediterranean, and the special authority that he had been granted to do this still had two and a half years to run – he had 'what it takes'. The Optimate faction was split: some of them thought Lucullus was being cheated and argued that so much power shouldn't be given to one man, also pointing out that there were other deserving people who wanted to hold the office, and that there were elected officials to do these jobs anyway. There was a certain degree of fear and jealousy, and a sense that Pompey wasn't really of the right party. Others respected Pompey's achievements and supported his appointment. The Popularis faction was very much pro the bill: Julius Caesar spoke in favour of it, and the people of Rome liked Pompey. The Equites were also supportive: Pompey's success against the pirates benefitted their trading activities very much, and peace in Asia would be greatly in their interests. Even Cicero, who generally disapproved of this type of thing, added his voice to those in favour.[33] He argued that the law was not unprecedented, the war itself was necessary, Pompey was eminently suited to the job, and was on the scene anyway. What he didn't say was what truly motivated him – he needed Pompey's support in his bid to become consul. Still, his involvement lent respectability to Manilius' cause, and the bill was passed by all thirty-five tribes. Pompey feigned displeasure at the new 'burden', but he had wanted it all along. Roman politicians were not slow to expose this cynical piece of play-acting for what it was.

In essence, Pompey had two things to do: (1) capture or kill Mithridates; and (2) make this seem more difficult than it was. In this respect, he was rather thrown off kilter when Mithridates immediately sought peace. Obviously, this posed a problem for Pompey, who was in Cilicia at the time: if he accepted the offer, his opponents would simply argue that the war against Mithridates had already been won before Pompey took over. So he offered Mithridates unacceptable terms that he knew Mithridates had no option but to reject: nothing short of an unconditional surrender would do.

Pompey could not afford an embarrassingly easy victory, and he had to make sure that all the work done in the east was his and his alone, so he reversed all the edicts of Lucullus. At an acrimonious meeting with Lucullus, Pompey accused Lucullus of avarice and mocked him as 'a Xerxes in a toga';[34] Lucullus' retort was that 'Pompey was going forth to fight an image and shadow of war, following his custom of alighting, like a lazy carrion-bird, on bodies that others had killed, and tearing to pieces the scattered remnants of wars'.[35]

When Lucullus had departed, Pompey took 50,000 men to attack Mithridates in Pontus. The Pontic king tried his level best to avoid an open battle, and when the two sides did engage, close to Dasteira by the River Euphrates, it was on a moonlit night where the Romans had the light behind them.

> First, all the [Roman] trumpeters together . . . sounded the attack, then the soldiers . . . raised a shout, while some clashed their spears against their shields and others struck stones against the bronze implements. The mountains surrounding the valley took up and gave back the din with most frightful effect, so that the barbarians, hearing them suddenly in the night and in the wilderness, were terribly alarmed, thinking they had encountered some supernatural phenomenon.[36]

The barbarians fell into disarray; the Romans closed on them; Mithridates' men pushed and trampled each in their panic; and the long shadows of the Romans baffled their opponents: 'The barbarians, thinking them near, would strike vainly into the air, and when they did come to close quarters in the shadow, they would be wounded when not expecting it. Thus many of them were killed and fewer taken captive. A considerable number also escaped, among them Mithridates.'[37]

Mithridates evaded capture with his concubine Hypsicratia, a woman who always displayed manly spirit and extravagant daring, which is why the king habitually called her Hypsicrates (the male form of her name), and two other companions.[38]

The king managed to rally a measly 3,000 troops on the Armenian border, while Pompey colonised Dasteira and renamed it Nicopolis (Victory City).[39] Mithridates' erstwhile ally Tigranes now decided that the Romans were far too strong for him, and offered a reward of 1,000 talents for the capture of Mithridates. The down-and-out king made an arduous overland march all round the eastern shore of the Black Sea to Panticapaeum in the Crimea, subduing a number of local tribes en route. He ousted his son Machares, sired on his queen-and-sister Laodice, and forced him into committing suicide. Mithridates was now lord of the Crimea, if no longer King of Pontus, which Pompey later reorganised as a Roman province.

Pompey tracked Mithridates as far as Colchis, but then abandoned the pursuit in favour of the conquest of several previously unheard-of tribes, which gave him good propaganda material back in Rome. Instead, he used his fleet to blockade Mithridates at Panticapaeum, before turning back to Pontus and conquering it. He returned Mithridates' concubines to their families, and one of these, Stratonice, surrendered the fortress of Sinoria to him. He also came across an extraordinary cache of Mithridates' letters, which shed fascinating light on his character:

> There were memoranda . . . from which it was discovered that, besides many others, he had poisoned to death his son Ariarathes, and also Alcaeus of Sardis, because he had surpassed him in driving race-horses. Among the writings were also interpretations of dreams, some of which he himself had dreamed, and others, some of his wives. There were also letters from Monime to him, of a lascivious nature, and answering letters from him to her. Moreover, Theophanes says there was found here an address of Rutilius, which incited the king to the massacre of the Romans in Asia.[40]

Mithridates, meanwhile, was levying troops, manufacturing weapons, and hatching an astonishing plan to raise another army, march up the Danube and invade Italy in alliance with the Gauls in imitation of Hannibal.[41]

It was a stalemate situation. Pompey turned his attention in the opposite direction, moving through Syria, which he annexed, and, in 63 BC, down into Judaea, where he found himself drawn into a three-month-long siege of Jerusalem. Finally, 'Fortune resolved the difficulty'[42] of Mithridates for him: when Pompey was at Jericho, news came through of Mithridates' death, which must have come as a big relief to him, since he'd had little luck over the last three years in securing his capture. Mithridates had finally taken his own life after losing the support of his subjects and facing a rebellion by another son, Pharnaces.[43]

> Mithridates then took out some poison that he always carried next to his sword, and mixed it. There two of his daughters, who were still girls growing up together . . . who had been betrothed to the kings of Egypt and of Cyprus, asked him to let them have some of the poison first, and insisted strenuously and prevented him from drinking it until they had taken some and swallowed it. The drug took effect on them at once; but upon Mithridates, although he walked around rapidly to hasten its action, it had no effect, because he had accustomed himself to other drugs by continually trying them as a means of protection against poisoners.[44] These are still called the Mithridatic drugs.[45]

So Mithridates asked his loyal Gaulish servant Bituitus to slay him. This he did. Pompey granted Mithridates' body an honourable funeral, and covered the cost of it.

Mithridates had been one of Rome's most tenacious enemies in the east, and there were celebrations on the streets when news of his death filtered through. Appian acknowledges that now, in consequence of the Mithridatic wars, Rome's empire had been advanced from Spain and the Pillars of Hercules to the Black Sea, and the sands which border Egypt, and the River Euphrates. To Roman eyes, they had achieved a great victory, and Pompey, who had commanded the army, was now truly 'the Great'. However, Mithridates never quite achieved the greatness to which he aspired. He had no grand design other than his own survival and aggrandisement, and despite his love of their culture, he had very little to offer the Greek population of the region. As far as they were concerned, it was a lose–lose situation: there was very little to choose between being ruled by Mithridates, a barbarian and so culturally alien, as our historical sources all emphasise, or by inefficient Roman provincial governors. It was ultimately the fact that barbarians, not Greeks, formed the base of his power that proved to be Mithridates' undoing.

Pompey's soldiers felt that in the person of Mithridates, 10,000 enemies had died; and the classical scholar and poet A. E. Houseman immortalised his death in *A Shropshire Lad* (1896):

> There was a king reigned in the east:
> There, when kings will sit to feast,
> They get their fill before they think
> With poisoned meat and poisoned drink.
> He gathered all that springs to birth
> From the many venomed earth;
> First a little, thence to more,
> He sampled all her killing store;
> And easy, smiling, seasoned sound,
> Sate the king when healths went round.

They put arsenic in his meat
And stared aghast to watch him eat;
They poured strychnine in his cup
And shook to see him drink it up:
They stood, they stared as white's their shirt:
Them it was their poison hurt.
– I tell the tale that I heard told.
Mithridates, he died old.

13

The Parthian Shot: Crassus at Carrhae

I think that a knowledge of the future would be a disadvantage . . . Take Marcus Crassus. What advantage, pray, do you think it would have been to him, when he was at the very summit of power and wealth, to know that he was destined to perish beyond the Euphrates in shame and dishonour, after his son had been killed and his own army had been destroyed?[1]

The First Triumvirate

When Pompey arrived back in Rome after the death of Mithridates VI he disbanded his army and celebrated a magnificent triumph, before running into a political brick wall. He needed land for his veteran soldiers as their pension on demobilisation and ratification of all the political arrangements that he had made in the east, and he wanted to marry into the family of the arch-Optimate Marcus Porcius Cato. But the Optimates closed ranks and frustrated him at every turn. Secondly, they also alienated the man who had once been Rome's richest individual, Marcus Licinius Crassus Dives ('the

Rich'; see p. 217): When Crassus made an inventory of his property just before he left for Parthia, he found that he was worth a staggering 7,100 talents, most of it gained by nefarious means.[2] As the spokesman for a syndicate of tax-farming Equites, he was currently trying to renegotiate a bad deal that they had made concerning collecting the taxes of Asia. But the Optimates were having none of this either. And thirdly, the Optimates annoyed the upwardly mobile Gaius Julius Caesar, who wanted both to celebrate a triumph for his recent campaigns in the Iberian peninsula, and to stand for the consulship of 59 BC. But legally he had to choose one or the other: either he could wait outside the city boundaries of Rome for the triumph, or appear in person inside the city to submit his candidacy. When the Optimates, who had never liked him, told him it was one thing or the other, Caesar wrong-footed them by giving up the triumph and arriving in Rome. Their response was to decree that if he got elected, his province would be the third-rate post of Commissioner for the Forests and Cattle Drifts of Italy. This was obviously totally unacceptable.

Pompey, Crassus and Caesar were not good friends, but they knew that if they cooperated they could get what they wanted in the short term. So they formed an *amicitia* (an informal political deal), which later became known as the First Triumvirate, and secured Caesar's election as consul for 59 BC. By fair means and foul, he ensured that each triumvir got what he wanted. From then on the alliance started to come under stress from inside and out, but self-interest again brought them together, and before the campaigning season of 56 BC they hammered out a new deal at Lucca in Italy that gave them total control of Rome: Caesar's command in Gaul was extended for five years (see pp. 262 ff.); Pompey and Crassus became joint consuls in 55 BC; Pompey got control of Spain for five years, but could stay in Rome; and Crassus took Syria for five years as his province.

Crassus couldn't believe his luck. He started to dream of conquering the eastern extremities of the world: 'But now, being altogether exalted and out of his senses, he would not consider Syria nor even Parthia as the boundaries of his success, but thought to make the campaigns of Lucullus against Tigranes and those of Pompey against Mithridates seem mere child's play, and flew on the wings of his hopes as far as Bactria and India and the Outer Sea.'[3]

No mention had been made of a Parthian war in his election, but everyone knew that Crassus wanted to wage one, despite the fact that the Parthians had done nothing to provoke Rome, and enjoyed treaty relations with her. The Tribune Gaius Ateius Capito tried to prevent him leaving the city, first by physical force, and then by dire curses which invoked strange and terrible gods, but Crassus could not be diverted from his goal.

Parthia and the Parthians

The Greeks and Romans called the people whom Crassus was about to attack 'Parthians'. They were originally 'Parni', who belonged to a semi-nomadic confederacy of people called the Dahae, who lived in the neighbourhood of Hyrcania on the southern coast of the Caspian Sea during the Hellenistic era. Their Greek name comes from Achaemenid Persian, and then a Seleucid administrative district called Parthia (*Parthava*), which they occupied, traditionally in 247 BC. That is the year in which the Parthian ('Arsacid') era begins, and in due course they came to have an empire that stretched from the River Euphrates in the west to the River Indus in the east. By the time they came into violent contact with Rome, the Parthian kings ruled an ethnically, politically, socially and culturally diverse population. When Crassus was leaving Rome, the man on the Parthian throne was Orodes II (aka Arsaces and Hyrodes; r. 57–37 BC). His queen was a culturally Greek princess from Commagene, called Laodice.

Modern scholarship has been keen to rehabilitate the Parthians, who have traditionally been regarded as culturally dependent on the Greeks and Romans, lacking serious political aspirations, and generally inferior to Rome on all counts. However, recent discoveries of texts from Mesopotamia, and archaeological remains throughout their territories, are present-ing a more nuanced picture. On the one hand, we certainly see philhellenic leanings in their coins and cultural dealings, but these run alongside what have been called the 'Iranian traits' of their rule, and the cultural mixing might well be one of the ways in which they tried to unite the diverse elements of their subjects. However, no amount of cultural assimilation could make them anything other than barbarian to Greek or Roman eyes. 'Parthian bowmen' and 'fierce Parthians with their painted quivers'[4] are used by Roman poets as bywords for eastern exoticism.

Orodes II and his subjects spoke Parthian, which is a western Middle Iranian language. They practised the Zoroastrian cult of fire, but they tolerated all other religions. The Parthians also played a vital role as middlemen in the trade between Syria, China and India. On the battlefield they were famous for their formidable mail-clad cavalry, but their expert lightly armed horse archers could also do incredible damage. They bred and rode the now extinct Nisaean horses, which Herodotus said were of remarkable size, and which were highly valued in antiquity.[5]

Crassus on the Offensive

Having levied the troops he needed, Crassus left Italy via the seaport of Brundisium (modern Brindisi) in 54 BC. In his impatience he sailed amid wintry storms, and lost a large number of ships. His remaining forces moved swiftly overland through the barbarian territory of Galatia, where he had a feisty exchange with King Deiotarus, who was a very old man but was founding a new city. Crassus mocked him: ' "O King, you are beginning to build at the twelfth hour." The Galatian laughed and said: "But you yourself, Imperator, as I see, are not marching very early in the day against the Parthians." '[6]

Deiotarus' jibe was that Crassus himself was aged over sixty, and looked older than he was. Cicero had also written to his friend Atticus, saying that Crassus 'sat in his official robes with less dignity than Lucius [Aemilius] Paullus did in the olden days',[7] his point being that when Paullus set out to confront Perseus in 168 BC (see p. 127) he was also sixty years old, and in his second consulship. However, Paullus had set out under good omens; Crassus under a curse.

Things went smoothly for Crassus at first. He bridged the River Euphrates without opposition, and took control of many cities in Mesopotamia, several of which went over to him voluntarily. He encountered slight resistance in capturing a city that the Greeks called Zenodotia, but showed his arrogance and small-mindedness by allowing his soldiers to salute him as 'Imperator' (the accolade for a truly victorious general), despite the insignificance of the conquest.[8] He then put garrisons into the cities that had taken, but lost the impetus by retreating into winter quarters in Syria, rather than pushing further on to Babylon and Seleucia (a city in Mesopotamia that had a large Greek population), which were traditionally hostile to the Parthians. Crassus' son Publius Licinius Crassus joined up with him, but Crassus senior focused on financial rather than military matters – Josephus says that he moved through Judaea, where he plundered the Temple at Jerusalem, to provide funds for the expedition[9] – giving the Parthians crucial breathing space.

At the start of the campaigning season of 53 BC, Orodes II sent envoys to Crassus to complain about his actions, and to ask what his grounds for invasion were. When Crassus responded that he would reveal the causes in Seleucia, the Parthian ambassador Vagises burst out laughing, and pointed to the palm of his hand with the words, 'Hair will grow there before you'll get to Seleucia!'[10] As the two sides parted, reports started to come in to Crassus about the weird nature of the Parthian warriors, and the challenges they posed: 'When the men pursued . . . there was no escaping them, and when they fled, there was no taking them; and strange missiles are the precursors of their appearance, which pierce through every obstacle before one sees who sent them; and as for the armour of their mail-clad horsemen, some of it is made to force its way through everything, and some of it to give way to nothing.'[11]

This was a shock. Crassus' men thought that the Parthians were not that much different from the Armenians and Cappadocians that Lucullus had defeated so easily (see pp. 232 ff.); the seers delivered omens that were universally inauspicious; but Crassus took no notice and pressed on, spurning an offer of 10,000 mail-clad horsemen and 30,000 infantrymen from King Artabazes II (aka Artavasdes) of Armenia in the process.

Crassus' army comprised seven legions, nearly 4,000 cavalry and around another 4,000 light-armed troops. They crossed out of Syria from Zeugma on the right bank of the River Euphrates, and marched along the river without encountering any Parthian presence other than horse-tracks in the sand. This bolstered Crassus' confidence, but his quaestor, Gaius Cassius Longinus, who would one day become one of Caesar's assassins, was more circumspect, and advised staying on the riverside and marching to Seleucia for strategic and logistical reasons.

While Crassus was weighing up his options, he was approached by an Arab chieftain called Ariamnes (or Abgarus, Mazaras or Mazzarus).[12] He had served under Pompey and everyone thought he was pro-Roman, but Plutarch describes the reality. He was 'a crafty and treacherous man, and one who proved to be, of all the mischiefs which fortune combined for the destruction of the Romans, the greatest and most consummate.'[13] He wanted to lure Crassus away from the safety of the river and get him to enter a large open plain: the Parthians would never consider a frontal attack, but wanted to be able to surround him. Ariamnes is specifically referenced as 'the Barbarian', and his facility as a plausible talker is acknowledged.[14]

The Barbarian urged Crassus to stop wasting time and to pursue the Parthian forces straight away, firstly because they were trying to flee, and secondly because the king wasn't present with his generals Surena and Sillaces. But this was fake news. Orodes was not scared of Crassus. On the contrary, he was busy devastating Armenia to punish Artabazes for holding himself in reserve for the conflict with Rome, while Surena wanted to confront the Romans, not escape from them.

To the Greeks and Romans, Surena was epitome of the eastern barbarian aristocrat:

> In valour and ability he was the foremost Parthian of his time, besides having no equal in stature and personal beauty. He used to travel on private business with a baggage train of a thousand camels, and was followed by two hundred wagons for his concubines, while a thousand mail-clad horsemen and a still greater number of light-armed cavalry served as his escort; and had altogether, as horsemen, vassals, and slaves, no fewer than ten thousand men.[15]

He was also prudent and clever, the complete antithesis of Crassus. As with many barbarians in Roman history, he is used to highlight the moral shortcomings of a Roman who did not measure up to the true vision of *Romanitas*.

Ariamnes the Barbarian convinced Crassus to follow him away from the river and into flat, sandy, treeless, waterless, open desert. As thirst, demoralisation and suspicion overtook Crassus' men, envoys from Artabazes arrived. The Armenian king said he couldn't help Crassus because he was fighting off Orodes, but he invited the Romans to join him, or if they could not, advised them at least to head for mountainous territory where the Parthian cavalry would be less effective. Perversely, Crassus told the messengers that he didn't have time to waste on the Armenians, and that in due course he would punish Artabazes for his treachery.[16] Cassius thought it was pointless to continue advising Crassus any more, but did abuse the Barbarian: ' "Basest of men," he said, "what evil spirit brought you to us? With what drugs and jugglery did you persuade Crassus to pour his army into a yawning and abysmal desert and follow a route more fit for a robber chief of Nomads than for a Roman imperator?" '[17]

The Barbarian just rode off before his treachery became obvious, leaving Crassus under the misapprehension that he was still working on his behalf.

Reports now came in that the Parthian army was approaching. Against Cassius' advice, Crassus drew his men up in a hollow square formation. They advanced to a stream, which they reached on 6 May 53 BC, but rather than allowing his soldiers to refresh themselves and bivouac overnight, Crassus ordered them into battle. They advanced more swiftly than was sensible in their fatigued state, and at first sight Surena's forces looked weak. But the Parthian had concealed his main forces behind the advance guard, and he had ordered them to cover their resplendent armour with skins and robes. Once they were close enough to the Romans, they filled the whole plain with terrifying, uncanny, barbarous sounds: 'The Parthians do not incite themselves to battle with horns or trumpets, but they have hollow drums of distended hide, covered with bronze bells, and on these they beat all at once in many quarters, and the instruments give forth a low and dismal tone, a blend of wild beast's roar and harsh thunder peal.'[18]

The Romans were completely disorientated by this, and the Parthians delivered a second shock when they threw aside the coverings of their armour to reveal dazzling helmets, breast-plates and weaponry, and their horses were similarly clad in plates of bronze and iron. Surena appeared in his full barbarian magnificence. He 'was the tallest and fairest of them all, although his effeminate beauty did not well correspond to his reputation for valour, but he was dressed more in the Median fashion,[19] with painted face and parted hair, while the rest of the Parthians still wore their hair long and bunched over their foreheads, in Scythian fashion, to make themselves look formidable.'[20]

The Parthians surrounded the Roman square. Crassus sent his light-armed troops against them, but they immediately retreated in the face of the density of the Parthian arrows, shot from composite bows that were 'large and mighty and curved'.[21] The velocity and power of the missiles could fracture any type of armour, and terror spread through the Roman ranks as they saw their devastating effect. Furthermore, the Roman formation meant that the Parthians didn't even need to aim carefully: they just couldn't miss. If the Romans maintained their formation, they were picked off at will, but if they tried to close with their enemies, they encountered the famous 'Parthian shot', as the horse archers fired as they fled.

The Romans' hopes that the Parthians would run out of ammunition were dashed when a camel train laden with arrows arrived. So Crassus ordered his son to force an engagement. Publius charged with 1,300 horsemen, 500 archers and eight cohorts of legionaries. But the Parthians simply turned and rode. Publius gave chase until it became obvious he had been tricked: the Parthian 'fugitives' about-faced; others joined them; they deployed their mail-clad cavalrymen in front of the Romans; and the light horsemen rode around them, kicking up clouds of sand that prevented the Romans from seeing or communicating properly. Carnage followed: 'In the agonies of convulsive pain, and writhing about the arrows, [the Romans] would break them off in their wounds, and then in trying to pull out by force the barbed heads which had pierced their veins and sinews, they tore and disfigured themselves even more.'[22]

The Parthians incapacitated many of the survivors by riveting their hands to their shields and nailing their feet to the ground. Publius made a desperate charge with his cavalry, most of whom were lightly armed Gauls, but the Parthian weapons, armour and desert heat were simply too much for them. Publius himself was severely wounded, and withdrew the remnants of his troops to a sandy hillock, which only allowed the Parthians even easier target practice. Only 500 Romans were taken alive, and Publius was not one of them: the Parthians cut off his head, and rode off to attack Crassus.[23]

Crassus had just started to advance when the Parthians arrived carrying Publius' head on a spear. In comparison to the noise of the barbarian war cries and drums, the Roman battle cry was weak and feeble, and for the rest of the day the Parthian cavalry assailed Crassus' main force, but without producing a conclusive outcome. Crassus spent the night lying on the ground all by himself, 'to the multitude an illustration of the ways of Fortune, but to the wise an example of foolish ambition'.[24]

The Battle of Carrhae

With Crassus in total despair, his officers called a council-of-war and decided to retreat. This was to be done at night and in silence, but would entail abandoning many of the wounded. What resulted was a chaotic march, but the army did make its way to the city of Carrhae (near Harran in modern south-eastern Turkey), where they were welcomed by the commander Coponius.[25] For their part, the Parthians elected to mop up the remnants of the forces around the Roman camp before establishing that Crassus really had made it through to Carrhae, and heading for the city. As Surena demanded the surrender of Crassus and Cassius, the Romans planned to sneak out of the city without the people of Carrhae knowing their plans. But, again, misguided trust brought disaster on Crassus: he confided the details to a faithless local called Andromachus, and also made him the guide for the journey; Andromachus simply passed on all the information to the Parthians.

Crassus' army exited Carrhae on a moonless night, led by Andromachus, who took them on a circuitous route into marshy terrain. Some of the Romans were deeply suspicious about this, notably Cassius, who headed back to Carrhae. When his Arab guides suggested he should stay there until the moon had passed Scorpio, he told them that he was more afraid of Sagittarius (the Archer – i.e. the Parthians), and made his escape into Syria with 500 horsemen.

At daybreak, the horror of the situation dawned on Crassus. He was isolated from the other Roman forces, and although he managed to get back onto a proper road, the Parthian attacks made him again seek a defensive position on a hill. His commander Octavius saw him, and the danger he was in, and brought his own contingent to drive off the attackers and form up in close order with Crassus' men. This posed a challenge for Surena: his men were getting weary of the fighting, and there was a danger that the Romans might slip out of his grasp. So again he employed subterfuge. Firstly, he released some Roman prisoners, who had heard his men saying, as they had been told to do, that Orodes did not want an endless war, and wanted to make a gesture of goodwill by treating Crassus kindly. Secondly, Surena called a halt to the fighting. And thirdly, he rode up the hill, unstrung his bow, and made Crassus an offer: 'I have put your valour and power to the test against the wishes of the king, who now of his own accord shows you the mildness and friendliness of his feelings by offering to make a truce with you if you will withdraw, and by affording you the means of safety.'[26]

Crassus was now not so trusting of barbarians as he once had been, but his misgivings were overridden by his soldiers, and he and Octavius set out to meet Surena.

Plutarch tells us that 'the first of the barbarians to meet him were two half-breed Greeks'.[27] It is likely that they traced their descent back to Alexander the Great's army, which had come through the region in the fourth century BC, and it is interesting to see who counts as a 'barbarian' in Plutarch's account here. The two men facilitated a very tense encounter between Crassus on foot and Surena on horseback, in which the Parthian announced a truce between Orodes II and the Romans, but said that they should go to the River Euphrates to set down the terms in writing, because Parthians didn't trust Romans at this stage. A scuffle then broke out when Surena's men produced a horse with a gold-studded bridle, unceremoniously hoisted Crassus onto it, and started to drive it along. Octavius and others surrounded the horse; swords were drawn; Octavius killed the groom of one of the barbarians; and Crassus was hacked down by a Parthian named Pomaxathres.[28]

There are other versions of Crassus' death, although Plutarch points out that these are all matters of conjecture. He mentions a different unnamed killer, who cut off Crassus' head and right hand as he lay on the ground; Dio Cassius records a version in which Crassus was slain by one of his own men so that he would not be captured alive.[29] There are also stories that his body was ritually humiliated. In one, the Parthians poured molten gold into his mouth to mock his wealth. In another, Surena staged a parody of a triumph, in which a captive who looked like Crassus was dressed in women's clothes, put on horseback, and preceded by trumpeters and lictors on camels. The lictors' *fasces* had purses suspended from them, and their axes were adorned with severed Roman heads. Behind them was a procession of prostitutes singing filthy songs about Crassus' effeminacy and cowardice. Surena also discovered a set of risqué books among the Roman baggage, notably the *Fabula Milesiaca* of Aristides, but his efforts to exploit these on moral grounds backfired. In one of Aesop's *Fables* there is the story of the two wallets, which everyone carries – one in front that contains his neighbour's faults, which he can always see, and one behind with his own faults in it, which he never sees. People were reminded of this when they saw Surena with a wallet of pornography from the *Milesiaca* in front of him, but trailing wagon-loads of concubines behind him: 'It was hypocritical of the Parthians to find fault with the *Milesiaca*, when many of the Arsacid royal line were sprung from Milesian . . . courtesans.'[30]

Plutarch also tells a bizarre tale of Crassus' severed head being used in a macabre re-enactment of Euripides' tragedy *The Bacchae* at Orodes' court. The king was well versed in Greek literature, and a celebrity actor was performing excerpts from the play, in which Queen Agave unknowingly dismembers her son Pentheus thinking he is a lion. As her delirium subsides, she realises she is actually holding his head. When Crassus' real head was tossed into the middle of the banqueters, the Parthians were ecstatic, and to universal delight the actor slipped seamlessly into the role of Agave, and sang as if inspired:

We bring from the mountain
A tendril fresh-cut to the palace,
A wonderful prey.[31]

Crassus' expedition had become a farcical tragedy. Some of his soldiers surrendered, but the ones who tried to escape were hunted down and cut to pieces. According to Plutarch 20,000 Romans lost their lives in the campaign, and 10,000 were taken prisoner.

The consequences of Surena's victory in 53 BC were far-reaching. On the personal level, he became a victim of his own success, since Orodes felt threatened by his burgeoning popularity and had him executed.[32] But Roman expansionism in the east was stopped in its tracks, Mesopotamia reverted to Parthian control, and the River Euphrates became the eastern border of the Roman Empire. The two powers were now very much on an equal footing, but they were also fierce rivals, and would remain so for the next 700 years. The Parthians do not seem to have developed any desire to conquer Rome at this stage, but Roman generals would periodically look to the east in their quests for glory.[33] In 44 BC Julius Caesar was planning an expedition to avenge Crassus' defeat, but the Sibylline Books prophesied that the Parthian Empire could only be destroyed by a king – a complete anathema to Roman Republican ideals – and on the eve of his departure Caesar was murdered by a group of conspirators that ironically included Crassus' ex-commander Cassius.[34]

14

Vercingetorix: Rebellion in Gaul

Rome and the Gauls

By 59 BC, Julius Caesar as consul had given the First Triumvirate the items on its wish list (see pp. 243 ff.). He had taken Cisalpine Gaul and Illyricum as his *provincia* for five years, and when the governor of Transalpine Gaul died at a convenient (though not suspicious) juncture, he had added this to his area of control. The following year he embarked on the conquest of the areas of Gaul that lay outside Roman dominion, on the pretext of terminating the supposed Gallic threat to Italy. Brennus' sack of Rome lived long in the memory, and Rome always regarded its imperial conquests as essentially defensive.

Caesar himself left a priceless first-hand account of his activities in Gaul, written in highly idiosyncratic prose: *De Bello Gallico* (*On the Gallic War*, aka *The Commentaries*). The work was designed as propaganda to inflate his image at Rome, in which it was very successful, but despite the heavy bias in favour of 'Caesar' (he always talks about himself in the third person), it also sheds invaluable light on how certain barbarians appeared to Roman eyes. There is, unfortunately, no written material from the Gaulish side, although archaeology can add to, or sometimes contradict, the ancient narratives.[1]

Caesar begins with the immortal statement '*Gallia est omnis divisa in partes tres . . .*' ('All Gaul is divided into three parts . . .'),[2] and tells his readers that these are inhabited by the Belgae, Aquitani and a people who call themselves Celts, though the Romans call them Gauls. Each of these three parts had its own language and laws, and was comprised of smaller tribes. Labelling them as 'Gauls', 'Celts' or suchlike can create a misleading sense of unity, since allegiances and identities were very localised, as Caesar himself explains: 'In Gaul there are factions not only in all the states, and in all the cantons and their divisions, but almost in each family, and of these factions those are the leaders who are considered according to their judgment to possess the greatest influence.'[3]

In terms of social hierarchy Caesar says that the Druids (see p. 334) and the Knights (the leading warriors) are the only two classes of men who have any rank and dignity, while the common people never act on their own initiative, take no part in political decision-making, and are practically treated as slaves. If the lower classes fall into debt, or if they are simply oppressed by more powerful people, they bind themselves to serve the nobles, who have the same rights over them as masters do over slaves.[4]

Barbarians are often characterised as being the exact opposite of the Romans, and so it is with Caesar's Gauls. They are extremely superstitious, and at times of major crisis they perform human sacrifices, carried out by the Druids, because they think that the gods can only be made favourable if the life of one man is offered for that of another. One method of doing this to build colossal wicker figures, fill their limbs with living men and set them alight. They think that criminals are the best people to use in these rites, because that is more acceptable to the gods, but they are happy to use innocent people if suitable villains can't be found.

The Gauls have divinities whom the Romans equate with their own. Mercury, the inventor of all arts, is particularly popular, and thought to act as a guide on their journeys, as well as overseeing commerce; Apollo, Mars, Jupiter and Minerva receive the same respect that they get from other peoples: Apollo averts disease; Minerva oversees industry and craft production; Jupiter is King of the Gods; and Mars is the war deity, to whom they dedicate all the booty that they capture, with transgressors punished by hideous torture and death.[5] They also claim descent from Dis, the god of Death and the Underworld, which is why they calculate all their dates using nights rather than days.[6]

Other barbarous customs that attract Caesar's interest are that the Gauls forbid their children to approach them until they have reached military age, and they think it is wrong for a son who is still a boy to stand with his father in public. Their women also receive strange treatment. Husbands match their wives dowries out of their own property, and whoever outlives the other inherits all the property, plus any profit made on the estate. Husbands have the power of life and death over their wives and children, and if a high-ranking male death looks suspicious, the wife is put on trial in the same way as a slave (which involves the use of torture), and if convicted she is put to death with extreme torture. Caesar says that, 'considering the state of civilization among the Gauls',[7] their funerals are magnificent and expensive. All their dearest possessions, including animals, are burned on the pyre, and in the period just prior to Caesar's arrival, he says, they also burned their slaves and favourite retainers after the funeral.

The tribes who were reckoned to have the best government also kept close control over their 'social media': anyone who heard a rumour or news from a neighbouring country that concerned the state, had to tell it straight to a magistrate, and not anyone else, because they felt that ignorant and impulsive people were often frightened by 'fake news' into subversive acts and meddling in important state affairs. The magistrates had control over what information the people were allowed to know, and it was illegal to talk politics outside a public assembly.

One recent discovery that appears to support the ancient texts comes from Le Cailar in France. Diodorus Siculus and Strabo both wrote about the Gauls severing the heads of their enemies and then preserving them using ingredients that included cedar oil, before displaying them in front of their dwellings, or draping them around the necks of their horses, and refusing to return them, no matter how much gold they were offered. Decapitated skulls, which had had their brains removed, showed evidence of the biomarkers of embalming, specifically contact with conifer resin, providing us with a possible dovetailing of the literary and archaeological evidence.[8]

Vercingetorix's Rebellion

By the end of 56 BC Caesar had subjugated the Helvetii, smashed the Belgae and dealt successfully with some serious resistance by the Veneti on the Atlantic coast. This put him in control of an area that reached the River Meuse in the north and what the Romans called the Ocean in the west, and after making a punitive foray against the Germanic tribes across the

Rhine, he invaded Britain in 55 and 54 BC. He is evasive about what his goals in Britain really were, and it may be that he had unfinished business there, but whatever plans he had, they were stymied by a revolt of the Gallic tribes that kicked off in the winter of 54/53 BC. The Belgic Eburones wiped out *Legio* XIV, and it would take Caesar an entire year to get a grip on the situation, which ultimately involved virtual genocide in the territory between the Meuse and the Rhine.

The consulship of Gnaeus Pompeius Magnus and Quintus Caecilius Metellus Pius Scipio, 52 BC, was a year of considerable political upheaval in Rome. This was so intense that some of the Gauls hoped it would prevent Caesar, who had returned to Italy for the winter, from rejoining his troops in northern Gaul at the start of the year. This was the perfect moment for a rebellion. The Gauls started to complain about Roman oppression, and to talk tactics for achieving their liberty: it would be freedom or death; the Carnutes agreed to strike the first blow; solemn oaths were sworn; and a date was set. When the Carnutes slaughtered the Roman civilians at Cenabum (modern Orléans), the news was spread across the region in the traditional Celtic fashion: in a world of little or no noise pollution they would shout to neighbouring communities, who would pass the message on in turn. By the end of the day, the information had reached the Arverni tribe, some 150 miles away,[9] where a chieftain called Vercingetorix (Ouergentorix in the Greek sources) was spurred into action.

Caesar describes Vercingetorix as 'a young man of supreme power'.[10] His father Celtillus had been an Arvernian chieftain and once 'held the supremacy of all Gaul',[11] but had been put to death by his own people because he wanted to become king.

Vercingetorix now attempted to mobilise the Arverni, but he was expelled from their capital Gergovia (near present-day Clermont-Ferrand and Gergovie) by a group of chiefs, including his uncle Gobannitio, who thought the project was too risky. But Vercingetorix was undeterred. He recruited beggars and outcasts from the fields, joined them up with other Arverni who shared his dreams, and expelled his opponents. He was now called 'King' (*Rex*) by his followers.[12]

His rallying cry for freedom brought the neighbouring tribes of the Senones, Parisii, Pictones, Cadurci, Turoni, Aulerci, Lemovices, Andi and various maritime peoples of the Atlantic coasts to his cause, and he was unanimously given the supreme command. He demanded hostages, specified the troop quotas for each tribe, insisted on the manufacture of weapons by a particular date, focused particularly on the cavalry contingents, and enforced his will by terrorism. Anyone who failed to comply was put to death with fire and torture, although for minor offences he merely sent people home with their ears cut off or one eye gouged out.[13]

Vercingetorix held the initial advantage: the new revolt was separating Caesar in Cisalpine Gaul to the south from his army in the north of Gaul; the southern and central parts of Gaul had not rebelled before, so Vercingetorix had surprise on his side; and because of this the Roman province of Transalpine Gaul was poorly defended. Vercingetorix sent Lucterius of the Cadurci south to attack the Ruteni on the border of the Transalpine Province, hoping to prevent Caesar moving north, while he himself moved northwards to attack the Bituriges of west-central Gaul. They initially looked to their overlords the Aedui for help, but when this was not forthcoming, they joined Vercingetorix's revolt.[14]

Caesar managed to confound Vercingetorix's plans by shoring up the defences of Transalpine Gaul, before doing a 'mini-Hannibal' and taking a small force across the snow-clad Cévennes Mountains, into Vercingetorix's homeland: 'He cleared away snow six feet deep and, having thus opened up the roads by a supreme effort of the troops, reached the borders of the Arverni. They were caught off their guard, for they thought themselves fortified by the Cevennes as by a wall, and not even a solitary traveller had ever found the paths open at that season of the year.'[15]

Plutarch remarks that 'the vigour and speed of his passage in so severe a winter showed the barbarians that an unconquered and invincible army was coming against them'.[16]

Caesar correctly anticipated that Vercingetorix would come back to protect his homeland, and used the diversion to move to Vienna (modern Vienne in south-east France), and then on through the territory of the Aedui into that of the Lingones, where he joined his legions in the north.

Vercingetorix responded by assaulting the town of Gorgobina in the territory of the Boii (precise location unknown). Caesar was effectively responsible for protecting Gorgobina, and he had to weigh up the drawbacks of allowing Vercingetorix to pick off his allies one by one against some pressing problems of logistics and supply. Electing to move his legions before he really wanted to, Caesar headed south and took Vellaunodunum (possibly modern Montargis or Château-Landon), where he acquired pack animals, followed by Cenabum on the Loire, before attacking the Bituriges' stronghold of Noviodunum Biturigum (probably modern Neung-sur-Beuvron). Vercingetorix raised the siege of Gorgobina to confront the Romans at Noviodunum, but by the time his cavalry outriders made visual contact with the town it was already in the process of surrendering. The sight of the Gallic cavalry convinced some of the townspeople to carry on fighting, but after the Romans got the better of a cavalry engagement outside the settlement, the Gauls fell into a panic, seized the ringleaders of the resistance, took them to Caesar and surrendered themselves as well.[17]

Avaricum

Vercingetorix's defeat at Noviodunum Biturigum in 52 BC changed the dynamics of the war. He now tried to deprive Caesar of supplies by using a comprehensive scorched-earth policy that involved the destruction of both crops and *oppida* (towns). Vercingetorix told the assembled chieftains that 'if these measures seemed grievous or cruel, they ought to take into account that it was far more grievous that their children and their wives should be dragged off into slavery, and that they themselves should be slaughtered – the inevitable fate of the conquered.'[18]

He received unanimous support. In one single day more than twenty towns of the Bituriges were torched. The fires could be seen everywhere, and though the Gauls found this incredibly upsetting, they consoled themselves with the thought that they would recover their losses in the inevitable victory that would follow. But they also dithered about what to do with Avaricum (modern Bourges), where there was a large supply of grain that the Romans desperately wanted. Burn it, or defend it? 'The Bituriges flung themselves at the feet of all the Gauls, entreating that they might not be compelled with their own hands to set light to almost the fairest city in all Gaul, the safeguard and the ornament of their state. They declared that they would easily defend themselves by its natural strength, for it was surrounded by river and marsh on almost every side, and had a single and a very narrow approach.'[19] Vercingetorix expressed his scepticism, but bowed to popular opinion.

Caesar began a twenty-seven-day siege. Initially Vercingetorix camped fifteen miles away and harassed the Roman foraging parties whenever he could. Amid heavy spring rain Caesar's men started to construct two towers, as well as an impressively high siege terrace. The Gauls made desperate attempts to counter these, raising towers of their own to match the height of Caesar's, attacking his soldiers as they worked and tunnelling under the terrace to undermine them.

As the Roman work neared completion, Vercingetorix moved his camp nearer to Avaricum and tried to lure a Roman foraging party into an ambush. But the Romans found out about his plan and, while Vercingetorix was away, Caesar led his army out and offered battle. But the Gauls were reluctant to engage in Vercingetorix's absence. Caesar returned to the siege, while the Gauls accused Vercingetorix of treason for riding off and leaving them vulnerable and leaderless. Had he made a deal with Caesar, they wondered? Vercingetorix needed all his verbal dexterity to convince them that he was genuine, and he also persuaded them that the Romans were weak, demoralised and on the point of giving up.[20]

The Romans were none of the above, but the Gauls sent 10,000 reinforcements to Avaricum. Roman persistence now met Gallic ingenuity, as the Romans built a ramp 25 metres high and 100 metres wide, which Vercingetorix's men tried to destroy with counter-mines, blazing torches and burning pitch. Their resistance has heroically desperate:

A certain Gaul before the gate of the town was hurling into the fire over against a turret lumps of grease and pitch that were handed to him. He was pierced by a dart from a 'scorpion'[21] in the right side and fell dead. One of the party next [to] him stepped over his prostrate body and went on with the same work; and when this second man had been killed in the same fashion by a scorpion-shot, a third succeeded, and to the third a fourth; and that spot was not left bare of defenders until the ramp had been extinguished, the enemy cleared away on every side, and a stop put to the fighting.[22]

When the Gallic warriors decided to try to escape silently from the city during the night, their wives begged them not to leave them and their children behind to whatever fate awaited them at Roman hands. The men remained implacable, so the women started to make as much noise as they could to alert the Romans to what was happening. The men abandoned the plan.

In the end, it was the weather that defeated the Gauls. When heavy wind and rain forced them to take their defensive duties less seriously than they should have done, Caesar's men seized the moment, made an all-out attack that took the Gauls by surprise, dislodged the defenders from the walls, trapped them in the city, and took vengeance for the massacre at Cenabum and the difficulty of the siege. Old men, women and children were slaughtered alongside the fighting men – 40,000 in total, if we believe Caesar. Just 800 made it across to Vercingetorix's camp.[23]

Despite the defeat, Vercingetorix's stock remained high. He was quick to point out that the defence of Avaricum had never been his idea, that the disaster had been brought about by the stupidity of the Bituriges, and that the Romans had prevailed because of their expertise in siege operations, not by courage on a conventional battlefield. He himself was undefeated, and the Gauls remained enthusiastic about his leadership.[24]

Gergovia

Vercingetorix's reputation went up another level in the next phase of the campaign. The Romans recuperated at Avaricum for a few days, and once their hunger and fatigue had worn off Caesar prepared to resume the campaign. He was distracted by envoys from the powerful pro-Roman Aedui, who were on the brink of civil war over the issue of which of their leaders should hold sovereign power for the year. He had to settle the dispute, and do it in person. This he did, travelling to Decatia (modern Decize in central France), deciding in favour of the wealthy young aristocrat Convictolitavis, promising the tribe rewards at the end of the war, and telling them to send him all their cavalry and 10,000 infantry. He then sent four legions north against the Senones and Parisii, while he himself led six legions through the territory of the Arverni along the River Allier (Elaver in Latin) to attack Gergovia.

Caesar needed to cross the river to get to Gergovia, but it wasn't fordable at that time of year, and Vercingetorix had destroyed all the bridges and was guarding the opposite bank. Caesar fooled Vercingetorix by sending four legions along the river, but keeping two of them hidden in a wooded area. While the Gauls shadowed the main contingent, the other legions came out of hiding, rebuilt one of the bridges and crossed over to the west bank. Vercingetorix was unwilling to fight a pitched battle, so he pressed on to Gergovia too:[25] 'Vercingetorix . . . pitched camp near the town, and then placed the forces of each state separately around himself at short distances. They occupied every ridge on the hills from where they could get a downward view, and they presented an awesome appearance.'[26]

The town of Gergovia stood on a steep hill with difficult approaches, and Caesar instantly realised that he couldn't take it by storm, so he prepared for a siege. Looking to secure his own food supplies and deprive the Gauls of theirs, he managed to capture a precipitous hill opposite the town, from where he could deny the defenders access to fresh water and restrict their foraging activities. Two legions were then stationed on the hill, while the other four set up camp on the plain. Caesar then linked the two camps with a 4-metre wide double trench to give his soldiers access between them.[27]

So far so good for Caesar. But then barbarian treachery ruined his plans. Convictolitavis of the Aedui repaid Caesar for his support by accepting bribes from the Arverni and defecting to Vercingetorix:

> The state of the Aedui was the only bar to the absolutely certain victory of Gaul [Convictolitavis said]; by its influence the rest were held in check; if it were brought over, the Romans would have no foothold in Gaul. It was true that he himself had received some benefit at Caesar's hands, but simply in the sense that he had won an entirely just cause before him, and he had a greater duty to the general liberty. Why should the Aedui come to Caesar to decide a question of their own right and law, rather than the Romans to the Aedui?[28]

Convictolitavis put his ally Litaviccus in charge of the 10,000 infantry who had been assigned to reinforce Caesar, and when they got to within a few days' march of the Roman camp, Litaviccus delivered some 'alternative truth': 'Whither, soldiers, are we proceeding? All our horsemen, all our chivalry is perished; Eporedorix and Viridomarus, chief men of our state, have been accused of treachery by the Romans, and put to death with their cause unheard.'[29]

He produced 'witnesses' who said they had seen this with their own eyes, and the Aedui responded by torturing and killing the Romans who were with the army, and by getting ready to join Vercingetorix. When Caesar heard this fake news, he countered it by leading four legions towards the oncoming Aeduan infantry and producing the supposedly dead Eporedorix and Viridomarus, who had been with him all along, for all to see. Litaviccus fled to Vercingetorix, and his men joined Caesar as originally planned.

The siege did not go well for Caesar. When an unexpected opportunity to attack the Gallic positions on the hill outside arose, he sent his legions in. Three Gallic camps were captured, but instead of halting the attack as they had been instructed, all except *Legio* X pressed on, motivated by greed and over-enthusiasm, and stormed the walls of Gergovia itself. Gallic reinforcements converged on the city, and 'when a great host of them had assembled, the matrons who a moment before were stretching out their hands to the Romans from the wall began to adjure their own men and, in Gallic fashion, to show dishevelled hair and to bring their children forward into view'.[30]

The Romans were outnumbered and exhausted. The attack ended in chaos, and the situation was only saved when *Legio* X and some cohorts of *Legio* XIII intervened. The Romans returned to camp having lost 46 centurions and almost 700 men.

Caesar needed to save face. The following day he repri-
manded his men for their impetuosity and for disobeying his
orders, and then, looking for a relatively honourable way of
retreating, he led his men out in full battle array on two
consecutive days. Vercingetorix wisely refused to accept the
invitation to an unequal fight, which allowed Caesar to claim
that he had subdued the Gaulish bravado, before he marched
back along the Allier and into the lands of the Aedui. Dio
Cassius sees the siege of Gergovia in a somewhat different light,
however: 'Caesar's time was being spent to no purpose . . . on
the whole he was being repulsed.'[31]

It is true that the successful defence of Gergovia in 52 BC
wasn't really down to any specific action by Vercingetorix, and
it represents just a thwarting of Roman intentions rather than
a significant defeat, but it was still enormously significant for
being the only time in the entire Gallic War that Caesar suffered
a major repulse with an army of which he was personally in
command. Vercingetorix' immortality rests largely on that fact.

Alesia

Vercingetorix's success may have influenced the Aedui to back
what they thought was the winning side. Convictolitavis and
Litaviccus concluded an alliance with Vercingetorix, and
proceeded to massacre the garrison and merchants at
Noviodunum on the Loire and to burn the town of Bibracte.
Rumours spread that Caesar had retired to Gallia Transalpina,
and other tribes joined the uprising, although the Remi and
Lingones stayed loyal to Rome, and the Treveri remained
neutral. The Aedui wanted to take command of the insurrection, but at a pan-Gallic council it was Vercingetorix who was

confirmed as leader, much to the annoyance of Eporedorix and Viridomarus. The strategy was again to conduct a scorched-earth policy to frustrate the Romans, while at the same time attacking other Gallic tribes who were not signed up to the revolt.

While Caesar was assembling and organising his resources, Vercingetorix decided to seek a battle and settle the issue once and for all:

> He called the cavalry commanders together to a council of war, and stated that the hour of victory was come. The Romans were fleeing to the Province and leaving Gaul. In his opinion that was enough to secure a temporary liberty, but it was too small a gain to give peace and quiet for the future; for they would return when they had collected a large force and would make no end of the war. Therefore, the Gauls must attack them while encumbered with baggage in column of route.[32]

The Gauls did attack, but they were no match for the well-organised Roman legionaries and their powerful auxiliary cavalry. There was now no option but for Vercingetorix to withdraw. The Romans pursued him to the stronghold of Alesia (*Alisiia* to its inhabitants; modern Alise-Sainte-Reine near Dijon), in the territory of the Mandubii, where he soon found himself facing the might of Roman picks and shovels.

Vercingetorix was able to send his cavalry away with orders to bring reinforcements, but Caesar intended to starve him out before any relief force might come to his rescue. The Roman circumvallation was one of the most astounding pieces of military engineering that they had ever achieved: a 15-kilometre-long network of defences: facing Alesia was a 7-metre-wide trench with perpendicular sides, to inhibit any surprise attack; 600 metres behind this they dug two 5-metre-wide trenches, the inner one filled with water; behind these trenches was a 4-metre-high palisaded rampart, with a battlemented breastwork with large forked branches projecting outwards to stop any attackers climbing up it; and towers were erected every 120 metres along the entire circuit of the fortification.[33]

Archaeological research suggests that the system was never fully completed, but it was sufficient to trap the Gauls in their *oppidum*, and as they fought to escape, the Romans added further elements: 'tombstones' – tree trunks and strong branches with sharp points were embedded in rows of five in front of the trenches to impale anyone who pushed into them; in front of them, they dug eight diagonal rows of pits, which they called 'lilies', 1 metre deep, with a thick sharpened stake at the bottom and covered with twigs and brushwood to conceal the trap; and in front of them they put 'spurs' – 30-centimetre-long logs that were buried in the ground with iron hooks attached to them.[34] And as if that wasn't enough, knowing that Vercingetorix had sent for reinforcements, Caesar constructed a similar line of fortifications, 22 kilometres long, facing outwards.

Each of Caesar's troops had rations for one month,[35] but Vercingetorix's people were running out of corn. The Gauls debated what to do, and Caesar records a speech of 'singularly transgressive cruelty'[36] made by Critognatus, advising them to do like their ancestors had when they had been assailed by the Cimbri and the Teutones: eat the flesh of those who were too old or too young to fight. They felt this should only be a last resort, but they did expel all the Mandubii, along with their wives and children. Vercingetorix hoped that they would be 'rescued' into slavery by the Romans, and that there would now be more supplies to go round; but Caesar refused to take them in. He didn't have enough food for them, and he fully expected the Gauls to take them back and so make their own lack of food worse. In the end, neither side took them, and they died of starvation in no-man's-land.[37]

Caesar gives a catalogue of the multi-tribal force that assembled to relieve the town: a quarter of a million infantry and 8,000 cavalry.[38] They revelled in their numbers and magnificence, and the defenders of Alesia were overjoyed at their arrival. Now it was the Romans who were surrounded. Still, they beat off the first assault by the relieving army in a day-long cavalry engagement, before the Gauls made a second strike at midnight on the next day. Vercingetorix led his men out of the town in support, but the engagement became hopelessly confused in the darkness, and the relieving Gauls could find no way of hurting the Romans. They just ended up caught on the 'spurs', impaled in the pits or shot by the Roman artillery on the rampart and the towers. Not one of them penetrated the Roman defences. Vercingetorix's inner force took too long to attack the entrenchments, and when they found out that their countrymen had withdrawn, they returned to the *oppidum*.

The relieving force held a council of war: 'Both sides felt that this was the hour of all others in which it was proper to make their greatest effort. The Gauls utterly despaired of safety unless they could break through the lines; the Romans anticipated an end of all toils if they could hold their own.'[39]

The third Gallic attack came closest to succeeding. They saw that Caesar had a camp on the northern side of Alesia, where a steep hill had made it impossible to include in the fortification ring. When they attacked it, Vercingetorix could see what was happening, and he responded by making a sortie from the *oppidum*. It was touch and go as the Romans struggled to cope with the simultaneous attacks. The Gauls made it into the fortification network, filled the trenches with soil, pulled down the ramparts and breastworks with grappling hooks, and dislodged the Romans from the towers. But, if we believe his account, Caesar had the situation under control. Resplendent in the scarlet cloak that he always wore in action,[40] he marshalled his squadrons and cohorts with consummate skill, urged his men to hold out and turned the battle in his favour. The relieving force fled the field: 'So quickly did so great a force, like a phantom or a dream, disperse and vanish out of sight, the greater part of them having fallen in the battle.'[41]

They dispersed to their homes, leaving Vercingetorix with no option but to surrender.

In Caesar's *Commentaries* the handover of Vercingetorix is a very mundane affair: the Arvernian tells his assembled tribal leaders that he had always acted in the interests of Gallic liberty, and instructs them either to kill or surrender him. They choose the latter. In Plutarch's *Life of Caesar*, however, the meeting between the two leaders is more dramatic: 'Vercingetorix, after putting on his most beautiful armour and decorating his horse, rode out through the gate. He made a circuit around Caesar, who remained seated, and then leaped down from his horse, stripped off his suit of armour, and seating himself at Caesar's feet remained motionless, until he was delivered up to be kept in custody for the Triumph.'[42]

Vercingetorix was deported to Rome and imprisoned in the same jail where Jugurtha had languished (the Tullianum; see p. 174). He remained there for a number of years, until he was brought out and displayed in the triumph that Caesar held in

46 BC, at the end of which he was executed.[43] The great Nobel Prize-winning, nineteenth-century classical historian Theodor Mommsen (1817–1903) stated, without evidence, that Vercingetorix was publicly beheaded,[44] but that is unlikely: beheading was the 'privilege' of the Roman elite; it is more likely that he was strangled.

It took Caesar another couple of years to mop up the final Gallic resistance, but the defeat of Vercingetorix had been a key moment. Caesar had reasserted control, and the Gauls had paid a horrifically high price: over the Gallic Wars around 1,000,000 of their people had died, and roughly the same number had been enslaved. That was the price of *Pax Romana* ('Roman Peace'), on Julius Caesar's terms: 'Accordingly, by addressing the states in terms of honour, by bestowing ample presents upon the chiefs, by imposing no new burdens, he easily kept Gaul at peace after the exhaustion of so many defeats, under improved conditions of obedience.'[45]

Caesar's conquests added a rich and populous area about twice the size of Italy to Rome's dominions, and established his reputation as one of the most effective generals in history. For his part, Vercingetorix's story illustrates just how dangerous even the developed 'barbarian' tribes of Gaul could be to Rome, but the aftermath of his revolt also shows how completely they submitted to Roman *imperium* once they had been brought to heel.

15

Cleopatra VII: The Whore Queen of Incestuous Canopus

The Ptolemies of Egypt

Caesar's conquests in Gaul radically altered the centre of gravity of the Roman Empire, and brought him adulation from the army and the Plebs. However, he continually faced opposition, obstruction and violent resistance from a hardcore of rivals within the Roman aristocracy, some of whom harboured a deep hatred of him as a person, and of everything he stood for. Once he had extinguished the embers of Vercingetorix's rebellion he became embroiled in an escalating series of events, which led to him crossing the River Rubicon in 49 BC and plunging the state into yet another series of civil wars: 'And in them what battles were fought, and what blood was shed, so that almost all the peoples of Italy, which formed the main strength of the Roman Empire, were conquered as if they were barbarians!'[1]

The ruler of Egypt at that time was a dynamic young woman who had come to the throne in 51 BC. Her name was Cleopatra. Egypt was no longer the mighty power that built the pyramids: when Alexander the Great took control of the country in

332 BC, it had already been ruled by the Persians for around 200 years. Alexander founded the city of Alexandria, which quickly grew into a vibrant multicultural centre, and after he died in 323 BC his general Ptolemy seized control and established a dynasty that was to rule Egypt, with varying degrees of effectiveness, for some three centuries. Cleopatra had an extraordinary gene pool. Ptolemy I 'the Saviour' was Macedonian, as were all the succeeding rulers, who, with the exception of Cleopatra, known as Cleopatra VII Thea Philopator ('Divine, Father-loving'), were all called Ptolemy. The majority of them practised brother–sister marriage, and the internal dynamics of the dynasty were, at times, complex and vicious. Barbara Chase-Riboud's poem 'Portrait of a Nude Woman as Cleopatra', in which Cleopatra VII is explaining her family history to one of her lovers, gives a wonderful flavour of this:

> But beware, beloved, Ptolemy women engender violence,
> Command money, men, and manumission.
> Cleopatra revels in infanticide, regicide and parricide.
> Ptolemy the builder of the museum[2] fathered
> Ptolemy II, who exiled his wife to marry his sister.
> Ptolemy IV murdered his father, brother, and mother;
> Married his sister but murdered her.
> Ptolemy V married Cleopatra and fathered
> Ptolemy VI, who married his sister Cleopatra, who
> Married both her two brothers, of which one brother,
> Ptolemy VIII, murdered his child Cleopatra out of
> Vengeance on his wife and sister when she became queen.
> He then married his wife Cleopatra's daughter by her
> Second husband, his brother and she, his niece.
> Ptolemy VII, murdered by his father and uncle, who had

Married his mother, who was also his sister, whom he
Murdered on her wedding night, was also brother to
Ptolemy IX, the other son murdered by his father,
Or his aunt, or his half sister.
Ptolemy X, married his sister Cleopatra, but
Ptolemy XI murdered his mother Cleopatra.
Ptolemy XII married his cousin Cleopatra but murdered
Her and was himself murdered by the people.
Ptolemy X, a son of Ptolemy XII, fathered a
Cleopatra whom he murdered to regain the throne,
Leaving this Cleopatra beside you.[3]

All those Ptolemy women are called Cleopatra because the name means 'Daughter of a Noble Father' in Greek. Yet the Romans feared and hated her to an extreme degree, and as W. W. Tarn very aptly put it: 'Rome, who had never condescended to fear any nation or people, did in her time fear two human beings. One was Hannibal, the other was a woman.'[4]

Cleopatra VII Thea Philopator

Cleopatra VII was born in 69 BC, and in 51 BC she succeeded her father, Ptolemy XII. He had a reputation for being a dissolute and arrogant ruler, and he earned himself the derisory title of 'the Flute Player'. He had spent much of his reign trying to win Roman approval and support, which he ultimately did with a massive bribe to Julius Caesar. His last will and testament decreed that Cleopatra should marry the elder of her two younger brothers, Ptolemy XIII, and reign jointly with him. So, this late-teenaged girl now possessed the once boundless powers of the pharaohs. This is illustrated by a relief dating from the first year of her reign, now in the Louvre, in which she is depicted as a male pharaoh wearing the crown of Upper and Lower Egypt, making an offering of two globular vases to the goddess Isis. The accompanying inscription reads: 'On behalf of Queen Cleopatra Thea Philopator, the (holy) place of the association of (Isis) Snonaitiake, of whom the president is the chief priest Onnophris. Year I, Epeiph I.'[5] It is interesting that Shakespeare's Octavius was to disparage Antony as

> . . . not more man-like
> Than Cleopatra; nor the queen of Ptolemy
> More womanly than he.[6]

Our historical evidence about Cleopatra's childhood is lacking, although we do know that the Ptolemies had the highest regard for Greek art and literature, which they promoted assiduously, and this included an education system that sought to develop children's overall culture, or *enkukleios paideia* – the phrase from which we get our word 'encyclopaedia'. Plutarch tells us that Cleopatra had an extraordinary voice, and a special talent for foreign, 'barbarian' languages: 'It was a pleasure merely to hear the sound of her voice, with which, like an instrument of many strings, she could pass from one language to another; so that there were few of the barbarian nations that she answered by an interpreter; to most of them she spoke herself; as to the Aethiopians, Troglodytes, Hebrews, Arabians, Syrians, Medes, Parthians, and many others.'[7]

Her Greco-Macedonian heritage meant that Cleopatra herself was no barbarian, but to Roman eyes she would come to represent everything that was transgressive and diametrically opposite to Romanness. To them, she was worse than barbarous, and yet she had the ability to captivate everyone who came into her presence. Plutarch tells us how 'the charm of her conversation, and the character that attended all she said or did, was something bewitching'.[8] Dio Cassius also remarks on her voice and her people skills: 'She also possessed a very elegant voice and knew how to use her charms to make herself attractive to every one.'[9]

Cleopatra's charisma seems undeniable, but unfortunately no contemporary text gives us a specific physical description of her. Dio Cassius simply says that she was 'brilliant to look upon and to listen to, with the power to subjugate every one, even Julius Caesar, a love-sated man already past his prime'.[10] Plutarch was more circumspect, however: 'Her actual beauty . . . was not in and of itself so utterly astonishing that it was completely incomparable.'[11]

Her allure was undoubtedly down to her personality, but she could well have known how to 'make the best of herself', and she is credited with writing a treatise on cosmetics, although the advice given seems not for the faint-hearted: 'Against hairloss: make a paste of arsenic monosulphide and blend it into oak gum, apply it to a cloth and place it where you have already cleaned as thoroughly as possible with sodium carbonate . . . another: rub in a pounded mixture of heads of mice. Another: anoint with a paste of mouse-dung, after rendering the spot raw with a cloth.'[12]

Cleopatra's coin portraits tend to show her in a quite unattractively 'realistic' manner, with a lively expression and large eyes, and a distinctive profile that features a strong hooked nose and prominent chin. Her hair is drawn back from the face in what scholars call the *Melonenfrisur* ('melon hairstyle'), with braids of hair held underneath a broad diadem, and tied into a bun at the nape of her neck. When Mark Antony abandoned Octavia for her (see p. 293), the couple had coins issued with portraits celebrating their union. On the obverse ('heads') Cleopatra appears with the legend 'Queen Cleopatra Thea II', but in the nominative case, as it generally is on Roman coins, rather than the genitive ('of Queen Cleopatra'), as it would be on a Greek one. Again her nose, eyes and chin are exaggerated, and she sports the *Melonenfrisur*, the diadem, the bun and the curls, as well as some elaborate and rich clothing, with the décolletage of her tunic edged with pearls.[13] Despite the resplendent jewellery, it is an image far removed from the glamorous creatures of Hollywood. As Blaise Pascal said, 'Cleopatra's nose, had it been shorter, the whole face of the world would have been changed.'[14]

In portrait statues and busts her physical appearance often matches the coin images. One marble head includes the melon hairstyle and the royal diadem, with a lump of marble on the crown of the head that may be the remnants of a *uraeus* (cobra), as worn by several Ptolemaic queens. She is also represented with an Egyptian tripartite wig with a vulture headdress, as she is on works ranging from portraits in Rome to the wall of the temple of Hathor at Dendera in Egypt, where she wears both a vulture headdress and the cobra crown. Free-standing statues can also be more purely Egyptian in style, depicting her wearing sheath-like drapery[15] and sometimes showing sculptured make-up lines.[16] And there are also Greco-Romano-Egyptian hybrid types where she wears a knotted Egyptian-style costume, albeit sculpted with a strong Hellenised influence, and has a corkscrew wig and carries a cornucopia, both of which are Greek in origin.[17] Both in portraits and on coins she often has a double cornucopia,[18] and a defining attribute can be a triple *uraeus*, which was possibly used to distinguish her from the much earlier Queen Arsinoë II, who also carries the double cornucopia but wears a double *uraeus*, and otherwise bears a strong family resemblance to Cleopatra.

Cleopatra VII's images were incredibly important. Her Egyptian subjects regarded them as divine, and one of them was still being cared for at Philae 400 years after her death. And astonishingly, one of her sacred images survived for a very long time in the centre of Rome itself. It had been commissioned by Julius Caesar during her stay in Rome as his guest (see p. 290), and he had it erected in the temple of Venus Genetrix (the protectress of Caesar's family). It was still on display as late as the third century AD, when Dio Cassius wrote about it: 'And so, despite being defeated and taken prisoner, Cleopatra was still glorified, because her adornments now lie as dedications in our temples, and she herself is seen in gold in the temple of Venus.'[19]

Her images can sometimes be hard to identify with certainty, but her hieroglyphs are now much less so. During the process of decipherment of the Rosetta Stone (see p. 119), which is written in hieroglyphs, demotic (a cursive version of hieroglyphics) and Greek, Jean-François Champollion noticed that the positions of names within the Greek text could correspond with the oval cartouches that clearly marked out significant words or phrases in the hieroglyphic section. Ultimately it was the names on the Rosetta Stone that provided the clue to the decipherment of the hieroglyphics. The values assigned by Champollion to the hieroglyphs in the names Ptolemy (*Ptolemaios* in Greek) and Cleopatra (*Kleopatra* in Greek, although this is a different Cleopatra) were based on the assumption that, being of non-Egyptian origin, they would need to be spelled phonetically. The 'o' in both Ptolemy and Cleopatra is indicated by a looped rope or lasso, which has the phonetic value 'wa'. Two different signs are used where we would expect a 't', which indicates that one of them was pronounced more like our 'd'. Also, the lion symbol that appears in both names seems to have been an Egyptian compromise, because the l-sound doesn't occur in ancient Egyptian and the Egyptians really struggled to pronounce it. In foreign words, the 'l' was usually replaced by 'r' or 'rw', which is the phonetic value of the lion sign. Added together, it seems that the Egyptians pronounced Ptolemaios as 'Ptwarwmys', and Cleopatra as 'Krwiwapadra'.

Regardless of how much some people want it to be otherwise for various ideological reasons, Cleopatra's origins are not Egyptian, and she wasn't black. This is a modern concern: for the Romans, skin colour was a far less significant indicator in defining a person's identity than their culture.[20] Theories of Cleopatra's ethnicity have been constructed around two areas of uncertainty in her genealogy, firstly the identity of her mother, and secondly that of her paternal grandmother.[21] The Ptolemies went to quite extreme lengths to keep themselves 'pure-bred': in Cleopatra's case she was married to both her brothers; elsewhere in the dynasty uncles married their nieces; and her grandfather Ptolemy IX Lathyrus ('Chickpea') married his own daughter Cleopatra Berenice III. Cleopatra VII's grandmother was Ptolemy IX's concubine, not his wife, but as Mary Lefkowitz pertinently points out, 'because the Ptolemies seemed to prefer to marry among themselves, even incestuously, it has always been assumed that Cleopatra's grandmother was closely connected with the family. If she had been a foreigner, one of the Roman writers of the time would have mentioned it in an invective against Cleopatra as an enemy of the Roman state.'²² Likewise with her mother: information about her is scant, but officially she was her father's sister, Cleopatra V Tryphaena. Hostile Roman sources regularly smear Cleopatra VII with taunts of incest,²³ but never with having a non-Greek appearance or of belonging to an 'alien' race. Essentially Cleopatra VII was of Macedonian descent and regarded herself culturally as a Ptolemy, and therefore Hellenic, although for political and religious reasons she cast herself as the daughter of Re, the Sun god, and used the royal name *netjeret mer-it-es*, 'Goddess, Beloved of her Father'. The vitriolic Roman sources would undoubtedly have taken even the slightest hint that Cleopatra was 'mixed-race' and exploited it to the maximum. But they never did.

Cleopatra and Julius Caesar

From the moment she ascended to the throne in 51 BC, Cleopatra had to fight for it. Egypt was in a bureaucratic mess, riddled with insurgency, its currency was weak, and these problems were aggravated by hostility within Cleopatra's own circle. Her youngest sister, Arsinoë, coveted her position, while her brother-husband was under the control of three hostile and manipulative advisors: a eunuch, Photinus; a soldier Achillas; and a rhetorician Theodotus. But the teenage queen soon demonstrated her political acumen. She devalued the currency, engaged in a new religious policy, and when two sons of the Roman proconsul of Syria were assassinated in Alexandria in 50 BC, she delivered the alleged killers to him to demonstrate her pro-Roman sentiments. Egypt was nominally independent, but that freedom was exercised very much at Rome's discretion. Cleopatra knew that a good relationship with Rome was essential to her ambitions, but choosing precisely who to deal with was always going to be fraught with difficulty, especially as Rome descended into civil war within two years of her accession. Interestingly Cleopatra sent soldiers to Pompey during his rivalry with Julius Caesar, and rumour had it that she had a liaison with Pompey's son, Gnaeus Pompeius, when he visited Alexandria as an envoy. Her stance is understandable, since Pompey had supported her father Ptolemy XII, accommodating him at Rome when he had been expelled by his subjects in 57 BC.

On home soil Cleopatra's younger siblings Ptolemy and Arsinoë fomented a revolt which forced her to flee from Alexandria in early 48 BC. She quickly raised an army of mercenaries, and the rival armies would have done battle had not Pompey himself arrived unexpectedly at Pelusium in Egypt on 28 September, in the aftermath of his crushing defeat by Caesar's troops at the Battle of Pharsalus in Greece.[24] Given his guest-friendship with Ptolemy XIII's father, Pompey had hoped to receive a favourable welcome. But he was disappointed. Theodotus recommended assassinating him: 'Then he smiled and, we are told, added the words: "Dead men don't bite." '[25]

Caesar described the murder:

The favourites of [Ptolemy XIII], who were administering the kingdom for him on account of his youth . . . either (as they alleged later) swayed by the fear that Pompey might suborn the royal army and seize Alexandria and Egypt, or from contempt of him in his misfortune (it is usually the case that friends become enemies in adversity), gave to all appearances a very generous response to the envoys he had sent and bade him come to the king; but they themselves conferred together secretly and then sent Achillas, an officer of the king, a man of singular audacity, and Lucius Septimius, a Military Tribune, to kill Pompey. Pompey was addressed by them courteously and was induced to approach by some acquaintance with Septimius, who had led a Century under him in the war against the pirates. So he boarded a little boat, with a few of his companions; and there he was killed by Achillas and Septimius.[26]

Cicero was saddened, but not surprised, by these events: 'I never had any doubt about what would be the end of Pompey. Such a complete despair of his success had taken possession of the minds of all the kings and nations, that I thought this would happen wherever he landed. I cannot but lament his fall: for I know him to have been honest, pure, and a man of principle.'[27]

Caesar arrived a few days later and summoned the warring parties to Alexandria, which is where one of the great meetings of history ensued:

Since there seemed to be no other way of getting in unobserved, Cleopatra stretched herself out at full length inside a sleeping bag, and [had it] carried indoors to Caesar. This little trick of Cleopatra's, which showed her provocative impudence, is said to have been the first thing about her which captivated Caesar, and, as he grew to know her better, he was overcome by her charm and arranged that she and her brother should be reconciled and should share the throne of Egypt together.[28]

Fundamentally Caesar was after money and Cleopatra was after power. Caesar's decision actually involved him in a full-scale war in which the great Library of Alexandria was very badly damaged, but Ptolemy XIII was defeated and lost his life by drowning on 27 March 47 BC. Caesar installed Cleopatra as Queen of Egypt, and she took her other brother, the eleven-year-old Ptolemy XIV, as her husband and co-ruler. After a fortnight's amorous respite with Cleopatra, Caesar left Egypt for Syria, where he won his famous *'veni, vidi, vici'* battle at Zela. Whether Caesar was in fact the father of Cleopatra's son Caesarion ('Little Caesar') cannot now be known, but as he was born on 23 June 47 BC, Caesar's paternity must be very doubtful.

When Caesar returned to Rome in 46 BC he celebrated a triumph in which both Vercingetorix and Cleopatra's younger hostile sister Arsinoë were displayed. Cleopatra made her way to Rome, bringing Caesarion with her, and Caesar gave her accommodation in one of his villas. She seems to have behaved with the utmost decorum, but many Romans hated 'the Egyptian woman' so virulently that they couldn't even bring themselves to speak her name: In a letter to his friend Atticus, Cicero wrote, 'I hate the Queen . . . And another thing – I can't recall the Queen's insolence without intense indignation, at the time when she was in the pleasure-gardens across the Tiber.'[29]

However unrealistic and unlikely it was, the idea of Caesar becoming king with Cleopatra as his consort appalled the Roman elite, and when Caesar was assassinated on the Ides of March 44 BC, she was quick to leave the city. 'The Queen's flight does not upset me', said Cicero.[30]

Caesar's assassination unleashed another round of civil wars even more unpleasant than the most recent ones, which meant that Cleopatra's plans for power had to be put on hold. So she retired to Egypt to await the outcome, and when her brother, at the age of fourteen, demanded his share in the government, Cleopatra poisoned him.

Cleopatra and Mark Antony

One of the major players in the Roman civil wars that followed Caesar's death was his right-hand man Mark Antony, whose main opponent would be Gaius Octavius. Octavius was the main beneficiary of Caesar's will, in which he was adopted as his heir, which allowed him to change his name: historians call him 'Octavian', but he was officially Gaius Julius Caesar Octavianus. Antony sneeringly told him, 'Boy, you owe everything to your name,'[31] and in a sense he was right. Antony now took military control of the eastern end of the Roman Empire, but Cleopatra took emotional control of Antony. Her liaison with him began when she visited him at Tarsus (in modern south-east Turkey) in 41 BC. Antony was planning to invade Parthia, and sent for Cleopatra. She was delighted. She'd known him when he'd been in Egypt as a young officer when she was fourteen, but she was now twenty-eight or twenty-nine, 'the age when a woman's beauty is at its most superb and her mind at its most mature',[32] and filled with unshakeable self-confidence. Antony's henchman Dellius, who delivered the summons,

> was struck by the charm and subtlety of Cleopatra's conversation . . . and he saw at once that such a woman, so far from having anything to fear from Antony, would probably gain the strongest influence over him . . . Cleopatra had already

seen for herself the power of her beauty to enchant Julius Caesar and the younger Pompey, and she expected to conquer Antony even more easily . . . She therefore provided herself with as lavish a supply of gifts, money, and orna-ments as the prosperity of her kingdom made it appropriate to take, but she relied above all upon her physical presence and the spell and enchantment which it could create.[33]

When she did arrive, she was fashionably late:

She came sailing up the river in a barge with a poop of gold, its purple sails billowing in the wind, while her rowers caressed the water with oars of silver which dipped in time to the music of the flute . . . Cleopatra herself reclined beneath a canopy of cloth of gold, dressed in the character of Venus . . . while on either side stood boys costumed as Cupids, who cooled her with their fans. The barge was lined with the most beautiful of her waiting-women attired as Nereids and Graces, some at the rudders, others at the tackle of the sails, and all the while an indescribably rich perfume . . . was wafted from the vessel to the river-banks.[34]

Antony didn't stand a chance. Spurning his wife Fulvia, who was in Italy doing all she could to champion his interests against the growing menace of Octavian, Antony postponed the Parthian expedition and went back to Alexandria with the Ptolemaic queen.

Cleopatra knew exactly how to exploit Antony's weaknesses. In Egypt they began to put on incredibly opulent banquets. Plutarch's grandfather knew a student doctor at Alexandria who once saw eight wild boars being roasted. 'You must have a vast number dining,' he said. 'No,' he was told, 'only about twelve.'[35] The 'Inimitable Livers' as they called themselves wallowed in this kind of extravagant debauchery until Antony's deteriorating relations with Octavian forced him to return to Italy in 40 BC, leaving behind newborn twins, Alexander Helios and Cleopatra Selene.

Antony made a temporary settlement with Octavian. Fulvia had recently died, so Antony married Octavian's newly widowed, virtuous and serenely beautiful sister Octavia. Octavia was the perfect antidote to 'bad women' such as Cleopatra and Fulvia, and within three years she had given birth to two daughters, Antonia Maior and Antonia Minor, whom she raised alongside her children from her first marriage, as well as her two stepsons from Antony's marriage to Fulvia. Antony went straight back to the east with his new bride in tow, and minted coins depicting the two of them – the first time a clearly identifiable living woman had appeared on official Roman coinage in her own right. In the spring of 37 BC, Octavia helped to iron out some further differences between her husband and her brother, which were settled by the Treaty of Tarentum, after which she was hailed as 'a wonder woman'.[36]

Antony then headed east to resurrect the Parthian campaign. But this time he left his wife at Rome, and immediately renewed his affair with Cleopatra. This scenario is possibly depicted on the famous Portland Vase in the British Museum, where Antony appears on the left, transfixed by Eros, whose mission is accomplished – his bow is held downwards; his torch is held up – and is seduced in a 'typically Egyptian' outdoor setting by Cleopatra, who is accompanied by a serpent. She pulls him towards her, watched by Anton, an otherwise unknown son of Hercules invented by Antony as the legendary founder of his family. On the other side of the vase Octavia reclines in the attitude of an abandoned female lover, languishing on the wreckage of a shattered home underneath a fig tree in the Roman Forum, consoled by Octavian in the presence of Venus Genetrix, the protectress of Octavian's family.

Cleopatra produced another child, Ptolemy Philadelphus, in 36 BC, and the insult to Octavia was compounded when the queen took her place on coins that Antony minted after he finally scored some military success in Armenia. Putting the image of a foreign female monarch on official Roman coinage was utterly monstrous to Roman eyes, and Antony's enemies portrayed Cleopatra as 'the whore queen of impious [or incestuous] Canopus',[37] in contrast to Octavia, the virtuous, betrayed wife. Antony told Octavian that his criticism was utterly hypocritical from a man of his reputation: 'What's changed you? Because I'm fucking the Queen like a beast? . . . So you're only boning Drusilla, then? Good health to you, if when you read this letter, you haven't shagged Tertullia, or Terentilla, or Rufilla, or Salvia Titsenia – or all of them. Does it make any difference where, or in which woman, you get a hard-on?'[38]

But Octavian's spin-doctors exploited the romance between the Roman general and the eastern queen to great effect. Antony's Parthian campaign ended in costly failure, but in the autumn of 34 BC he still celebrated a fantastic triumph in Alexandria, and staged the event known as the 'Donations of Alexandria', which was seen as 'theatrical, arrogant, and anti-Roman'.[39] This provided an enormous propaganda gift to Octavian: Antony and Cleopatra held a ceremony where they sat on golden thrones, along with Caesarion and their own three children; Cleopatra was hailed as Queen of Kings,

Caesarion as King of Kings; and Antony granted to Cleopatra and her children huge tracts of territory in the east that were not his to give.

Hatred for 'the Egyptian' escalated at Rome throughout the following year, but even so, not everyone backed Octavian: both consuls and over 300 senators left Rome to join Antony early in 32 BC; Octavian nominated fresh consuls; Antony divorced Octavia; completely illegally Octavian published Antony's will, which allegedly showed that he wanted to relocate the capital from Rome to Alexandria; Antony moved into Greece with Cleopatra; Octavian secured a declaration of war against Cleopatra (it was essential that it was not seen as a civil war), and crossed to Greece for the final showdown.

The history of the ensuing events was almost entirely concocted by the winning side, and Octavian tells us that 'the whole of Italy of its own accord took an oath of allegiance to me and demanded that I should be its leader in the war . . . The same oath was taken by the provinces of Gaul and Spain, and by Africa, Sicily, and Sardinia.'[40]

He had a slight superiority in forces, and an excellent admiral in Marcus Vipsanius Agrippa, whereas Cleopatra's presence among Antony's troops was disruptive. Quite what happened at the crucial Battle of Actium, fought on 2 September 31 BC, is hard to ascertain in detail, but the end result was that Cleopatra's squadron escaped, Antony followed in her wake, and the remainder of their forces surrendered. Octavian placed a victory monument overlooking the battle site at Nicopolis ('Victory-City'), and the pro-Octavian poet Virgil later presented the battle as a clash between virtuous Romans and obscene barbarians:

On one side Augustus Caesar, high up on the poop, is
    leading
The Italians into battle, the Senate and People with him . . .
On the other side, with barbaric wealth and motley
    equipment,
Is Anthony, fresh from his triumphs in the East . . .
Egypt [*and*] the powers of the Orient . . .
Sail with him; also – a shameful thing – his Egyptian
    wife . . .
She cannot yet see the two serpents of death behind her.[41]

In a poem written soon after the battle of Actium, Horace
also brilliantly captured the Roman horror at what Antony's
relationship with Cleopatra implied:

Now Roman soldiers – lies, you'll say in later times –
Made over to a woman, bear
Weapons and stakes for her, can bring themselves to do
Whatever wrinkled eunuchs bid.
While, reared among our battle-standards – shameful sight! –
The sun can see mosquito-nets.[42]

His point is that a Roman soldier should take his insect bites
like a man: nothing could be more effete, more appalling, or
more un-Roman, more barbarian, than this.

Cleopatra and Octavian

Antony and Cleopatra fled to Egypt, where the final act of the
drama was played out as Octavian's army took Alexandria
around a year later. We have to treat the historical accounts

with caution, but it seems that Cleopatra barricaded herself into a mausoleum, which she had already constructed for herself, along with Eiras, Carmian and (according to Dio) a eunuch, and then sent messengers to tell Antony that she was dead. He responded by making a botched suicide attempt, but when he discovered that Cleopatra was still alive he ordered his slaves to carry him to the mausoleum. Cleopatra let ropes down and pulled him up with the help of her two waiting women. Plutarch describes Antony, covered with blood, struggling in his death throes, and stretching out his hands towards Cleopatra as he swung helplessly in the air.[43] When she had got him up, she laid him on a bed, tore her dress and spread it over him, beat and lacerated her breasts, and smeared her face with the blood from his wounds.

With Antony dead, Cleopatra still had to meet Octavian. Dio says that 'she remembered that she was queen and preferred to die bearing the title and majesty of a sovereign rather than live in a private station. At any rate she kept ready fire to destroy her treasure, and asps and other reptiles to end her life; she had experimented before on human beings to discover how these creatures caused death in each case.'[44]

The asp (Greek *aspis*) is the Egyptian cobra, which grows to around 2 metres long. Plutarch adds that she discovered that asp venom brought on a kind of drowsy listlessness and numbness, and that its victims resisted any attempt to revive them, like people do when they are in a deep natural sleep:[45] '[The asp] has four fangs, their underside hollow, hooked, and long, rooted in its jaws, containing poison, and at their base a covering of membranes hides them. Thence it belches forth poison unassuageable on a body . . . No bite appears on the flesh, no deadly swelling with inflammation, but the man dies without pain, and a slumberous lethargy brings life's end.'[46]

The sources are unanimous in stating that Octavian wanted her alive. They talked and she deployed all her sexy tricks: 'She dressed herself with studied negligence – indeed her appearance in mourning wonderfully enhanced her beauty – and seated herself on [a richly ornamented] couch. Beside her she arranged many different portraits and busts of Julius Caesar, and in her bosom she carried all the letters Caesar had sent her.'[47]

She read these letters to Octavian, but he remained the good virtuous Roman, impervious to her seduction attempts, although she did convince him that she wanted to live. He departed, smugly imagining that she would be the star attraction in his triumph in Rome.

In Plutarch's brilliant account of her death (17 August 30 BC) she bathes and eats an exquisite meal, after which an Egyptian peasant arrives carrying a basket, and when the guards ask him what is in it, he strips away the leaves at the top to reveal a load of figs. Cleopatra then sends a sealed writing tablet to Octavian, dismisses all her attendants except for her two faithful waiting women, and closes the doors of the mausoleum.[48]

Actually, nobody had any sure knowledge about how Cleopatra really died. Our sources mention the asp (or asps) in the figs, or in a pitcher, perhaps covered beneath some flowers, or alternatively a comb filled with poison, or a pin smeared with it. They also say that the asp was never discovered, and that her body showed no symptoms of poisoning, although there were two tiny punctures on her arm.

The Roman propaganda machine did its best to demonise Cleopatra. A terracotta lamp, made in Italy in the first century

AD, and possibly showing the influence of Propertius' line 'whore queen of incestuous Canopus', shows a caricature of an eastern woman, very probably Cleopatra, in a Nile landscape, sitting on a giant phallus on the back of a crocodile. But Cleopatra's image underwent constant modification. Octavian needed to have defeated a genuinely dangerous opponent, and worthy foes often elicited Roman pity and admiration. Not long after news of Cleopatra's death reached Rome, Horace produced his 'Cleopatra Ode;, which brilliantly captures the mood of the day:

> Today is the day to drink and dance on. Dance, then,
> Merrily, friends, till the earth shakes.[49] Now let us
> Rival the priests of Mars
> With feasts to deck the couches of the gods.
>
> Not long ago it would have been high treason
> To fetch the Caecuban[50] from family store-rooms,
> When the wild Queen[51] was still
> Plotting destruction to our Capitol
>
> And ruin to the Empire with her squalid
> Pack of diseased half-men – mad, wishful grandeur,
> Tipsy with sweet good luck!
> But all her fleet burnt, scarcely one ship saved –
>
> That tamed her rage; and Caesar,[52] when his galleys
> Chased her from Italy, soon brought her, dreaming
> And drugged with native wine,
> Back to the hard realities of fear.

As swiftly as the hawk follows the feeble
Dove, or in snowy Thessaly the hunter
The hare, so he sailed forth
To bind this fatal prodigy in chains.[53]

To the writers of her time, Cleopatra was 'She Who Must
Not Be Named': the phrases they use are all disparaging, and
the poets avoid telling her tale in direct narrative form. Lucan
is an exception, however, naming Cleopatra and describing her
entertaining Julius Caesar in her beautiful, shameless and jaw-
droppingly sexy, if rather obvious, way. But even so there
remains something that must not be mentioned: the price she
negotiates for Julius Caesar's support is a 'night of unspeakable
shame', so unspeakably shameful that it is left unspoken.[54]

One of the best epitaphs for Cleopatra was penned by Dio
Cassius:

Cleopatra was a woman of insatiable sexuality and insatiable
avarice. She often displayed an estimable ambition, but
equally often an overweening arrogance. It was by means of
the power of love that she acquired the sovereignty of the
Egyptians, and when she aspired to obtain dominion over
the Romans in the same fashion, she failed in the attempt
and lost her kingdom besides. Through her own unaided
genius she captivated the two greatest Romans of her time,
and because of the third, she destroyed herself.[55]

Octavian spared her children by Antony, but had his rival's
eldest son by Fulvia put to death, and Caesarion too. When
Appian had summed up Rome's status after the Mithridatic
Wars, he said that 'Egypt alone was lacking to their grasp of the

whole Mediterranean'.[56] Octavian now finished the job: Egypt was annexed, ending 300 years of Ptolemaic rule. Octavian took it under his own personal administration, typically muddying the waters in his propaganda: 'I added Egypt to the Empire of the Roman people.'[57]

First-hand evidence about Cleopatra's life is elusive. However, there is one document that provides a wonderful exception to this rule. It is written on papyrus, and comes from the Roman cemeteries at Abusir el-Melek, where it was reused as mummy cartonnage, and is now in the Ägyptisches Museum und Papyrussammlung, Berlin. It is a royal ordinance granting duty-free tax privileges to Antony's right-hand man, P. Canidius, dated to 23 February 33 BC. Below the main text, written by a scribe, Cleopatra signs off the document in her own handwriting, not with her name, but with just one word. And if it is the only word she could have left to posterity, it is a wonderfully appropriate one: γινέσθοι (*ginesthoi*) = 'make it happen'.[58]

16

Arminius: Bring Me Back My Legions!

Augustus versus the Barbarians

The deaths of Antony and Cleopatra left Octavian with no military or political rivals. He was master of the Roman world. In 29 BC he returned to Rome and celebrated a triple triumph, and he himself tells us that he went on to make an extraordinary gesture in January 27 BC: 'After I had put an end to the civil wars, having by universal consent acquired control of all affairs, I transferred government from my own authority to the discretion of the Senate and people of Rome.'[1]

In fact, he did nothing of the sort. Under an arrangement known as the 'First Settlement', he took control of the provinces where the majority of the legions were stationed, retained control of Rome's foreign policy, assumed the name 'Augustus', which carried quasi-religious overtones of fruitfulness (Latin *augeo* = 'I increase/enlarge/enrich/embellish'), and became known as *Princeps* ('first citizen'/'first among equals'), even though his *auctoritas* (authority) meant that his will would be done in all key areas. But the historians of the day sang his praises: 'There is no boon that men can desire of the gods or

303

gods grant to mankind, no conceivable wish or blessing which [Octavian] did not bestow on the Republic, the Roman people, and the world.'²

He had become Rome's first emperor.

Defining and securing the interface between his empire and Barbaria was one of Augustus' key priorities. Parthia remained a major worry in the east, where he envisaged the River Euphrates and the Arabian Desert as the frontier, but in 20 BC, when dynastic problems broke out there, Augustus exploited the opportunity and 'compelled the Parthians to give back . . . the booty and the standards of three Roman armies and to seek the friendship of the Roman people as suppliants'.³

The reference is to the eagles lost by Crassus at Carrhae (see pp. 253–257). It was a massive propaganda coup.

The several thousand kilometres of Rome's northern frontier were even more concerning. From 16 to 15 BC, in what Augustus told the Romans was a 'just' war,⁴ his stepsons Tiberius (the future emperor) and Nero Claudius Drusus conquered the territory north of the Alps as far as the River Danube. The area was duly organised into the provinces of Raetia⁵ and Noricum, and an inscription from the triumphal arch in La Turbie on the French Riviera commemorates the conquest: 'To the Emperor Augustus, son of the late lamented Caesar . . . erected by the Senate and People of Rome, to commemorate that under his leadership and auspices all the Alpine races stretching from the Adriatic Sea to the Mediterranean were brought under the dominion of the Roman people. Alpine races conquered − [a list of forty-six barbarian tribes follows].'⁶

In 14 BC the area between Gaul and Italy became the province of Alpes Maritimae, and Augustus boasted that 'the peoples of Pannonia,[7] where no army of the Roman people had ever been before my Principate, [were] completely defeated through Tiberius Nero . . . and brought under the rule of the Roman people'.[8]

Further to the east, Moesia was provincialised in AD 6, bringing the frontier between the Roman Empire and Barbaria into line with the River Danube, but since Europe's major rivers tend to unify adjacent peoples rather than separate them, and since political, cultural, linguistic, religious and economic frontiers seldom coincide, the frontier was always relatively permeable, with much movement across it in both directions.

For Augustus, the Rhine frontier was so problematical that he planned to create a province of Germania Magna, with its eastern border on the River Elbe but with its capital on the Rhine at Colonia Agrippinensis (modern Cologne). Nero Claudius Drusus was engaged in that project between 12 and 9 BC, until he was killed in a fall from his horse. Tiberius then continued the process until a major uprising among the Pannonians and Dalmatians in Illyricum broke out in AD 6 which took him three years, fifteen legions and an equal number of auxiliary forces to put down. But then, 'scarcely had [he] put the finishing touch upon the Pannonian and Dalmatian war, when, within five days of the completion of this task, dispatches from Germany brought . . . baleful news'.[9]

The Roman governor Publius Quinctilius Varus' arrogant attitude towards the Germans had provoked a backlash that brought about a defeat that would change Roman ambitions in Barbaria forever.

Germania and Germani

The Germans came only second to the Celts as the major linguistic and cultural grouping encountered by the Greeks and Romans in northern Europe. Quite how the early Germanic peoples developed is extremely hard to ascertain. Our two main ancient literary sources are Caesar in his *Gallic War* and Tacitus, particularly in his *Germania*, completed in AD 98 and designed to enlighten educated Romans about the Germani and their character, habits, institutions, folklore, religion and climate, and to emphasise the seriousness of the 'German menace' because of the disasters inflicted on Romans by 'German' peoples, who lived in great numbers in the areas on the other side of the Rhine and the Danube.

The opinions that the Roman writers may have picked up from the Celtic Gauls might also have muddied the waters, since the designation 'German' seems to have been a Gallic one that 'Germans' didn't apply to themselves, and more modern studies are frequently infused with nationalism and ideologies that are inapplicable to the ancient world. The standard view is that German language and culture originated in what is now northern Germany and the territories around the western Baltic from about 500 BC onwards. Movements of peoples then brought Germanic contact with the Mediterranean world from about 300 BC, and included the migration of the Cimbri and Teutones in the second century BC (see pp. 175 ff.), which is probably when there was also German settlement across the lower Rhine, while the Suebi arrived on the upper Rhine in the early first century BC.

Tacitus opened his account by saying that Germania as a whole (by which he means the lands east of the Rhine rather than the Celticised and Romanised Germanic peoples of the Roman provinces Germania Superior and Germania Inferior) 'is separated from the Gauls and from Raetians and Pannonians by the rivers Rhine and Danube: from the Sarmatians[10] and Dacians[11] by mutual misgivings or mountains: the rest of it is surrounded by the Ocean.'[12]

In analysing Germanic society we must factor in the wide geographical spread of Germanic settlement and the deep cultural differences and diversity among its many peoples, even though Tacitus regards them as indigenous rather than 'mixed race':

Who would have left Asia or Africa or Italy to look for Germany? With its wild scenery and harsh climate it is pleasant neither to live in nor look upon unless it be one's fatherland . . . Personally I associate myself with the opinions of those who hold that in the peoples of Germany there has been given to the world a race unmixed by intermarriage with other races, a peculiar people and pure . . . whence it comes that their physique, so far as can be said with their vast numbers, is identical: fierce blue eyes, red hair, tall frames, powerful only spasmodically, not correspondingly tolerant of labour and hard work, and by no means habituated to bearing thirst and heat; to cold and hunger, thanks to the climate and the soil, they are accustomed.[13]

However, our archaeological evidence allows us to construct a picture of a simple Iron Age society, at least by comparison with their Celtic neighbours, but one that was on an upward trajectory, and which had permanent farms and villages. Their agriculture was both arable and pastoral, although Caesar says their priorities lay elsewhere:

> For agriculture they have no zeal, and the greater part of their food consists of milk, cheese, and flesh. No man has a definite quantity of land or estate of his own [and] they adduce many reasons for that practice – the fear that they may be tempted by continuous association [with one specific homeland] to substitute agriculture for their warrior zeal; that they may become zealous for the acquisition of broad territories, and so the more powerful may drive the lower sort from their holdings; that they may build with greater care to avoid the extremes of cold and heat; that some passion for money may arise to be the parent of parties and of quarrels. It is their aim to keep common people in contentment, when each man sees that his own wealth is equal to that of the most powerful.[14]

Though there could be nominal kings, chosen, says Tacitus, on the grounds of birth, but not granted unlimited or arbitrary authority, the real political power was diffused among local clan chiefs who controlled the people by example rather than force, and by the admiration that they won by fighting in front of the line.[15] Major decisions were made by the whole community, albeit in quite chaotic and therefore, in Tacitus' eyes, barbarous ways. The assemblies were usually held at the new or full moon:

> It is a foible of their freedom that they do not meet at once and as if commanded, but a second and a third day is wasted by dilatoriness in assembling: when the mob is pleased to

begin, they take their seats carrying arms. Silence is called for by the priests . . . then a king or a chief is listened to, in order of age, birth, glory in war, or eloquence, with the prestige which belongs to their counsel rather than with any prescriptive right to command. If the advice tendered be displeasing, they reject it with groans; if it please them, they clash their spears.[16]

A relative scarcity of iron determined the style of their weapons, with short spears that they called *frameae* (singular *framea* in Latin) being the most common. These had a small, very sharp, narrow iron head, and were so wieldy that they were equally effective on foot or on horseback, hand-to-hand or at a distance.

The infantry launch showers of missiles . . . and hurl these to great distances, for they wear no outer clothing, or at most a light cloak . . . their shields only are picked out with choice colours. Few have breast-plates: scarcely one or two at most have metal or hide helmets. The horses are conspicuous neither for beauty nor speed [and] on a broad view there is more strength in their infantry . . . the swift-footed infantryman, whom they pick out of the whole body of warriors and place in front of the line, being well-adapted and suitable for cavalry battles . . .

The battle-line itself is arranged in wedges: to retire, provided you press on again, they treat as a question of tactics, not of cowardice . . . to have abandoned one's shield is the height of disgrace; the man so shamed cannot be present at religious rites, nor attend a council: many survivors of war have ended their infamy with a noose.[17]

Caesar was impressed by the aggressiveness of their warriors, who would devastate their own borders to create large areas of wilderness around their territory, and who regarded it as a real index of courage when no one would dare to settle near them. They happily sanctioned acts of brigandage outside their communities, because these gave their young men something 'useful' to do, and if their own community happened to become 'drugged with long years of peace and quiet',[18] the high-born young men would proactively seek out other tribes who were engaged in war: 'for rest is unwelcome to the race, and they distinguish themselves more readily in the midst of uncertainties: besides, you cannot keep up a great retinue except by war and violence.'[19]

Once upon a time the Gauls had been the Germans' superiors in valour, says Caesar, but the proximity of Gaul to the Roman provinces, the ready availability of exotic luxury goods and the constant experience of defeat had emasculated the Gauls, leaving them second best to the Germans in fighting prowess.[20]

Caesar says that their entire life is composed of hunting expeditions and military activities, and that they embrace toil and hardship from an early age.[21] Children were breastfed by their mothers, not by nursemaids and wet nurses, and grew up amid filth, squalor and poverty into adults whose height and physique greatly impressed the Romans.[22] 'Love comes late to the young men'[23] and chastity was highly prized: no one in Germania found vice amusing, or called it 'fashionable' to seduce or be seduced; clandestine love letters were, apparently, unknown; adultery was rare; it was disgraceful to have had carnal knowledge of a woman before the age of twenty, and 'there is no secrecy in the matter, for both sexes bathe in the rivers and wear skins or small cloaks of reindeer hide, leaving the great part of the body bare'.[24]

Tacitus expands on the Germanic dress code, saying that everyone wears a cloak, fastened with a brooch or just a thorn. Elite males might wear underclothes – 'not loose, like those of Parthians and Sarmatians, but drawn tight, throwing each limb into relief'[25] – and many people wear the skins of wild beasts, while the women dress like the men, except that they often wear trailing linen garments with purple stripes, whose upper parts don't widen into sleeves, but leave the arms, shoulders, and the adjoining part of the chest exposed.

The Roman view of German women follows the standard 'barbarian stereotype': formidable, weird and un-Roman. They were said to have turned losing battles into victories by pleading heroically with their men and thrusting forward their bared breasts, to show them that slavery, which the warriors feared much more on their women's behalf than on their own, was imminent.[26] Like all ancient societies, the Germans were slave-owning, although along a different model to that of the Romans – their slaves were more like serfs with obligations of service, control of a land-holding and homes of their own: barbarian women and children did their own housework.[27]

Germanic women were felt to have uncanny prophetic powers, so they were often consulted, and their answers were accorded great respect. Unlike the Gauls and Britons, they had no Druids to regulate divine worship, and, Caesar says, 'no zeal for sacrifices'.[28] He says that they only acknowledge the gods that they see, and by whom they are openly assisted – the equivalents of the Roman Sol (the Sun), Vulcan (the Fire god) and Luna (the Moon) – and have never heard of any other divinities. Tacitus, however, adds Mercury (i.e. Wotan), who receives human sacrifices, and Hercules (Fonar) and Mars (Tiu), who are appeased with animals. They have enormous respect for omens and casting lots, and 'they regard it as incompatible with the majesty of the gods to confine them within walls, or to portray them with the likeness of any human face: they consecrate groves and woods, and they give the names of gods to that "mysterious otherness" which is only visible to the eyes of reverence'.[29]

They have strong rules of guest-friendship, are generous in sharing food – wild fruits, fresh game, curdled milk – and prone to twenty-four-hour drinking sessions, which often end in injury or killing. The tribes nearest the Rhine, being slightly more 'civilised' than the rest, buy wine, but for most of them the alcohol of choice is, typically for barbarians, beer: 'For drink they use the liquid distilled from barley or wheat, after fermentation has given it a certain resemblance to wine . . . if you humour their drunkenness by supplying as much as they crave, they will be vanquished through their vices as easily as on the battlefield.'[30]

Tacitus is not implying, however, that it was Roman policy to conquer the Germans by getting them inebriated: he is telling his sophisticated, wine-drinking Roman readership than the Germans are weak, primitive and barbaric.

Unlike the Celtic peoples, the Germani did not have any proto-urban settlements that could accommodate any kind of central administration. Loyalties were local and tribal, and there was no real encompassing sense of overall 'Germanness': they only ever effectively unified in wartime under a battle leader, but their lack of a clearly defined state structure allowed them a degree of flexibility in their response to Roman aggression, and helped to preserve them from conquest.

Arminius, Varus and the Saltus Teutoburgiensis

The 'baleful news' that the messengers conveyed to Augustus in AD 9 concerned the fate of a number of Roman legions commanded by Publius Quinctilius Varus in Germania. Varus came from a famous, rather than a high-born family, and is described by Velleius Paterculus as being a man of mild character and quiet disposition, a little sluggish in mind and body, and more accustomed to the leisure of the camp than to actual service in war.[31] He had gone out to govern Syria as a poor man, but when he had returned, he was rich and the province was poor. Having been appointed to his command in Germania he had completely misjudged the feisty nature of the Germans, issuing orders to them as though they were Roman slaves and exacting money like he would from a subject nation.[32] Furthermore, he had 'entered the heart of Germany as though he were going among a people enjoying the blessings of peace, and sitting on his tribunal he wasted the time of a summer campaign in holding court and observing the proper details of legal procedure'.[33]

In the opinion of Velleius Paterculus, who becomes our main source at this point, this was a big mistake. He describes the Germans as duplicitous to a degree that anyone without experience of them couldn't possibly understand: they are a race of born liars; they trump up fictitious lawsuits; they deliberately provoke disputes; and they keep telling Varus that they are eternally grateful that Roman justice is settling their disputes, and that their own barbarous nature is being softened by this new method of settling quarrels by law rather than war.[34] Varus saw himself as a civilian praetor administering justice in the Forum, rather than a military commander in the heart of Germany.

At this point a young German of noble birth came on the scene, who was 'brave in action and alert in mind, possessing an intelligence quite beyond the ordinary barbarian'.[35]

His name was Arminius, son of Sigimer, war chief of the Cherusci. In Tacitus' day this tribe had gone soft:

> For long years they have been unassailed and have encouraged an abnormal and languid peacefulness. It has been a pleasant rather than a sound policy: with lawlessness and strength on either side of you, you will find peacefulness vanity; where might is right, self-control and righteousness are titles reserved for the stronger. Accordingly, the Cherusci, who were once styled just and generous, are now described as indolent and blind.[36]

But in AD 9 they were much more formidable. Arminius himself had become a Roman citizen, having served in Rome's auxiliary forces, and he had even attained Equestrian rank. But he exploited Varus' negligence to perpetrate some extreme treachery, 'sagaciously seeing that no one could be more quickly overpowered than the man who feared nothing, and that the most common beginning of disaster was a sense of security'.[37]

He slowly accumulated accomplices, convinced them that Rome could be crushed and set a date for executing the plot. At this point a German called Segestes turned informer, but Varus didn't believe his story. There would be no second chance.[38]

Arminius managed to lure three Roman legions, XVIII, XIX and possibly XVII, into difficult terrain at Kalkriese near the Saltus Teutoburgiensis (Teutoburg Forest).[39] The precise details of the engagement remain sketchy, although Dio Cassius gives a vivid picture of the way the nightmare unfolded for Varus' army. They were struggling to fell trees, build roads and make bridges because of the density of the forest; just like in peacetime they were encumbered with wagons, pack animals, women and children, and a large retinue of servants; violent rain and wind hampered their progress; slippery ground around the roots and logs made walking treacherous; and the tops of the trees kept breaking off and falling on them. In the midst of these difficulties,

> the barbarians suddenly surrounded them on all sides at once, coming through the densest thickets, as they were acquainted with the paths. At first they hurled their volleys from a distance; then, as no one defended himself and many were wounded, they approached closer to them. For the Romans were not proceeding in any regular order, but were mixed in helter-skelter with the waggons and the unarmed, and so, being unable to form readily anywhere in a body, and being fewer at every point than their assailants, they suffered greatly and could offer no resistance at all.[40]

The overall picture was crystal clear: 'An army unexcelled in bravery, the first of Roman armies in discipline, in energy, and in experience in the field, through the negligence of its general, the perfidy of the enemy, and the unkindness of fortune was surrounded . . . Hemmed in by forests and marshes and ambuscades, it was exterminated almost to a man by the very enemy whom it had always slaughtered like cattle.'[41]

It was total annihilation, the heaviest Roman defeat on foreign soil since the disaster of Crassus in Parthia: '[The Germans] put out the eyes of some men and cut off the hands of others. They cut off the tongue of one man and sewed up his mouth, and one of the barbarians, holding the tongue in his hand, exclaimed, "That stopped your hissing, you viper." '⁴²

The *Praefectus Castrorum* (Camp Prefect) Lucius Eggius opted to die by torture at the hands of the enemy rather than in battle. Caldus Caelius escaped a similar fate by grabbing a section of the chain with which he was bound, and smashing it over his own head so that 'both his brains and his blood gushed from the wound'.⁴³ Varus himself followed the example of his father Sextus Quinctilius Varus, who had fought on the losing side at Philippi, and ran himself through with his sword. His partially burned body was mutilated by the Germans 'in their barbarity',⁴⁴ and his severed head was ultimately sent to Augustus at Rome.

Six years later, a Roman force was back in the area and found the eagle of *Legio* XIX where the remains of Varus' army still lay unburied. They discovered Varus' first camp, with a half-ruined wall and a shallow ditch that showed where some of the remnants had taken cover: 'In the plain between were bleaching bones, scattered or in little heaps, as the men had fallen, fleeing or standing fast. Hard by lay splintered spears and limbs of horses, while human skulls were nailed prominently on the tree-trunks. In the neighbouring groves stood the savage altars at which they had slaughtered the Tribunes and chief Centurions.'⁴⁵

Survivors from the disaster told their comrades about the tribunal from which Arminius made his harangue, the gibbets and torture pits for the prisoners, and the arrogance with which he insulted Rome's standards and eagles. The Roman army then buried the bones of the three legions, mourning their fellow-soldiers and hating the barbarians. In recent years archaeologists have excavated pits in the neighbourhood of

Kalkriese that contained dismembered human remains whose bones show deep cuts: these are probably the mass graves of which Tacitus speaks.[46]

Arminius versus Germanicus

Arminius' massacre of Varus' legions effectively put a stop to Roman expansion east of the Rhine. Dio Cassius tells us that the Germans eradicated all the Roman strongholds apart from one, which Velleius Paterculus calls Aliso,[47] in the Lippe valley. Archaeological finds at Haltern am See, east of the Rhine, show evidence of hasty evacuation: at least twenty-four soldiers buried in potters' pits; weapons stored away; coins buried in hoards; and a great deal of pottery in pristine condition. The *Praefectus Castrorum* Lucius Caedicius found himself under siege by an immense force of Germans, but was able to fight his way to safety on a stormy night.[48]

As news of the catastrophe spread, Varus' nephew Lucius Nonius Asprenas, who was in command of *Legiones* I *Germanica* and V *Alaudae* at Moguntiacum (modern Mainz) led his forces northward, occupied the fortresses of Cologne and Xanten, and rescued what survivors he could, but found himself accused of appropriating the property of the dead officers. The Emperor Augustus' stepson Tiberius marched to the Rhine from the Danube with *Legiones* XX *Valeria Victrix* and XXI *Rapax*. At Rome there was great unease, and Augustus apparently refused to shave his beard or cut his hair for months, and used to bang his head against a door and shout, 'Quinctilius Varus, give me back my Legions!'[49]

Arminius now tried to assemble a coalition of German tribes, while Tiberius effectively shored up the Rhine fortifications, successfully enough for him to celebrate a triumph in AD 12. However, the lost territory was never recovered. On the Rhine itself the military districts of Germania Superior and Germania Inferior were created, each with an army of four legions. Augustus then left a recommendation that the empire should be kept within the existing confines of the Rhine, Danube and Euphrates, and when Tiberius succeeded him as emperor in AD 14, he stuck to that advice.

Nevertheless, there was still plenty of activity on the northern frontier. During the autumn of AD 14, the army of Germania Inferior, commanded by Tiberius' nephew Germanicus,[50] made a foray into 'free' Germania, possibly to distract the soldiers of the powerful Rhine army who were becoming restless after the death of Augustus, rather than for any far-reaching strategic objectives. However, the campaign continued in AD 15, when Germanicus took the army of Germania Superior as far as the upper Weser. He was looking to exploit the divisions between Arminius 'the troubler of Germany'[51] and the pro-Roman Germanic leader Segestes, who had tried to warn Varus about Arminius (see p. 314). Tacitus says that Segestes had been forced into the war by the will of his people, and that there was also a bitter domestic feud between him and Arminius, who had carried off his daughter even though she was betrothed to someone else. When Segestes found himself under siege by his fellow countrymen, he turned to Rome for help: 'Arminius [was] now the dominant figure, since he advocated war. For with barbarians the readier a man is to take a risk so much the more is he the man to trust, the leader to prefer when action is afoot.'[52]

Germanicus rescued Segestes and also captured Arminius' wife Thusnelda. She was pregnant at the time, and Arminius was driven crazy by her capture and the enslavement of their unborn child. While he tried to whip up the Cherusci to make war on Segestes and on Rome, Tiberius granted an indemnity to Segestes' relatives and children, and Thusnelda gave birth to a son called Thumelicus, who was brought up at Ravenna.[53]

This was the point at which Germanicus' troops visited the site of the slaughter of Varus' army (see p. 316 f.), and after some inconclusive skirmishing Germanicus withdrew his men from the theatre of operations. Arminius turned his attention to the force commanded by Aulus Caecina Severus, who had been campaigning against the Germanic Chatti tribe, and was now returning via a narrow causeway known as the *Pontes Longi* (Long Bridges), which traversed an area of foul, muddy marshland.[54] Caecina had a terrible dream in which he saw Varus covered in blood, rising from the marsh, and heard him calling, although he refused to obey and pushed him back when he extended his hand.[55] Arminius' Cherusci were at home fighting in these conditions, but failed to exploit their successes by becoming distracted by plunder. When the Romans made it onto solid ground, Arminius proposed allowing them to march out and then entrapping them again in wet and broken country. However, Arminius' uncle, Inguiomerus, 'advocated the more drastic measures dear to the barbarian: – "Let them encircle the rampart in arms. Storming would be easy, captives more plentiful, the booty intact!"'[56] Inguiomerus won the argument about strategy, but the Romans won the ensuing battle.

In AD 16 Germanicus changed his tactics and built a huge fleet designed to transport his troops along the major European rivers. They assembled in the territory of the Batavians, near modern Nijmegen in the Netherlands, before sailing through the 3-kilometre-long Fossa Drususiana (Canal of Drusus),[57] which linked the northern branch of the Rhine near Arnhem with the Issel (IJssel in Dutch), and then through the lands of the Frisians and Chauci, before disembarking in the valley of the upper Ems. From here Germanicus marched east, to where Arminius and his Cherusci were waiting for him on the east bank of the River Weser, at a place called Idistaviso (location unknown).

At this point Arminius asked if he could speak with his brother Flavus, who was serving in the Roman forces and was well known both for his loyalty and for the loss of one eye. Arminius inquired about this facial disfigurement; Flavus told him how it happened; Arminius asked what reward he had received; Flavus listed increased pay and various military decorations; Arminius laughed at the cheap rewards of servitude.[58] They each argued for their own position: Flavus praised Roman greatness, the heavy penalties for the vanquished, and the mercy bestowed on those who submitted, using Arminius' wife and child as examples; Arminius' appeal was to the sacred call of his homeland, ancestral liberty, the gods of the German hearths, and their mother, who wanted Arminius to be a liberator of the Cherusci, not a traitor. They parted shouting threats and abuse at one another, Flavus using quite a lot of choice Latin, which he had picked up from his time in the Roman army.[59]

Germanicus crossed the Weser using his auxiliary cavalry in the initial assault, in which, on behalf of the Romans, the Batavian commander Chariovalda distinguished himself before going down under a hail of missiles. Prior to the main engagement, Germanicus prepared his men for the prospect of fighting in wooded areas, with some classic barbarian stereotyping:

The barbarians' huge shields, their enormous spears, could not be so manageable among tree-trunks and springing brushwood as the *pilum*, the *gladius*, and close-fitting body-armour. Their policy was to strike thick and fast, and to direct the point to the face. The Germans carried neither corselet nor headpiece – not even shields with a toughening of metal or hide, but targes of wickerwork or thin, painted board. Their first line alone carried spears of a fashion: the remainder had only darts, fire-pointed or too short. Their bodies, again, while grim enough to the eye and powerful enough for a short-lived onset, lacked the stamina to support a wound. They were men who could turn and run without a blush for their disgrace and without a thought for their leaders, faint-hearted in adversity, in success regardless of divine and human law.[60]

Arminius' rallying cry was a denunciation of Roman greed, cruelty and arrogance: for him it was freedom or death.

Germanicus deployed eight legions, plus Gallic, German, Raetian and Vindelician auxiliaries, themselves technically barbarian. It was Roman discipline versus German impetuosity, and the outcome was never in doubt. Arminius was in the thick of the action, striking, yelling, wounded, trying to motivate his men, and smearing his own blood over himself to avoid recognition. But as his Cherusci were pushed back he fought his way through the auxiliary contingents and got away, possibly with the complicity of some Chauci, who let him go. Inguiomerus was also saved by a similar use of 'manliness or treachery'.[61] Tacitus dryly observes that it was a brilliant Roman victory achieved at low cost. But it was not the end of the war.

The defeat spurred the German tribes into a renewed war effort, and a second engagement was fought on the Cheruscian frontier in a narrow swampy space between a river and a forest, where the Angrivarii had also erected a wide earthwork to mark the boundary between them and the Cherusci. Here the adaptability of Rome's legionaries won the day – slingers and artillery inflicted severe casualties on the defenders of the earthwork, while the Germans were hampered by their numbers and the terrain, which made it too awkward to wield their weapons effectively. As they closed to hand-to-hand fighting, the Romans, with their 'shields tight to the breast and hand on hilt, kept thrusting at the barbarians' great limbs and bare heads and opening a bloody passage through their antagonists – Arminius being now less active, whether owing to the succession of dangers or to the hampering effects of his recent wound. Inguiomerus, moreover, as he flew over the battle-field, found himself deserted less by his courage than by fortune.'[62]

Germanicus could afford himself the luxury of withdrawing one legion from the action to build a camp, while their comrades satiated themselves on barbarian blood until nightfall. A victory monument was erected, surrenders were offered and accepted, Germanicus returned to winter quarters, and an arch was erected at Rome to celebrate the recapture of the eagles lost with Varus: the inscription stated that Germanicus had avenged the 'deceitful destruction of an army of the Roman people'.[63]

On 26 May in the consulship of Gaius Caelius (or Caecilius) and Lucius Pomponius Germanicus Caesar (AD 17), Germanicus celebrated a triumph over the Cherusci, Chatti, Angrivarii and all other German tribes on Rome's side of the River Elbe. In Roman terms, the honours were well merited: he had reconquered the Lippe valley and the North Sea coast, defeated Arminius and restored Roman prestige. The Emperor Tiberius now had a decision to make: (1) maintain the aggression, or (2) leave the Germani alone. Wisely, he chose option two, withdrew the Roman forces from the Lippe valley, sent his son Drusus Julius Caesar to Illyricum, and redeployed Germanicus to the east, where he fell ill and died at Antioch on 10 October AD 19, in circumstances that many felt were suspicious.[64] But Rome's frontier became fixed along the Rhine, and it remained relatively secure for some 200 years. One other aspect of Germanicus' legacy to Rome was his son Gaius Julius Caesar, who accompanied Germanicus and his wife Agrippina the Elder on the Rhine campaigns when he was a child. They paraded him to the troops dressed up in a miniature military uniform, from which he acquired the affectionate nickname meaning 'Little Boot' – Caligula.[65]

Arminius versus the Germans

The Roman withdrawal allowed the barbarian Germani to revert to the 'typical behaviour of their tribes':[66] fighting one another. The rival factions were led by the neutral but Romanised King Maroboduus of the Marcomanni, and Arminius, 'fighting for liberty'.[67] Arminius' Cherusci were joined by two rebel Suebian tribes, the Semnones and Langobardi, but his uncle Inguiomerus deserted to Maroboduus. Battle was joined by armies who had learned much from their campaigns against the Romans in terms of organisation and discipline. Casting Maroboduus as a spineless fugitive and a betrayer of his country, Arminius inspired his warriors by reminding them of the freedoms they had recovered, the legions they had slaughtered, and the booty and weaponry, torn from Roman dead, which they were now brandishing. Maroboduus retorted by accusing Arminius of bringing disaster on both himself and his people, because of his act of perfidy in entrapping 'three wandering legions and a general who was oblivious to deception'.[68] Arminius got the upper hand, and when Maroboduus asked the Emperor Tiberius for assistance he was told in no uncertain terms that his former neutrality disqualified him from receiving Roman aid. Tacitus says that Drusus was then sent out to establish peaceful conditions,[69] but goes on to narrate how he distinguished himself by stirring up barbarian-on-barbarian conflicts that damaged Maroboduus even more: he appealed to Tiberius' mercy once again, and after a discussion in the Senate he was allowed to enter Italy, and spent the last eighteen years of his life at Ravenna.

Tacitus had some rare primary source material for the circumstances surrounding Arminius' final demise:

I find from contemporary authors, who were members of the Senate, that a letter was read in the Senate House from the Chattan chief Adgandestrius, promising the death of Arminius, if poison were sent to do the work; to which the reply went back that 'it was not by treason nor in the dark but openly and in arms that the Roman people took vengeance on their foes': a high saying intended to place Tiberius on a level with the old commanders who prohibited, and disclosed, the offer to poison King Pyrrhus.[70]

Arminius tried to exploit the Roman withdrawal and Maroboduus' expulsion to aim at wider dominance over the Germanic tribes, but this alienated too many people, and in the end it was barbarian infighting, not Roman legions, that brought his rather low-key downfall: 'He was attacked by arms, and, while defending himself with chequered results, fell by the treachery of his relatives.'[71]

Tacitus wrote an influential epitaph for Arminus, acknowledging his achievements and lamenting the lack of interest he received from other ancient historians:

> Undoubtedly the liberator of Germany; a man who ... threw down the challenge to the Roman nation, in battle with ambiguous results, in war without defeat; he completed thirty-seven years of life, twelve of power, and to this day is sung in tribal lays, though he is an unknown being to the Greek historians, who admire only the history of Greece, and receives less than his due from us of Rome, who glorify the ancient days and show little concern for our own.[72]

This idea of Arminius as a German 'national hero' ('Hermann the German') became highly influential in the late nineteenth century, when Tacitus' assessment of him as 'undoubtedly the liberator of Germany' was frequently quoted, even though his career shows very clearly that in his lifetime the concept of a united Germany was never an ideal, let alone a reality.

17

Boudicca: Queen of the Iceni, Scourge of Rome

Britannia: A Distant, Mysterious, Barbaric Country

It was Julius Caesar's descriptions of his two expeditions to Britain in 55 and 54 BC that really opened the island up to the Roman consciousness (see p. 263). His narrative includes a fascinating and influential overview of the barbarian British ethnography, climate, resources and orientation:

> The interior of Britain is inhabited by people who claim . . . to be indigenous. The coastal areas are inhabited by invaders who crossed from Belgium for the sake of plunder . . . The population is extremely large, there are very many farm buildings . . . and the cattle are very numerous. There is timber of every kind . . . but no beech or fir. They think it wrong to eat hares, chickens, or geese, and keep these creatures only for pleasure and amusement . . .
>
> The island is triangular in shape, with one side facing Gaul. One corner of this side points east and is on the coast of Kent . . . The lower corner points south . . . The second

side of the island faces westward, towards Spain. In this direction lies Ireland . . . It is believed that there are several smaller islands too, where, some writers say, there is continual darkness for 30 days in midwinter . . . The third side of the island faces north; there is no land opposite this side, but the eastern corner of it points roughly towards Germany.[1]

The erroneous idea that the west side of Britain points towards Spain became the received wisdom, glibly repeated by the geographer Strabo: 'Britain is triangular in shape. Its longest side lies parallel to Gaul . . . Each [side] measures about 860–880 km. [The British shore] extends from Kantion [Kent] (which is directly opposite the mouth of the Rhine), as far as the westerly end of the island which lies opposite Aquitania and the Pyrenees.'[2]

Caesar's descriptions of the inhabitants of the island were equally influential in fixing the image of its barbarian population:

By far the most civilized of the Britons are those who live in Kent [whose] way of life is very like that of the Gauls. Most of the tribes living in the interior do not grow grain; they live on milk and meat and wear skins. All the Britons dye their bodies with woad, which produces a blue colour and gives them a wild appearance in battle. They wear their hair long; every other part of the body, except for the upper lip, they shave. Wives are shared between groups of ten or twelve men, especially between brothers and between fathers and sons; but the children of such unions are counted as belonging to the man with whom the woman first cohabited.[3]

The stereotype of watery Britain's bestial blueness persisted for over 500 years, when the poet Claudian personified Britannia as 'veiled with the skin of a wild beast of Caledonia, her cheeks tattooed, her blue cloak sweeping over her footprints like the surge of Ocean'.[4]

Strabo goes on to provide some information about the resources of the island and the way of life of its inhabitants, who are true barbarians:

It produces corn, cattle, gold, silver and iron. These things are exported along with hides, slaves and dogs suitable for hunting . . . The men of Britain are taller than the Gauls and not so yellow-haired. Their bodies are more loosely built [and] some of their customs are more primitive and barbarous. Thus for example some of them are well supplied with milk but do not know how to make cheese; they know nothing of planting crops or of farming in general . . . Their cities are the forests, for they fell trees and fence in large circular enclosures in which they build huts and pen in their cattle, but not for any great length of time. The weather tends to rain rather than snow. Mist is very common, so that for whole days at a stretch the sun is seen only for three or four hours around midday.[5]

This idea that Britannia was located much further north than it really is became part of the conventional picture:

The length of the days is beyond the measure of our world: the nights are clear and, in the distant parts of Britain, short, so that there is but a brief space separating the evening and the morning twilight. If there be no clouds to hinder, the sun's brilliance – they maintain – is visible throughout the night: it does not set and then rise again, but simply passes over.[6]

Some of this is correct, but much of it is just a conventional picture, which bears only a tangential relation to reality, notably the supposed British ignorance about agriculture. Strabo had never travelled to Britain, and Britain had not been definitively conquered in his day, and we often learn far more about what was *thought* to be interesting or important to the Romans than we do about the actual facts. Tacitus, writing in around AD 98, even after Roman armies had been up into northern Scotland, still trots out some of the conventional-yet-erroneous information:

The question of who were the first inhabitants of Britain and whether they were indigenous or immigrant is one which, as one would expect among barbarous people, has never received attention. The physique of the people presents many varieties, whence inferences are drawn: the red hair and the large limbs of the inhabitants of Caledonia [modern Scotland] proclaim their German origin; the swarthy faces of the Silures [roughly from modern Monmouthshire, in South Wales], the curly quality, in general, of their hair, and the position of Spain opposite their shores, attest the passage of Iberians in old days and the occupation by them of these districts; those peoples, again, who adjoin Gaul are also like Gauls, whether because the influence of heredity persists, or because when two lands project in opposite directions till they face each other the climatic condition stamps a certain physique on the human body; but, taking a general view of

the case, we can readily believe that the Gauls took possession of the adjacent island. You would find there Gallic
ceremonies and Gallic religious beliefs; the language is not
very different; there is the same recklessness in courting
danger, and, when it comes, the same anxiety to escape it;
but the Britons display a higher spirit, not having yet been
emasculated by long years of peace.[7]

Tacitus then produced a final cost/benefit analysis that was
probably the key to his discussion: 'Britain produces gold and
silver and other metals: conquest is worthwhile.'[8]

So Britain is presented as a distant, quasi-mythical land
across the ocean, near the ends of the earth – the poet Horace
spoke of its inhabitants as 'the very last of the world',[9] and of
'the whale-burdened sea that bursts on the exotic British coast'[10]
– but also as a place that is rich in potential tribute. It would be
both prestigious and profitable to conquer, and the sheer
barbarity of its inhabitants would add to the interest.

British Barbarians Conquered (1)

The Emperor Gaius 'Caligula' had made preparations for an
invasion of Britain, which, for reasons that are rather inscrut-
able, were never followed through. When he was assassinated
in AD 41, his uncle Claudius, who had been hiding behind
some curtains, found himself unceremoniously hoisted onto
the throne of Rome by the Praetorian Guard (or so his official
version of events spun it[11]). The ideal way for him to secure his
bond with the army, and hence his own safety, was conquest,
and Britannia was the perfect target. He could outdo Julius
Caesar, who had visited the island twice and received the

submission of various tribal chieftains, but never made any lasting acquisitions;[12] the logistical work had all been done by Caligula; the economic rewards of victory were attractive; the Druids had now moved their headquarters to Mona (modern Anglesey) but might still use their influence to stir up trouble in Gaul; Claudius was a practising historian; and there was a ready-made pretext in that the expansionist activities of the powerful Catuvellauni tribe, under Caratacus[13] and Togodumnus, the sons of the late Cunobel(l)inus 'King of the Britons',[14] were upsetting Britain's status as a stable and profitable neighbour of the Roman Empire.

So in AD 43 Claudius assembled a well-balanced and expertly led invasion force: the battle-hardened *Legio* IX *Hispana* under the overall commander Aulus Plautius; first-rate officers such as Gnaeus Hosidius Geta, Titus Flavius Vespasianus ('Vespasian', the future emperor), and his elder brother Flavius Sabinus; *Legiones* II *Augusta*, XIIII *Gemina* and XX (later entitled *Valeria Victrix*), and perhaps a *vexillatio* (detachment) of *Legio* VIII *Augusta*, all augmented by auxiliaries who provided a strong cavalry contingent, giving a total of around 40,000 men. The crossing and landings were unproblematical; Caratacus and Togodumnus were located and defeated; 'a river which the Barbarians thought the Romans would be unable to cross without a bridge'[15] – either the Medway or the Thames – was indeed crossed, with the help of Plautius' auxiliary unit of 'Celts' who were specially trained in swimming over rivers; and Togodumnus was killed in guerrilla fighting in the Vale of St Albans. Claudius arrived in August, assumed the command, defeated the barbarians, captured their tribal capital at Camulodunum (modern Colchester), and celebrated a spectacular triumph back in Rome. A triumphal arch in Rome was

'Set up by the Senate and People of Rome because he received the formal submission of eleven Kings of the Britons, overcome without any loss, and because he was the first to bring barbarian peoples across the Ocean under the sway of the Roman people.'[16]

It was a perfect example of how the conquest of barbarian peoples could bring immense kudos to a Roman ruler.

The post-invasion period saw a combination of conquest and consolidation as the hitherto barbarian territories made their first tottering steps towards becoming a fully fledged Roman province. Under her first governors, the Fosse Way was developed into a major line of communication from the south-west to the north-east; settlements such as Verulamium (modern St Albans) and Londinium (modern London) were starting to thrive; and anti-Roman insurgency against the Governor Ostorius Scapula by Caratacus, who had escaped across the River Severn into the territory of the swarthy Silures, was eradicated when he was defeated in the hills of the Welsh borders. In AD 51 Caratacus fled to Queen Cartimandua of the Brigantes, who ruled a tribal confederacy that covered much of modern Yorkshire and Lancashire and extended into the Scottish Lowlands. She handed him over to the Romans. Tacitus puts into Caratacus' mouth a brilliant speech delivered at Rome to Claudius:

Had my lineage and my rank been matched by my moderation in success, I should have entered this city rather as a friend than as a captive; nor would you have scorned to admit to a peaceful league a king sprung from famous ancestors and holding sway over many peoples. My present lot, if to me a degradation, is to you a glory. I had horses and men, arms and riches: what wonder if I lost them with a pang? For if you would rule the world, does it follow that the world must welcome servitude? If I were dragged before you after surrendering without a blow, there would have been little heard either of my fall or of your triumph: punishment of me will be followed by oblivion; but save me alive, and I shall be an everlasting memorial of your clemency.[17]

The Emperor spared him, after which Dio Cassius relates that he wandered around Rome, admiring its size and splendour, commenting, 'And can you, then, who have got such possessions and so many of them, covet our poor tents?'[18]

We get an indication of the confidence that the Romans had in their control of Britannia by the fact that the fifth governor, Gaius Suetonius Paulinus (governed AD 58–61), was using *Legiones* XIIII *Gemina* and XX to eradicate Druidism on Mona, a long way north-west of the Fosse Way line. We get the Roman perspective on the Druids from Caesar's *Commentaries*, where he informs his readers that they carry out public and private sacrifices, interpret all matters of religion, don't pay taxes and are exempt from military service. They also act as educators of young men in the Druidic arts, and make judicial decisions about murder, inheritance and boundary disputes. They also have the power to excommunicate people from religious practices. There is one Chief Druid who has absolute authority, selected on the basis of his pre-eminence in dignity, or, if there are several worthy candidates, by vote or violence.

Caesar says that anyone seeking to gain a deep knowledge of Druidism goes to Britain.[19] It can take twenty years to learn the relevant doctrines, many of them transmitted in verse, but none of them written down. This is partly to make them inaccessible to the mass of the people, and partly because they think dependence on writing leads to sloppy learning and poor memory. A key Druidic religious belief is that souls transmigrate from one body to another after death, which makes men brave because they don't fear dying, and Caesar concludes 'they likewise discuss and impart to the youth many things respecting the stars and their motion, respecting the extent of the world and of our earth, respecting the nature of things, respecting the power and the majesty of the immortal gods'.[20]

So the Druids were highly influential in British society. But as Paulinus was carrying out his mission, a disaster struck that was so bad that the reigning emperor, Nero, 'even thought about withdrawing the army from Britain, and only decided against it because he did not want to seem to diminish the glory of his father [i.e. Claudius]'.[21]

Boudicca's Revolt[22]

The crisis facing Rome had arisen after King Prasutagus of the Iceni, a tribe located chiefly in modern Norfolk, had died without a son and had bequeathed half of his kingdom to Rome, and half to his daughters. Unfortunately such an arrangement was inadmissible in Roman law: 'Ulpian in the 16th book "ad edictum": It is a special feature of the imperial *procurator* that by his order a slave of the Emperor can enter on an inheritance and that the procurator can, if the Emperor should be named as heir, intermeddle with a rich inheritance and thereby perfect the Emperor's heirship.'[23]

Presumably the barbarian Prasutagus had no detailed knowledge of the Roman legal system, and his wishes were not respected: 'As if they were war booty his kingdom was devastated by centurions and his household by slaves ... To begin with, his wife Boudicca was whipped and his daughters raped. Various Icenian nobles were forcibly deprived of their ancestral estates ... and the king's relatives were treated like slaves.'[24]

The Trinovantes[25] of Essex were similarly treated as 'prisoners and slaves', although their specific grievances centred on the establishment of the temple of the Divine Claudius in the new colony at Camulodunum,[26] which was seen as a symbol of everlasting slavery, and which cost them a fortune to administer. To make matters worse, to pay for this kind of thing, the Britons had accepted cash donations from Claudius, and taken on loans from speculators such as Nero's tutor Seneca the Younger, who had lent the islanders 40,000,000 *sestertii* plus interest.[27] Tacitus also singles out the greed and rapacity of Decianus Catus, the procurator of the island, who now demanded that the donations be returned,[28] while Seneca called in his loan.

This level of insensitivity and blatant misrule violated the Britons' deeply held sense of honour:

Once they had had only one king to a tribe: now they had two. The Governor oppressed their persons, the *Procurator* their property ... they were as one in ruining their subjects. From the one came centurions, from the other slaves, both to inflict violence and insult. No excess of greed or lust was omitted. In battle it was the strong who gained the spoils, but now it was at the hands of cowards and men totally unfit for war that they were being driven out of their homes and suffering both loss of their children and conscription of themselves into the Roman Army. Indeed that last indignity suggested that it was only for their own country that Britons did not know how to die.[29]

Back in AD 48, the terror tactics of the second governor Publius Ostorius Scapula had provoked a short-lived revolt among the Iceni when he tried to disarm them.[30] Now, between AD 60 and 61 – the exact date has been much disputed[31] – a new and much more serious rebellion broke out among the Iceni, led by Queen Boudicca, which swiftly spread to the Trinovantes, 'together with some others who, not yet broken to servitude, had bound themselves by secret oaths to resume their independence'.[32] The British grievances had clearly been brewing for some time, and although the outbreak of the war can be blamed on highly experienced Romans such as Seneca, much of the responsibility for allowing them to get out of hand must be attributed to the Governor Suetonius Paulinus.

The Roman historical tradition is incredibly anti-Nero and, although at this stage his rule was generally quite benign, the rebellion was used to disparage his reputation. And in Boudicca the ancient historians found a perfect foil to the emperor: she might be a barbarian female, but she is given all the virtues that Nero lacked, spiced up with a little exotic eroticism: 'Buduika [i.e. Boudicca] had uncommon intelligence for a woman . . . She was very tall and grim; her gaze was penetrating and her voice was harsh; she grew her long auburn hair to the hips and wore a large golden torque and a voluminous patterned cloak with a thick plaid fastened over it. This was how she always dressed.'[33]

Her rebel army, about 120,000 strong, attacked, captured and razed Camulodunum. The Roman commanders had been guilty of providing it with amenities rather than seeing to its needs, and it was practically defenceless: the veterans who lived there were old; the town had no walls; misled by secret pro-rebels, they even dispensed with ramparts or trenches; the governor was on the other side of the island; the procurator only sent 200 incompletely armed men; they failed to evacuate the old people and women; they put their trust in the temple's protection, but their gods looked the other way:

> For no visible reason, the statue of Victory at Camulodunum fell down – with its back turned as though it were fleeing the enemy. Delirious women chanted of destruction at hand. They cried that in the local senate-house outlandish yells had been heard; the theatre had echoed with shrieks; at the mouth of the Thames a phantom settlement had been seen in ruins. A blood-red colour in the sea, too, and shapes like human corpses left by the ebb tide, were interpreted hopefully by the Britons – and with terror by the settlers.[34]

A *vexillatio* of *Legio* IX *Hispana* commanded by Quintus Petillius Cerialis Caesius Rufus marched south from his fortress – either at Longthorpe or Lincoln – and attempted to relieve Camulodunum, but he was ambushed and routed, perhaps with losses of 2,000 men,[35] although he himself escaped. The 'native horde' took the town after two days' siege, focusing their violence on the temple of the Divine Claudius.[36]

Suetonius Paulinus responded as soon as he received the news. *Legiones* XIIII *Gemina* and XX started the two-week journey back from Mona, while he went ahead with his cavalry to try to defend Londinium. He also sent for *Legio* II *Augusta* from Isca (modern Exeter), but their *Legatus* was in Gaul and Poenius Postumus, the *Praefectus Castrorum*, refused to march.

Paulinus rode through the disaffected territory to Londinium, where he immediately realised that he didn't have the resources to defend it, so he decided to sacrifice the city to save the province, and headed back to rejoin his legions. He allowed the inhabitants to accompany him, but anyone who stayed behind – women, the elderly or those who were just attached to the place – were slaughtered: 'For the British did not take or sell prisoners, or practise other war-time exchanges. They could not wait to cut throats, hang, burn, and crucify – as though avenging, in advance, the retribution that was on its way.'[37]

Terrible massacres, in which the ancient sources say in excess of 70,000 people lost their lives, took place at Londinium and then at Verulamium, where Boudicca's barbarians committed some stomach-churning atrocities:

They hung up naked the noblest and best-looking women. They cut off their breasts and stitched them to their mouths, so that the women seemed to be eating them, and after this they impaled them on sharp stakes run right up the body. While they were doing all this in the grove of Andate . . . they performed sacrifices, feasted, and abandoned all restraint. (Andate was their name for victory, and she enjoyed their especial reverence.)[38]

Reunited with his infantry, Paulinus could only deploy around 10,000 men (*Legio* XIIII, *vexilationes* of *Legio* XX, plus auxiliaries) who by now were outnumbered by approximately twenty to one. Yet even so he realised that things would get even worse if he didn't fight immediately, and it was essential that he should neutralise the expert British charioteers (*essedarii*): 'They combine the mobility of cavalry with the staying power of infantry; and by daily training and practice they attain such proficiency that even on a steep incline they are able to control the horses at full gallop, and to check and turn them in a moment. They can run along the chariot pole, stand on the yoke, and get back into the chariot as quick as lightning.'[39]

It was rare for them to have accidents. In Juvenal's *Satire* 4, Domitian's councillor Veiento makes a prophecy: 'You have a huge omen of a great and famous triumph. You will capture some king or other, or else Arviragus[40] will fall off his British chariot pole.'[41]

The image of Boudicca's chariot in the popular imagination is of a vehicle equipped with scythed wheels. This goes back to mistaken Roman sources, though. Pomponius Mela, writing about twenty years before the reign of Boudicca, says that the Britons 'fight not only on horseback and on foot, but also in two-horsed chariots and war-chariots [*bigis et curribus*[42]] in the Gallic style . . . They call those chariots *covinni*, and they are equipped with scythes around the axle-trees [*falcatis axibus*].'[43]

Other writers of the time reference *covinni*. Lucan says that the Belgae are 'drivers of remarkable *covinni*',[44] and Silius Italicus trots out the stereotype that 'the blue-painted inhabitant of Thule drives his scythed chariot [*falcigero . . . couinno*] around the close-packed battle lines'.[45]

In normal Roman usage the *covinnus* was a private civilian vehicle, which seems to be why the writers are intrigued by the addition of scythes.

Sextus Julius Frontinus, who governed Britain shortly after Boudicca's revolt,[46] also talks about scythe-bearing, four-horsed chariots (*falcatas quadrigas*) deployed by the Gauls against Caesar,[47] but Caesar himself uses different terms: the Celtic term *essedum* rather than *covinnus* for the vehicle, and *essedarii* for the drivers, as does Jordanes, writing in Greek in the sixth century AD: '[The Britons] paint their bodies with iron-red, whether by way of adornment or perhaps for some other reason [and] fight not only on horseback or on foot, but even with scythed two-horse chariots, which they commonly call *essedae*.'[48]

But Caesar, who often fought against them, never refers to British scythed chariots, and nor does Tacitus in describing his father-in-law Agricola's encounter with charioteers at the Battle of Mons Graupius (see p. 345): it seems clear that there is good reason for this – none of the sources who attribute scythe-bearing chariots to the Britons were eyewitnesses. Indeed, the second-century AD Greek historian Arrian makes an import-ant distinction between British and Persian practice: The Britons 'used two-horse chariots, with small, bad horses. Their light, two-wheeled chariots are well adapted to running across all sorts of terrain and the wretched horses to enduring hard-ships. Of the Asians, the Persians long ago practiced the use of scythe-bearing chariots and armoured horses, beginning in the time of Cyrus.'[49]

Neither is there any archaeological evidence for British scythed chariots, and it may be significant that on the *denarii* minted at Rome in 48 BC by the moneyer Lucius Hostilius Saserna, which depict a *biga* driven by a charioteer holding a whip in his left hand and the reins in his right, with a warrior standing on the chariot, facing backwards and holding a shield in his left hand and hurling a spear with his right, the scythes are conspicuous by their absence.[50] Boudicca's famed scythed chariot is probably bogus.

So Paulinus selected a battle site just off Watling Street some-where between Mancetter and St Albans,[51] where his flanks and the rear were protected by woods and hills. He drew up his forces in textbook fashion, with the legionaries in close order, light-armed auxiliaries on their flanks, and the cavalry massed on the wings; Boudicca's warriors formed a huge, seething, amorphous, barbaric mass.[52]

It was traditional for Greek and Roman historians to put speeches into the mouths of the rival commanders before they described major battles. In Dio Cassius, Boudicca harangues her warriors, contrasting her hard, manly Britons with the soft, effeminate Romans ruled by Nero: they live in luxury, drink unmixed wine, anoint themselves with oil, take warm baths and sleep with young men, and ones who are past their prime at that. While Nero may have the name of 'man', she scoffed, 'he is in fact a woman, and the evidence for this is that he sings and plays the lyre'.[53] Tacitus also plays on the 'woman theme', inventing a speech designed to explain barbarian customs to his Roman readership, rather than to inspire British warriors:

Boudicca drove round all the tribes in a chariot with her daughters in front of her. 'We British are used to woman commanders in war,' she cried. 'I am descended from mighty men! But now I am not fighting for my kingdom and wealth. I am fighting as an ordinary person for my lost freedom, my bruised body, and my outraged daughters. Nowadays Roman rapacity does not even spare our bodies. Old people are killed, virgins raped. But the gods will grant us the vengeance we deserve! The Roman division which dared to fight is annihilated. The others cower in their camps, or watch for a chance to escape. They will never face even the din and roar of all our thousands, much less the shock of our onslaught. Consider how many of you are fighting – and why. Then you will win this battle, or perish. That is what I, a woman, plan to do! – let the men live in slavery if they will.'[54]

The Britons were so confident that they brought their wives along to see the victory, installing them in carts at the edge of the battlefield.

As it so often was when faced with a Roman army in a set-piece engagement, the barbarian optimism was sadly misplaced. Precisely as Paulinus had instructed them, the Romans stood their ground, launched their *pila* at the onrushing enemy, and then charged in wedge formation. They instantly eradicated all serious resistance; Boudicca's fleeing fighters were impeded by the ring of wagons; the Romans spared neither the women nor the baggage animals; and Tacitus was impressed: 'It was a glorious victory, comparable with bygone triumphs. According to one report almost 80,000 Britons fell . . . Boudicca poisoned herself.'[55] In Dio Cassius' account, however, Boudicca just gets ill and dies.

Boudicca's revolt had come close to ending Roman involvement in Britannia, and after his battlefield victory Suetonius Paulinus embarked on a policy of reprisals so savage that it even caused friction between himself and the new procurator, Gaius Julius Alpinus Classicianus. This was only defused by the diplomatic efforts of Nero's freedman Polyclitus,[56] and the appointment of a new governor, Marcus Trebellius Maximus, who achieved some much-needed post-Boudiccan consolidation.

British Barbarians Conquered (2)

The next phase in the history of Roman Britain revolved around another queen, but this time a pro-Roman one, Cartimandua of the Brigantes. A series of military revolts led to the suicide of Nero in AD 68, and the so-called Year of the Four Emperors the year after.[57] Amid the turbulence across the Channel, mutinies among the troops in Britain, and a running feud between Trebellius and Marcus Roscius Coelius, commander of *Legio* XX *Valeria Victrix*, Cartimandua's ex-husband Venutius, 'a man of barbarous spirit who hated the Roman power',[58] tried to rekindle the opposition to Rome:

> In addition he had motives of personal hostility against Queen Cartimandua ... Her power had grown when she captured King Caratacus by treachery and handed him over to embellish the triumph of the Emperor Claudius ... Venutius had been her husband. Spurning him, she made his armour-bearer Vellocatus her husband, and her partner in government ... The people of the tribe declared for Venutius [who] summoned his supporters. The Brigantes rallied to him, reducing Cartimandua to the last extremity. She besought Roman protection. Our *alae* and cohorts fought indecisive battles, but at length rescued the queen from danger. The kingdom went to Venutius; we were left with a war to fight.[59]

Rome's post-Nero Flavian dynasty, whose first ruler was Vespasian, was faced with a binary choice between comprehensive conquest of the island or total withdrawal. Given that Vespasian was a veteran of campaigns in Britain, it was obvious which option he would choose. The swashbuckling Petillius Cerialis, the *Legatus* of *Legio* IX *Hispana* during Boudicca's revolt, was appointed governor in AD 71. He advanced northwards, established IX *Hispana* at Eboracum (York), and smashed the power of the Brigantes; his capable successor, Sextus Julius Frontinus, overran south Wales; and towards the end of Vespasian's reign, Tacitus' father-in-law Gnaeus Julius Agricola (governor from AD 77 or 78 – our sources make the dates tricky to establish definitively) subdued north Wales and sent his auxiliary cavalry swimming across the Menai Strait to finish off the conquest of Mona, before pushing northwards to the River Tay and consolidating the Forth–Clyde line, which Titus (then emperor) may have envisaged as the limit of Roman expansion. Under Domitian, who acceded to the purple in AD 81, Agricola became uneasy about a possible uprising by the northern tribes, so he moved into the territory of the Caledonii (aka Caledones), who responded by attacking Roman installations 'without provocation',[60] which allowed him to fight a 'defensive' war to eliminate any potential threat.

During Agricola's first campaign beyond the Forth–Clyde line, *Legio* IX *Hispana's* camp suffered a night attack and was only saved by the intervention of XX *Valeria Victrix*, but the following year (AD 83 or 84) Agricola confronted the Caledonii under their leader Calgacus in the major Battle of Mons Graupius. The Romans won so easily that Agricola didn't even have to engage his legions: his auxiliaries inflicted 10,000 casualties on their own. Agricola was recalled soon afterwards, and his campaigns, which are brilliantly described by Tacitus,[61] said to be probably a better biographer than Agricola was a general, marked the end of Roman expansion in Britain for some time. At this point, history was very much being written by the victors, but the vanquished barbarians are often given the best lines. Calgacus couldn't inspire his warriors to victory, but the immortal denunciation of Roman imperialism that Tacitus put into his mouth just before the battle would resonate throughout the barbarian world for centuries: 'The Romans are the robbers of the world . . . If their enemy is opulent, they are greedy for wealth; if he is poverty-stricken, they are eager for glory . . . They alone out of everyone lust for wealth and poverty with equal passion. They call plunder, murder and rape by the spurious names of "empire", and where they make a desert they call it "peace".'[62]

18

Judaea Capta: Revolts in Judaea

Judaea

No sooner had Nero's generals established some semblance of order in the far-flung western reaches of the empire, than the emperor had to confront rebellion and resistance in Judea. By the time the unrest erupted, Judaea had been an official Roman province for six decades, albeit with almost six centuries of turbulent history prior to that. Back in 586 BC, King Nebuchadnezzar II had despoiled the Temple at Jerusalem, razed the city to the ground and deported the people to Babylonia; the area had then fallen under the administration of the Persian Empire (538–332 BC), the Ptolemies of Egypt (332–200 BC), the Seleucids of Syria (200–142 BC), and the hereditary Hasmonean high priests descended from Mattathias, the father of Judas Maccabaeus (142–63 BC). The Hasmoneans carved out a Jewish state whose area matched that of David's biblical kingdom, and which prospered until Pompey the Great reduced the territory in 63 BC (see p. 239). Pompey had been dragged into a dispute between Hyrcanus II and Aristobulus, the two sons of the ex-queen, Salome Alexandra (r. 76–67 BC), and had installed Hyrcanus II as 'ethnarch', after which the kingdom came to be administered by Rome. In 57 BC Aulus Gabinius, the governor of Syria, reorganised it into five districts, although Hyrcanus remained ethnarch until the Parthians invaded in 40 BC. Having captured Hyrcanus, they mutilated him in order to disqualify him for the priesthood, and replaced him with one of Aristobulus' sons, Mattathias Antigonus, who issued the last Hasmonean coinage.

One man who escaped the Parthian invasion was Herod 'the Great'. With the backing of Mark Antony and the Roman Senate, Herod was declared king of Judaea. He married Mariamme, the granddaughter of both Hyrcanus and Aristobulus, which enabled him finally to unite the feuding Hasmonean factions, and, with the assistance of Gaius Sosius, the governor of Syria and Cilicia, he took Jerusalem in 37 BC. Mark Antony duly had Mattathias Antigonus beheaded.

Herod was an effective and financially astute ruler, whose building projects included the fortress-palace of Masada. However, when he started an unauthorised war against the Nabataeans in 9 BC, his gloss began to wear off at Rome, and his cruelty towards his extensive family – the product of nine other wives as well as Mariamme, whom he executed in 29 BC – made the situation worse. When he died in 4 BC, the Romans stepped in. Herod's son Archelaus became ethnarch of Judaea, Samaria and Idumaea, but after deputations of Jews and Samaritans approached Augustus in AD 6 he was banished to Vienna (Vienne). Judaea was annexed along with Samaria and Idumaea, which collectively became the Roman province of Judaea.

In some ways the Romans were supportive of the Jews. Various decrees enforced their right to observe their traditional practices throughout the empire, certain exemptions were granted to facilitate the observance of the Sabbath, and even Christian writers would come to categorise Judaism as a legitimate religion (*religio licita*). However, a census conducted in AD 6 also served as a catalyst for resistance to Rome in Judaea, which Josephus termed the 'fourth philosophy', and general misgovernment engendered anti-Roman feeling in the Jewish population of Jerusalem, as well as among the Galilean non-landowners. In AD 19 the Emperor Tiberius forced 4,000 Jewish youths into military service in the bandit-infested, fever-ridden island of Sardinia, and expelled all the other Jews from Rome on pain of slavery, after a Roman matron had been swindled by a gang of Jewish conmen.

Gaius 'Caligula' (r. AD 37–41) also had a somewhat fractious relationship with the Jews. He appointed his friend Herod Agrippa I, the grandson of Herod the Great (he is called Herod in the Acts of the Apostles but Agrippa on his coins), as king of the substantially Jewish area of Galilee and Peraea. Yet Agrippa's zealous Judaism did little to mollify the discord between the emperor and his Jewish subjects. The prefect of Egypt, Aulus Avillius Flaccus, became worried about his personal safety under Gaius' regime and, egged on by an anti-Semitic Greek faction in Alexandria, presided over the first pogrom in Jewish history in AD 38. The flashpoint occurred when Agrippa tried to transit through Alexandria in secret on his way from Rome to Judaea, but was discovered. Flaccus suspected that Agrippa was there to undermine him, and far from trying to prevent the anti-Jewish mob violence that ensued, he actively encouraged it. Synagogues were torched, shops looted, and many Jews were rounded up in the theatre, where members of the Jewish Council were flogged and some Jewish women were forced to eat pork. Possibly prompted by complaints from Agrippa,

Caligula had Flaccus arrested, replaced and executed, but he spurned the delegations sent to Rome by both the Jewish and the Greek factions, and the conflict was still unresolved when he was assassinated.

The overall situation was not helped by Caligula instructing Publius Petronius, the *Legatus Augusti pro praetore* of Syria, to erect a cult statue of him in the Holy of Holies of the Temple at Jerusalem, although Petronius' nicely judged delaying tactics, alongside intervention by Herod Agrippa I, ensured that Caligula died before the scheme could be carried out.

Barbarian Jews

The resistance of the Jews to the imperial cult was one of the factors that made them, in Roman eyes, barbarians. Their religion, and its ramifications for their lifestyle, diet, culture and social identity, was one of the defining features of their 'otherness', and hence their 'barbarity'. Jewish monotheism was diametrically opposed to Roman polytheism, and numerous Romans felt that they dishonoured the gods. Pliny the Elder said that 'the Jews are a race remarkable for their contempt of the divine powers'.[1]

At a later period, the second-century AD Christian philosopher Tatian called the Hebrew Bible 'barbaric'.[2] And to Tacitus the Jews were completely contrary: 'They regard as profane all that we hold sacred; on the other hand, they permit all that we abhor.'[3] He expressed and explained his anti-Semitic feelings very forcefully in Book 5 of his *Histories*:

The . . . customs of the Jews are base and abominable, and owe their persistence to their depravity. For the worst rascals among other peoples, renouncing their ancestral religions, always kept sending tribute and contributions to Jerusalem, thereby increasing the wealth of the Jews; again, the Jews are extremely loyal toward one another, and always ready to show compassion, but toward every other people they feel only hate and enmity. They sit apart at meals, and they sleep apart, and although as a race they are prone to lust, they abstain from intercourse with foreign women; yet among themselves nothing is unlawful. They adopted circumcision to distinguish themselves from other peoples by this difference. Those who are converted to their ways follow the same practice, and the earliest lesson they receive is to despise the gods, to disown their country, and to regard their parents, children, and brothers as of little account. However, they take thought to increase their numbers; for they regard it as a crime to kill any late-born child, and they believe that the souls of those who are killed in battle or by the executioner are immortal: hence comes their passion for begetting children, and their scorn of death . . . The Jews conceive of one god only, and that with the mind alone: they regard as impious those who make from perishable materials representations of gods in man's image; that supreme and eternal being is to them incapable of representation and without end. Therefore they set up no statues in their cities, still less in their temples; this flattery is not paid their kings, nor this honour given to the Caesars . . . The ways of the Jews are preposterous and mean.[4]

The Jews were also categorised as barbarians on linguistic grounds. Joseph ben Mattathias, aka Flavius Josephus (his assumed Roman name), who wrote an important account of the Jewish rebellion (*Jewish War*) and a Jewish history (*Jewish Antiquities*), was an aristocratic Jewish priest and scholar who boasted matrilineal Hasmonean descent. He had been to Rome on a diplomatic mission, but had ended up staying there for two years before returning, with quite pro-Roman sentiments, to Jerusalem. And he was completely explicit about Jewish barbarism, using the word 'barbarian' to describe his own people several times. As a historian he regarded Hebrew sources as part of barbarian culture: 'the tradition of keeping chronicles of antiquity is found rather among the barbarian races than among Greeks'.[5]

Josephus also acknowledges that the Jews were barbarians because of their eastern, Semitic origin, as when he says that the Chaldaeans were 'the original ancestors of our race, and this blood-relationship accounts for the mention of the Jews in their annals'.[6]

Finally, Josephus was acutely aware that the Jews were barbarians because of their Semitic language and script, which also set them apart from Greek and Latin speakers.[7] He himself wrote in Greek, but struggled with the language because 'the habitual use of my native tongue has prevented my attaining precision in the pronunciation. For our people do not favour those persons who have mastered the speech of many nations.'[8]

The Great Jewish Revolt

The simmering unrest in Judaea in Nero's reign is well illustrated by the events surrounding the return of the Apostle Paul to Jerusalem after his third missionary journey. He was both a Jew and a Roman citizen, describing himself as being 'of the stock of Israel, of the tribe of Benjamin, a Hebrew of the

Hebrews; according to the law, a Pharisee',[9] and he was quoted as saying 'I am a Pharisee, the son of a Pharisee'.[10] He admitted that prior to his conversion he had been a violent persecutor of the church of God,[11] and although he could certainly speak Hebrew, Greek was his first language: he stood on the border-line between barbarian and Roman.

In AD 58, after his arrival in Jerusalem, he went to the Temple with four Jewish converts and was spotted by some Jews from Asia who vociferously accused him of wrongdoing.[12] A riot broke out, and Paul was dragged from the Temple by a mob, who started to beat him up. Roman soldiers were able to put a stop to this,[13] and although they arrested Paul they gave him permission to address the people.[14] This just made the situation worse. Paul was led away to the Roman barracks. He was famously about to be publicly flogged, only to receive an eleventh-hour reprieve: 'And as they bound him with thongs, Paul said unto the centurion that stood by, Is it lawful for you to scourge a man that is Roman, and uncondemned? When the centurion heard that, he went and told the chief captain, saying, Take heed what thou doest; for this man is a Roman. Then the chief captain came, and said unto him. Tell me, art thou a Roman? He said, Yea.'[15]

The whole situation exposed a number of problems with Rome's imperialism for both rulers and subjects. The Jews did make concessions by sacrificing twice a day to both the divine Roman emperor and to the Roman people, and back in Tiberius' reign Jesus had advocated consensus by telling the Pharisees to 'Render therefore unto Caesar the things which are Caesar's; and unto God the things that are God's',[16] effectively acknowledging that taxes paid both to Rome and to the Jewish Temple could exist side by side. For his part, John the Baptist told Roman soldiers, 'Do violence to no man, neither accuse any falsely; and be content with your wages.'[17] However, it was not simply a case of Romans versus Jews: many tax-gatherers in Judaea came from a Jewish elite that did very well out of the Roman Empire, making taxation a real bone of contention within Jewish society. Judaea was a place where compromise was hard to achieve.

Other Jews were not always as fortunate as Paul. In AD 63, when they assembled in Caesarea to protest that they were being discriminated against, they clashed with the local Greek citizens. The Roman procurator, Marcus Antonius Felix, sent in the army; the philhellenic Emperor Nero took the side of the Greeks, and the Jews were incensed.

By AD 66 Judaea had become a time bomb, and we have an eyewitness account from Josephus of how it exploded. In May of that year the Roman procurator,[18] Gessius Florus, who needed to make up a budget deficit of 400,000 *sestertii*, ordered his soldiers to seize seventeen talents (435 kilograms) of silver from the Temple treasury in Jerusalem. From the Jewish perspective, this was a sacrilegious violation of their most holy place, especially when Florus ordered his Gentile soldiers to force their way in.

The incident inevitably caused unrest. Florus' reaction was to march in person from Caesarea to Jerusalem to restore order and get hold of the treasure. The twenty-nine-year-old Josephus and the moderate high priest Hanan made conciliatory noises, but Florus was completely uncompromising. He sent in the cavalry, and more than 3,000 innocent people lost their lives. The instigators of the riot were crucified, leading to further Jewish protests and another bloodbath, after which Jewish popular opinion swung in favour of nationalism and armed resistance. Sacrifices for the emperor's welfare in the Temple stopped and 'freedom coinage' was issued.

The nationalist backlash pushed the Romans onto the defensive. Florus and most of his cohorts were driven back to Caesarea, and the pro-Roman client king, Marcus Julius Agrippa, aka Herod Agrippa II, the great-grandson of Herod the Great and client king of Chalcis, north-east of Judaea, was called in, but he was stoned and expelled. With the Jewish insurgents assuming a measure of control throughout Judaea, Nero now turned to Gaius Cestius Gallus, the newly appointed *Legatus Augusti pro Praetore* of Syria. Gallus marched to Jerusalem with 30,000 troops in the October of AD 66. But he still failed to take the city, and as he retreated he found himself trapped in a narrow defile near Beth-horon, where a sizeable army of Jewish rebels slaughtered around 6,000 of his men.

In Jerusalem, meanwhile, the moderates had managed to regain control of the city and of the management of the war. A 'losing draw' would have suited them, but Nero was still smarting from Boudicca's revolt and was fearful that this rebellion might spread to the numerous Jews in Antioch, Alexandria or, worse, Parthia, and so destabilise the whole eastern end of his empire. So he turned to Titus Flavius Vespasianus ('Vespasian'), a veteran of Claudius' invasion of Britain (see p. 332). Vespasian brought in his eldest son, also called Titus Flavius Vespasianus (aka Titus), and made him *Legatus* of *Legio* XV *Apollinaris* based in Alexandria, while he himself took command of *Legiones* X *Fretensis* and V *Macedonica* based in Syria (although he decided against deploying XII *Fulminata*, defeated at Beth-horon). Vespasian gathered his army, augmented by auxiliaries and allies, in Syria during the winter of AD 66–7.

When the Roman forces moved into Judaea in AD 67, they laid siege to Jotapata (Yodfat) in Galilee. It was brutal. Vespasian himself was wounded, and horrendous injuries were inflicted on the defenders by the Roman catapults. One man's 'head was knocked clean off by a stone, and his skull was thrown for over half a kilometre. In the day time as well, a pregnant woman who had just come out of her house had her stomach struck so violently that the foetus was ripped out to about a hundred metres away. Such was the power of the stone-thrower.'[19]

As Titus led the final assault, the Jewish commander, Joseph ben Mattathias, hid in a cave with forty other rebels. They made a suicide pact. On Joseph's suggestion they drew lots for each man to kill the one next to him. Joseph made it through to the final two, persuaded his companion to surrender, and prophesied Vespasian's elevation to the purple. Having been spared, he defected to Rome and was henceforth known as Flavius Josephus (see p. 351 f.).

Titus was bearing down on Jerusalem in the summer of AD 68 when the news broke that Nero had taken his own life.[20] Military activity in Judaea was temporarily suspended, and Vespasian sent Titus to greet the new Emperor Galba. Events conspired to prevent him making it to Rome, though, and while Rome tore itself apart in the civil wars of the so-called 'Year of the Four Emperors' (AD 69), from which his father Vespasian emerged as ruler of the empire, Titus returned to Judaea to assume the supreme command against the uprising. Jerusalem became the focus of operations once again.

The siege of Jerusalem began in the spring of AD 70 and took 140 days. With two pro-Roman Jews, Josephus and Vespasian's early backer Tiberius Julius Alexander, on Titus' staff, the Romans followed their best military practice and deployed *Legiones* V *Macedonica,* XII *Fulminata,* XV *Apollinaris* and X *Fretensis* to make terraces, ramps, towers and battering rams to smash through the city's fortifications. Titus breached the walls of the New City, completed the circumvallation of the Inner City, inflicted starvation on the defenders and stormed the outer Temple court. Amid utter carnage, the Temple was burned to the ground – something that friendly sources such as Josephus assert that Titus tried to avoid, and more hostile ones see as a deliberate policy decision.[21]

Overall, it had been 'job done' with typical Roman efficiency. Vespasian placed Judaea under an imperial *Legatus* and installed *Legio* X *Fretensis* as a permanent garrison in Jerusalem; Jewish-owned land in Judaea was expropriated; propaganda-coinage celebrated *IUDAEA CAPTA*; and the Temple's treasures were displayed in the triumph celebrated by Titus and Vespasian in AD 71: the golden menorah, silver trumpets and the table for the showbread are still visible carved in relief on the Arch of Titus in the Forum at Rome.

The last remnants of the resistance were mopped up in spring AD 74 when the new governor of Judaea, Lucius Flavius Silva, with *Legio* X *Fretensis* and assorted auxiliaries, took the seemingly impregnable fortress of Masada, held by Eleazar ben Yair and a group of extremists often called Zealots but better termed *Sicarii* after their characteristic curved flick-knives.

> The *Sicarii* clubbed together against those who consented to submit to Rome and in every way treated them as enemies, plundering their property, rounding up their cattle, and setting fire to their habitations; protesting that such persons were no other than aliens, who so ignobly sacrificed the hard-won liberty of the Jews and admitted

their preference for the Roman yoke. Yet, after all, this was but a pretext, put forward by them as a cloak for their cruelty and avarice, as was made plain by their actions. For the people did join with them in the revolt and take their part in the war with Rome, only, however, to suffer at their hands still worse atrocities; and when they were again convicted of falsehood in this pretext, they only oppressed the more those who in righteous self-defence reproached them with their villainy.[22]

Silva enclosed Masada's steep-sided rocky hill with a line of circumvallation and constructed a quite astonishing siege ramp, up which a tower with a massive battering ram was deployed. Josephus records that the *Sicarii* killed their families and then themselves rather than surrender:

> They had died in the belief that they had left not a soul of them alive to fall into Roman hands; but an old woman and another, a relative of Eleazar, superior in sagacity and training to most of her sex, with five children, escaped by concealing themselves in the subterranean aqueducts, while the rest were absorbed in the slaughter. The victims numbered nine hundred and sixty, including women and children.[23]

The Romans were astounded by the survivors' story, and rather than exulting over the heaps of corpses, they developed a deep admiration for their single-minded contempt for death. But all Judaea had now been subdued: 'The fortress being thus taken, the general left a garrison on the spot and himself departed with his army to Caesarea. For not an enemy remained throughout the country, the whole having now been subdued by this protracted war, which had been felt by many even in the remotest parts, exposing them to risk of disorder.'[24]

Following the war in Judaea, Titus enjoyed an illicit romantic interlude in the already complex love life of the Jewish princess Berenice of Cilicia, the sister and, some said, lover of Marcus Julius Agrippa. In Juvenal's *Satires*, a lady called Bibula goes on a shopping spree that includes 'a famous diamond ring – once flaunted by Berenice, which adds to its price: a gift from her brother, that barbarous prince Agrippa, a token of their incest, in the land where monarchs observe the Sabbath barefoot, and tradition leaves pigs to attain ripe old age'.[25]

To the Romans Berenice looked rather too much like another Cleopatra VII, and although she went to Rome in AD 75, her relationship with Titus had to end (with mutual sorrow) when he became emperor in AD 79.

One of the first crises that Titus had to deal with as emperor was the eruption of Mount Vesuvius, which destroyed Pompeii, and Marcus Julius Agrippa's nephew, also called Agrippa, was one of the few victims whose names we know.[26] The apocalyptic nature of the eruption provoked Jewish writers, responding to the sack of Jerusalem by Vespasian and Titus, to predict the fall of the Roman Empire: 'Then know the wrath of the heavenly God, on those who destroyed the blameless race of the pious.'[27]

The response of Vespasian and Titus to the suppression of the revolt was somewhat different. Vespasian began the work on the iconic Flavian Amphitheatre or 'Hunting Theatre', known since medieval times as the Colosseum (or Coliseum), and Titus inaugurated it in AD 80 with a hundred-day festival at venues all across Rome. According to one specialist in reconstructing 'ghost' inscriptions from the pinholes that once held bronze letters, the original building inscription of the amphitheatre read: 'Imperator Caesar Vespasianus Augustus ordered this new amphitheatre erected from the spoils of war.'[28] The war in question was the Jewish War.

Bar Kokhba: The Redemption of Israel

Efforts at amicable coexistence and accommodation were still punctuated by occasional flashpoints. The Emperor Domitian (r. AD 81–96) is often portrayed, on the basis of scant and ambivalent evidence, as a persecutor of Christians on a par with Nero, but the Jews certainly felt the impact of his extension of the *fiscus Iudaicus* (Jewish tax), which came to include not only those who were born Jewish or had converted to Judaism, but also people who kept the fact that they were Jews a secret or lived as Jews without professing Judaism. Suetonius was an eyewitness to this process in action: 'I recall being present in my youth when the person of a man ninety years old was examined before the *Procurator* and a very crowded court, to see whether he was circumcised.'[29]

Domitian's cousin, the Consul Titus Flavius Clemens, was put to death in AD 95 on a charge of 'atheism', and a number of others who had 'drifted away into Jewish customs' were similarly condemned.[30] Romans at this date generally regarded Christians as a Jewish sect, and it may be that those who 'lived as Jews without professing Judaism' were in fact Christians. Spurning Rome's state religion if you weren't a Jew counted as atheism, which became a common accusation against Christians.

In AD 115 the Emperor Trajan embarked on a massive invasion of Parthia, which took him as far east as the Persian Gulf in the area of modern Basra in Iraq. While he was away, the

Jewish population in Cyrenaica in North Africa turned against the Roman authorities and perpetrated considerable destruction, focusing particularly on pagan temples. There must have been some deep-seated ill-feeling, and before the end of AD 116 the insurgency had spread to Alexandria and other parts of Egypt, Palestine and Cyprus, while another rebellion in Trajan's newly formed Mesopotamian province involved the Jews of Babylonia. Mesopotamia was soon handed over to the Parthian prince Parthamaspates as a client ruler but, although Trajan's coinage claimed that he had 'given the Parthians a king' (*REX PARTHIS DATUS*), Parthamaspates was never acknowledged by the Parthians. The revolts in Cyrenaica and Egypt were suppressed by Quintus Marcius Turbo with considerable loss of life, while Palestine was brought back under control by the Berber governor of Judaea, Lusius Quietus, who, by a corruption of his name, became the eponym of what became known as the Kitos War.

Another relatively peaceful interlude ensued until Hadrian (r. AD 117–38), Trajan's successor, attempted to refound Jerusalem and provoked a horrendously bloody rebellion. The city had not been officially rebuilt after the damage perpetrated in the Great Jewish Revolt of AD 66, but if Hadrian expected the Jews to respond favourably to his decision to turn it into a Roman colony under the name of Colonia Aelia Capitolina, he was horribly mistaken. Jewish unhappiness was made worse by Hadrian's earlier decision to outlaw circumcision ('they were forbidden to mutilate their genitals' is how the *Historia Augusta* puts it[31]), not to mention the fact that *Legio* X *Fretensis'* insignia of a boar was displayed on one of the city gates, and there was a plan to construct a temple to Jupiter Optimus Maximus on the site of the old Temple of Solomon.

Why Hadrian behaved so insensitively towards his Jewish subjects is hard to fathom, especially given that the contemporary writer Pausanias describes him as the emperor 'who has gone furthest to honour religion, and among all sovereigns done most for the happiness of each of his subjects [and who] has never willingly gone to war'.[32]

But, willingly or not, a war had to be waged. In AD 132 there was an enormous uprising centred on Judaea led by Shimon bar Kosba.[33] He took on the name Bar Kokhba, meaning 'Son of the Star' in Aramaic, giving him a link with the messianic prophecy in Numbers 24.17: 'I shall see Him, but not now; I shall behold Him, but not nigh. There shall come a Star out of Jacob, and a Scepter shall rise out of Israel, and shall smite the corners of Moab and destroy all the children of Sheth.'

On the other hand, his detractors (often Christian) dubbed him Bar Koziba, meaning 'Son of the Lie', and Saint Jerome later claimed that he used to fan a lighted straw in his mouth with puffs of breath so that he appeared to be breathing fire.[34] The Palestinian Bishop Eusebius of Caesaraea (AD 260–c.340) described him as 'a man who was murderous and a bandit, but relied on his name, as if dealing with slaves, and claimed to be a luminary come from heaven and was magically enlightening those who were in misery'.[35]

Bar Kokhba was clearly a charismatic leader: he took the title nsy' Ysr'l (Prince of Israel); his rebels declared the 'Redemption/ Liberation of Israel', which they dated to 1 Tishri (October) AD 131; the premier Jewish religious authority, Rabbi Akiba, was on his side; his brilliantly executed guerrilla tactics created havoc among the Roman troops; and Judaea quickly became his.

Details of the actual course of the revolt are vague, but finds related to the uprising from the so-called 'Cave of Letters' in Nahal Hever in the Judean Desert include coins with the legend 'Shimeon' on one side, and 'to the Freedom of Jerusalem' on the other, as well as various letters between Bar Kokhba and his subordinates Ionathes and Masabala in the important rebel base at En Gedi. One of these, from Soumaios, is written in Greek, because 'we can't find anyone who knows how to write in Hebrew'.[36] This might indicate that non-Jews were also involved in the revolt, which is an inference that can also be drawn from Dio Cassius' statement that 'many outside nations were joining for the eagerness of gain'.[37] On the other hand, it might simply show that none of the Jewish soldiers in the camp could write Hebrew, but it is clear that Bar Kokhba's revolt was serious enough for Hadrian to deploy a major legionary force and bring in his finest general, Sextus Julius Severus, all the way from Britannia.

Severus embarked on a process of extermination and ethnic cleansing, and Bar Kokhba made his last stand at Bethar near Jerusalem in AD 135: 'The siege lasted a long time before the rebels were driven to final destruction by famine and thirst and the instigator of their madness paid the penalty he deserved.'[38]

His death ended a war that had seen, according to Dio Cassius, 50 fortresses and 985 villages razed to the ground, 585,000 people killed in the various engagements, many Jews sold into slavery, and 'as for the numbers who perished from starvation, disease or fire, that was impossible to establish'.[39] Other finds from the Cave of Letters included mirrors, a glass plate, bronze jugs and house keys, hidden there during the fighting. But no one came back for them. At Rome Hadrian was hailed as Imperator, although he did not accept the usual greeting 'I and the legions are in health' because the attrition rates of the Roman troops had been so enormous.

Judaea was literally wiped off the map by being renamed Syria-Palestina, *Legio* VI *Ferrata* was stationed in Galilee, and Eusebius says that the Jewish population was forbidden even to set foot in the district around Jerusalem, except for one annual visit.[40]

19

Decebalus: Genocide in Dacia

Domitian and the Chatti

Shortly after Gnaeus Julius Agricola had won his victory over Calgacus' Caledoni at the Battle of Mons Graupius in AD 83 (see p. 345 f.), he was recalled by the Emperor Domitian. Tacitus disapproved. Overstating both aspects, he said that 'Britain was totally subdued and immediately abandoned',[1] and attributed this to Domitian's jealousy of Agricola's success. However, the reality was that troops were desperately needed to face another barbarian threat in central Europe: a *vexillatio* of *Legio* II *Adiutrix* was transferred from Britannia to the Danube in AD 85, and the rest of the legion followed shortly afterwards; all the British territory beyond the River Forth was given up and the British garrison was cut down to three legions: II *Augusta*, IX *Hispana* and XX *Valeria Victrix*.

One of Domitian's military problems was a war that had broken out along the middle sector of the Rhine frontier against the Germanic Chatti tribe in AD 82 or 83. Tacitus tells us that hardy frames, close-knit limbs, fierce countenances, and a peculiarly vigorous courage, mark the tribe. For Germans, they have much intelligence and sagacity; they promote their picked men to power, and obey those whom they promote; they keep their ranks, note their opportunities, check their impulses, portion out the day, intrench themselves by night, regard fortune as a doubtful, valour as an unfailing, resource.[2]

Their infantry was impressive, and they had a tendency to wage entire wars rather than individual battles.

Tacitus also takes an interest in the significance of their hair and beards:

A practice, rare among the other German tribes, and simply characteristic of individual prowess, has become general among the Chatti, of letting the hair and beard grow as soon as they have attained manhood, and not till they have slain a foe laying aside that peculiar aspect which devotes and pledges them to valour. Over the spoiled and bleeding enemy they show their faces once more; then, and not till then, proclaiming that they have discharged the obligations of their birth, and proved themselves worthy of their country and of their parents. The coward and the unwarlike remain unshorn.[3]

In the past the Chatti had been part of Arminius' alliance that had destroyed Varus' legions in the Teutoburg Forest in AD 9 (see p. 313 ff.), and during the first century AD they had expanded from their homeland near the upper Visurgis (modern Weser) River in northern Germany, across the Taunus highlands to the Moenus (modern Main) River valley, defeating the Cherusci and other neighbouring tribes in the process. Now Domitian took the field against them in person, smashed their power, expanded the area of Roman control in the Wetterau region of Germany, established a permanent boundary there as well as along the eastern edge of the *Decumates Agri* (broadly the Black Forest area), and celebrated a triumph in the summer of AD 83 (even though the war dragged on for a few more years). The poet Martial sang his praises:

> Crete gave a great name, Africa a greater one:
> Scipio the victor has one, and Metellus has the other.
> Germany granted a nobler name when the Rhine was
>   tamed,
> and even as a boy, Caesar, you were worthy of this name.
> Your brother earned Idumaean triumphs together alongside
>   your father,
> but the laurel given for the Chatti is totally yours.[4]

Domitian and Decebalus

The picture painted of Domitian by most Roman sources is extremely negative, but he was generally popular with his soldiers, not least because he gave them a 33 per cent pay rise – their first since Augustus – and he would come to rely heavily on their loyalty in confronting another serious barbarian threat, this time on the River Danube frontier. This came from the Dacians, whose lands lay in the loop of the lower Danube, mostly comprising the plateau of Transylvania, but also stretching eastwards to the River Hierasus (modern Siret/ Sireth) and north to the River Vistula – essentially modern north-central and western Romania. The Dacians spoke a

Thracian dialect – the Greeks often mixed them up with the
Thracian Getae – and were an agricultural and cattle-breeding
people who had assimilated a degree of Celtic and Scythian
culture, worshipping the Scythian deity Zalmoxis. They also
exploited gold, silver and iron mines in the Carpathian
Mountains, and traded with both Greeks and Romans, import-
ing a good deal of wine.

The power of the Dacians had ebbed and flowed since the
mid-first century BC, when their leader Burebistas had united
their disparate tribes, subdued various Celtic and Illyrian
communities to the south and west, and menaced Roman
Macedonia. Prior to his assassination, Julius Caesar had
intended to campaign against them;[5] Octavian had sought a
marriage alliance with the Dacian King Cotiso during his
struggles with Mark Antony;[6] and once Octavian had become
Augustus, there was very little friction for several decades.

The origins of Domitian's conflict with Dacia are elusive,
although Roman provocation is a distinct possibility: Dacia's
mines might have been an alluring target. But under their
leader Decebalus, the Dacians invaded Roman territory in
AD 85. Dio Cassius describes Decebalus as 'shrewd in his
understanding of warfare and shrewd also in the waging of war;
he judged well when to attack and chose the right moment to
retreat; he was an expert in ambuscades and a master in pitched
battles; and he knew not only how to follow up a victory well,
but also how to manage well a defeat. Hence he showed himself
a worthy antagonist of the Romans for a long time.'[7]

The weapon of choice for Decebalus' warriors was called the
ensis falcatus[8] ('sickle-shaped sword') or *falx supina*[9] ('curved sickle').
It was a highly effective, single-edged, scythe-like weapon, sharpened just on the inside, that came in two versions: the shorter

one-handed type, which the Dacians called a *sica*,[10] had a curved iron blade about 40 centimetres long, fastened to a handle of about 55 centimetres;[11] the more aggressive two-handed weapon, which is often just called a *falx*, used a blade of around 90 centimetres attached to a handle of similar length. The sharp point of the *falx* could pierce helmets, chop shields in half, hack through armour, and inflict crippling and deadly wounds.

Brandishing their awesome *falces*, Decebalus' Dacians made their way into the Roman Empire and slew Oppius Sabinus, the governor of Moesia. Domitian's punitive response, led by the *Praefectus Praetorio* Cornelius Fuscus, was successful enough for Domitian to celebrate a triumph in AD 86. But Fuscus then got himself killed in further fighting and Domitian had to return to the region, where Tettius Julianus, the new governor of Upper Moesia, defeated the Dacians at Tapae (modern Zeicani, Romania), which guarded their main political centre of Sarmizegethusa, in (probably) AD 88. Domitian and Decebalus then tried to normalise relations by striking a deal in which the Dacian would become a nominal client king and protect the lower Danube in return for the help of Roman engineers and financial subsidies.

Decebalus and Trajan

Decebalus' accommodation with Domitian had been extraordinarily favourable to the Dacians, but after Domitian's demise and the accession to the throne of the bellicose Emperor Trajan in AD 98, it started to look just too good. He reappraised the arrangements, 'and was grieved at the amount of money [the Dacians] were receiving annually, and he also observed that their power and their pride were increasing'.[12]

Decebalus had reason to be fearful. Trajan was fond of fighting, popular with his troops, and willing to share hardships and dangers with them: 'And even if he did delight in war, nevertheless he was satisfied when success had been achieved, a most bitter foe overthrown and his countrymen exalted.'[13]

In AD 101 Trajan assembled legions and auxiliaries from Germany, Britain and elsewhere, and formed two new ones, XX *Ulpia* and (probably later) II *Traiana*. He then struck hard into Decebalus' territory.

The *falx*-wielding Dacian warriors posed serious challenges to Trajan's soldiers, who made specific modifications to their own kit to try to neutralise the power of the barbarian weaponry: they added special iron reinforcements to their helmets; went back to wearing *lorica hamata* (chainmail) and *lorica squamata* (scale armour), which were both more flexible and more protective than the more modern segmented cuirasses of the *lorica segmentata*; added leather strips called *pteruges* ('feathers') to their sleeves and skirts; and put thick layers of padding underneath. There was savage fighting near Tapae again, and towards the end of AD 101 Decebalus had been defeated, his counter-attack repulsed, his sister captured, and Trajan's forces had advanced to his base at Sarmizegethusa (modern Várhely, Romania). In autumn 102 Decebalus sought peace:

He reluctantly engaged to surrender his arms, engines and engine-makers, to give back the deserters, to demolish the forts, to withdraw from captured territory, and furthermore to consider the same persons enemies and friends as the Romans did, and neither to give shelter to any of the deserters nor to employ any soldier from their empire; for he had been acquiring the largest and best part of his force by persuading men to come to him from Roman territory. This was after he had come to Trajan, fallen upon the ground and done obeisance and thrown away his arms.[14]

Decebalus was still allowed to retain his throne as a client king, but Roman garrisons were installed in his territory. An amazing bridge, 1,135 metres long with twenty stone piers connected by arches, was then constructed over the Danube by Trajan's master engineer and architect Apollodorus of Damascus. The emperor returned to Rome, celebrated a triumph and put on gladiatorial games, and the Senate awarded him the title *Dacicus*.

Once again Decebalus had got off very lightly, but unfortunately for his people he broke the treaty in AD 105. By stockpiling arms, giving refuge to deserters, repairing his forts, sending envoys to his neighbours, attacking people who had previously differed with him and annexing a portion of the territory of the Iazyges, he prompted the Senate to declare him an enemy. And this time Trajan's response was practically genocidal. He marched into Dacia via Apollodorus' bridge in the early summer of AD 106. Decebalus favoured guerrilla tactics over a pitched battle, and tried to assassinate Trajan in his camp and to secure a settlement by capturing and ransoming his senior officers. All to no avail: the assassination plot was betrayed, and Gnaeus Pompeius Longinus, whom he had captured by trickery, poisoned himself.[15] Trajan's troops bore down on Sarmizegethusa and swiftly captured it. Decebalus committed suicide rather than be paraded in a Roman triumph, and so the Romans had to make do with exhibiting his severed head on the steps of the Capitol. The *Fasti Ostienses* confirm that the war was over by the autumn of AD 106.

Dacia became the first Roman province north of the Danube; a colony ultimately called Colonia Ulpia Traiana Augusta Dacica Sarmizegethusa was founded close to Sarmizegethusa; Dacia's gold mines were exploited; and the war booty was enormous:

> The treasures of Decebalus were also discovered, though hidden beneath the river Sargetia, which ran past his palace. With the help of some captives Decebalus had diverted the course of the river, made an excavation in its bed, and into the cavity had thrown a large amount of silver and gold and other objects of great value that could stand a certain amount of moisture; then he had heaped stones over them and piled on earth, afterwards bringing the river back into his course.[16]

Reputedly (although no doubt exaggeratedly) Trajan took more than 2.25 million kilograms of gold, twice as much silver and over 500,000 prisoners. He ploughed these barbarian funds back into infrastructure, social projects and handouts for the people. He could afford to be generous, and his coins said as much by featuring the image of *Abundantia* (Abundance personified). Ten thousand gladiators fought and 11,000 animals were killed in a victory celebration that lasted 123 days.[17]

A monument to Trajan's Dacian campaigns still stands in Rome: Trajan's Column, 'set up to serve at once as a monument to himself and as a memorial of the work in the Forum'.[18] Designed by Apollodorus of Damascus, and dedicated on 2 May AD 113, it has a pedestal with carvings depicting barbarian military equipment on its four sides, and an inscription ascribing its construction to the Senate and People of Rome.[19]

Made from Parian marble, the column is 100 Roman feet (about 30 metres) high, was topped by a statue of the emperor in gilt bronze, and features a continuous 200-metre-long, 0.85–1.45-metre-high spiral of relief sculpture that wraps itself twenty-three times around the column's exterior. On it there are 2,600 figures portrayed taking part in 155 distinct scenes from the Dacian Wars. Trajan is there, planning, sacrificing, supervising, consulting, haranguing his troops, who defeat a series of conventionally stereotyped barbarians. At the top, the column culminates with Decebalus' suicide, the pursuit of the Dacian leaders and mass deportations. It is an astonishing monument to regime change and ethnic cleansing perpetrated by the Romans in the barbarian world.

20

Parthia, Persia and Palmyra

The Demise of Parthia

Trajan's reign fell into what Edward Gibbon famously described as 'the period in the history of the world during which the condition of the human race was most happy and prosperous'.[1] But the hurt of Crassus' defeat at Carrhae some 250 years ago had not gone away, and during this 'happy and prosperous' period the Romans received an unwelcome Parthian wake-up call. Vologaeses IV (r. AD 147–91) invaded Armenia, installed his own nominee as king, and destroyed the Roman legion that was sent in to restore order, which might have been *Legio* IX *Hispana*, last attested at York under Trajan and in the early second century at Nijmegen, but perhaps then transferred to the east by Hadrian. The Parthians subsequently moved into Syria, so in the summer of AD 162 Marcus Aurelius dispatched his co-emperor Lucius Verus with a massive army and several top-flight generals, including the redoubtable Statius Priscus, who Lucian says merely shouted out and twenty-seven enemy fighters dropped dead.[2] He managed to seize the Armenian capital Artaxata in AD 163, founded a new one, and garrisoned it.

Lucius Verus' commander Marcus Pontius Laelianus also did much to restore discipline in the Syrian army by rigorous kit inspections and a clampdown on drinking and gambling, and Fronto writes that Lucius himself acted as a role model, marching

> on foot at the head of his men as often as he rode on horse-back, putting up with the blazing sun and choking dust, his head exposed to sun and shower, hail and snow – and to missiles. He sweated unconcernedly as if engaged in sport . . . He took a belated bath after his work was done and ate simple camp-food, drank local wine. He often slept on leaves of turf. Through so many provinces, so many open dangers of sieges, battles, citadels, posts and forts stormed, he lavished his care and advice.[3]

Other sources see it rather differently, however, and make him party all along the warpath and spend a lot of time at the resort of Daphne near Antioch, where he struck up an affair with the gorgeous and gifted Panthea from Smyrna. Marcus Aurelius responded by sending out Lucilla, Lucius' fourteen-year-old intended bride, to Ephesus, where the marriage took place in AD 164.

Lucius Verus was certainly a good delegator, though, and this allowed the professionalism of the Roman army to see the campaign through: they installed the pro-Roman Mannus on the throne of Osrhoene; followed up by capturing the frontier outpost of Nisibis (modern Nusaybin in Turkey, right on the Syrian border), where the Parthian general narrowly escaped by swimming the Tigris; and they advanced down the Euphrates, scored a victory at Dura-Europus, destroyed Seleucia-on-the-Tigris, and sacked Ctesiphon, the winter capital of the Parthian

Empire, situated on the left bank of the River Tigris (32 kilometres south-east of modern Baghdad, in Iraq). Lucius took the title *Parthicus Maximus*. The next year Gaius Avidius Cassius took Rome's legions over the Tigris into Medea (modern Iran), further east than any Roman army had gone before, whereupon Lucius started calling himself *Medicus*, 'of Medea' (as did Marcus Aurelius). Vologaeses IV fled, while the Romans consolidated their grip on the border regions and finally withdrew in AD 166. Lucius and Marcus celebrated a joint triumph, and the *Historia Augusta* jokes that, because of Lucius' behaviour on campaign, the Parthian War was described as the 'Histrionic/Theatrical' War.

Gibbon's happy era came to an end with the debauchery and conspiracy that characterised the reign of Commodus (r. AD 180–92), who liked to think of himself as a gladiator and the 'Roman Hercules', after which there was a 'Year of the Five Emperors' in which the Roman Empire was effectively sold at auction to Didius Julianus, before Septimius Severus (r. AD 193–211) emerged as Rome's first African emperor.[4] Within the boundaries of the empire, at least, the old distinctions between Romans and those who would have once been considered barbarians were breaking apart.

Those outside the borders of the empire were still definitively barbarian in Roman eyes, however, and the Parthians once again imprinted themselves on the Roman consciousness when King Vologaeses V (r. AD 191–208) retaliated against a Roman incursion of AD 195 by attacking Nisibis. Septimius Severus escalated the conflict by raising three new legions, of which I and III *Parthica* were quartered in Mesopotamia. In the late summer of AD 197, Septimius' invasion force sailed along the Euphrates before marching against Ctesiphon and capturing it without difficulty. Although incidents of the sort were not uncommon in antiquity, Roman barbarism manifested itself at Ctesiphon when all the adult males were killed, the women and children enslaved, and the Parthian royal treasury looted. Northern Mesopotamia once again became a Roman province, and on 28 January AD 198, the centenary of Trajan's accession, Severus took the title of *Parthicus Maximus*. He had become the greatest expander of the empire since Trajan, but rather than annexing the territory he had just conquered, he withdrew his loot-laden army, making two costly and unsuccessful assaults on the fortress city of Hatra, in the Al Jazirah region of present-day Iraq, on the way home.

Septimius Severus died in AD 211, leaving Gibbon to label him the 'principal author of the decline and fall of the Roman empire',[5] and his eldest son Caracalla to not only murder his own younger brother Geta, but to secure his *damnatio memoriae* (the damnation of his memory) and have his name expunged from the records. The following year Caracalla issued an edict that was deeply significant for the extension of 'Romanness' across the empire's ever-increasingly ethnically diverse population. It was known as the *Constitutio Antoniniana*, and it granted Roman citizenship to virtually all free inhabitants of the empire.[6] From this moment, any free person born in the formerly barbarian areas of Britain, Gaul, Spain, Egypt, Syria, or wherever, could say those famous words, 'I am a Roman citizen.'

Caracalla's greatest ambition was to outdo both Alexander the Great and Trajan by conquering the east. So he relocated to Antioch and sought to exploit the internal tension in Parthia. When Vologaeses V died in AD 208, his successor and eldest son Vologaeses VI found himself challenged by the younger son, Artabanus V. Caracalla backed the latter, agreed to marry his daughter, crossed the Euphrates and Tigris rivers, and penetrated deep into Parthian territory, where his army was welcomed with flowers, wild dancing, pounding drums and copious amounts of alcohol. But when the Parthians abandoned their horses and put their quivers and bows away, Caracalla gave the order to attack. After massacring the Parthians, the Romans took large amounts of booty and prisoners, and marched away unopposed, burning and pillaging towns and villages at will.

When the Roman army wintered at Edessa (modern Şanlıurfa in Turkey), Caracalla was probably very pleased with himself, but a retrospective analysis of the situation a decade into the future might have given him a different viewpoint. Like his hero Alexander the Great, Caracalla died in the east. On 8 April AD 217, he was heading for Carrhae, but was assassinated while he was taking a toilet break. He had unquestionably avenged Crassus and hastened the demise of the Parthian Empire, whose overthrow by the Sasanian (aka Sassanian, Sasanid or Sassanid) dynasty in Persia was started by Ardashir I, but in doing so he had taken Rome out of the frying pan and into the fire.

Ardashir I was descended from Sasan, after whom the dynasty is named. Our conflicting and incomplete sources only allow a very vague picture to emerge, but over the first two decades of the third century AD, amid family infighting and localised conflicts, Ardashir became the ruler of Pars (roughly coterminous with the modern province of Fars in Iran), established his capital at Ardashir-Khwarrah (modern Firuzabad), and expanded into western Iran to such an extent that Artabanus V was forced to respond. Two Parthian defeats later, Artabanus V took personal command of his forces and faced Ardashir in a decisive battle at Hormozgan, near the modern city of Bandar Abbas, in AD 224. The Parthian army was comprehensively defeated, and Artabanus V was killed, thereby terminating four centuries of rule by the Parthian Arsacid dynasty. Ardashir took possession of Ctesiphon, and was acknowledged as *Shahanshah* ('King of Kings').

The Romans did not always make clear-cut distinctions between Parthians and Persians, frequently regarding them as generic eastern barbarians. The new Sasanian dynasty were often wrongly referred to by Roman historians as 'Parthians' or 'Medes', partly because those writers formed part of a fixed tradition going back to the Greek writers of the fifth century BC, which had a very distinctive style, content and vocabulary, and where there were no Sasanians but huge numbers of Medes, and partly because of the Roman view that barbarians from any one area were all the same, regardless of what you called them. Procopius, for instance, said that in ancient times 'the Goths, Vandals, Visigoths, and Gepaedes . . . were named Sauromatae and Melanchlaeni ['Black-cloaks']; and there were some too who called these nations Getic. All these, while they are distinguished from one another by their names, as has been said, do not differ in anything else at all.'[7]

Regardless of who the Romans thought the Sasanians were, they would pose a series of new challenges. And, in addition, Rome faced a degree of internal barbarism during Ardashir I's reign, as she stumbled onto five decades of what some historians see as 'transition', but which was in fact an omnishambles. As the sixth-century historian Zosimus put it, 'the Roman Empire degenerated to a species of barbarity, and fell to decay'.[8]

Amid a seemingly endless list of emperors, usurpers, rebels and outlaws, nearly all of whom were assassinated, the empire

faced dangerous challenges from barbarians outside its borders
and economic meltdown within them.

Shapur I 'the Great'

While Rome was imploding the second Sasanian *Shahanshah*,
Ardashir I's son Shapur I ('Son of a King', known to the Romans
as Sapores and/or Sapor) came to the throne. The *Res Gestae
Divi Saporis*, a trilingual inscription from the walls of the Cube
of Zoroaster (Ka'ba-ye Zartosht) at Naqsh-e Rustam near
Persepolis in Iran, informs us that Shapur's mother was the
exceptionally beautiful Arsacid princess Lady Myrod.[9] Shapur
had been involved in his father's campaigns against the
Parthians, was judged to be 'the gentlest, wisest, bravest and
ablest of all his children',[10] and seems to have become co-ruler
with Ardashir I at some stage: the Cologne Mani Codex[11] implies
that they were ruling together when it states that Ardashir
'subjugated the city of Hatra[12] and King Shapur, his son, placed
on his head the great (royal) diadem' in AD 240;[13] in AD 242,
the Roman Emperor Gordian III (r. AD 238–44[14]) informed
the Senate that he had removed the threat of *reges Persarum*
('Kings [in the plural] of the Persians');[15] Ardashir I's late coins
show him facing a young prince, clearly Shapur, and carry the
legend, 'Divine Shapur King of Iran whose seed is from gods';[16]
and rock reliefs at Salmas in Azerbaijan and at Darábgerd in
southern Iran, where Ardashir I started his career as its *argbad*
(military commander/governor), both show Shapur I wearing
Ardashir's crown.

Once installed as ruler in his own right, Shapur I became
embroiled in hostilities with Rome. The Parthians had
moved into Mesopotamia, and now, in AD 242, the

seventeen-year-old Gordian III opened the gates of the temple of Janus, and set out against Shapur in the company of Gaius Furius Sabinus Aquila Timesitheus, the *Praefectus Praetorio*, whose daughter Tranquilliana he married, 'with so huge an army and so much gold as easily to conquer the Persians'.[17] He arrived in Syria:

> There he fought and won repeated battles, and drove out Shapur, the Persians' king. After this he recovered Artaxanses [unknown], Antioch, Carrhae, and Nisibis, all of which had been included in the Persian Empire. Indeed the king of the Persians became so fearful of the Emperor Gordian that . . . he evacuated the cities and restored them unharmed to their citizens; nor did he injure their possessions in any way. All this, however, was accomplished by Timesitheus, Gordian's father-in-law and prefect. And in the end Gordian's campaign forced the Persians, who were then dreaded even in Italy, to return to their own kingdom, and the Roman power occupied the whole of the East.[18]

Gordian III wrote to the Senate to say that if it were pleasing to the gods, he would get to Ctesiphon.[19] But it wasn't. Timesitheus died of a very nasty bout of diarrhoea and was replaced as *Praefectus Praetorio* by Marcus Julius Philippus, aka Philip the Arab,[20] who could well have connived in the assassination of Gordian III in the spring of AD 244. Other accounts have Gordian III killed in action, or falling from his horse, but 'Philippus Arabs' was undoubtedly proclaimed emperor and made peace with Shapur in order to focus on other enemies elsewhere in the empire. He minted coins proudly announcing *PAX FUNDATA CUM PERSIS* ('Peace Achieved with the Persians').[21]

That is the Roman version. Shapur I's account is inscribed on the Cube of Zoroaster at Naqsh-e Rustam, and is very different:

> Just as we were established on the throne, the emperor Gordian gathered in all of the Roman Empire an army of Goths and Germans and marched . . . against us . . . There was a great frontal battle. And Gordian Caesar perished, and we destroyed the Roman army. And the Romans proclaimed Philip emperor. And Philip Caesar came to us for terms, and paid us 500,000 *denarii* as ransom for his life and became tributary to us.[22]

The *Shahanshah* rammed home the propaganda on a rock relief at Darábgerd, which shows a defeated foe (Gordian III, possibly) under Shapur's horse, and two pleading figures in front of it, one of whom may be Philip the Arab,[23] and at Bishapur (relief I), which illustrates a combination of Shapur's investiture and triumph, with the Persian again on horseback, and Gordian under his horse and Philip kneeling in front of him. However, Shapur might be overstating the matter somewhat: Philip later reneged on the treaty, recovered the lost territory, and called himself *Parthicus Adiabenicus* (Victor over Parthia and Adiabene in Assyria), *Persicus Maximus* and *Parthicus Maximus*.

Regardless of who actually won the first war, there was a short-lived lull until Shapur I became the aggressor once more, using the excuse that 'the Caesar lied and did harm to Armenia'[24] and was probably not paying the agreed 'tribute'. Shapur invaded Mesopotamia around AD 250, but got distracted by troubles in his Persian heartlands, which 'necessitated his presence there'.[25] Having dealt with these he resumed the anti-Roman campaign, and inflicted a crushing defeat on them at the Battle of Barbalissus (near modern Aleppo in Syria) in AD 252. The *Res Gestae Divi Saporis*, inscribed on the Cube of Zoroaster at Naqsh-e Rustam, tells the story in Shapur I's own words: 'We attacked the Roman Empire and we destroyed an army of 60,000 men at Barbalissus. Syria and its surrounding areas we burned, devastated and plundered. In this one campaign we captured of the Roman Empire 37 cities.'[26] Among these cities was Antioch.

Although Shapur I burned and pillaged the Roman province of Syria right up to the Mediterranean coast, he had no serious intention of retaining all the territory he passed through. And neither did the current incumbent on the Roman throne have any intention of allowing Shapur I to run amok in the eastern end of his empire. By AD 257 Valerian (r. AD 253–60) had brought both Antioch and the province of Syria back under Roman control, but then he pushed on into Mesopotamia, where he tried to rescue the city of Edessa, which was besieged by the Persian army. The Naqsh-e Rustam inscription gives Shapur's version of events:

In the third campaign . . . as we were besieging Carrhae and Edessa, Valerian Caesar came against us [with troops from] Germania, Raetia [plus the names of some 29 Roman provinces], a force of 70,000 men. Beyond [i.e. west of] Carrhae and Edessa there was a great battle between the Emperor Valerian and us. We made the Emperor Valerian prisoner with our own hands; and the commanders of that army, the *Praefectus Praetorio*, Senators and officers, we made them all prisoner, and we transported them to Persia. We burned, devastated and plundered Cilicia and Cappadocia [the names of 36 cities follow].[27]

Once again Shapur I commemorated his victories over Rome on various rock reliefs: one at Bishapur (relief II) depicts Gordian III prostrate and Shapur I on horseback, holding Valerian by the wrist; another at Naqsh-e Rustam shows Philip the Arab kneeling and Valerian standing; and the largest, also at Bishapur (relief III), shows the *Shahanshah* with all three of the aforementioned emperors, although Valerian is shown unfettered and in full imperial regalia, and shows no sign of maltreatment.

Valerian had been a persecutor of Christians, and later Christian writers could barely conceal their schadenfreude at the fate of their oppressor, which they saw as a lesson for future 'adversaries of Heaven':

[Valerian] wasted the remainder of his days in the vilest condition of slavery: for Shapur, the king of the Persians, who had made him prisoner, whenever he chose to get into his carriage or to mount on horseback, commanded the Roman to stoop and present his back . . . Afterward, when he had finished this shameful life under so great dishonour, he was flayed, and his skin, stripped from the flesh, was dyed with vermilion, and placed in the temple of the gods of the barbarians . . . as an admonition to the Romans.[28]

Valerian's son Gallienus probably heard about his capture in AD 259. The *Historia Augusta* says that he adapted a well-known quotation from a philosopher about the death of his son – 'I knew that I had begotten a mortal' – to, 'I knew that my father was mortal',[29] and rather than asking for him back, simply claimed the whole empire and devoted himself to a life of feckless pleasure-seeking:

> born for his belly and his pleasures, [Gallienus] wasted his days and nights in wine and debauchery and caused the world to be laid waste by pretenders . . . so that even women ruled better than he . . . He built castles of apples, preserved grapes for three years, and served melons in the depth of winter . . . always served out of season green figs and apples fresh from the trees. He always spread his tables with golden covers . . . He used a jewelled sword-belt and he fastened jewels to his boot-laces . . . In summer he would bathe six or seven times in the day, and in the winter twice or thrice. He always drank out of golden cups, for he scorned glass, declaring that there was nothing more common . . . His concubines frequently reclined in his dining-halls, and he always had near at hand a second table for the jesters and actors . . . The prefects and the chiefs of all the staffs . . . were invited to his banquets and bathed in the pools along with the prince. Women, too, were often sent in, beautiful girls with the emperor, but with the others ugly old hags. And he used to say that he was making merry, whereas he had brought the world on all sides to ruin.[30]

For his part, Shapur exploited both the riches that he acquired from his plunder and the technical expertise of many of the Romans that he deported, to rejuvenate the urban centres, industries and agriculture of his realm. Christians lived free from persecution, and thriving communities established churches and monasteries. The Greek and Syriac languages came into wider use, and some significant works on science and astronomy, including Ptolemy's *Almagest*, were translated into the Sasanian Empire's Pahlavi language. The new influx of people into Shapur I's realm led to him assuming the title of 'King of Iranians and un-Iranians'. After ruling his multi-ethnic subjects for another decade or so, he died of illness at Bishapur in May AD 270.

Zenobia: The Most Lovely and Most Heroic of Her Sex

One of the subplots of Rome's dealings with the Parthians and Persians was the rise of Septimius Odenathus (also spelled Odenaethus, Odenatus or Odainath) to become the ruler of the great Syrian oasis caravan city of Palmyra. He belonged to an aristocratic family from Palmyra that had been granted Roman citizenship in the AD 190s, but he exploited the weaknesses of Rome and Persia in the mid-third century to make himself a major player in the region, although he was careful to acknowledge Rome's supremacy.

In the aftermath of the defeat and capture of Valerian, his *Praefectus Praetorio* Balista (aka Ballista or Callistus) and a high-ranking fiscal official called Fulvius Macrianus routed a Persian force that was returning from pillaging Cilicia. The Persians then provoked a rebellion by proclaiming Macrianus' sons, Macrianus Minor and Quietus, as emperors. The usurpation by the Macriani was quickly stamped out, with Odenathus ultimately, if not initially, playing a significant pro-Gallienus role, and from AD 262 he led successful incursions over the River Euphrates into Persian territory, in which he captured Shapur's harem, recovered Carrhae and Nisibis, and besieged Ctesiphon (briefly and unsuccessfully), before declaring himself

Shahanshah with his son Hairan I as co-ruler. Emperor Gallienus also granted Odenathus the title of *Dux* and *Corrector Totius Orientis* ('General' and 'Regulator of the Whole East') for his services rendered. However, Odenathus and Hairan were both murdered in suspicious circumstances in AD 267. His widow, Zenobia (*Bath Zabbai* in Aramaic), then took control of the Palmyrene Empire as regent in the name of their eight-year-old son, Vaballathus. His name is a Latinisation of the Palmyrene Wahballat, meaning Gift of Allat, an Arabian goddess who was equated with Athena: so Vaballathus used Athenodorus ('Gift of Athena') as the Greek form of his name.

Zenobia was one of the great female figures of antiquity: 'Her face was dusky and of a swarthy colour, her eyes were black and unusually powerful, her spirit was divine, and she was unbelievably attractive.'[31] She was also ferociously intelligent and well educated, having been tutored by the old-school Platonist and literary critic Cassius Longinus.

As they so often do with barbarian queens, the Roman sources use her to highlight Gallienus' failings – she is everything that he is not: 'Zenobia ruled . . . not in feminine fashion or with the ways of a woman, but surpassing in courage and skill not merely Gallienus, than whom any girl could have ruled more successfully, but also many an Emperor.'[32]

Morally unimpeachable, cultured, fond of hunting and drinking, falsely claiming descent from Cleopatra VII of Egypt, and 'ruling Palmyra and most of the East with the vigour of a man',[33] she had grand ideas for the Palmyrene state but, for the moment, provided that she kept the east secure, Gallienus was prepared to tolerate her regime. Internal threats were more on his mind than exotic Palmyrene queens anyway, and so they should have been: in AD 268 he fell victim to a conspiracy, impaled on the spear of Cecropius, the commander of the Dalmatian cavalry.[34]

Gallienus was succeeded by a series of very competent, highly energetic and extremely aggressive soldier-emperors, the first of which was Claudius II Gothicus, born in the one-time barbarian territory of Illyria. He reigned from AD 268 to 270, and the ancient tradition about him is one of unadulterated hero-worship: 'Claudius, a venerated man and justly respected, dear to all good men, a friend to his native land, a friend to the laws, acceptable to the senate, and favourably known to the people, received the imperial power.'[35] The *Historia Augusta* describes him as a man of gravitas, purity and abstemiousness who was so strong that he could knock a horse's teeth out with his bare fists, and concludes: 'Both the senate and people adored him so much both before, during and after his rule that it is universally agreed that neither Trajan, nor the Antonines, nor any other Emperor was so loved.'[36]

Yet he was powerless to stop Zenobia moving into Asia Minor, and if we accept the account in the *Historia Augusta*, she wiped out a Roman army that was setting out against the Persians.[37] Syria would soon be hers.

Claudius II Gothicus contracted a plague and died at Sirmium in August AD 270. Then his brother Quintillus became emperor, maybe for as little as seventeen days,[38] before the Danube legions threw their weight behind a no-nonsense, bullet-headed cavalry commander with a crew cut and designer stubble called Lucius Domitius Aurelianus ('Aurelian'), who assumed the purple in September.

Aurelian immediately faced pressing issues in the form of barbarian invasions by the Vandali ('Vandals') and Sarmatians, who penetrated the Danube valley, and the Germanic Alemanni (aka Alamanni = 'Men United'/'All Men') and Iuthungi (or

Juthungi = 'Descendants'/'Offsprings'), who got as far as Placentia (modern Piacenza in Italy) before they were repulsed in AD 271. There were also three usurpers – Domitianus, Septimius and Urbanus – who were also swiftly eradicated. Zenobia exploited Aurelian's preoccupations to send her general Septimius Zabdas into the Roman province of Arabia Petraea, where he overcame *Legio* III *Cyrenaica*, sacked the city of Bostra and destroyed the temple of Zeus Ammon, before proceeding to subdue Judaea. At that point

> Zenobia . . . sent Zabdas into Egypt, because Timagenes an Egyptian attempted to place Egypt under the government of the Palmyrenians. Zabdas had for this purpose raised an army of Palmyrenians, Syrians, and barbarians, to the number of 70,000, which was opposed by 50,000 Egyptians. A sharp engagement ensued between them, in which the Palmyrenians had greatly the advantage. He then departed, leaving them a garrison of five thousand men.[39]

The Zenobia/Zabdas problem was initially confronted by Aurelian's *Praefectus Aegypti* Tenagino Probus, who had been away clearing the seas of pirates. With his own forces, augmented by anti-Palmyran Egyptians, he dislodged Zabdas' garrisons: 'But as Probus was encamped on a mountain near Babylon [i.e. the Babylon Fortress, situated in modern Cairo in Egypt], thereby cutting off the passage of the enemy into Syria, Timagenes, who was well acquainted with the country, seized the summit of the mountain with two thousand men, and attacked the Egyptians by surprise. Probus being taken with the rest killed himself.'[40] Zabdas completed the conquest, and Zenobia was declared Queen of Egypt.

In AD 271, Zenobia's general Zabbai opened up a new front in Asia Minor. He was joined by Septimius Zabdas, and together they occupied Galatia and seized Ancyra (modern Ankara in Turkey). This marked the zenith of Zenobia's power: Roman emperors had previously appeared on the Palmyrene coinage, but Aurelian now disappears; the legends on coins dubbed Vaballathus 'King, Emperor, and *Dux Romanum* (leader of the Romans)'; Zenobia and Vaballathus took the titles *Augusta* (Empress) and *Augustus* (Emperor) respectively; and Zenobia's court became a magnet for the intellectuals of the region. All in all, she was now a serious menace to Rome.

Despite difficulties elsewhere in his empire, Aurelian could not let the situation deteriorate any further. With an army that included some new units raised specifically for or during the campaign, such as *Legio* I *Illyricorum*, he had reclaimed all the territory between Ancyra and Antioch by AD 272. Zenobia's main shock troops were her *clibanarii* (heavily armoured cavalry who get their name from the word for an iron bread oven), and when the two sides engaged at Immae about 40 kilometres north of Antioch, the lighter Roman cavalry lured them into a chase, which exhausted them and their steeds in the viciously hot sun. Then, 'as soon as the cavalry of the Emperor saw their enemy tired, and that their horses were scarcely able to stand under them, or themselves to move, they drew up the reins of their horses, and, wheeling round, charged them, and trod them under foot as they fell from their horses. By which means the slaughter was promiscuous, some falling by the sword, and others by their own and the enemies' horses.'[41]

Zenobia was not present at the battle, which had been fought under Zabdas' command. She was at Antioch, to where Zabdas fled. There they engaged in some skulduggery. They pretended that they had won, chose a man who looked like Aurelian, dressed him in imperial clothing, and paraded him through the city as if he were a prisoner.[42] They then evacuated Antioch and headed to Emesa.

The people of Antioch were somewhat surprised, albeit pleasantly, when Aurelian turned up there shortly afterwards. He then gave chase to Zenobia, captured the fort at Daphne in the suburbs of Emesa by the adept use of the *testudo* formation, consolidated his position, and received reinforcements who included some Palestinians who fought with clubs.

Zenobia offered battle and Aurelian, who could deploy 70,000 fighting men,[43] accepted. The issue was largely decided in his favour by the Palestinian clubmen,[44] and Zenobia's forces ended up besieged in Palmyra. Zosimus tells a tale about a Palmyran soldier who uttered indecent taunts against Aurelian:

> Upon this, a Persian who stood by the emperor said, 'If you will allow me, sir, you shall see me kill that insolent soldier.' To which the Emperor consented, and the Persian, placing himself behind some other men that he might not be seen, shot at the man while in the act of looking over the battlements, and hit him whilst still uttering his insulting language, so that he fell down from the wall before the soldiers and the Emperor.[45]

Zenobia escaped from the city 'on a female camel, which is the swiftest of that kind of animals, and much more swift than horses',[46] but she was intercepted and captured by Aurelian's men at the Euphrates. There are two accounts of what happened to her: Zosimus' mundane one in which she perished from disease or lack of food en route to Rome, and a much sexier one in which she was paraded in Aurelian's triumph there: 'She was decked out with gems that were so enormous that she struggled under the burden of her ornaments . . . Furthermore, her feet were bound with gold, her hands with golden chains, and not even her neck was without a chain of gold, the weight of which was supported by a Persian jester.'⁴⁷

While Zenobia was subsequently accommodated close to Hadrian's villa at Tivoli, her subjects rebelled again. They clothed Septimius Antiochus, who may or may not have been a son of Zenobia, in purple, but Aurelian responded instantly, and Palmyra was so savagely sacked and looted that it never really recovered. A revolt in Egypt by partisans of Zenobia was given similarly short shrift, and Aurelian took the title *Restitutor Orientis* (Restorer of the East).

The Barbarisation of the Roman Army

After his successes against Zenobia, Aurelian aimed to upgrade himself to *Restitutor Orbis* ('Restorer of the World'). He was the first Roman emperor to assume the official title of *Deus* (God) in his lifetime: inscriptions refer to *Deus Aurelianus* (the god Aurelian), and his coins carry the legend *DEO ET DOMINO NATO AURELIANO AVG* on one side and *RESTITUT ORBIS* on the other. In other words, Aurelian is not just 'Restorer of the World' but 'Born [*nato*] god [*deo*] and master [*domino*]'. He died in AD 275, and was quite a hard act to follow: Marcus Claudius Tacitus, Florianus (for two months and twenty days), and Marcus Aurelius Probus (Probus in Latin means 'excellent in a moral sense') were the next to assume the purple. Probus' epitaph reads: 'Here lies the Emperor Probus, and indeed a man of probity, the victor over all barbarian tribes and also the victor over pretenders.'[48]

The phrase 'all barbarian tribes' conjures up a rather misleading image of hundreds of thousands of barbarians overwhelming Rome's borders, but although they were very frightening and often destructive, their actual numbers were probably relatively small.

The barbarians who needed Probus' attention were the Franks and the Alemanni, who were devastating Gaul and the Rhineland, the Burgundiones (a Germanic people) and the Vandali, who were terrorising Raetia, and the Goths, who needed to be expelled from the Danubian provinces. Probus rose manfully to the task, and by AD 279 he could focus on Asia Minor, where a brigand called Lydius the Isaurian was pillaging Pamphylia and Lycia. Lydius was shot by a turncoat artillery expert, after which the final item on Probus' 'to-do list' was a rebellion in Upper Egypt by the Blemmyae. By the end of AD 279 he seemed to have a secure grasp of both the eastern and the western provinces.

One interesting decision that Probus took was to allow large numbers of Bastarnae from Scythia (roughly modern Moldova), Goths, Vandali, Alemanni and Franks to settle in Gaul and in the Danubian provinces, perhaps to rectify depopulation caused by warfare and plague. For their part, the barbarians probably felt that they would be better off inside the Roman frontiers: essentially they were looking for lands to farm, not to destroy Rome, and many of them served as recruits in the Roman army. The pleasure felt by the barbarians at being allowed to settle within the empire is perhaps reflected in the name that some of them were given: *laeti*, 'the Happy Ones' in

Latin (although the term may also be a Germanic one denoting serfs).

Probus' policy would cause difficulties later on, but for now he seemed sufficiently pleased with himself to assume the title *Persicus Maximus*, implying triumphs over the Sasanian Persians, although precisely why is not specified. Towards the end of AD 281 Probus celebrated a triumph: the Circus Maximus was turned into a temporary forest for a beast hunt where the people were allowed to take thousands of ostriches, stags, wild boars and other animals; 100 lions, 100 lionesses, 200 leopards and 300 bears made a spectacle 'bigger than it was enjoyable'[49] in the Colosseum; and many captive Blemmyae, Germans, Sarmatians and Isaurian brigands were made to fight as gladiators after being displayed in the triumph.

The following spring Probus was intending to campaign against the Persians, and had reached the vicinity of his birthplace, Sirmium, when Marcus Aurelius Carus, the *Praefectus Praetorio*, proclaimed himself emperor. Probus' soldiers defected, and killed him as he took refuge in an iron-clad watchtower. Carus now set out with his son Numerianus to complete his predecessor's unfinished business with Persia. This can have only been a vanity project, since Persia under Vahram II was by now a shadow of what it had been under Shapur I. The Roman battle group advanced through Mesopotamia and took Ctesiphon, and Carus assumed the title *Persicus Maximus*. But there, in July or August AD 283, both the vanity and the expedition stopped. Most of the ancient sources say that Carus was hit by a thunderbolt, although disease and assassination cannot be ruled out (or definitively ruled in).

Numerianus had started to oversee an orderly withdrawal of the Roman troops from Persia when it was said that he had contracted a serious eye infection, which meant that he had to travel in a closed litter. No one thought any more about this until a hideous stench started to emanate from the litter, and his rotting corpse was discovered. On 20 November AD 284, a military assembly acclaimed the Dalmatian-born commander of the *domestici* (imperial guards), Gaius Aurelius Valerius Diocles, as emperor.

He assumed the name Diocletianus (Diocletian), saw off Carus' other son Carinus, and proceeded to impose his dominance onto the Roman world. The empire changed its nature from a Principate (*Princeps* = 'First Among Equals') to the Dominate (*Dominus* = 'Lord and Master'). There was root and branch reform of the governmental, administrative, economic and military systems of the empire.[50]

Under Diocletian the army's strength was increased to some sixty legions, although archaeological evidence shows that legionary fortresses were now much smaller, so estimating the overall size of the Roman army at this time is an inexact science. Figures of around 350,000 to 400,000 men are commonly quoted. The old-school legions of around 5,000 high-quality infantrymen now metamorphosed into something more flexible. The legions, auxiliary cavalry *alae* and cohorts of this 'New Model Army' now functioned alongside other units sometimes vaguely designated *numeri* ('numbers') while the cavalry of the field armies were organised into *vexillationes*. Overall, the army was now divided into a central mobile field force (*comitatenses*, 'companions') commanded by *magistri militum*, and static frontier garrisons (*ripenses* – riverside troops, referring to the Rhine and Danube – and *limitanei*, 'borderers') commanded by *duces* ('Dukes', singular *dux*). *Limitanei* who became permanently attached to the *comitatenses* were designated *pseudocomitatenses.* There was a hierarchy descending from the imperial guards (the *scholae* and the *domestici*) down to the elite 'palatine' units (*palatinae*), the 'praesental' field armies (those 'in the presence of' the emperor), the regional field armies and the *limitanei*, who got less pay and fewer privileges than the *comitatenses*, but still seem to have operated pretty effectively as a rule.

The basic kit of the Roman infantry came to be trousers and a shortish, long-sleeved tunic, belted at the waist. Belt buckles and the brooches that fastened their cloaks served as the badges of the different ranks. Armour comprised a mass-produced helmet, scale or mail body armour rather like the medieval hauberk but with sleeves and a hood, plus a circular or oval shield sporting the regimental insignia. Offensive weaponry included a sword called a *spatha* (longer than the old *gladius*), various combinations of thrusting and throwing spears (the *spiculum* – rather like a *pilum* – *verutum* and *lancea*), and lead-weighted darts called *plumbatae* or *mattiobarbuli*. Archers, slingers and *manuballistae* (cart-mounted catapults) were also deployed. The cavalry arm featured heavily armoured *clibanarii* and *cataphracti,* especially in the east, as well as lighter-armed *scutarii, promoti, stablesiani,* mounted archers, and units of Moors and Dalmatians.

All this, especially the trousers and long swords, had a some-what 'barbarian' flavour to it. Within the borders of the Roman Empire, and especially within the ranks of the army, the old binary Roman/barbarian distinctions were becoming ever more fluid. The *duces* were often of non-Roman stock, as is shown by names such as Fullofaudes, Duke of Britain; in the *Notitia Dignitatum*, the workshops that produced ornamented armour are called *barbaricaria*; the later imperial army also adopted the *draco*, a sort of windsock in the form of a dragon, which the Dacians on Trajan's Column used as a standard; the units of the field army started to assume somewhat 'barbarous', almost animalistic, titles; and the war cry, the *barritus*, was often, if mistakenly, said to have a barbarian origin:

> [The Germans] have also those cries by the recital of which – '*barritus*' is the name they use – they inspire courage; and they divine the fortunes of the coming battle from the circumstances of the cry. Intimidation or timidity depends on the intonation of the warriors; it seems to them to mean not so much unison of voices as union of hearts; the object they specially seek is a certain volume of hoarseness, a crashing roar, their shields being brought up to their lips, that the voice may swell to a fuller and deeper note by means of the echo.[51]

Rome's new-look army was put to the test when the new Sasanian king, Shapur I's son Narses (r. AD 293–302), resurrected his father's ambitions and incited uprisings by the Blemmyae in Egypt and the Saracens in the Syrian desert. Diocletian dealt with the Egyptian problem easily enough, but an invasion of Armenia, Osrhoene and part of Syria by Narses was more problematical. Diocletian's 'Caesar' (emperor-in-waiting) Galerius initially suffered a defeat near Carrhae, but then comprehensively destroyed Narses' forces in AD 298, captured Ctesiphon, extended Rome's possessions beyond the Tigris, and most importantly secured peace in the region for several decades.

An indication of Rome's suspicion of 'barbaric' Persian customs comes from Diocletian's Edict Against Manichaeism. Manichaeism had been founded by a Babylonian prophet called Mani in the middle of the third century AD. The cult offered redemption, and would become an important religion, but for now it was persecuted by both the Roman and indeed the Persian authorities. Around AD 297, Rome's rulers wrote to the proconsul of Africa. They were concerned that 'the accursed customs and perverse laws of the Persians' might 'infect men of a more innocent nature, namely the temperate and tranquil Roman people':

> They lure on many others to accept the authority of their erroneous doctrine. But the age-old religion [ought not to] be disparaged by a new one. For it is the height of criminality to re-examine doctrines once and for all settled and fixed by the ancients . . . Now, therefore, we order that the founders and heads be subjected to severe punishment: together with their abominable writings they are to be burned in the flames. We instruct that their followers, and particularly the fanatics, shall suffer a capital penalty, and we ordain that their property be confiscated.[52]

Barbarophobia was still alive and well.

Shapur II 'the Great'

On 1 May AD 305, as he had always intended to do, Diocletian abdicated, and retired to his enormous fortified palace at Spalato (modern Split, in Croatia), where he remained, contentedly growing vegetables, until his death on 3 December AD 311. In Persia, the tenth and longest-reigning *Shahanshah*, Shapur II the Great, came to the throne in AD 309 even before he was born – legend saying that the crown was placed on his mother Ifra Hormizd's womb by the courtiers and the clergy while she was pregnant, although it doesn't specify how they knew the child was male. During his childhood and adolescence Rome underwent further civil wars and witnessed the conversion to Christianity of Constantine I the Great, who issued the Edict of Milan in AD 313, thereby guaranteeing, at least in theory, that no Christian in the Roman Empire could be persecuted for his or her faith. Shapur was less tolerant: Christians in his realm came to be seen as collaborators with his Roman adversaries, and there was a rise in discrimination and persecutions against them.[53]

The peace that had been concluded between Narses and Diocletian in the late AD 290s lasted until AD 337, when Shapur II started to threaten Rome's eastern borders, partly in response to the conversion of Armenia to Christianity. A diplomatic solution proved elusive, so Constantine put together an expedition to conquer and Christianise Persia, during which he intended to be baptised in the River Jordan. However, he fell ill on the way, and his baptism took place near Nicomedia, just before he died on 22 May AD 337. Poorly documented hostilities dragged on until the war ended in stalemate in AD 350.

One of the factors that diverted Shapur II's attention from Rome was the appearance of tribes of Huns, probably the Kidarites,[54] who were making incursions into his territory.[55] But by AD 358 the *Shahanshah* could refocus his energies westwards, and operations against Constantine's son Constantius II ebbed and flowed until the latter died at the age of forty-four at a road station between Tarsus and the Cilician Gates, on 3 November AD 361. Constantius II was succeeded by his cousin Julian, who already had a proven military track record from successful operations against the Alemanni and Franks on the Rhine frontier, and who shocked the entire Roman world by announcing that he was pagan.

Shapur II seems to have been prepared to negotiate at this point, but Julian was not. Under the auspices of Rome' traditional deities, he took the offensive. He left Constantinople in May AD 362 and arrived in Antioch, where he spent the rest of the year assembling his forces and alienating the local population. Julian finally hit the campaign trail under sunny skies on 5 March AD 363 with 65,000 men, including the great Roman historian Ammianus Marcellinus. Things went well up to and including an engagement outside Ctesiphon where Julian's 'Homeric tactics'[56] brought him victory. But the Roman high command decided not to besiege the city, descended into disorder and pillaging,[57] lost focus concerning their objectives, made some serious errors, which included burning the boats of their river-going fleet, and started to pull back. In a skirmish on 23 June, Julian neglected to put on his breastplate, leaving him undefended against a spear thrown, as Ammianus Marcellinus says, 'by whom no one knows'.[58] Various other sources spin the story to suit their pro- or anti-Julian agendas: the unknown warrior can be a Saracen (fighting on either the Persian or the Roman side), a Persian or a Roman, and can be Christian or pagan. In any case, the wound was fatal. Julian had, somewhat prematurely, erected an inscription in the upper Jordan valley to himself as *BARBARORVM EXTINCTORI* ('Annihilator of the Barbarians'),[59] but history was depicted by the Sasanian victors in the form of a relief at Taq-e Bostan in north-west Iran, on which Julian's body, recognisable by his thin features and goatee beard, is trampled by Shapur II.[60]

So Roman officers selected 'a passable candidate' as emperor[61] in the shape of the *protector domesticus* (senior staff officer)

Flavius Iovianus ('Jovian'). He succeeded in extricating the Roman forces by negotiating a 'shameful treaty'[62] with Shapur II under which he ceded large portions of Galerius' conquests from the end of the previous century (notably Nisibis) and vacated Armenia. Shapur II ruled until his death in AD 379, having earned himself the nickname 'he who pierces shoulders' from his harsh treatment of Arab prisoners, but leaving the Sasanian Empire in its strongest ever condition; Jovian, however, was found dead in his bed at Dadastana, a border town between Galatia and Bithynia, on his journey back to Constantinople early in AD 364, either overcome by the noxious smell of fresh plaster in his bedroom, by fumes from a large fire or by indigestion brought on by overeating.[63] Ammianus Marcellinus regarded Jovian's death as the end of an era: 'This dreadful period of uncertainty came to a sad end.'[64]

It took less than a week after Jovian's death for the army to install a soldier from the Danube region of Pannonia as emperor. We know him as Valentinian I. He appears in our sources as an energetic and decisive disciplinarian who was noted for his religious tolerance, even though he could be cruel, greedy, envious and grasping. In less than a month he had appointed his rather indecisive, boorish, visually impaired, bow-legged, Arian-Christian-fundamentalist brother Valens as co-emperor. They took the consular robes on 1 January 365, which was the normal protocol at the beginning of a new reign, having held a meeting at Naïssus (modern Niš in Serbia), where they had agreed to divide the military commanders, troops and court officials between them, before going their deeply signifi-cant separate ways: 'Valentinian departed to Mediolanum [modern Milan], Valens to Constantinople.'[65]

Rome had effectively made its East–West split.

21

Fritigern: The Gothic Hannibal

The 'Barbarian Conspiracy' in Britain

Ammianus Marcellinus eloquently expressed the barbarian challenges confronting Rome's newly divided empire in the AD 360s: 'During this time, when the bolts of our frontiers were unfastened, bands of armed barbarians were pouring forth like glowing ashes from Mount Etna.'[1] And an anonymous fourth-century AD source put it similarly: 'Above all it must be noted that wild nations are pressing upon the Roman Empire and howling about it everywhere, and treacherous barbarians ... are assailing every frontier.'[2] But in the west, the Emperor Valentinian I was doing his utmost to keep the situation under control: 'Even his harshest critic cannot find fault with his unfailing shrewdness in matters of state, especially if he bears in mind that it was a greater service to keep the barbarians in check by frontier barriers than to defeat them in battle.'[3]

Valentinian I's policy involved enlisting barbarians and provincials in Gaul to ensure that Rome's armies were at full strength, alongside the construction and/or refurbishment of forts, lookout stations and bridgeheads along the Rhine.

When it came to domestic politics, Valentinian I lived in perpetual fear of conspiracy. But whether or not those particular fears were justified, the Western emperor did have to confront a very real *Barbarica Conspiratio* ('Barbarian Conspiracy') in Britain in AD 367. The term 'Barbarian Conspiracy' is, in fact, somewhat misleading, since there was never any overarching sense of barbarian identity among the various Celtic and Germanic tribes. In the far north of Britain were people that the Romans called *Picti* ('Picts'). However, *Picti* is not the name of an ethnic group. It means 'the Painted Men', and was a generic name by which the Romans, in another typical piece of 'barbarian stereotyping', referred to all the tribes north of Hadrian's Wall. How the Picts differed from neighbouring British tribes, if at all, is unclear, although they appear to have spoken a P-Celtic language like the Britons. However, because they left no written records, we have no idea what they called themselves, although Irish sources refer to them as Cruithne, which is a Q-Celtic version of a P-Celtic word like *Pritani*: *Cruithne* = *Pritani* = *Britanni*, i.e. Britons in Latin.

Back in AD 360, the Emperor Julian had responded to reports that the Picti were harassing territory along Hadrian's Wall by sending in a field force under his *Magister Militum* (Master of Soldiers – the chief military commander), Lupicinus, who stabilised the situation. Ammianus Marcellinus says that the storm broke in AD 367 when two Pictish tribes, the Dicalydones and Venturiones, banded together with the warlike Attacotti and the Scotti from Ireland. The Roman *Areani* (frontier scouts) were supposed to have raised the alarm, but instead they collaborated with the Picti, and the wall was overrun and/or bypassed by sea. Meanwhile, in the south, Saxons and Franks had killed Nectaridus, the *Comes Litoris Saxonici* (Count of the Saxon Shore), who commanded the coastal forts, and overwhelmed Fullofaudes, the *Dux Britanniarum* (Duke/General of Britain). There was a complete collapse of army discipline, soldiers deserted, slaves escaped and chaos ensued.

However, these barbarians were not acting in a carefully choreographed, conspiratorial way, and were neither attempting, nor even contemplating, a conquest of Rome. The Western Emperor Valentinian I himself was preoccupied with fighting against the Alemanni, so he delegated the task to his *Comes Rei Militaris* Count Theodosius, who marched with four contingents of *comitatenses*, started operations as far south as Londinium (modern London), appointed a new *Comes Britanniarum* (Count of Britain) and a new *Vicarius* (provincial governor), and expelled the invaders within a couple of years.

He embarked on some major reconstruction projects, and although the historical and archaeological sources leave the details rather vague, it seems that towns were refortified with towers for ballistae; a naval base was established at Holyhead to face down the Irish; lookout stations were installed on the Yorkshire coast to prevent anyone trying to sail past Hadrian's Wall, which itself was strengthened; and the *Areani* were disbanded. It is also possible that local kings were established in the Lowlands of Scotland to provide a buffer zone between the wall and the Picti. These chieftains assumed Latinised names – Antonius (formerly Annwn), Quintilius (Cinhil), Clemens (Cluim) and Paternus (Padarn), with the latter also being known as Pesrut ('the Man of the Red Cloak', as used by Roman soldiers), which may be an indication of their allegiance to Rome, although the complete lack of Roman pottery in this area might also indicate that they were anti-Roman and that their names are a result of conversion to Christianity. Nevertheless, Count Theodosius' measures seem to have been effective enough to initiate a quarter of a century of prosperity for the towns and villas of Britannia.

Fritigern the Goth: The Hannibal of the North

Over in the eastern half of the empire, Valentinian I's brother, the Eastern Emperor Valens, had a personal vendetta with the Goths, 3,000 of whom had supported Julian's pagan relative Procopius back in AD 365, when he had made a farcically unsuccessful attempt to usurp power.[4] When we first hear about Goths, in the first century AD, we find them living in what is now Poland. But, needless to say, there has been great (and often vested) interest in their origins and early history. The copious modern writings about them come in varying degrees of scholarliness, and often generate a lot of heat but little light. A broad spectrum of people – from Swedish kings to Hapsburg monarchs to Romantic German nationalists to Nazi imperialists – have all used and misused Gothic history to suit their own purposes.[5] However, our prime ancient source for the history and culture of the Goths is a work written in Latin and entitled *De Origine Actibusque Getarum* ('On the Origin and Deeds of the Getae'), usually just called the *Getica*, which was completed in AD 551 by Jordanes, who was not a scholar, but was a Goth. As the title of the work shows, Jordanes fell into the familiar barbarian-related trap of confusing the Goths with the Getae, who were an entirely different people, but nonetheless the *Getica* is valuable because it gives us a near-contemporary account from a relatively neutral standpoint. It is a single-volume abridgement of Magnus Aurelius Cassiodorus' twelve-volume history of the Goths,[6] although Jordanes says that he only had access to that work for three days, and could only replicate it in a very general way. However, he says that he also included material from various Greek and Latin authors, and wrote the beginning and end himself. The final result is a fascinating hotchpotch.

According to the *Getica*, the Goths were a Germanic people coming from what is now Sweden, although archaeologically the Gothic confederacy is associated with the Sîntana de Mureş–Černjachov culture, which spreads from Romania to Ukraine. They spoke an east Germanic language, used Germanic personal names, and were physically tall, sporting beards and long blond or red hair. They wore skins and furs, were adept horsemen, capable agriculturalists and stock raisers, and fought very effectively by forming their wagons into a defensive laager that protected their formidable cavalry strike force. There are traces of an inferiority complex when they compared themselves to the Romans, memorably expressed by their ruler Theodoric (493–526), who observed that 'an able Goth wants to be like a Roman; only a poor Roman would want to be a like a Goth'.[7]

The fact that they were archetypal barbarians does not mean that they were pagan, however: Bishop Ulfilas ('Little Wolf', c.311– c.382), who produced a Gothic translation of the Bible, was crucial to their conversion to the Arian form of Christianity.

Rome had fought sporadic conflicts with the Goths since the third century AD, when Timesitheus drove them back in AD 238, and again repulsed them in AD 242 before he set out with the Emperor Gordian III to fight the Persians (see pp. 381 ff.). In AD 250 the Goths under King Cuiva had crossed into Moesia Inferior, overrun Macedonia and Thrace, including

Philippopolis (modern Plovdiv in Bulgaria), and inflicted a stinging defeat on the Roman army at the Battle of Abritus (or Abrittus, and also known as the Battle of Forum Terebronii/ Trebonii, close to Razgrad in modern Bulgaria) in July the following year, much to the delight of the fourth-century AD Christian apologist Lactantius, who gleefully described the death of the Emperor Decius, who had been a notorious persecutor: 'He was suddenly surrounded by the barbarians, and slain, together with great part of his army; nor could he be honoured with the rites of sepulture, but, stripped and naked, he lay to be devoured by wild beasts and birds, a fit end for the enemy of God.'[8]

Treaties were made, but in AD 268 further Gothic incursions into Greece and Asia Minor, in concert with a Germanic people called the Heruli, brought about the sack of Athens, before the Emperor Gallienus defeated them in a significant engagement at Naïssus. Later that same year, the next emperor, Claudius II, earned his nickname 'Gothicus Maximus' by smashing an invasion by the Goths and Alemanni near Lake Benacus (Garda), and liberating Illyria.

Now, a century or so later, Valens invaded Gothic territory from Marcianopolis in Lower Moesia (modern Devnya in Bulgaria) by bridging the Danube. He harassed the Gothic Greuthungi (variously spelled Grauthingi, Greothingi, Greothyngi, Gruthungi or Grouthingoi, and also called Ostrogothi or Austrogoti by ancient writers), and forced Athanaric, the Iudex ('Judge', i.e. head of the royal clan) of the Tervingi (whose name could be derived from the Gothic triu = 'tree', and who can also be referred to as Thervingi or Visi) to flee and sue for peace.

It was actually the disruption of their trade, rather than military defeat, that hit the Goths hardest, and in AD 369, having conducted a cost-benefit analysis of the conflict, both sides were ready to negotiate. Athanaric and the Eastern Emperor Valens met on boats in the middle of the Danube and made an agreement that suited Rome very well: the Goths were only allowed to trade at two crossing points on the river, and the Gothic chieftains would no longer be subsidised by Rome: 'No one saw gold coin counted out for the barbarians, countless talents of silver, ships freighted with fabrics or any of the things we were in the habit of tolerating before, enjoying the fruits of peace and quiet that was more burdensome than the incursions, and paying yearly tribute, which we were not ashamed to do, although we refused to call it by that name.'[9]

Subsequently there was internal warfare among the Goths as a chieftain called Fritigern challenged the humiliated and presumably discredited Athanaric with the support of Roman *limitanei*.

Valentinian I of the Western Roman Empire had a rather different relationship with the barbarians then his brother. He campaigned effectively against the Alemanni, Sarmatians and the Germanic Quadi, but died because he couldn't cope with what he regarded as the barbarian 'attitude problem'. In AD 375 some peace envoys of the Quadi approached him and were allowed to state their case. They initially blamed foreign brigands for their hostile behaviour, but then they referred to a 'wrongful and untimely' attempt by the Romans to build a fort across the Danube. Valentinian I's wrath was uncontrollable: 'He tried to speak or give some order; this was clear from the gasps that racked his sides, and from the way in which he ground his teeth and made movements with his arms as if he were boxing. Finally, he could do no more. His body was covered with livid spots, and after a long struggle he breathed his last.'[10]

Barbarian bare-faced arrogance could even kill a Roman emperor. Valentinian I was succeeded by the four-year-old Valentinian II, who initially 'governed' under the guardian-ship/influence of his teenaged half-brother Gratian, the Frankish general Merobaudes and Valentinian I's ambitious widow, Justina. Gratian became progressively more powerful, and was soon the effective leader of parts of the Western Roman Empire despite his brother's title.

At this point chaos erupted on the Danube. The Huns were on the move (see pp. 435–437). Writers at the time painted a picture of them driving other peoples before them, but the reality may not be quite so clear-cut, and it could have been that changing economic conditions in the area between the Rivers Tanais (Don) and Danastius (Dniester) were a factor. Nevertheless, the ancient accounts say that they caused various tribes to flinch away from them in the direction of the Roman Empire as they moved south-eastwards from the steppes, displaced the Alani,[11] who were themselves no pushover, from north of the Caucasus, vanquished the Greuthungian realm of Ermanaric, and smashed Athanaric's Tervingian army as they kept on coming across the river valleys of the Tanais, Borysthenes (Dnieper) and Danastius. Writing around five years after the Western Emperor Valentinian I's death, Bishop Ambrose of Mediolanum said, 'the Huns threw themselves upon the Alani, the Alani upon the Goths, and the Goths upon the Taifals and Sarmatians'.[12]

These various displaced populations started to encroach closer to the Danube and the Rhine. The Goths' powers of resistance had not been helped by their prior defeats by the Eastern Emperor Valens, and when they were now assaulted by the Huns, the 'greater part of the people' (Ammianus

Marcellinus is vague about who exactly they were) deserted Athanaric and, under their new co-rulers Alavivus and Fritigern, the Tervingi fled to the Danube, where in AD 376 they begged Valens to give them a safe space inside the empire.

Precisely how many people there were, and what sort of threat they really posed, are tough questions to answer. The Romans certainly regarded the Tervingi as an innumerable horde, and Ammianus Marcellinus quotes Virgil to make his point:

> If you wish to know their number, go and tot up the grains
> Of sand that are whirled around by a sand-storm in the
> Sahara.[13]

Most modern scholarly analysis rejects this, and current guesses average out at between 15,000 and 20,000 warriors plus their dependants. Rome's armies should not have found this an invincible force, but the Eastern Emperor Valens was preoccupied with new hostilities against Shapur II's Sasanians (see pp. 399 ff.), and so he granted their request. Ever since its earliest days, Rome had welcomed barbarian immigrants – one of her strengths had been the ability to assimilate outsiders – and Valens' hope was that the Tervingi would provide an important military resource, cultivate the land and increase his tax revenue. So he let them into Thrace. The Romans even helped to ferry the Goths across.

Some modern commentators feel that 'the best course of action would have been to refuse entry',[14] and Ammianus Marcellinus saw the consequences with 20/20 hindsight: 'Diligent care was taken that no future destroyer of the Roman state be left behind, even if he were smitten with a fatal disease.'[15]

The crossing degenerated into farcical chaos, and if the immigrants were supposed to be disarmed on the other side, the job was not well done. To make matters worse, the Roman commanders Lupicinus and Maximus treated them appallingly, and food shortages became so extreme that the 'exchange-rate' became one dead Roman dog for one Gothic slave. Around the same time the Greuthungi crossed the Danube without Roman authorisation, and the two Gothic contingents came together at Marcianopolis, which is where the Roman commanders were based. Here Lupicinus invited Fritigern and Alavivus to a showy banquet, but wouldn't allow their starving people into the city to buy food. Things turned violent: the Romans had Fritigern and Alavivus' bodyguard butchered; Fritigern was allowed to return to his people to calm them down; but instead he hurried away to 'set in motion the various incitements that lead to wars'.[16]

The Romans had missed a golden opportunity: as allies, the Goths could have been a great source of strength to Valens; but as enemies they would perpetrate immense damage. They reverted to their 'stereotypical barbarian' behaviour: they burned and pillaged; they defeated Lupicinus; they received reinforcements from Gothic contingents in the Roman army; they ravaged Rome's Balkan provinces; they got penned in north of the Haemus mountains, but repelled a Roman attack by forming their wagons into a laager at Ad Salices (in modern Dobruja) in AD 377; they broke out again, aided by some Huns and Alani; and the storm of destruction resumed, 'as if the Furies were putting everything in motion'.[17]

Valens had to respond, and he needed help. He sent for Gratian, extricated himself and his *comitatenses* from the conflict with Shapur II's Sasanians, and moved westwards to

Adrianople (Hadrianopolis, sometimes called Hadrianople – modern Edirne in Turkey). Here he was the victim of some 'alternative facts': there were far more Goths there than he had been led to believe. Yet he made the decision to engage without waiting for Gratian to arrive. However, before he could do this, Fritigern, who followed the same Arian brand of Christianity as Valens,[18] sent a deputation led by a priest, which proposed peace in exchange for a Gothic homeland in Thrace. 'Loyalty for land' would become a Gothic mantra over the next decades, but the Roman response would always be the same: stonewall rejection.

Valens would be the last Roman emperor personally to lead his men into battle for two centuries. He did so on a hot sunny day in August AD 378, and made his men march 8 Roman miles to get at the enemy. Fritigern's warriors had set light to the surrounding countryside, formed their wagons into the customary circle, and were raising their uncanny war cry. Valens then rejected another Gothic peace mission because he felt the envoys were not high ranking enough, but the delay suited Fritigern. He was waiting for reinforcements led by the Greuthungian chieftains Alatheus and Saphrax, and he sent yet another envoy who proposed an exchange of hostages and a personal parley with Valens. This seemed a reasonable proposal, but as the Roman emissary headed for the Gothic ramparts, Fate intervened.

Some Roman soldiers launched an unauthorised attack; Fritigern's Goths, having now been joined by Alatheus, Saphrax and also some Alani, struck back with a devastating cavalry charge; the Romans rallied; the main battle lines clashed; the Roman left wing drove the Goths back to their laager, but became isolated and 'collapsed like a broken dyke'; the Roman infantry became so compacted that they couldn't wield their swords effectively; the dust cloud that was thrown up meant that no one could see or avoid incoming missiles; the Goths overwhelmed the Roman baggage trains; and in the end the Romans couldn't organise an orderly retreat.

Ammianus Marcellinus called it the biggest military defeat in Roman history since the Battle of Cannae nearly 600 years before. Fritigern had become the Hannibal of the North. Casualty estimates vary between 10,000 and 20,000, and the Eastern Emperor Valens' body was never recovered. Various accounts of his death became current. In one, he was simply killed outright by an arrow, in another he did not die instantly, but was taken to a fortified farmhouse, which was surrounded by Goths who burned the house and everyone in it.[19]

The Goths continued to indulge their appetite for plunder. They occupied Thrace and Illyricum, driving a wedge between the Roman Empire's eastern and western halves, but their assaults on Adrianople and Constantinople were beaten back. They were especially overawed by Constantinople's mighty fortifications and the cultural splendours inside them, but also by Rome's Saracen allies, one of whom, clad only in a loincloth, hurled himself into the midst of the Gothic forces, slit a man's throat, put his lips to the wound and sucked out the gushing blood. Such barbarity appalled even Rome's barbarian foes.

Land for Peace

Ammianus Marcellinus concluded his work by describing how a large number of Goths who had enrolled in the Roman army were treacherously massacred in order to protect the eastern provinces. Thereafter, our lack of reliable sources makes it tricky to piece the events together, but it is clear that Gratian responded decisively to the disaster at Adrianople. If that defeat had been Imperial Rome's Cannae, she now needed a latter-day Scipio Africanus, and Gratian's choice to assume the role was Theodosius I, the son of the recently deceased Count Theodosius (see p. 405 f.). He acceded to the purple as co-Augustus on 19 January AD 379, and took charge of the Eastern Roman Empire, along with the *dioceses* of Dacia and Macedonia, with Valentinian II still the nominal head of the Western Roman Empire. Theodosius I's task was made easier by the death of the Sasanian King Shapur II that year, which caused instability in Persia, and allowed the emperor to focus on the Goths, who by now had taken over the whole of Thrace, made incursions into Greece and devastated Pannonia, where, in AD 380, Gratian finally agreed to let some of them settle on vacant lands under their own chiefs.

The tide started to turn back Rome's way when Athanaric died early in AD 381, and Gratian's barbarian generals, the Frankish Bauto and Arbogastes ('Arbogast'), expelled the Goths from Macedonia and Thessaly. Illyricum was cleared by September AD 382, paving the way for an accord to be reached in October. At the beginning of AD 383, Emperor Theodosius I celebrated his victory and the philosopher Themistius delivered a speech, 'A Thanksgiving for the Peace', to the emperor's court:

> We have seen their leaders and chiefs, not making a show of surrendering a tattered standard, but giving up the weapons and swords with which up to that day they had held power, and clinging to the [Emperor Theodosius I's] knees . . . At present their offences are still fresh, but in the not too distant

future we shall have them sharing our religious ceremonies, joining our banquets, serving along with us in the army and paying taxes with us.[20]

It was a highly optimistic assessment. The Romans knew that they had only narrowly won a difficult war, and that the Danube defences were very vulnerable. So at this point they were prepared to grant the Tervingi land in exchange for peace. Emperor Theodosius I and Gratian (who died later in AD 383) allowed them and some of the Greuthungi to settle as a group on the empire side of the Danube in the provinces of Thracia and Dacia Ripensis. Again, Themistius spun the events as a great victory, and made comparisons with Hannibal:

For you [Theodosius I] have not destroyed those who wronged us but appropriated them. You did not punish them by seizing their land but have acquired more farmers for us. You did not slaughter them like wild beasts but charmed away their savagery just as if someone, after trapping a lion or a leopard in nets, were not to kill it but to accustom it to being a beast of burden. These fire-breathers, harder on the Romans than Hannibal was, have now come over to our side. Tame and submissive, they entrust their persons and their arms to us, whether the emperor wants to employ them as farmers or as soldiers.[21]

It should have been a win–win situation, but within thirty years the Goths would do what Hannibal conspicuously failed to do: sack Rome.

22

Alaric the Goth: Sacker of Rome

The Rise of Alaric the (Visi)Goth

In the Eastern Roman Empire, Theodosius I's next battles were fought on the spiritual plane, principally against his nemesis Bishop Ambrose of Mediolanum, but with a significant Gothic involvement. In AD 390, Butheric, the Gothic garrison commander at Thessalonica, had imprisoned a celebrity charioteer for an alleged homosexual rape. This sparked a riot in which Butheric was killed, bringing retribution from Theodosius I's Gothic troops in which the church historian Theodoret says 7,000 people died, cut down like ears of wheat at harvest time.[1] The non-binary nature of the relationship between the Romans and the barbarians at this point in history was becoming abundantly clear:[2] for the Eastern emperor to order Goths to slaughter Roman citizens was utterly shocking. Ambrose refused to give Theodosius I Holy Communion until he had done penance for eight months – the famous Penance of Milan.

Theodosius I also mobilised large numbers of Goths to confront Flavius Eugenius, who tried to usurp the throne of the Western Roman Empire after Valentinian II was found hanged at Vienna (Vienne) in AD 392. Whether Valentinian II's death was due to suicide, as Arbogast asserted, or criminality, Theodosius I responded by elevating his younger son Honorius to the rank of Augustus, and mobilising a formidable army to eradicate Eugenius in AD 394.

Among Theodosius' Gothic *foederati* – warriors from tribes who were subsidised by Rome in return for them supplying troops to fight in her armies – was a young, talented, loyal, brave, nobly born, Christian, Tervingian warrior called Alaric ('Alaricus' in Latin), whose name meant 'Lord of All' in his native language. Alaric 'is a mysterious figure'.[3] Born in *c*.AD 370, Claudian claims that he came from Peuce Island in the Danube delta in modern Romania. Details of his early career remain obscure, although we know that he married the sister of the Gothic leader Ataulf, and certainly held Roman offices, but what their specific titles were is often unclear. But he was present when the armies engaged at the River Frigidus (modern Vipava in Slovenia) on 5 September AD 394.

Each side made its religious affiliations clear: the Western usurper Eugenius set up a statue of Jupiter, and adorned his banners with images of Hercules; the Eastern Emperor Theodosius led his troops under the Christian *labarum*:

A long gilded spear with a horizontal bar formed the sign of the cross. At the top was a circlet of gold and costly jewels, in the centre of which was the symbol of our Saviour's name [the chi-rho symbol]. From the crossbar of the spear hung a royal banner, richly embroidered and shimmering with precious stones, all lavishly stitched with gold thread. It is impossible to describe its beauty – or its effect on those who saw it. The banner was square. On its upper part, beneath the sign of the cross and immediately above the embroidered panel, it bore a half-length portrait [*ikon*] of the devout emperor.⁴

Unusually for an ancient battle, the fighting lasted two days. During the intervening night Theodosius I supposedly prayed for a storm, and had his prayers granted: 'Such a fierce wind arose as to turn the weapons of the enemy back on those who hurled them. When the wind persisted with great force and every missile launched by the enemy was foiled, their spirit gave way, or rather it was shattered by the divine power.'⁵

Eugenius was captured and executed; Arbogast escaped but committed suicide; Theodosius I's Gothic allies reportedly suffered 10,000 casualties, which seems to have pleased some commentators: 'In this case too, the fires of civil war were quenched . . . leaving out of account the ten thousand Goths, who, it is said, were sent ahead by Theodosius and destroyed to a man by Arbogast; for the loss of these was certainly a gain and their defeat a victory.'⁶

However, Rome's Eastern emperor had little time to enjoy the fruits of victory: he died at Mediolanum in January AD 395, prompting the contemporary historian Eunapius to assess the situation like this:

It is recorded that Theodosius I's sons succeeded him as Emperor [the late-teenaged Arcadius in the Eastern Roman Empire at Constantinople; the eleven-year-old Honorius in the Western at Mediolanum]. But if one were to give a truer picture of what happened (and truth is, after all, the purpose of history), they took the title of Emperors, while in reality total power lay with [the *Praefectus Praetorio* Flavius] Rufinus in the East and [the half-Vandal general Flavius] Stilicho in the West.[7]

Rufinus' background was in Aquitaine Gaul. Born in c.AD 335 he comes across as a clever, driven, avaricious, unprincipled Christian who had trouble speaking Greek, but the existence of a vitriolic verse invective entitled *Against Rufinus* by Stilicho's Alexandrian Greek poetical spin-doctor Claudian certainly gives us a distorted view. Stilicho (born in AD 365) was the son of a provincial Roman woman and a Vandal cavalry officer serving in the Roman army. But he regarded himself as Roman, not barbarian, and had risen through the ranks under Theodosius I, taking part in a successful embassy to Shapur III (r. AD 383–8), marrying Theodosius I's favourite niece Serena, developing a deep animosity between himself and Rufinus, leading Theodosian troops to victory at the Battle of the Frigidus, and securing promotion to *Magister Militum* around AD 393. On Theodosius I's death Stilicho claimed that the Eastern emperor's final wish was that he, Stilicho, should be regent for both Honorius in the west and Arcadius in the east. This was not a solution that was acceptable to the Eastern court, and the inevitable conflict brought him head-to-head with the twenty-something Gothic leader Alaric.

In the shake-up of offices that marked the transition of power, Alaric was disappointed not to receive the high-level command that he had hoped for. So he exploited the unhappiness of the Gothic warriors who had suffered so disproportionately at the Battle of the Frigidus:

After Theodosius, the lover of peace and of the Gothic race, had passed from human cares, his sons began to ruin both empires by their luxurious living and to deprive their Allies, that is to say the Goths, of the customary gifts. The contempt of the Goths for the Romans soon increased, and for fear their valour would be destroyed by long peace, they appointed Alaric king over them. He was of a famous stock, and his nobility was second only to that of the Amali, for he came from the family of the Balthi, who because of their daring valour had long ago received among their race the name *Baltha*, that is, The Bold. Now when this Alaric was made king, he took counsel with his men and persuaded them to seek a kingdom by their own exertions rather than serve others in idleness.[8]

When, or indeed whether, Alaric became king of the Goths is a difficult issue. Roman sources call him *rex* (king), although at different points in his career; Greek ones use *phylarkhos* (tribal chieftain), *hegemon* (leader) and *tyrannos* (tyrant/king); while some sources quite pointedly give him no title at all. It is similarly tricky to establish the precise nature of his forces, their activities and their demands, although what seems to have mattered most at the time was that they were simply thought of as 'the Goths'. Modern works frequently call him 'Alaric the Visigoth', although the designation *Visi*, as in 'Visigoths', does not appear until the *Notitia Dignitatum*, a document produced in AD 400 (give or take twenty-five years each way) and preserved in medieval manuscripts.

Regardless of his official status, Alaric led his Goths into Thrace and Macedonia, where he caused havoc, before menacing Constantinople. Rufinus may have tried to buy him off, and Stilicho was told to return the contingents that had marched west during the River Frigidus campaign to their bases in the east. This he did, under the Gothic *Comes Rei Militaris* Gaïnas. But Gaïnas may have had secret instructions: 'The Emperor [Arcadius] was persuaded to come out before the city. Rufinus, the City Prefect, accompanied him. But, once Gaïnas and his men had prostrated themselves and received due welcome from the Emperor, Gaïnas gave the signal. All at once they surrounded Rufinus, falling on him with their swords. One sliced off his right hand, another his left, while another cut off his head and ran off singing a victory song.'[9]

The main beneficiary of this incident was not the half-Vandal Stilicho but a eunuch named Eutropius who was the *Praepositus Sacri Cubiculi* (Provost of the Sacred Bedchamber) to the Eastern Emperor Arcadius, and whose power led him to become a bizarre role model: 'Even some who were already grown men, craving to be eunuchs and yearning to become Eutropiuses, disposed of both their sense and their testicles that they might enjoy the condition of Eutropius.'[10]

Claudian had a field day with him in a lengthy abusive poem entitled *Against Eutropius*,[11] but the eunuch became the dominant figure in Constantinople; Gaïnas became *Magister Militum* in Thrace; and Alaric didn't have the resources to take Constantinople, so he chose a softer target and went on the rampage in Greece (AD 395–6), where he sacked Athens. How much destruction was perpetrated is unknown, although it has been suggested that a certain amount of damage was inflicted on the pagan sculptures on the Acropolis, but that the sculpture later designated 'Metope North 32' from the Parthenon, depicting the winged Hebe interacting with the seated goddess Hera, was spared because the Christian Goths mistakenly read the scene as the Annunciation. Stilicho intervened in the Peloponnese, which he tried to detach from the Eastern Roman

Empire, but Alaric, to whom Eutropius granted the title of *Magister Militum per Illyricum* around now, fought him off and moved into Illyricum.

Stilicho, who had been declared a public enemy by Eutropius, had allegedly become diverted by luxury, comic actors and shameless women, but more important distractions were threats to the Italian grain supply because of unrest in Africa, and seaborne barbarian incursions into Britain, both of which he dealt with effectively. Claudian also tells us that the Eastern court made the barbarian Goth Alaric their *Magister Utriusque Militiae* (commander of both infantry and cavalry) in AD 399, which gave him crucial access to supplies via legitimate Roman military channels. But this was short-lived: a foray into Asia Minor by some Huns indirectly led to the execution of Eutropius, a failed attempt by Gaïnas to take over Constantinople, in which he was killed and the Constantinopolitans slaughtered 7,000 of his Gothic troops, and a general groundswell of anti-Gothic feeling that had a negative impact on Alaric, who may have lost his military command.

With no official resources to feed and pay his men, Alaric invaded Italy late in AD 401, catching Stilicho off guard. The half-Vandal was currently sorting out frontier issues in Raetia, where another independent Gothic leader, Radagaisus, had violated the empire's borders. The Emperor Honorius and the court of the Western Empire relocated to Ravenna, which was better fortified than Mediolanum, but Stilicho still managed to hold Alaric off in battles fought at Pollentia (modern Pollenzo) on Easter Day AD 402, where Alaric's wife and family were taken prisoner, and some months later at Verona. However, Stilicho was not in a position to destroy Alaric completely, and instead he probably returned Alaric's family, let the Goths withdraw to Pannonia, and actually started using Goths as his allies.

The Great Invasion

Alaric now drops off our sources' radar for several years, but other Goth barbarians remained very much at the forefront of the Roman consciousness. Radagaisus was soon back on the scene, leading a terrifying army that his contemporaries numbered at 200,000 or even twice that number. He may well have been under threat from the Huns, and was either looking for safety within Rome's borders or to secure his position in Barbaria via the prestige and booty of a military success. But he achieved neither: Stilicho deployed thirty units of the Roman field army, plus some allied Huns and Alani, surrounded him in the hills of Fiesole (near modern Florence), and captured and executed him on 23 August AD 406. Some 12,000 of Radagaisus' warriors were drafted into the Roman army, and so many others were enslaved that the price of slaves in Italy dropped through the floor.

Renegade Goths were not Rome's only problem at the time. On New Year's Eve AD 405 or 406 (there is dispute over the date: some authorities give AD 406; Prosper of Aquitaine's *Chronicle* can be read either way; Zosimus implies it was 31 December AD 405; Orosius says the attack happened in AD 408[12]) Rome faced what historians call 'The Great Invasion'. A vast horde of Silingi and Hasdingi Vandals (from Silesia in modern Poland, and the border with Dacia respectively), Germanic Suevi (aka Suebi) and Alani crossed the Rhine. Edward Gibbon propagated a myth that they crossed the river when it was frozen, but no ancient source actually says they did. The Franks put up some stiff resistance and slew the Vandal king, but were unable to hold out,[13] and the Christian Bishop Orientius later wrote that 'all of Gaul smoked as a single funeral pyre'.[14] In Britannia the army elected a soldier called Flavius Claudius Constantinus (Constantine III) as emperor, possibly because they felt that the central authorities were doing nothing to protect the province, but it immediately became more than a local issue. Channelling Constantine I the Great, who had also been proclaimed in Britain, Constantine III decided to sacrifice Britain, now effectively cut off from Rome, in order to save Gaul from the barbarian menace.

As the invaders swept onwards (their precise itinerary is unclear, but Moguntiacum, Borbetomagus [modern Worms in Germany], Remi [Reims in France] and Treveri were all overrun), the field army of Britannia stepped in. Constantine III secured most of Gaul and then won over Spain, from where Emperor Honorius' relatives Didymus and Verenianus tried to dislodge him, but Constantine III's general Gerontius defeated, captured and executed them, and Constantine III's son Constans was placed in charge there. Stilicho was uncharacteristically slow off the mark, and when he did dispatch a Gothic officer called Sarus to stop Constantine III, the choice proved to be a gross miscalculation: he was soon in retreat back to Italy. Constantine III took the area around Arelate (modern Arles), and in due course would secure recognition from Honorius, who would provide unequivocal acknowledgement that he was his fellow emperor by sending him an imperial robe.

The barbarian Goth Alaric now reappears in the narrative. Stilicho had suffered a temporary crisis when his daughter Maria, who had married the Western Emperor Honorius in *c.*AD 398, died in AD 307. But the familial ties were quickly restored when Honorius married Maria's sister, Thermantia. For his part, Alaric also saw new opportunities in the upheavals caused by the Great Invasion. He moved to Noricum, from where he could either menace Italy, with or without Constantine III's collaboration, or block the Alpine passes and keep him out. From this position of strength Alaric demanded an exorbitant 4,000 pounds of gold for 'services rendered' to Rome, and sought permission to take his army into Pannonia, which would presumably have become a Gothic homeland. At Ravenna, Honorius remained intransigent, though, and at Rome the senators, who would be the ones to find the gold, voted to resist. However, Stilicho persuaded them otherwise, prompting the Senator Lampadius famously to quote Cicero's elegant *'non est ista pax sed pactio servitutis'* ('that is not peace, but a bargain of servitude!') before taking refuge in a church.[15]

Just to complicate matters, the Eastern Emperor Arcadius died on 1 May AD 408, leaving Honorius' seven year-old nephew, Theodosius II, as successor. Stilicho saw the new situation in the Eastern Roman Empire as the perfect opportunity to assert his authority over the Balkan region. So he now made a deal with Alaric: the Goth would attack Constantine III, freeing the half-Vandal to take control of the succession in the east. However, Stilicho's plans unravelled when Emperor Honorius' *Magister Officiorum*, the eunuch Olympius, propagated a conspiracy theory that Stilicho was plotting to overthrow Emperor Theodosius II and to install his own son, Eucherius, in his place. Olympius' fake news seemed convincing because Stilicho's son Eucherius had been betrothed to Galla Placidia, the half-sister of Arcadius and Honorius, and the gullible army at Ticinum (modern Pavia) in Liguria fell for it. A number of

Stilicho's supporters were slaughtered, while he himself headed for Ravenna, but when his Gothic officer Sarus defected to Olympius and massacred Stilicho's Hunnic bodyguards in a night-time stealth attack, the half-Vandal was forced to take refuge in a church. In the early hours of 22 August AD 408, Olympius' henchmen lured Stilicho out with a promise that he was only going to be arrested, and promptly executed him.

Alaric: The Sacker of Rome

Anti-Stilicho reprisals now took place; the Western Emperor Honorius divorced Stilicho's daughter Thermantia; Eucherius was assassinated; and when Honorius' soldiers massacred thousands of barbarian men, women and children in Italy, 30,000 survivors started to look to the Goth Alaric for protection and vengeance. But Alaric was in a difficult position himself: he had no formal command, his legitimacy was shaky and his 4,000 pounds of gold had not been paid. So he decided to strike at Rome itself. The Senate panicked. They accused Stilicho's widow Serena of having treacherous contact with the Goths, and asked her cousin and former foster daughter Galla Placidia to endorse a death sentence, which she did.

Strangling Serena made no difference, because by October AD 408 Alaric was strangling the Eternal City. The Goth had Rome surrounded, and he controlled Portus at the mouth of the River Tiber. Jerome relates stories of mothers having to eat their newborn babies,[16] while the pagans blamed the Christians, arguing that when the old deities had been honoured, Rome had ruled the world, whereas Christianity had brought famine and pestilence. With Honorius still at Ravenna, the Senate decided to strike a deal. But when their negotiators told Alaric that although Rome was ready to make peace, she was also well prepared for war, and not afraid of Goths, Alaric simply upped the ante: 'He said that he would not end the siege unless he got all the gold in the city; and all the silver too; not to mention any movable property that there might be in Rome; and all the Barbarian slaves. When one of the ambassadors asked, "If you take all this, what will you leave us?", Alaric replied, "Your lives."'[17]

The senators caved in; Alaric made fresh demands: 5,000 pounds of gold, 30,000 pounds of silver, 4,000 silk tunics, 3,000 scarlet-dyed skins and 3,000 pounds of pepper; the senator Palladius calculated how much each senator needed to contribute, but could only balance the books by ordering the gold and silver statues of the gods to be melted down. The destruction of the statue of *Virtus* (Manliness/Courage) was especially symbolic: 'When it was taken away, such bravery and virtue as the Romans possessed went with it.'[18]

Alaric now made Honorius an offer: if he would ratify the treaty, give him land and provide hostages, the Goths would not only make peace, but would join Rome against her enemies.

Honorius said that he accepted, and Alaric was naive enough to trust him. The Goth decreed a seventy-two-hour suspension of hostilities, but the hostages never arrived. The Senate sent a deputation, including a certain Priscus Attalus, to Ravenna to persuade Honorius to honour the agreement. Unfortunately, the eunuch Olympius opposed any deal that had any hint of his old nemesis Stilicho's policy of cooperation with Alaric, and so Honorius didn't deliver. Instead, he sent the ambassadors back, having appointed Priscus Attalus as his *Comes Sacrarum Largitionum* (finance minister), and summoned five legions from Dalmatia to go to Rome. But they were ambushed by

Alaric, and of the 6,000 soldiers who set out, a mere 100, including Priscus Attalus, made it to Rome.

The senators at Rome were at their wits' end. They sent a second deputation to Honorius, which included Pope Innocent I and probably Priscus Attalus, which needed special permission and an escort from Alaric to make the journey. By now, though, the imperial court at Ravenna was in chaos, a situation that wasn't helped by the fact that Alaric's brother-in-law Ataulf (Ataulfus to the Romans; Athavulf, 'Noble Wolf', to the Goths) was now in Italy bringing Goth reinforcements. Honorius dispatched Olympius and 300 Huns to make a pre-emptive strike against Ataulf, but although the Huns made a successful night raid, they soon realised how heavily outnumbered they were. Olympius knew his days were numbered, and so he fled to Dalmatia. Honorius sent Priscus Attalus back to Rome, having promoted him to *Praefectus Urbi*.

At this point the Roman garrison at Ravenna mutinied, leaving the city cut off by both land and sea. The spineless Honorius simply hid, leaving a character called Iovius to sort out the troops and try to ratify the agreement with Alaric. In a meeting held at Ariminum (modern Rimini), Alaric reiterated his request for money and a homeland in Histria and Venetia as well as Dalmatia and the two Noricums. Unfortunately, Iovius also told the court at Ravenna that Alaric wanted Stilicho's old title of *Magister Utriusque Militiae*, and he was in Alaric's tent when their response was read out: under no circumstances would Honorius bestow any honour on Alaric whatsoever.

Iovius went back to Ravenna, promising never to make peace with Alaric. For his part, the Goth was more flexible: peace and a homeland were still his preferred options, and he offered to settle for just 'the two Noricums, which lie at the furthest reaches of the Danube for they are regularly under attack and pay little in the way of tax. In addition, he would be content with however much corn the Emperor saw fit to give him on an annual basis. Forget about the gold; instead there would be friendship and military alliance between Alaric and the Romans.'[19]

Alaric now arranged to be invited into Rome to address the Senate. His plan was simple. He would appoint the Senator Priscus Attalus as the next emperor of the West, and on 4 November AD 409 the new Augustus delegated the day-to-day running of the state to the Senate, and control of the army to Alaric as *Magister Utriusque Militiae*, with Ataulf as commander of the household cavalry. Priscus Attalus' new coins showed the personified Rome seated on a throne holding Victory on a globe, and carried the unwittingly ironic legend *INVICTA ROMA AETERNA* ('Unconquerable Eternal Rome').

The negotiations continued. On Honorius' behalf, Iovius proposed that Priscus Attalus could become co-Augustus of the West, but with Constantine III already preening himself in the purple cloak that Honorius had sent him the previous year (see p. 425), a three-emperor solution was not realistic. So Priscus Attalus made Honorius a counter offer: Honorius could abdicate and live like an emperor for the rest of his life. However, Iovius insisted that Honorius should be symbolically mutilated, most likely in his right hand, the fingers of which were usually extended in a gesture symbolising legitimacy whenever any emperor spoke. Obviously this was unacceptable to Honorius, but while he was assessing the pros and cons of a life of left-handed leisure, a fleet from the Eastern Roman Empire arrived in Ravenna, bringing 4,000 troops to Honorius from his nephew Emperor Theodosius II in Constantinople. Iovius defected to Priscus Attalus.

While Honorius had been pondering the effects of having his fingers cut off, his ruthless henchman Heraclianus had severed the grain supply from Africa to Rome. Alaric and Iovius relocated to the Eternal City, where, at an emergency meeting of the Senate, it was decided to adopt Priscus Attalus' proposal to despatch a Roman army, rather than a Gothic one, to Africa. Alaric was livid, but any schadenfreude he may have felt when the expeditionary force was defeated was probably offset by seeing the population of Rome asking for the legalisation of cannibalism: 'Put a price on human flesh!' they begged.[20]

Alaric and Honorius finally came to an agreement to end the hostilities. They met outside Ravenna, where Alaric's men relieved Attalus Priscus of his imperial regalia, and delivered them to Honorius. Peace should have broken out at this point, but there were other players who had vested interests in it not doing so, one of whom was Sarus, the Goth who had betrayed Stilicho. He detested his fellow-Goth Alaric, and just as the negotiations were being finalised he attacked Alaric's camp with 300 warriors. Alaric assumed that Honorius was behind this, and with his dream of a Gothic homeland morphing into a diplomatic nightmare, he decided to destroy Rome.

About a hundred years earlier, the Christian writer Lactantius[21] had written that: 'The fall and ruin of the world will soon take place, but it seems that nothing of the kind is to be feared as long as the city of Rome stands intact. But when the capital of the world has fallen . . . who can doubt that the end will have come for the affairs of men and the whole world?'[22]

Now his worst fears were realised. On 24 August AD 410
Alaric's Goths entered the Eternal City. According to Procopius,
either a band of 300 of Alaric's finest fighters dressed up as
slaves, infiltrated the city and opened the Salarian gate, or a
well-to-do woman called Proba, who was motivated by pity
for Rome's starving populace, let them in. For the pagans it
was obvious that Rome fell because she had spurned her old
gods, who reciprocated by spurning her, but the events posed
major problems for Christians: Rome was now a Christian
city, so where was God when it was sacked? And, what's more,
sacked by Christians. Some Christian sources suggest that
Alaric's Goths sacked Rome in a gentle and caring kind of
way: God had authorised the city's capture; the Goths were
doing His will; so obviously they obeyed God's laws. The
contemporary Christian historian Orosius attributed the
destruction of the imperial palaces and the mausoleums of
Augustus and Hadrian to thunderbolts, rather than Gothic
violence.[23] There are other tales such as that of Alaric ordering
that anyone sheltering in a church should be spared, and one
about an elderly nun who was in possession of the sacred
vessels of the apostle Peter and became the centre of a joyous,
hymn-singing procession to St Peter's that was protected by
the merciful Goths and escalated into a huge Romano-Gothic
carnival. On the other hand, the story of the wealthy octogen-
arian Marcella probably gives a more accurate picture. She had
given away most of her inherited wealth and founded what is
sometimes regarded as the first convent in the history of the
Roman Church, and a letter written by St Jerome to her young
pupil Principia, who was there at the time, relives the terror
for her:

They say that, when the [Gothic] soldiers burst into Marcella's house [and] asked for the Golden hidden treasure, she pointed to her old worn tunic as a sign of her poverty. But they did not believe that she had really chosen the path of poverty. They say that, even when she was being beaten with clubs and whips, she felt no pain, but lay face down before them; and begged through her tears that you, Principia, might not be taken from her; nor that your youth might mean you would suffer what her old age meant that she had no need to fear. Christ softened their hard hearts and, amidst those bloodstained swords, piety found a place. The Barbarians escorted both you and Marcella to the Basilica of the Blessed and Paul, that it might be your place of refuge, or your tomb.[24]

Marcella died, just one victim of innumerable atrocities. Even St Augustine writes of Romans being put to death in a 'hideous variety of cruel ways',[25] and of bodies left unburied in the streets, arson, pillage, rape, people trafficking and enslavement. Jerome describes the behaviour of Heraclianus: 'To him, nothing was sweeter than wine or money. He claimed to serve the meekest emperor [Honorius], while being himself the cruellest of all tyrants . . . "From mothers' arms he snatched their daughters-in-law betrothed", and sold noble girls in marriage to Syrian businessmen – the most grasping of any in the human race.'[26]

Neither was this simply barbarian versus Roman or pagan versus Christian. The inhabitants of Rome pursued old personal vendettas amid the chaos. All in all, it had been an apocalyptic event. Jerome reflected: 'Who could believe that after being raised up by victories over the whole world Rome should come crashing down, and become at once the mother and the grave of her peoples?'[27]

Yet Alaric gained almost nothing politically. The barbarian Goth spent just three days in Rome before moving on. If the grain supplies from Africa would not come to Rome, he would go there to get them. He moved south into Campania and on down to Rhegium, but inclement weather prevented him crossing to Sicily. Alaric then became extremely ill. His followers put him in a wagon and moved back northwards, but he died early in AD 411 at Consentia in Bruttium (modern Calabria).

His people mourned him with the greatest devotion. Near the city of Consentia, the life-giving waters of the River Busentus tumble down from the foot of the mountain. After diverting the river from its course, his people gathered a workforce of captives . . . to dig a grave for Alaric in the middle of the river bed. At the centre of this pit, they buried their leader, surrounded by many treasures. Then they turned back the waters of the river to flow along its old course. So that no one should ever know exactly where Alaric was buried, they killed everyone who had dug his grave.[28]

On 18 October 2017, the specialist search company Merlin Burrows announced that they had 'found and pin-pointed the exact location of the lost treasure and tomb of King Alaric I . . . turning this myth and legend into a reality'.[29] The scholarly community now awaits the publication of the findings in peer-reviewed journals.

23

Attila the Hun: Born to Shake the Nations

The Huns

The disruptions that had forced the Goths and other barbarian tribes to seek protection within the boundaries of the Roman Empire in the last quarter of the fourth century AD had been caused largely by 'the race of the Hunni, fiercer than ferocity itself'.[1] Their origins are hard to pinpoint, and although the vague vicinity of modern Kazakhstan is frequently cited in modern works, the Roman world had a far more lurid picture:

> We learn from old traditions that their origin was as follows: Filimer, king of the Goths . . . found among his people certain witches, whom he called in his native tongue Haliurunnae. Suspecting these women, he expelled them from the midst of his race and compelled them to wander in solitary exile afar from his army. There the unclean spirits, who beheld them as they wandered through the wilderness, bestowed their embraces upon them and begat this savage race, which dwelt at first in the swamps – a stunted, foul and puny tribe, scarcely human, and having no language save

one which bore but slight resemblance to human speech. Such was the descent of the Huns who came to the country of the Goths. This cruel tribe . . . were fond of hunting and had no skill in any other art. After they had grown to a nation, they disturbed the peace of neighbouring races by theft and rapine.[2]

Ammianus Marcellinus' famous description of the Huns defined their image for posterity:

The very moment they are born, they make deep cuts in their children's cheeks, so that, when hair appears in the course of time, its vigour might be checked by these furrowed scars . . . They have squat bodies, strong limbs, and thick necks, and are so prodigiously ugly and bent that they might be two-legged animals, or the figures crudely carved from stumps which are seen on the parapets of bridges . . . They live on the roots of wild plants and the half-raw flesh of any sort of animal, which they warm by placing it between their thighs and the backs of their horses . . . They wear clothes made out of linen or the skins of field mice sewn together; and, once they have put on some shabby shirt, they will not take it off again or change it until it has rotted away . . . On their heads they wear round hats made of skins, and goatskins on their hairy legs . . . They are virtually joined onto their horses, which are tough but deformed . . . Whatever they do by day or night, buying or selling, eating or drinking, they do on horseback, even leaning over their horses' narrow necks to sleep . . . They are totally ignorant of the difference between right and wrong, their speech is shifty and obscure, and they are under no constraint from religion or superstition.[3]

Their 'weapons of mass destruction' were their formidable composite bows, and their fanaticism and unorthodox battle tactics made them particularly frightening:

> They are lightly armed and so fast and unpredictable that they will scatter suddenly and gallop here and there chaotically, inflicting untold slaughter . . . They can fire missiles from far off, arrows tipped not with the usual arrowheads but with sharp splintered bones, which they attach onto the shafts with extraordinary skill. They fight close-to without any fear for their own lives; and while the enemy is busy watching out for sword-thrusts, they catch him with lassoes made out of plaited cloth, so that his limbs get all entangled and he cannot walk or ride.[4]

Once again we are presented with some standard Roman stereotyping of barbarians. The further removed from the Mediterranean a people was, the stranger and more savage it was thought to be: out to the north-east were the Vidini and Geloni who clothed themselves with the skins of their dead enemies; the Agathyrsi who painted themselves blue; the cannibal Melanchlaenae ('Black-cloaks') and Anthropophagoi ('Man-eaters'); the female-warrior race of the Amazons; and, the most extreme of all, the Huns.[5]

Yet for all the fear and paranoia, the Romans had, at times, developed good enough relations with the Huns to use them in their own armies: as ever with Rome's relations with barbarians, the struggles would not necessarily be ones of binary opposites, and many of the conflicts of the later Roman Empire were as much barbarian-on-barbarian as Roman-on-barbarian.

Attila the Hun

Attila was born into a powerful Hunnic family in the early fifth century AD, somewhere to the north of the Danube River: 'Attila was the son of Mundiuch, and his brothers were Octar and Ruas who are said to have ruled [during the AD 420s and early 430s] before Attila, though not over quite so many tribes as he. After their death [in AD 434] he succeeded to the throne of the Huns, together with his brother Bleda.'⁶

Jordanes provides a snapshot of his character and appearance:

> He was a man born into the world to shake the nations, the scourge of all lands, who in some way terrified all mankind by the dreadful rumours noised abroad concerning him. He was haughty in his walk, rolling his eyes hither and thither, so that the power of his proud spirit appeared in the movement of his body. He was indeed a lover of war, yet restrained in action, mighty in counsel, gracious to suppliants and lenient to those who were once received into his protection. He was short of stature, with a broad chest and a large head; his eyes were small, his beard thin and sprinkled with gray; and he had a flat nose and a swarthy complexion, showing the evidences of his origin.⁷

The Hunnic Empire at this point encompassed territory from the Rhine to the borders of the Sasanian Empire in the east, and Attila's brother Ruas had been a constant thorn in the side of the Eastern Emperor Theodosius II (r. AD 408–50), demanding tribute and threatening the Balkans and Thrace if the payments weren't sufficiently generous. Predictably the price of peace escalated: the payments to Ruas in AD 422 had been 350 pounds of gold per annum, but the first known action of Attila and Bleda was to renegotiate the deal, and at the Treaty of Margus (modern Požarevac in Serbia) the payments went up by 100 per cent. By AD 447 the figure had gone up to 2,100 pounds, although it was still probably worth it from Theodosius II's point of view:

> The Romans complied with all Attila's instructions, and treated them as the command of their master. For not only were they taking precautions not to engage in a war against him, but they also were afraid that the Persians were preparing war, and that the Vandals were disturbing the peace at sea, and that the Isaurians were inclined to engage in brigandage, and the Saracens were mounting raids into their Eastern Empire, and that the tribes of Ethiopia were in rebellion. For this reason they swallowed their pride and obeyed Attila, but tried to prepare for military action against the other peoples, gathering their forces and appointing commanders.[8]

Over in the western half of Rome's empire, the Huns had been happy to fight alongside Romans in the various conflicts that had developed in the aftermath of Alaric's sack of Rome. The Roman general Flavius Aetius had spent a good deal of his youth as a hostage, first with the Goth Alaric, and later with the Huns. In AD 423 he initially supported John the Notary's attempt to supplant the four-year-old Valentinian III as emperor of the West, allegedly deploying 60,000 friendly Huns, but when John was betrayed and decapitated, Flavius Aetius persuaded the Huns to return back over the Danube, received a pardon, switched sides, and fought effectively against some awkward Goths and Franks in Gaul for the rest of the 420s. His machinations enabled him to become *Magister Utriusque Militiae* in AD 430, although he duly faced a challenge from a rival Roman commander by the name of Bonifacius ('Boniface'; for his career prior to this, see pp. 459 ff.), which was settled in a battle near Ariminum in AD 432 in which Bonifacius would probably have claimed the victory had he not been killed. Flavius Aetius then used another awesome force of Huns to eradicate Bonifacius' son Sebastian, and secure total dominance over Valentinian III and become the Western Emperor in all but name. Huns could be emperor-makers.

As virtual emperor, Flavius Aetius fought hard to control a situation in which barbarian incursions were threatening the very existence of Rome: Britannia was completely out on a limb and being assailed by Picti, Scotti, Angles, Saxons and Jutes, and Flavius Aetius may be referenced in the famous *gemitus Britannorum Agitio ter consuli* ('groans of the Britons to Agitius, three times Consul'), since 'Agitius' is usually held to be Aetius.[9] The Britons groaned that: 'The barbarians drive us to the sea, the sea drives us back to the barbarians; death comes by one means or another: we are either slaughtered or drowned.'[10]

In addition, the Rhine frontier had collapsed; northern Gaul was no longer under Roman administration; the Goths in Aquitania II and Novempopulana may have been in revolt; in Spain, a large kingdom of Suevi was allying itself to the Visigoths of Theodoric I, who were settled around the Garonne; and the Vandals had official control of Numidia and the Mauretanias. There was still a reasonably effective regular Roman army, but Flavius Aetius would need to strengthen it with barbarian allies from outside the empire if he was going to realise his ambitious plans to restore the Western Empire.

In Gaul, in alliance with the Huns, Flavius Aetius recovered Arelate and Narbo (modern Narbonne in France) from the Goths in AD 436, pushed some Frankish tribes back across the Rhine (or incorporated them as *foederati*), and completely eradicated the Burgundian kingdom of King Gundigar on the middle Rhine, in an episode that later inspired the Nibelungen saga. He also subdued several rebellious local leaders in Gaul that the Ravenna government called Bagaudae (or Bacaudae: 'the Warriors' in Celtic), who are sometimes regarded as bands of insurgent peasant-farmers-cum-dispossessed-outlaws driven to brigandage by Roman oppression, although more recent work suggests that they were characters who took positions of local leadership without Roman authorisation, making them bandits or rebels only in the eyes of the empire.

Attila versus the Eastern Roman Empire

The exact nature of Attila's activities in the late AD 430s is unclear, but it seems that by AD 441 the Eastern Emperor Theodosius II was no longer sticking to the terms of the Treaty of Margus. So when the Eastern Roman Empire sent a rather half-hearted naval expedition to the western Mediterranean to try to dislodge the Vandal ruler Gaiseric[11] from Sicily (see p. 462), the Huns Attila and Bleda seized the opportunity to wreak havoc in Rome's Balkan territories. Singidunum (modern Belgrade in Serbia) was razed to the ground. A truce was arranged in AD 442 which allowed Theodosius II to recall his forces from the Western Empire, but the following year Attila went on the offensive again, destroying Naïssus and Serdica, taking Philippopolis, defeating Theodosius' soldiers in a series of engagements, and arriving outside Constantinople. There was no way that the Huns could realistically hope to assault the mighty walls of Rome's eastern capital, but the damage they inflicted on the forces of the Eastern Roman Empire enabled them to reimpose the tribute at a vastly increased rate, along with a lump-sum payment of 6,000 pounds of gold to cover the arrears.

Attila then briefly drops off the historical radar, but by AD 445 he had murdered Bleda and as sole ruler of the Huns he planned to extend the tentacles of his power: 'In order that he might first be equal to the expedition he was preparing, he sought to increase his strength by murder. Thus he proceeded from the destruction of his own kindred to the menace of all others.'[12]

Attila launched another assault on the Eastern Roman Empire in AD 447. Again the details are hazy, although it seems that the attrition rates on both sides were high, and that the barbarian got as far south as Greece, until he was finally stopped at Thermopylae.

Amid the military actions between Attila and the Eastern Emperor Theodosius II there was also considerable diplomatic engagement, and we have an invaluable first-hand account of this in the *History* of Priscus of Panion, who made the long and hazardous trip from Constantinople to Attila's headquarters, escorted by barbarian guides, as part of a Roman embassy in AD 449:

I entered the enclosure of Attila's palace, bearing gifts to his wife, whose name was Kreka. [She lived in a beautifully constructed wooden house, where], having been admitted by the barbarians at the door, I found her reclining on a soft couch. The floor of the room was covered with woolen mats for walking on. A number of servants stood round her, and maids sitting on the floor in front of her embroidered with coloured linen cloths intended to be placed over the Scythian dress for ornament. Having approached, saluted her, and presented the gifts, I went out and walked to the other houses, where Attila was.[13]

Attila then invited the Roman delegation to a banquet:

The cupbearers gave us a cup, according to the national custom, that we might pray before we sat down. Having tasted the cup, we proceeded to take our seats, all the chairs being ranged along the walls of the room on either side. Attila sat in the middle on a couch; a second couch was set behind him, and from it steps led up to his bed, which was covered with linen sheets and wrought coverlets for orna-ment, such as Greeks and Romans used to deck bridal beds. The places on the right of Attila were held chief in honour – those on the left, where we sat, were only second . . .

[Toasts were drunk.] Tables, large enough for three or four, or even more, to sit at, were placed next the table of Attila, so that each could take of the food on the dishes with-out leaving his seat . . . A luxurious meal, served on silver plate, had been made ready for us and the barbarian guests, but Attila ate nothing but meat on a wooden trencher. In everything else, too, he showed himself temperate – his cup was of wood, while to the guests were given goblets of gold and silver. His dress, too, was quite simple, affecting only to be clean. The sword he carried at his side, the ratchets of his

Scythian shoes, the bridle of his horse were not adorned, like those of the other Scythians, with gold or gems or anything costly.[14]

Feasting gave way to song, and in the final negotiations the Romans agreed to vacate a swathe of territory south of the Danube, and to continue paying the tribute.

Attila versus the Western Roman Empire

The Eastern Emperor Theodosius II died as a result of a riding accident on 28 July AD 450, to be succeeded on 25 August by a Thracian military officer called Flavius Marcianus ('Marcian'). As far as foreign policy was concerned, Marcian benefited from the settlement of Rome's differences with Persia, and his approach to Attila became quite uncompromising. Unlike their fellow-barbarian Goths, the Huns had no interest in securing a permanent residence inside the empire and regarded blackmail and extortion as completely acceptable. Marcian, however, did not. He took steps to recover the Balkans, and he stopped paying off the Huns. The policy bore fruit: Attila simply decided that the Western Roman Empire was a softer target, which allowed Emperor Marcian some breathing space to establish a modicum of peace and prosperity throughout his own realm.

Attila's attitude to the Western Empire was, in part, determined by some extremely bizarre events that involved Emperor Valentinian III's thirty-two-year-old sister Honoria in a strange love triangle. In her teenage years she had got pregnant. Her lover had been executed, after which she had been sent to Constantinople to live with her ultra-chaste cousin Pulcheria, and when she had ultimately been allowed back to Ravenna she had been given a worthy, admirable but unremarkable husband in the person of Herculanus Bassus. Honoria clearly wanted someone more exciting, and she rebelled against her family in the most extreme way imaginable: she wrote a letter explaining her predicament, enclosed her ring with it, gave it to her eunuch Hyacinthus, and told him to deliver it to Attila the Hun.

Attila just couldn't believe his luck. As far as he was concerned Honoria's letter amounted to a marriage proposal. So he demanded that Valentinian III should give her to him, along with her share of what he called the 'sceptre of Empire' – i.e. half of the Western Roman Empire. Ravenna responded that it had no intention of doing this, and that anyway females didn't hold the 'sceptre of Empire'. This gave Attila the excuse that he needed to declare war, on the (spurious) grounds that he was defending the honour of his 'bride'. Obviously Attila's demands were rejected, and he went on the warpath.

Prior to receiving Honoria's letter, Attila had maintained pretty cordial relations with Flavius Aetius, who was still the effective ruler of Valentinian III's half of the empire. But that changed when the Huns moved into Gaul in AD 451. They crossed the Rhine, destroyed Divodurum Mediomatricum (modern Metz in Germany) and several other cities, and arrived at the River Loire. Attila was held at bay at Aureliana Civitas (formerly Cenabum, and now Orléans), which gave Flavius Aetius breathing space to garner the support of various Gauls and Aquitanian Visigoths led by Theoderic I, the latter brought onside by a Gallic noble called Avitus. Getting these Goths to join Flavius Aetius might have proved impossible, since back in the early AD 440s Huneric, the son of the Vandal King Gaiseric, had been betrothed to the Emperor Valentinian III's five-year-old daughter Eudocia, despite the fact that Huneric was already married to one of Theoderic I's daughters. Gaiseric had marked the new engagement by accusing Theoderic I's daughter of trying to assassinate him, cutting off her nose and ears, and sending her back to her father. But when Gaiseric allied himself with Attila, Theoderic I took a pragmatic approach and linked up with the Romans, possibly as the lesser of two evils. Flavius Aetius was also joined by a Frankish faction, some Alani and several contingents of northern Gallic Bagaudae, who started to be called by the more respectable name of Aremoricani once they were on the Roman side. Flavius Aetius may also have been able to deploy some of the former Rhine *limitanei* and some remnants of the old British *comitatenses*.

It was practically barbarian versus barbarian. Flavius Aetius' multi-ethnic army forced Attila to back off, and finally engaged with him at the Battle of the Catalaunian Fields (known to the ancient authorities as *Campus Mauriacus*), which modern scholarly consensus places between Troyes and Châlons-sur-Marne. Prosper of Aquitaine described the incalculable slaughter; Hydatius numbered the dead at 300,000; the *Gallic Chronicle of 511* spoke of innumerable cadavers; the Goth Theoderic I was killed in action; but crucially Attila got the worse of things and retreated to Pannonia.

The victorious Romano-barbarian army was too badly weakened to give chase, however, and by the following year Attila was back attacking Italy with fresh forces. Flavius Aetius was powerless to repel him. Aquileia (the ancient ancestor of Venice), Patavium (Padua), Verona, Brixia (Brescia), Bergomum (Bergamo), Mediolanum and Ticinum all fell but, rather unexpectedly, Attila did not attempt to sack Rome. Legend has it that Pope Leo I talked him out of it (he certainly asked him to withdraw, although he may have paid him off); another version says that the Huns thought that there was a curse on anyone who sacked Rome (look at what happened to Alaric, they said); or Attila's forces may have been suffering from malaria or dysentery, which commonly affected armies in Italy at that time; or again the Eastern Roman army may have attacked Attila's trans-Danubian heartland.

Whatever his reasons for withdrawing were, Attila and his barbarians headed back across the Danube, where, in AD 453, he met a slightly bizarre and unheroic end:

> He took in marriage a very beautiful girl named Ildico, after countless other wives, as was the custom of his race. He had given himself up to excessive joy at his wedding, and as he lay on his back, heavy with wine and sleep, a rush of super-fluous blood, which would ordinarily have flowed from his nose, streamed in deadly course down his throat and killed him, since it was hindered in the usual passages. Thus did drunkenness put a disgraceful end to a king renowned in war.[15]

The Huns accorded their leader all the appropriate honours for a man of his status, and Jordanes quotes the funeral dirge, which they sang before they disposed of his body in three coffins, bound respectively with gold, silver and iron, and slew the workers who had dug his grave:

> The chief of the Huns, King Attila, born of his sire Mundiuch, lord of bravest tribes, sole possessor of the Scythian and German realms – powers unknown before – captured cities and terrified both Empires of the Roman world and, appeased by their prayers, took annual tribute to save the rest from

plunder. And when he had accomplished all this by the favor of fortune, he fell, not by wound of the foe, nor by treachery of friends, but in the midst of his nation at peace, happy in his joy and without sense of pain. Who can rate this as death, when none believes it calls for vengeance?[16]

Attila had been the glue that held the whole Hunnic project together, and was probably the greatest barbarian threat to the empire since Hannibal. His unexpected death was an enormous bonus, not just for Rome, but for numerous barbarian tribes, who went on to smash Attila's heirs in a huge multi-barbarian battle in Pannonia: 'And so the bravest nations tore themselves to pieces. For then, I think, must have occurred a most remarkable spectacle, where one might see the Goths fighting with pikes, the Gepidae raging with the sword, the Rugi breaking off the spears in their own wounds, the Suevi fighting on foot, the Huns with bows, the Alani drawing up a battle line of heavy-armed and the Heruli of light-armed warriors.'[17]

Attila and the Huns' reputation for destructiveness has persisted, although there remain nuances of response in which he can be either demonised or idolised. British propaganda made derogatory use of 'the Hun' for the Germans during the First World War, but this had its origin in an address made on 27 July 1900 by Kaiser Wilhelm II to German soldiers bound for China, in which Attila was presented as a role model: 'Just as a thousand year ago, the Huns under Attila won a reputation of might that lives on in legends, so too may you assert the name of the Germans in China in such a way that no Chinaman will ever again dare so much as to pull a face at a German.'[18]

24

Barbarian Warlords: Gaiseric and the Fall of Rome

Vandalism and the Vandals

During the period of the Enlightenment, whenever thinkers looked to the ancient world for examples of barbaric destructiveness, it was the Goths who tended to spring to mind. In his great *The History of the Decline and Fall of the Roman Empire*, Edward Gibbon commented very pertinently on their image: 'So memorable was the part which they acted in the subversion of the Western empire, that the name of the GOTHS is frequently but improperly used as a general appellation of rude and warlike barbarism.'[1] But nowadays it is the Vandals who are the byword for mindless destruction. They were certainly invoked in this context at times, as when the artist Raphael (1483–1520) wrote to the Medici Pope Leo X in 1517 complaining about the 'recycling' of ancient ruins by the builders of sixteenth-century AD Rome, whom he described as 'Goths and Vandals'.[2] The twenty-two-year-old Alexander Pope also raged against the 'holy Vandals' of the Catholic Church in his *Essay on Criticism* of 1711:

Learning and Rome alike in empire grew,
And arts still follow'd where her eagles flew;
From the same foes, at last, both felt their doom,
And the same age saw learning fall, and Rome.
With tyranny, then superstition join'd,
As that the body, this enslav'd the mind;
Much was believ'd, but little understood,
And to be dull was constru'd to be good;
A second deluge learning thus o'er-run,
And the monks finish'd what the Goths begun.
    At length Erasmus, that great, injur'd name,
(The glory of the priesthood, and the shame!)
Stemm'd the wild torrent of a barb'rous age,
And drove those holy Vandals off the stage.[3]

Similarly, in his *Course in Experimental Philosophy* (1714), John Theophilus Desaguliers attacked the 'army of Goths and Vandals in the philosophical world'[4] who were opposed to Isaac Newton, and the English poet William Cowper bewailed the destruction of Lord Mansfield's library in the Gordon Riots:

On the Burning of Lord Mansfield's Library, Together with his MSS. by the Mob, in the Month of June 1780.
So then – the Vandals of our isle,
Sworn foes to sense and law,
Have burnt to dust a nobler pile
Than ever Romans saw![5]

However, it was really the French Abbé Henri Grégoire de Blois, referring to the destruction of artworks during and after the French Revolution in his '*Rapport sur les destructions opérées par le vandalisme, et sur les moyens de le réprimer*',[6] who coined the term '*Vandalisme*' in the sense that we use it now. Some of his contemporaries found this extremely offensive, racist even, as he acknowledged: 'Those respected scholars, born in that part of Germany, whence the Vandals had once come, claimed that the meaning which I gave to the term "vandalisme" was an insult to their ancestors, who were warriors, and not destroyers.'[7] But the term stuck.

The Vandals (Vandali, Vandili or Vandilii to the Romans, Bandaloi to the Greeks) were usually understood by our earlier sources as a loose grouping of Germanic tribes. Pliny told his readers that 'There are five German races: the Vandals, who include the Burgodiones, Varinnae, Charini and Gutones [i.e. Goths]; [and four others].'[8]

In his *Germania*, Tacitus was at pains to point out that it was the Romans who lumped all the Germanic tribes under the generic name of 'Germani', although the barbarians saw it differently:

Their ancient hymns – the only style of record or history which they possess – celebrate a god Tuisto . . . To him they ascribe a son Mannus, the beginning of their race, and to Mannus three sons, its founders; from whose names the tribes nearest the Ocean are to be known as Ingaevones, the central tribes as Herminones, and the rest as Istaevones. Some authorities, using the licence which pertains to antiquity, pronounce for more sons to the god and a larger number of race names, Marsi, Gambrivii, Suebi, Vandilii; these are, they say, real and ancient names, while the name of 'Germani' is new and a recent application.[9]

This transpired, says Tacitus, because after the first Germanic people crossed the Rhine into Gaul, what had originally been just the name of one individual tribe was applied to the whole people. 'Germani,' he says, is an 'artificial name'.[10] He also seems to regard the Vandilii as the same people as the Lugii, who comprised several states in the southern parts of eastern Germany, one of whose tribes, the Nahanarvali, followed a strange prehistoric ritual, which the Romans regarded as equivalent to their cult of Castor and Pollux, in which a priest presided in female dress.[11] This tribe may be the same people as the Silingai (Silingae in Latin), first mentioned by the second-century AD geographer Ptolemy, who lived north of the Carpathian Mountains around what now is Silesia, mostly in modern Poland, to which they give their name.[12]

The first occurrence in our sources of Vandali as a tribal name comes in the so-called Marcomannic War, which broke out in around AD 166 in the Danube frontier zone, during the joint reign of Marcus Aurelius (AD 161–80) and Lucius Verus (AD 161–9),[13] and which came to be known also as the German War, the Northern War or the War of Many Nations as more tribes entered the picture. Population movements in what is now Poland and Ukraine started to affect various tribes on Rome's borders. These peoples sought sanctuary within the Roman Empire and threatened war unless they were taken in, at a time when the Danube frontier had been weakened by the deployment of many of its troops to the east. The eponymous Germanic Marcomanni, along with the Quadi and the Sarmatian Iazyges, moved into Roman territory, across Raetia, Noricum and Pannonia, raided northern Italy, and laid siege to Aquileia.

The Germanic incursion coincided with troops returning from the east (see p. 375 ff.) bringing what is often called the Antonine Plague, an illness incurable at the time whose symptoms were described by the contemporary Greek physician Galen as diarrhoea, high fever and the appearance of pustules on the skin after nine days. It was possibly smallpox. Mortality estimates vary, but the death toll may have run into millions. Military operations had to be curtailed, but ultimately the two emperors forced 'several kings to retreat, together with their peoples'.[14] Lucius Verus was keen to return to Rome, but Marcus Aurelius insisted on addressing the problems on the Danube, and so they crossed the Alps, 'pressed further on, and settled everything that pertained to the defence of Italy and Illyricum'.[15] The fighting was typically barbaric. Dio Cassius tells us that 'Among the corpses of the barbarians were found even those of women in full body armour.'[16]

So far so good for Rome. Some tribes surrendered, and a number of their tribespeople were conscripted into Rome's armies. But in AD 171, a barbarian group called the Astingi, usually assumed to be Vandals, led by their chieftains Raus and Raptus,

came into Dacia with their entire households, hoping to secure both money and land in return for their alliance. But failing of their purpose, they left their wives and children under the protection of [the Roman governor of Dacia, Cornelius] Clemens, until they should acquire the land of the Costoboci by their arms; but upon conquering that people, they proceeded to injure Dacia no less than before. The Lacringi, fearing that Clemens in his dread of them might lead these newcomers into the land which they themselves were inhabiting, attacked them while off their guard and won a decisive victory.[17]

The end result was that the Astingi ceased their aggression against the Romans. The siege of Aquileia was raised, and by the end of AD 171, the barbarians had been pushed out of Roman territory. The Astingi became quite useful allies for a while.

Marcus Aurelius was succeeded by the somewhat unhinged Emperor Commodus[18] (sole rule AD 180–92), who did, however, try to restrict barbarian-on-barbarian fighting, and prohibited the Marcomanni and Quadi from making war on various tribes, including the Vandili.[19] On the other hand, in AD 212 or 213, the equally bizarre Emperor Caracalla did the opposite: 'He commended [Gaius] Fabricius Luscinus because he had been unwilling to secure the death of Pyrrhus through the treachery of a friend (see p. 71); and yet he took pride in having stirred up enmity with the Vandili and the Marcomani, who had been friends.'[20]

The Vandals are conspicuous by their absence in the literary sources until Rome's third-century 'Age of Chaos',[21] and only emerge towards the end of that period with the accession of Emperor Aurelian around September AD 270:

Aurelian, having regulated the empire, went . . . into Pannonia, which he was informed the Scythians [who were in fact Vandals, Sarmatians, Alemanni and Iuthungi] were preparing to invade. For this reason he sent orders to the inhabitants of that country to carry into the towns all their corn and cattle, and every thing that could be of use to the enemy, in order to distress them with famine, with which they were already afflicted. The barbarians having crossed the river [near Aquincum, modern Budapest] into Pannonia had an engagement, the result of which was nearly equal. But the same night, the barbarians recrossed the river, and as soon as day appeared, sent ambassadors to treat for peace.[22]

The peace agreement saw the Vandals remain outside Rome's frontiers, surrender their plunder and supply 2,000 cavalrymen for Rome's armies, and although they immediately tried to cheat on the deal, the Emperor Aurelian brought them to heel.[23] Nevertheless, a decade later, in the reign of Probus (AD 276–82), we find them fighting in Dacia:

[Probus] made war on the Burgundi and the Vandals. But seeing that his forces were too weak, he endeavored to separate those of his enemies, and engage only with a part. His design was favoured by fortune; for the armies lying on both sides of the river, the Romans challenged the barbarians that were on the further side to fight. This so incensed them, that many of them crossed over, and fought until the barbarians were all either slain or taken by the Romans.[24]

All those who were taken alive were sent to Britain and settled there.

Typically, the Vandals' conflicts were not just with Rome. During the reign of Constantine I 'the Great', the Gothic chieftain Geberich sought to expand his realm at Vandal expense, and inflicted a devastating and humiliating defeat on Visimar of the Asdingi: 'The remnant of the Vandals who had escaped, collecting a band of their unwarlike folk, left their ill-fated country and asked the Emperor Constantine for Pannonia.

Here they made their home for about sixty years and obeyed the commands of the Emperors like subjects.'[25]

Into the Roman Empire

Up until this point in their history, the Vandals had only really been bit-part players in the events on Rome's northern border, but in the first decade of the fifth-century AD they took centre stage: 'A long time afterward they were summoned [from Pannonia] by Stilicho, Master of the Soldiery, Ex-Consul and Patrician, and took possession of Gaul. Here they plundered their neighbours and had no settled place of abode.'[26]

This was as part of the 'Great Invasion' (see pp. 424–427), when alongside immense numbers of Suevi and Alani, the Silingi and Hasdingi Vandals crossed the Rhine, somewhere between Moguntiacum and Borbetomagus, according to some writers at the instigation of the semi-Vandal Stilicho, and gradually worked their way south-west through Gaul. They effectively isolated Britain from the Roman Empire, and prompted the usurpation by Constantine III (see p. 425), which is of much greater interest to our written sources than the Vandals themselves, but in any case it seems that Constantine III himself didn't regard these barbarians as his main priority, and he dealt with them using a shrewd combination of force and diplomacy.[27] Nevertheless, writing in c.AD 408, Saint Jerome gives a vivid account of the devastation caused:

I shall now say a few words of our present miseries . . . Savage tribes in countless numbers have overrun all parts of Gaul. The whole country between the Alps and the Pyrenees, between the Rhine and the Ocean, has been laid waste by hordes of Quadi, Vandals, Sarmatians, Alani, Gepidae, Heruli, Saxons, Burgundians, Allemanni and ... even Pannonians. For [quoting Psalm 83.3] 'Assur also is joined with them'. The once noble city of Moguntiacum has been captured and destroyed. In its church many thousands have been massacred. The Vangiones [inhabitants of Worms] after standing a long siege have been extirpated. The powerful city of Remi, the Ambiani [of modern Amiens], the Altrebatae [modern Arras], the Morini on the skirts of the world, Tornacus [modern Tournay], Menetae [modern Speyer], and Agentorate [modern Strasbourg] have fallen to Germania: while the provinces of Aquitaine and of Novempopulana, of Lugdunensis [modern Lyons] and of Narbonensis [modern Narbonne] are, with the exception of a few cities, one universal scene of desolation. And those which the sword spares without, famine ravages within. I cannot speak without tears of Tolosa, which has been kept from falling hitherto by the merits of its reverend bishop Exuperius. Even the Spains are on the brink of ruin and tremble daily as they recall the invasion of the Cymbricae; and, while others suffer misfortunes once in actual fact, they suffer them continually in anticipation.[28]

The Spanish anticipation turned to reality as the Vandals, Suevi and Alani invaded the Iberian peninsula in the autumn of AD 409. The results, to Christian eyes, were literally apocalyptic:

As the barbarians ran wild through Spain ... a famine ran riot, so dire that driven by hunger human beings devoured human flesh; mothers too feasted upon the bodies of their own children whom they had killed and cooked with their own hands; wild beasts, habituated to feeding on the bodies of those slain by the sword, famine or pestilence, killed all the braver individuals and feasting on their flesh everywhere became brutally set upon the destruction of the human race. And thus with the four plagues of sword, famine, pestilence and wild beasts raging everywhere throughout the world, the annunciations foretold by the Lord through his prophets came to fulfilment.[29]

Yet the region recovered once the barbarian ravages abated, and the various tribes divided the five Roman provinces of Hispania by drawing lots:

> They then apportioned to themselves by lot areas of the provinces for settlement: the Vandals took possession of Gallaecia and the Sueves that part of Gallaecia which is situated on the very western edge of the Ocean. The Alans were allotted the provinces of Lusitania and Carthaginiensis, and the Siling Vandals Baetica. The Spaniards in the cities and forts who had survived the disasters surrendered themselves to servitude under the barbarians who held sway throughout the provinces.[30]

A brief interlude of relative calm was then shattered when Alaric the Goth's successor Ataulf was driven out of Gaul and into Tarraco (modern Tarragona) and Barcino (modern Barcelona) in Spain by the Roman generalissimo Flavius Constantius. Ataulf was assassinated by one of his own men in AD 415; his successor Singeric was murdered and replaced by Wallia; and the Vandals taunted the Goths when they were reduced to starvation by Flavius Constantius, selling them grain at the exorbitant rate of one gold *solidus* per *trula* ('spoonful'), and calling them by the derogatory nickname *truli* – 'the Spoonies'.[31] But Wallia had his revenge: having agreed to provide military service to the Western Roman Emperor Honorius, he took the offensive against the Alani in Lusitania and Vandal Silingi in Baetica with considerable success. By AD 418 he had harassed the Silingi Vandals, killed King Addax of the Alani in AD 418, and forced the Alani survivors to seek refuge with Gunderic, leader of the Hasdingi Vandals in Gallaecia. Wallia's Goths were rewarded with a permanent residence in Aquitania in southern Gaul.

Around AD 420 there was some inter-barbarian fighting between the Hasdingi and the Suevi in Gallaecia. A Roman army under Asterius, the *Comes Hispanorum*, stepped in on the Suevic side, and forced the Vandals to move into Baetica. The unintended consequence of this was to turn the Vandals into a serious threat to the rich territories of southern Spain. The Roman *Comes Domesticorum* Castinus was sent in to sort out the situation, along with his co-commander the *Magister Militum* Bonifacius ('Boniface') and a large number of Gothic *foederati*, but when he had all but forced the Vandals to surrender he was defeated in AD 422 thanks to some unspecified Gothic treachery. He also had a major disagreement with Bonifacius, who took umbrage and crossed over to Africa and started to build a power base there. Meanwhile, the Hasdingi Vandals came to dominate southern Spain, and although they left very little in the way of archaeological remains, Andalusia is still probably named after them.

By the mid-420s AD the Vandals were attacking the Balearic Islands and plundering Rome's province of Mauretania

Tingitania in North Africa.[32] Hydatius' *Chronicle* informs us that in AD 428 'Gunderic, the king of the Vandals, captured Hispalis [modern Seville], but soon after, when with overwhelming impiety he tried to lay hands on the church of that very city, by the will of god he was seized by a demon and died'.[33]

Gunderic was succeeded by his bastard brother Gaiseric (aka Geiseric or, less correctly, Genseric). His people already occupied some very rich grain-growing land, but now they looked across the Strait of Gibraltar at the wealthy, fertile, vulnerable and lightly defended regions of North Africa.

Gaiseric: Into Africa

In the May of either AD 428 or, more probably, AD 429,[34] the Vandals embarked on a hugely significant enterprise. Gaiseric organised them into eighty groups of 1,000 people, and ferried them across the Strait of Gibraltar into Africa. This incursion was, of course, of great concern to the now African-based *Comes Domesticorum et Africae* Bonifacius, even though his main worries happened to be centred on the court at Ravenna, where the Augusta, Galla Placidia, currently acting as regent for her underage son, the Western Roman Emperor Valentinian III, had been duped into thinking that Bonifacius was plotting against her. When he took her general Flavius Aetius' advice not to obey her command to return to Italy, this simply confirmed her suspicions. Nevertheless, a Gothic commander called Sigisvult managed to smooth things over, which allowed Bonifacius to confront the barbarians in Africa on behalf of the empire.

Bonifacius tried diplomacy and then battle.[35] But he was defeated, and sought refuge inside the walls of Hippo Regius (modern Bone/Bona/Annaba in Algeria), where St Augustine had been bishop since AD 395. The Vandal siege of the city ended in failure, but Augustine was smitten with a fatal illness and died on 28 August AD 430. Elsewhere the Vandals ranged through North Africa, raping and pillaging as they went: a rescript (reply to a petition) of Pope Leo I gives a small but chilling insight, allowing virgins who had been raped still to receive the sacraments, even though they no longer counted as undefiled.[36] The Vandals were themselves Christian, but Arians, and they inflicted considerable brutality against the Nicaean Christians. Although some modern scholarship has tried to rehabilitate the Vandals' image, contemporary Christian sources portray their activities in Africa as utterly terrifying: 'A man such as [Augustine] had to see cities overthrown and destroyed and within them their inhabitants and their buildings on their estates wiped out by a murderous enemy, and others put to flight and scattered. He saw churches denuded of priests and ministers, holy virgins and others vowed to chastity dispersed, some amongst them succumbing to tortures, others perishing by the sword.'[37]

But the Romans regrouped, and the Eastern and Western Empires combined to try to dislodge Gaiseric's people:

> Bonifacius and the Romans in Libya, since a numerous army had come from both Rome and Byzantium [Constantinople] and Aspar [the Eastern Emperor Theodosius II's Alano-Gothic *Magister Militum*] with them as general, decided to renew the struggle, and a fierce battle was fought in which they were badly beaten by the enemy, and they made haste to flee as each one could. And Aspar betook himself homeward, and Bonifacius, coming before [Galla] Placidia,

acquitted himself of the suspicion, showing that it had arisen against him for no true cause.[38]

A peace agreement was reached in AD 435, under which the empire granted Gaiseric quite extensive tracts of land in Africa, based on the two Mauretanias and Numidia.

The agreement was short-lived, though. In AD 439 Gaiseric's Vandals made a surprise assault on the Roman province of Africa and seized its capital, Carthage, where, we are told, most of the inhabitants were watching chariot racing in the hippo-drome. This was a real game-changer: one of the Mediterranean's premier cities was now under firm barbarian control; Gaiseric had acquired a first-rate naval base; Rome's grain supply was at risk; Constantinople's access to the eastern Mediterranean was inhibited; Sicily was under threat; and the court at Ravenna, with the Western Emperor Valentinian III now ruling in his own right, was understandably nervous about the safety of southern Italy.

The Fall of Rome

In AD 440 Valentinian III's fears were realised: Gaiseric attacked Sicily. Valentinian III took defensive measures in Italy, which included bolstering the fortifications of some major urban centres, and the Eastern Emperor Theodosius II some-what sluggishly sent a naval expedition to the western Mediterranean in spring AD 441, but this was not done with any real conviction, since he was already preoccupied with Persia and the Huns. Valentinian III was forced to look to diplomacy, and in AD 442 the Western Roman Empire signed a treaty with the Vandals that acknowledged their control over

Numidia, Byzacena and Proconsularis, and though the less attractive Mauretanian provinces were returned to the Romans, the Spanish situation precluded them exercising any effective government there either. The agreement was cemented by a dynastic marriage: Gaiseric's son Huneric was betrothed to Valentinian III's five-year-old daughter Eudocia and sent to Ravenna, creating an important political realignment of the Vandals away from the Visigoths and towards the Roman imperial family (see p. 445).

Once again, we have a slight hiatus in our historical sources, as the focus of the ancient writers turns more towards the Huns than the Vandals. But the death of Attila in AD 453 sent shockwaves through the Western court at Ravenna that resulted in some highly complex dynastic infighting. On 21 September AD 454 Attila's nemesis Flavius Aetius was assassinated in a plot organised by a wealthy senator called Petronius Maximus and the eunuch Heracleius, with Valentinian III possibly administering the coup de grâce. But then, on 16 March AD 455, two of Flavius Aetius' bodyguards, possibly Huns but with the Gothic names of Optila and Thraustila, avenged their master's death: 'Valentinian rode in the [Campus Martius] with a few bodyguards and the followers of Optila and Thraustila. When he had dismounted from his horse and proceeded to archery, Optila and his friends attacked him. Optila struck Valentinian on his temple and when turned around to see the striker he dealt him a second blow on the face and felled him.'[39]

Petronius Maximus might simply have wanted the throne of the Western Roman Empire for himself, since he now bribed his way into power and cemented his position by marrying Valentinian III's widow Licinia Eudoxia, whose daughter

Eudocia was now offered to his son Palladius.[40] The problem with the latter arrangement was, of course, that Eudocia was already betrothed to Gaiseric's son Huneric and, in addition, Licinia Eudoxia detested her new husband. A number of sources, albeit with a degree of scepticism, tell us that Licinia Eudoxia emulated her sister-in-law Honoria's tactics for escaping her unwelcome marriage (see p. 444) by appealing to Gaiseric.[41] If the story is genuine, this gave Gaiseric a convenient pretext for getting hold of Huneric's fiancée Eudocia, but regardless of the truth of the matter, he set sail for Rome.

The arrival of the Vandal fleet at the mouth of the Tiber created pandemonium at Rome, in the midst of which Petronius Maximus was hacked down by some imperial slaves on 22 May AD 455. His dismembered body was thrown into the Tiber. Pope Leo I allegedly met the barbarian Gaiseric at the gates of Rome, but unlike his supposed success with Attila, he failed to divert the Vandal king. Gaiseric now perpetrated another sack of Rome, but this one lasted for a fortnight, and was far more destructive than Alaric's. Rome was comprehensively vandalised in both the literal and the figurative senses: the material plunder included the menorah that Titus had looted from Jerusalem in AD 70 (see p. 357), bronze statues from the palace and the gilded bronze roof of the temple of Jupiter Capitolinus,[42] but the human booty was even more valuable to Gaiseric:

He even led away as captives surviving Senators, accompanied by their wives; along with them he also carried off to Carthage in Africa the empress Licinia Eudoxia, who had summoned him; her daughter [Galla] Placidia [the Younger], the wife of the patrician Olybrius, who then was staying at Constantinople; and even the maiden Eudocia. After he had returned, Gaiseric gave the younger Eudocia, a maiden, the daughter of the empress Eudoxia, to his son Huneric in marriage, and he held them both, the mother and the daughter, in great honour.[43]

Huneric's marriage to Eudocia was dynastically crucial: she was the granddaughter of the Eastern Emperor Theodosius II, and from Gaiseric's perspective, any legitimate male offspring would be the heirs to the the throne of the Western Roman Empire. Satisfied with a job well done, Gaiseric returned to Carthage, from where, in random fashion, he raided Italy, Sardinia, Sicily, Corsica, the Balearic Islands, Spain, Dalmatia and Greece, so violently that the young poet Sidonius referred to the fighting as the Fourth Punic War, even if equating the Vandals with the third- and second-century BC Carthaginians is stretching historical veracity a little.[44]

Gaiseric's pillage and destruction were facilitated by the fact that both halves of the Roman Empire had new rulers: the Gallic Avitus, who had taken over in the West with the backing of Gallic nobility and the Gothic army of Theoderic II and his brother Frederic, and the Thracian Marcian in the East (for Marcian's dealings with Attila the Hun, see p. 444). The whole empire was now ruled by men who in earlier times would have been considered barbarians by the Romans. Diplomacy proved ineffectual, until a more robust response was formulated by Majorian and Flavius Ricimer, the commanders of the Italian army. Majorian was a young man, perhaps of Egyptian descent, whose father had been a financial official under Flavius Aetius, while Ricimer was the Suevo-Gothic grandson of Wallia.

The Western Emperor Avitus set his sights on Africa, and the omens were good. On 1 January AD 456, Sidonius delivered a panegyric that talked up the benefits that Avitus would bring to Rome: 'He will restore Libya to you a fourth time in chains . . . it is easy to feel sure even now of what he can do by waging war, how he shall, time and again, bring nations under your yoke . . . Lo, this prince of riper years shall bring back youth to you whom child-princes have made old.'[45]

Avitus paid his Visigothic troops with money raised by selling bronze fittings stripped from public buildings to metal merchants, and focused initially on Spain. But all he did was to create chaos there, primarily because he had to deal with more pressing issues in Italy.

Gaiseric's Vandals always had the option of cutting off Italy's grain supplies: 'When Avitus was Emperor of Rome there was famine at the same time. The mob put the blame on Avitus and compelled him to dismiss from the city of the Romans his allies who had entered with him from Gaul.'[46]

To make matters worse, Ricimer and Majorian rebelled. The Emperor Avitus faced them on the battlefield at Placentia on 17 October AD 456, but was defeated. His life was spared, and he was made into a bishop.

The uncertainty in the West was compounded by the fact that the Eastern Emperor Marcian died shortly after Avitus' deposition. His successor Leo I, another Thracian, appointed Majorian as *Magister Utriusque Militiae* in February AD 457, and the Italian army proclaimed Majorian as the Western Roman emperor in April. Majorian was a genuinely talented emperor, and he needed to be. Successful operations in Raetia, Campania, Gaul and Spain allowed him then to focus solely on the Vandals. So in AD 460, he gathered a fleet at Cartagena, redeployed his general Marcellinus from Dalmatia to secure Sicily, and spurned Gaiseric's overtures of peace.

With a conflict seeming unavoidable, the Vandal then conducted a scorched-earth policy in Mauretania, where he also poisoned the wells – Majorian's invasion force would have to transit that region in order to get to grips with him – and then hit back with a highly effective pre-emptive strike on the Roman fleet at Cartagena. That scuppered Majorian's plans, and he signed a treaty with Gaiseric under which he accepted 'shameful', but unspecified, terms. No Roman emperor could afford that kind of setback, and no sooner had he set foot on Italian soil than he was apprehended by Ricimer and decapitated on 2 August AD 461.

A power vacuum now ensued in the Western Roman Empire, which suited Gaiseric perfectly. He wanted Olybrius, the husband of Valentinian III's daughter Galla Placidia the Younger, to take the purple (thereby making Gaiseric's son, Huneric, the emperor's brother-in-law). Adopting an aggressive stance, he took Sardinia and Sicily, and no one could do anything to curtail his widespread seaborne raids, although the Eastern Emperor Leo I at Constantinople did get him to agree to release Galla Placidia the Younger and Eudoxia (for a large ransom).

By AD 467 the Western Empire had finally acquired a highly competent man on its throne in the person of Procopius Anthemius, and, as usual, the Vandals were still public enemy number one. The new Western emperor formulated a plan, backed by the East, the ambition of which was matched by its vast expense: 64,000 pounds of gold and 700,000 of silver. But the cost-benefit analysis made it a gamble worth taking, and in AD 468 a mighty armada of 1,100 ships was assembled to transport a formidable army to Africa under the command of Leo I's brother-in-law Basiliscus, while a land army under

Heraclius, who was probably the Eastern *Comes Rei Militaris*, was to march simultaneously into Vandal territory. The general Marcellinus was to complete the offensive by invading Sardinia.

All three prongs of the attack had initial success: Heraclius kicked the Vandals out of the province of Tripolitania; Marcellinus captured Sardinia, and pushed the Vandals out of Sicily; and Basiliscus defeated one of Gaiseric's naval squadrons close to the island. Unfortunately for the Romans, rather than driving home his advantage, Basiliscus allowed Gaiseric to negotiate a five-day truce. The Vandal exploited this to assemble a fleet that included fireships, and when he unleashed them against Basiliscus' fleet, which was now lying at anchor off Mercurium on the African coast, they caused pandemonium. Gaiseric's conventional vessels exploited the chaos, and the outcome was catastrophic for the Romans: Sardinia and Sicily fell back under Vandal control; Marcellinus was assassinated; and by *c.*AD 470 some form of peace had been agreed. In AD 476 Gaiseric's position as a major player in the Mediterranean world was formally acknowledged with the signing of the 'Perpetual Peace' with the new Eastern Emperor Zeno, an Isaurian, which allowed Gaiseric to keep possession of all of his territorial acquisitions in return for ending the persecution of Nicaeans and releasing Roman prisoners.

Whether the people living at the time would have seen it that way is not clear, but a new era was coming into being: the Eastern Roman Empire was metamorphosing into the Byzantine Empire, and would live on for another millennium, still based in Constantinople, until the fall of the city to the Ottoman Turks under Mehmet II the Conqueror in AD 1453.

Gaiseric died at Carthage in AD 477, having lived just long enough to hear about the final demise of the Roman Empire in the West. Orestes, a Pannonian officer who had served at Attila's court, installed his own son Romulus Augustulus ('Little Augustus') – an ironic name in as much as it carried the names of Rome's founder Romulus, and her first emperor Augustus, albeit in the diminutive – as emperor, although for what it was worth the Western Roman Empire had by now been whittled away to just Italy and southern Provence, and Romulus Augustulus was not recognised by Zeno in Constantinople anyway. In any case, Orestes lost the loyalty of his troops, who mutinied under their German commander Odoacer in August AD 476. Orestes was killed, but Romulus Augustulus was not even worth putting to death. He was placed under house arrest, given a living allowance, and may have established a monastery in Campania with his mother. Odoacer assumed control, but the Western Empire didn't need an emperor any more, so he simply took the title of *Rex* (King) instead, and governed his own kingdom, not the Roman Empire, from Ravenna, not Rome.

Epilogue

Edward Gibbon said in his autobiography that he sat 'musing amidst the ruins of the Capitol' in Rome one evening in 1764, and there became inspired to write his iconic *The History of the Decline and Fall of the Roman Empire*. It seemed to him that one of the highest points of human achievement had been destroyed by barbarian invaders, and his work in many ways defined how the trajectory of Rome's history would be seen for the next two centuries. The idea was humorously picked up in Sellar and Yeatman's delightfully satirical 'history' book entitled *1066 and All That: A Memorable History of England, comprising all the parts you can remember, including 103 Good Things, 5 Bad Kings and 2 Genuine Dates*, which parodies the teaching of history in English schools in the 1920s and 1930s:

> The withdrawal of the Roman legions to take part in Gibbon's Decline and Fall of the Roman Empire (due to a clamour among the Romans for pompous amusements such as bread and circumstances) left Britain defenceless and subjected Europe to that long succession of Waves of which History is chiefly composed. While the Roman Empire was overrun by

waves not only of Ostrogoths, Vizigoths, and even Goths, but also of Vandals (who destroyed works of art) and Huns (who destroyed everything and everybody, including Goths, Ostrogoths, Vizigoths, and even Vandals), Britain was attacked by waves of Picts (and, of course, Scots) who had recently learnt how to climb the wall.[1]

On a more serious note, in 1971 Peter Brown published *The World of Late Antiquity*, which was enormously influential in making people reappraise the era from around AD 200 to 800, which, he argued, should not be seen as one of decay, but as one of 'religious and cultural revolution'.[2] This has been particularly influential among scholars in the United States, and also on a major 1990s European Science Foundation-funded research project, called 'The Transformation of the Roman World', on the period between AD 300 and 800.

This 'transformation' approach is still probably the favourite one among scholars today, who prefer to talk about the 'transformation' (or 'transition', 'change' or suchlike), rather than the 'decline', 'fall', 'crisis' or indeed the 'end' of the Roman world at all. The negative (and moral) connotations of 'decline' are felt to be unacceptable, and the whole notion that the break-up of the Roman world in the west was caused by hostile or violent invasions has been vigorously challenged. Scholars favouring this standpoint tend to talk about 'accommodation' when they analyse how peoples from outside the Roman Empire ended up occupying it: 'what we call the Fall of the Western Roman Empire was an imaginative experiment that got a little out of hand', writes Walter Goffart,[3] while Ralph W. Mathisen and Danuta Shanzer note an academic consensus that the barbarian settlements occurred 'in a natural, organic, and generally eirenic manner', and assert that it is wrong to 'demonize the barbarians and problematize the barbarian settlements'.[4] They feel that 'the barbarian settlement of the west was accomplished with a minimal, relatively speaking, level of disruption, and . . . barbarian populations were integrated . . . seamlessly into the old Roman world'.[5]

Sellar and Yeatman make much in their book of the idea of 'Good Thing'/'Bad Thing' (with capital letters and inverted commas), and the question of whether the fall/transformation of Rome was a 'Good Thing' or a 'Bad Thing' has often exercised the commentators. For the German philosopher Johann Gottfried Herder, writing in the late eighteenth century, it was the former: 'Expiring Rome lay for centuries on her death-bed . . . a deathbed extending over the whole World . . . which could . . . render her no assistance, but that of accelerating her death. Barbarians came to perform this office; northern giants, to whom the enervated Romans appeared dwarfs; they ravaged Rome, and infused new life into expiring Italy.'[6]

But Herder's younger contemporary Lord Byron saw the process very differently:

> There is the moral of all human tales;
> 'Tis but the same rehearsal of the past,
> First Freedom, and then Glory – when that fails,
> Wealth, vice, corruption – barbarism at last.[7]

The arguments continue to rage, but the people that we know as barbarians have left an indelible mark on world history, and created, for better or worse, a benchmark by which we often judge ourselves and others. There is, perhaps, a sense in which we still cannot live without them:

Why are the streets and squares emptying so rapidly,
everyone going home lost in thought?

Because night has fallen and the barbarians haven't come
And some of our men just in from the border say
There are no barbarians any longer.

Now what's going to happen to us without the barbarians?
Those people were a kind of solution.[8]

Notes

What is a Barbarian?

1 *Corpus Inscriptionum Latinarum* (*CIL*) IV 1880, trans. V. Hunink, *Oh Happy Place! Pompeii in 1000 Graffiti* (Sant'Oreste: Apeiron, 2014), p. 252 f. The words from 'AT' to 'EST' form a pentameter verse.

2 *CIL IV* 4235, trans. V. Hunink, op. cit., p. 124.

3 See, for example, G. Halsall, 'Why Do We Need the Barbarians?' (15 July 2011), https://600transformer.blogspot.com/2011/07/why-do-we-need-barbarians.html, accessed 18 September 2013.

4 G. Halsall, *Barbarian Migrations and the Roman West, 376–568* (Cambridge: Cambridge University Press, reprinted with corrections, 2009), p. 42.

5 This is much more of a modern preoccupation than an ancient one: 'The sheer spectrum of skin pigmentation (or hair colours), especially around the Mediterranean, makes it very hard to define a sharp dividing line between "black" and "white" skin . . . The failure to appreciate [this has] produced heated debate over the extent of "black" input into Classical culture. Certain individuals might or might not have had skin that we would today think of as "black" but "black" and "white" are modern racial constructs. Both parties in this debate divide past society according to contingent, modern notions of race, which is far from helpful.' G. Halsall (2009), op. cit., p. 44 f.

6 G. Halsall (2009), op. cit., p. 56.

7 The question is raised by R. W. Mathisen and D. Shanzer (eds), *Romans, Barbarians, and the Transformation of the Roman World* (Farnham: Ashgate, 2011), p. 2.

8 M. Ventris and J. Chadwick, *Documents in Mycenaean Greek* (2nd edn, Cambridge: Cambridge University Press, 1974), p. 568.

9 Aristophanes, *Birds* 1700f.; cf. Theocritus, *Idyll* 15.

10 Plato, *Protagoras* 341c.

11 E. Hall, *Inventing the Barbarian: Greek Self-Definition through Tragedy* (Oxford: Oxford University Press, 1989), p. 5.

12 Thucydides 1.3.3, trans. S. Kershaw.

13 See E. Hall, op. cit., *passim*.

14 Euripides, *Iphigeneia in Aulis* 1400.

15 Aristotle, *Politics* 1252b.8 ff., trans. S. Kershaw.

16 This is made explicit by Laelius, speaking in Cicero's *De Re Publica* 1.37.58, see p. 10.

17 Pliny, *Natural History* (*NH*) 2.80.189–90, trans. H. Rackham, in Pliny, *Natural History, Volume I: Books 1–2* (Cambridge, MA: Harvard University Press, 1938).

1. Mythical and Semi-Mythical Resistance: Aeneas to Tarquin the Proud

1 Homer, *Iliad* 20.187 ff., trans. R. Lattimore, in Homer, *The Iliad of Homer* (Chicago, IL: University of Chicago Press, 1951).

2 Homer, *Iliad* 5.297–317; 5.431–459.

3 Virgil, *Aeneid* 1.1–7, trans. C. Day Lewis, in Virgil, *The Eclogues, Georgics and Aeneid of Virgil* (Oxford: Oxford University Press, 1966).

4 Lived *c.*59 BC–AD 17.

5 Livy 1.1.5, trans. A. de Selincourt, in Livy, *The Early History of Rome: Books I–V of The History of Rome from its Foundation* (Harmondsworth: Penguin, 1960).

6 Livy 1.1.8, trans. A. de Selincourt (1960), op. cit.

7 The tradition regarding Ascanius is confused and contradictory. See p. 6.

8 Virgil, *Aeneid* 8.485 ff., trans. C. Day Lewis, op. cit.

9 See S. Kershaw, *A Brief Guide to the Greek Myths* (London: Robinson, 2007), pp. 264, 318 ff.

10 Virgil, *Aeneid* 8.614 ff.

11 Livy 1.2.6, trans. S. Kershaw.

12 Livy 1.3.2–3, trans. A. de Selincourt (1960), op. cit.

13 Virgil, *Aeneid* 6.763–5.

14 Livy 1.3.6.

15 Livy 1.3.11, trans. A. de Selincourt (1960), op. cit.

16 See, for example, https://www.archaeology.org/news/2028-140414-rome-forum-dates, accessed 12 August 2018.

17 Lived *c.*200–*c.*118 BC.

18 Lived *c.*60–after 7 BC.

19 Livy 1.4.1–3, trans. S. Kershaw.

20 Livy 1.4.7.

21 See, for example, T. A. J. McGinn, *The Economy of Prostitution in the Roman World: A Study of Social History and the Brothel* (Ann Arbor: University of Michigan Press, 2004), p. 7 f.

22 Livy 1.7.1–2, trans. A. de Selincourt (1960), op. cit.

23 Livy 1.7.2, trans. S. Kershaw.

24 Cicero, *De Re Publica* 1.37.58, trans. C. W. Keyes, in Cicero, *On the Republic. On the Laws* (Cambridge, MA: Harvard University Press, 1928).

25 Vitruvius 6.1.10–11, trans. P. Jones and K. Sidwell, *The World of Rome: An Introduction to Roman Culture* (Cambridge: Cambridge University Press, 1997), p. 2; cf. p. xxiv f.

26 Virgil, *Aeneid* 6.777–84, trans. C. Day Lewis, op. cit.

27 The Latin adjective he uses is *agrestis* = 'rustic', 'rude', 'wild', 'savage'. They are barbaric.

28 Lictors were essentially bodyguards. See p. 45.

29 Livy 1.8.1–2, trans. A. de Selincourt (1960), op. cit.

30 Livy 1.8.6, trans. A. de Selincourt (1960), op. cit.

31 Livy 1.8.6–7. See p. 42.

32 Livy 1.9.5, trans. A. de Selincourt (1960), op. cit.

33 It was in honour of Neptune, patron of the horse.

34 Livy 1.9.10–11, trans. B. O. Foster, in Livy, *History of Rome, Volume I: Books 1–2* (Cambridge, MA: Harvard University Press, 1919).

35 Livy 1.9.14–16, trans. A. de Selincourt (1960), op. cit.

36 See H. I. Flower, 'The Tradition of the Spolia Opima: M. Claudius Marcellus and Augustus', *Classical Antiquity*, vol. 19, no. 1 (2000), pp. 34–64; S. J. Harrison, 'Augustus, the Poets, and the Spolia Opima', *Classical Quarterly*, vol. 39, no. 2 (1989), pp. 408–14.

37 Livy 1.11.5–9.

38 Livy 1.13.2–3, trans. A. de Selincourt (1960), op. cit.

39 Livy 1.13.4–5.

40 Livy 1.16.1, trans. S. Kershaw.

41 Virgil, *Aeneid* 6.812 ff., trans. C. Day Lewis, op. cit.

42 Livy 1.26.4–5.

43 Livy 1.27.1–3.

44 Livy 1.28.6.

45 Livy 1.28.9, trans. B. O. Foster (1919), op. cit.

46 Virgil, *Aeneid* 8.642–5, trans. C. Day Lewis, op. cit.

47 Livy 1.28.11, trans. B. O. Foster (1919), op. cit.

48 Livy 1.57.2–5, trans. A. de Selincourt (1960), op. cit.

49 Livy 1.58. 10–11, trans. S. Kershaw.

50 Virgil, *Aeneid* 8.647–52, trans. C. Day Lewis, op. cit.

51 Livy 2.10.1–6, trans. S. Kershaw.

52 Livy 2.10.11, trans. S. Kershaw.

53 Livy 2.10.12, trans. S. Kershaw.

54 Livy 2.13.

55 Livy 2.14.

56 Tacitus, *Histories* 3.72; Pliny, *NH* 34.139.

57 Dionysius of Halicarnassus 7.5–6.

58 Dionysius of Halicarnassus 6.95.2, trans. E. Cary, in Dionysius of Halicarnassus, *Roman Antiquities, Volume IV: Books 6.49–7* (Cambridge, MA: Harvard University Press, 1943).

2. Brennus: The Gaul who Sacked Rome

1 Plutarch, *Camillus* 15.1–16.2.

2 Pliny, *NH* 35.25, trans. H. Rackham, in Pliny, *Natural History, Volume IX: Books 33–35* (Cambridge, MA: Harvard University Press, 1952); cf. the Gaul who fights Titus Manlius, see p. 56 f.

3 Dionysius of Halicarnassus 13.10–11.

4 In Plutarch's account the father is not named and the boy is called Lucumo.

5 Dionysius of Halicarnassus 13.10.2. In Plutarch's version the corruption is mutual, *Camillus* 15.3.

6 Dionysius of Halicarnassus 13.11.1, trans. E. Cary, in Dionysius of Halicarnassus, *Roman Antiquities, Volume VII: Books 11–20* (Cambridge, MA: Harvard University Press, 1950).

7 Plutarch, *Camillus* 15.2, trans. B. Perrin, in Plutarch, *Lives, Volume II: Themistocles and Camillus. Aristides and Cato Major. Cimon and Lucullus* (Cambridge, MA: Harvard University Press, 1914).

8 Plutarch, *Camillus* 16.2; cf. Polybius 2.18.1.

9 See R. Stillwell et al. (eds), *The Princeton Encyclopedia of Classical Sites*, http://www.perseus.tufts.edu/hopper/text?doc=Perseus:text:1999.04.0006:entry=sena-gallica, accessed 17 May 2018.

10 Plutarch, *Camillus* 17.8–12, trans. B. Perrin (1914), op. cit.

11 Pliny, *NH* 14.149, trans. H. A. Rackham, in Pliny, *Natural History, Volume IV, Books 12–16* (Cambridge, MA: Harvard University Press, 1945).

12 Ammianus Marcellinus 15.12.4, trans. W. Hamilton, in Ammianus Marcellinus, *The Later Roman Empire (AD 345–378)*, selected and translated by Walter Hamilton with an introduction and notes by Andrew Wallace-Hadrill (London: Penguin, 1986).

13 Plutarch, *Camillus* 17.1.

14 Plutarch, *Camillus* 17.2–4, trans. B. Perrin (1914), op. cit.

15 Diodorus Siculus 14.113.5.

16 Plutarch, *Camillus* 18.1, trans. B. Perrin (1914), op. cit.

17 Plutarch, *Camillus* 18.2, trans. B. Perrin (1914), op. cit.

18 Diodorus Siculus 14.114.1.

19 See A. Drummond, 'Fabius Ambustus, Quintus', in S. Hornblower and A. Spawforth (eds), *The Oxford Classical Dictionary* (3rd edn, Oxford: Oxford University Press, 1996).

20 Dionysius of Halicarnassus (13.12.2) numbers the Romans at four entire legions of well-trained, picked troops, augmented by a greater number of other citizens who led indoor or easy lives and had less experience of fighting.

21 Plutarch, *Camillus* 18.6, trans. B. Perrin (1914), op. cit.

22 For example, Plutarch, *Camillus* 18.7.

23 Plutarch, *Camillus* 18.4–5.

24 This would date the battle to mid-July. The year in question is problematical. See p. 37 ff.

25 Plutarch, *Camillus* 19.7–8, trans. B. Perrin (1914), op. cit.

26 Beards do not necessarily equal barbarity.

27 Livy 5.41, trans. A. de Selincourt (1960), op. cit.; cf. Plutarch, *Camillus* 21.2–22.6.

28 Livy 5.42.8, trans. S. Kershaw.

29 Camillus is prominent in the accounts of Plutarch, Dionysius of Halicarnassus, Appian and Dio Cassius, although he is relatively unimportant in Diodorus, and not mentioned at all by Polybius.

30 Plutarch, *Camillus* 23.3, trans. B. Perrin (1914), op. cit.

31 Plutarch, *Camillus* 23.3, trans. B. Perrin (1914), op. cit.

32 Plutarch, *Camillus* 23.5, trans. B. Perrin (1914), op. cit.

33 Dionysius of Halicarnassus 13.6.4, trans. E. Cary (1950), op. cit.

34 Cf. Diodorus Siculus 14.116.3–4.

35 Dionysius of Halicarnassus 13.6.4, trans. E. Cary (1950), op. cit.

36 Diodorus Siculus 14.116.5–7.

37 Plutarch, *Camillus* 18.3. This attack is not attested elsewhere. It is not implausible, but may not be authentic.

38 Livy uses the word *regulus* to describe Brennus – a disparaging diminutive = 'Little King'.

39 Livy 5.48.8–9, trans. S. Kershaw.

40 'Τοῖς νενικημένοις ὀδύνη', Plutarch, *Camillus* 28.5.

41 Livy 5.49.3; cf. Plutarch, *Camillus* 29.2, where Camillus says it was the custom of the Romans to deliver their city with iron and not with gold. Wikipedia, and other popular internet sources derived from it, wrongly quote Camillus as saying, '*non auro, sed ferro, recuperanda est patria*' (https://en.wikipedia.org/wiki/Brennus_(4th_century_BC), accessed 23 May 2018). In Livy, his words come in reported speech (*ferroque non auro reciperare* [or *recuperare*] *patriam iubet*), and Plutarch is writing in Greek.

42 Livy 5.49.6.

43 Plutarch, *Camillus* 22.1.

44 Plutarch, *Camillus* 30.1. The Ides fall on the fifteenth of March, May, July and October, and on the thirteenth of the other months.

45 Historians and archaeologists use 'relative' chronology to indicate the order in which events happen, and 'absolute' chronology to specify the precise dates on which they occur.

46 Polybius 1.6.1, trans. S. Kershaw.

47 See, for example, F. Walbank, *A Historical Commentary on Polybius: Vol. 1, Commentary on Books I–VI* (Oxford: Oxford University Press, 1970), ad. 1.6.1–2, p. 46 f., ad. 2.18.6, pp. 185–7, pp. 35–7.

48 *CIL* IV.1842, trans. S. Kershaw. The nones fall on the seventh of March, May, July and October, and on the fifth of the other months. The Romans counted inclusively, so five days before the seventh is the third, not the second.

49 The six invented consuls are: Papirius and Vivius; Sacraviensis and Caeliomontanus; and Priscus and Cominius. They feature in the *Chronography of 354 AD*. See http://www.tertullian.org/fathers/chronography_of_354_00_eintro.htm, accessed 21 May 2018.

50 Varro lived from 116 to 27 BC. For Varronian chronology, see J. Lendering, 'Varronian Chronology', at http://www.livius.org/articles/concept/varronian-chronology, accessed 20 May 2018; H. A. Sanders, 'The Chronology of Early Rome', *Classical Philology*, vol. 3, no. 3 (1908), pp. 316–29.

51 Fragments from it, known as the *Fasti Capitolini*, are on display in the Capitoline Museums in Rome.

52 See, for example, 'History of Rome', https://en.wikipedia.org/wiki/History_of_Rome, accessed 21 May 2018.

53 Plutarch, *Camillus* 30.1, trans. S. Kershaw. The Greek words he uses are παραλόγως (*paralogos* = beyond calculation, unexpected, unlooked for) and its comparative παραλογώτερον (*paralogoteron*).

54 Livy 5.43.1 ff., 47.1 ff.

55 See, for example, F. Walbank, op. cit., ad. 2.18.2, p. 185.

56 See H. Bellen, *Metus Gallicus – Metus Punicus. Zum Furchtmotiv in der römischen Republik* (Wiesbaden: Steiner, 1985); J. Wankenne,

'Heinz Bellen, *Metus Gallicus – Metus Punicus. Zum Furchtmotiv in der römischen Republik*', *L'antiquité classique*, no. 56 (1987), pp. 463–4; A. Kneppe, *Metus temporum: zur Bedeutung von Angst in Politik und Gesellschaft der römischen Kaiserzeit des 1. und 2. Jhdts. n. Chr.* (Wiesbaden: Steiner, 1994).

3. The Plebs: Barbarous Insiders and Internal Resistors

1 Polybius 1.6.3, trans. W. R. Paton, in Polybius, *The Histories, Volume I: Books 1–2*, translated by W. R. Paton, revised by F. W. Walbank and C. Habicht (Loeb Classical Library 128, Cambridge, MA: Harvard University Press, 2010).

2 Polybius 2.18.9. Livy, however, makes no mention of this peace.

3 See Menenius Agrippa's fable of the body parts of society, quoted on p. 44.

4 The usual caveats concerning the dating of early Roman history apply throughout this discussion, see pp 37–9. xxx. Also, see M. Breaugh, *The Plebeian Experience: A Discontinuous History of Political Freedom* (New York: Columbia University Press, 2013), pp. 4–11.

5 Livy 2.32.2 remarks that the historian Piso said they went to the Aventine Hill, although that is not the generally accepted version.

6 Livy 2.32.8, trans. S. Kershaw.

7 Livy 2.32.9-11, trans. A. de Selincourt (1960), op. cit.

8 Livy 3.55.10, trans. B. O. Foster, in Livy, *History of Rome, Volume II: Books 3–4* (Cambridge, MA: Harvard University Press, 1922).

9 Who the other two were is uncertain.

10 'Less' and 'more' might possibly be interchanged here (*minore* and *maiore* look quite alike in Latin handwriting).

11 Gellius XX.1.42, trans. S. Kershaw.

12 Gellius XX.1.42, trans. E. H. Warmington, *Remains of Old Latin, Volume III: Lucilius. The Twelve Tables* (Cambridge, MA: Harvard University Press, 1938).

13 Cicero, *De Legibus* III.8.9, trans. E. H. Warmington, op. cit.

14 Ulpian, *Tituli ex corpore Ulpiani* 10.1, trans. E. H. Warmington, op. cit.

15 Cicero, *Philippics* 2.28.69, trans. S. Kershaw. Cicero is in fact referring to Mark Antony's extramarital affair with Cytheris, but treating
   it like a legal marriage for rhetorical effect.

16 Gaius, *Institutes* 1.144–5, trans. E. H. Warmington, op. cit.

17 Livy 3.55.1, trans. A. de Selincourt (1960), op. cit.

18 Livy 6.10–20.

19 Livy 6.11.7.

20 Livy 6.11.6–8, trans. Revd Canon Roberts, in Livy, *History of Rome*
   (New York: E. P. Dutton and Co., 1912).

21 The *Magister Equitum* (Master of Horse) was a *Dictator's* right-hand man.

22 Livy 6.11.10, trans. S. Kershaw.

23 Livy 6.14.10, trans. S. Kershaw.

24 Livy 6.15.4–5, trans. Revd Canon Roberts, op. cit.

25 Livy 6.15.13, trans. Revd Canon Roberts, op. cit.

26 Livy 6.18.16, trans. Revd Canon Roberts, op. cit.

27 Livy 6.19.3, trans. S. Kershaw.

28 Livy 6.19.6–7, trans. Revd Canon Roberts, op. cit.

29 Livy 6.11.8.

30 Livy 6.34.3, trans. S. Kershaw.

31 Livy 6.34.5, trans. B. O. Foster, in Livy, *History of Rome, Volume III:
   Books 5–7* (Cambridge, MA: Harvard University Press, 1924).

32 Livy 6.34.11, trans. B. O. Foster (1924), op. cit.

33 Ironically, Licinius was later punished for violating his own law:
   Livy 7.16.9.

34 Livy, 6.35.5–6.

35 Livy 6.37.2–11, trans. B. O. Foster (1924), op. cit.

36 Livy 7.10.5–11, trans. B. O. Foster (1924), op. cit.

37 Livy 8.15.9.

38 Livy 6.42.12.

39 In 366 BC, AUC 388; Livy 6.42.12–13, 7.1.4–6.

4. Pyrrhus of Epirus: Cadmean and Pyrrhic Victories

1 A reference to the Sack of Rome by the Gauls.

2 Polybius 1.12.7, trans. I. Scott-Kilvert, in Polybius, *The Rise of the
   Roman Empire* (Harmondsworth: Penguin, 1979).

3 The ancient region of Epirus encompasses parts of modern north-western Greece and Albania.

4 Livy 8.17.9–10.

5 Livy 8.24. See J. Lendering, 'Alexander of Molossis' (2004), http://www.livius.org/articles/person/alexander-of-molossis/?, accessed 3 June 2018.

6 Thucydides 2.80.5–7, trans. C. F. Smith, in Thucydides, *History of the Peloponnesian War, Volume I: Books 1–2* (Cambridge, MA: Harvard University Press, 1919).

7 Euripides, *Andromache* 663–6, trans. D. Kovacs, in Euripides, *Children of Heracles. Hippolytus. Andromache. Hecuba* (Cambridge, MA: Harvard University Press, 1995).

8 He was the son of Priam and Hecuba of Troy.

9 He was the grandfather of Achilles.

10 Euripides, *Andromache* 1243–9, trans. D. Kovacs, op. cit.

11 Plutarch, *Pyrrhus* 1.3, trans. B. Perrin, in Plutarch, *Lives, Volume IX: Demetrius and Antony. Pyrrhus and Gaius Marius* (Cambridge, MA: Harvard University Press, 1920).

12 Plutarch, *Pyrrhus* 1.3, trans. B. Perrin (1920).

13 Plutarch, *Pyrrhus* 3.2, trans. B. Perrin (1920).

14 Plutarch, *Pyrrhus* 5.1, trans. B. Perrin (1920).

15 Antigone was Berenice's daughter by an obscure Macedonian called Philip, born before Berenice's marriage to Ptolemy.

16 Plutarch, *Pyrrhus* 7.2, trans. B. Perrin (1920), op. cit.; cf. *Demetrius*, 36.2–6, 37, 40.1.

17 Plutarch, *Pyrrhus* 7.4.

18 Herodotus 2.52.

19 Plutarch, *Pyrrhus* 13.1.

20 Plutarch, *Pyrrhus* 3.4–5, trans. B. Perrin (1920), op. cit.

21 Homer, *Iliad* 1.491 f., trans. B. Perrin (1920), op. cit.

22 Plutarch, *Pyrrhus* 14.1–8, trans. B. Perrin (1920), op. cit.

23 Plutarch, *Pyrrhus* 16.4.

24 Plutarch, *Pyrrhus* 16.5, trans. S. Kershaw.

25 Plutarch, *Pyrrhus* 16.57–8, trans. B. Perrin (1920), op. cit.

26 See, for example, Herodotus 1.166.1–2; Plato, *Laws* 641c. See also Henry George Liddell (compiler), Robert Scott (compiler), Henry

Stuart Jones (ed.), Roderick McKenzie (ed.), *A Greek-English Lexicon* (9th edn, New York: Oxford University Press, 1995).

27 See S. Kershaw (2007), op. cit., pp. 212 ff.

28 See S. Kershaw (2007), op. cit., pp. 156 ff.

29 Plutarch, *Pyrrhus* 19.5.

30 Plutarch, *Pyrrhus* 21.1–4.

31 Plutarch (*Pyrrhus* 21.9) says that one of his sources, Dionysius, didn't mention two battles at Asculum, but said that the two armies fought until sunset on one day. Apparently he made no reference to an acknowledged Roman defeat either.

32 Plutarch, *Pyrrhus* 21.7, trans. I. Scott-Kilvert, in Plutarch, *The Age of Alexander: Nine Greek Lives* (Harmondsworth: Penguin, 1973).

33 Plutarch, *Pyrrhus* 21.9–10, trans. I. Scott-Kilvert (1973), op. cit.

34 Polybius 3.25.3–5, trans. I. Scott-Kilvert (1979), op. cit.

35 Polybius' dating is vague; Livy dates it to 279/8 BC (ep. 13, *quarto foedus renovatum*).

36 Justin 18.2.

37 Plutarch, *Pyrrhus* 22.6, trans. B. Perrin (1920), op. cit.

38 Plutarch, *Pyrrhus* 22.4, 24.1.

39 Plutarch, *Pyrrhus* 23.3, trans. B. Perrin (1920), op. cit.

40 Cf. Dionysius of Halicarnassus, *Excerpta ex lib. xx* 8.

41 Plutarch, *Pyrrhus* 23.3, trans. S. Kershaw.

42 Plutarch, *Pyrrhus* 24.3–4, trans. B. Perrin (1920), op. cit.

43 Dionysius of Halicarnassus 20.9.1, trans. E. Cary (1950), op. cit.

44 Dionysius of Halicarnassus 20.9.2, trans. E. Cary (1950), op. cit.

45 Dionysius of Halicarnassus 20.10.1, trans. E. Cary (1950), op. cit.

46 Livy, *Periochae* 13–14.

47 Pliny, *NH* 7.68.

48 Livy, *Periochae* 14.

49 Dionysius of Halicarnassus, 20.10.1. Orosius (4.2.5) gives Pyrrhus 86,000 troops. See J. Champion, *Pyrrhus of Epirus* (Barnsley: Pen & Sword Military, 2009), p. 120.

50 Dionysius of Halicarnassus 20.11.1, trans. E. Cary (1950), op. cit.

51 Plutarch, *Pyrrhus* 25.3; Dionysius of Halicarnassus 20.12.3.

52 Frontinus, *Stratagems* 2.2.1, trans. C. E. Bennett and M. B. McElwain, in Frontinus, *Stratagems. Aqueducts of Rome* (Cambridge, MA: Harvard University Press, 1925).

53 Plutarch, *Pyrrhus* 25.4–5, trans. B. Perrin (1920), op. cit.

54 Orosius, *Histories Against the Pagans* 4.2.5, trans. I. W. Raymond, in Paulus Orosius, *Seven Books of History Against the Pagans: The Apology of Paulus Orosius* (New York: Columbia University Press, 1936).

55 Aelian, *On Animals* 1.38, 2.36, trans. A. F. Scholfield, in Aelian, *On Animals, Volume III: Books 12–17* (Cambridge, MA: Harvard University Press, 1959). The example he gives here is of a use of the stratagem by the Megarians against Antigonus II Gonatas' Macedonians in 266 BC, but he is clearly suggesting that the Romans did likewise.

56 See Pliny, *NH* 3.105. The town was called Maloeis ('Sheeptown' or 'Appletown') in Greek, and the accusative case Maloenta gets Latinised to Maleventum. Combining *male* (= 'badly') with *venio*, *ventus* or *eventus* produces 'Badly Come', 'Ill Wind' or 'Bad Result' to Roman ears.

57 Plutarch, *Pyrrhus* 26.1–2, trans. B. Perrin (1920), op. cit.

58 Quoted by Plutarch, *Pyrrhus* 26.5, trans. B. Perrin (1920), op. cit.

59 Plutarch, *Pyrrhus* 26.6, trans. B. Perrin (1920), op. cit.

60 Chilonis also seems to have had her eye on Areus' handsome son Acrotatus (Plutarch, *Pyrrhus* 28.3).

61 Pyrrhus' death is described in these terms by Plutarch, *Pyrrhus* 34. Orosius says that he died after being hit by a rock (Orosius, *Histories Against the Pagans* 4.2.5).

5. Hannibal at the Gates

1 Livy 21.1.1, trans. S. Kershaw.

2 *The Importance of Being Earnest* (1895), Act I.

3 Virgil, *Aeneid* 4.621 ff., trans. H. Rushton Fairclough, in Virgil, *Eclogues. Georgics. Aeneid: Books 1–6* (Cambridge, MA: Harvard University Press, 1916).

4 Lived *c.*254–184 BC.

5 See S. Kershaw, *A Brief Guide to Classical Civilization* (London: Robinson, 2010), pp. 244–9.

6 Punic, which was spoken throughout the Carthaginian Empire, is a northern-central Semitic language, a later form of Phoenician, which is very close to Hebrew and Moabite.

7 Plautus, *Poenulus* 994–1029, trans. S. Kershaw.

8 Cicero, *De Lege Agraria* 2.95, trans. J. H. Freese, in Cicero, *Pro Quinctio. Pro Roscio Amerino. Pro Roscio Comoedo. On the Agrarian Law* (Cambridge, MA: Harvard University Press, 1930).

9 Polybius 3.22.

10 The dating of this is controversial. See F. Walbank, op. cit., ad. 2.22–5, p. 337 f.

11 Polybius 3.24.

12 Polybius 3.25, trans. I. Scott-Kilvert (1979), op. cit. See p. 73.

13 See Polybius 1.8–10.

14 Livy names him Quintus Fulvius Flaccus. See T. R. S. Broughton, *The Magistrates of the Roman Republic, Vol. 1: 509 BC–100 BC* (Cleveland, Ohio: Case Western Reserve University Press, 1951), p. 202.

15 Polybius 1.11.

16 Polybius 1.12.5, trans. S. Kershaw.

17 Silius Italicus, *Punica* 1.71–7.

18 Valerius Maximus 9.3.2.

19 Polybius 1.20.2.

20 The device and its use are described in detail by Polybius 1.22. See also *Inscriptiones Latinae Selectae* (*ILS*) 65.

21 Polybius 1.11–64 is the main source for the war.

22 Polybius 1.62–3.

23 Polybius 1.81.4–82.2, trans. W. R. Paton (2010), op. cit.

24 Livy 21.4, trans. S. Kershaw.

25 Polybius 2.1.7–8.

26 Diodorus Siculus 25.10.3–4 (at Helice, possibly modern Elche); Livy 24.41.3 (at Castrum Album, possibly modern Alicante).

27 Polybius 3.29.3, trans. S. Kershaw.

28 Livy 21.3.1.

29 Livy 21.4.5–9, trans. S. Kershaw.

30 See, for example, Horace, *Odes* 3.6.36, 4.4.49. See also B. Isaac, *The Invention of Racism in Classical Antiquity* (Princeton and Oxford: Princeton University Press, 2004), pp. 326 ff.

31 Polybius 9.26.11, trans. I. Scott-Kilvert (1979), op. cit.; cf. 9.22.8, 9.24.8.

32 Livy 21.4.2.

33 See G. K. Jenkins, *Coins of Punic Sicily* (Lancaster, PA: Classical Numismatic Group, 1997); G. K. Jenkins and R. B. Lewis, *Carthaginian Gold and Electrum Coins* (London: Royal Numismatic Society, 1963); http://www.livius.org/pictures/a/carthaginian-art/melqart-on-a-coin-of-hannibal, accessed 17 June 2018.

34 See, for example, I. Van Sertima (ed.), *African Presence in Early Europe* (New Brunswick and Oxford: Transaction Books, 1985); J. A. Rogers, *Sex and Race: Negro-Caucasian Mixture in All Ages and All Lands* (New York: Rogers, 1967); J. A. Rogers, *World's Great Men of Color I* (New York: Simon & Schuster 1996). Against this see, for example, F. M. Snowden, 'Misconceptions about African Blacks in the Ancient Mediterranean World: Specialists and Afrocentrists', *Arion: A Journal of Humanities and the Classics*, Third Series, vol. 4, no. 3 (Winter 1997), pp. 28–50; M. Lefkowitz, *Not Out of Africa: How Afrocentrism Became an Excuse to Teach Myth as History* (New York: New Republic and Basic Books, 1997).

35 Possibly as far back as 230 to 228 BC, and certainly prior to the Ebro River Treaty.

36 Polybius 3.33.2–4, trans. I. Scott-Kilvert (1979), op. cit.

37 Livy 21.1.2–3, trans. A. de Selincourt, in Livy, *The War with Hannibal: Books XXI–XXX of The History of Rome from its Foundation* (Harmondsworth: Penguin, 1965).

38 There are three men called Publius Cornelius Scipio who feature in Rome's conflicts with Carthage, two of whom are also called Africanus: (1) P. Cornelius Scipio (consul 218 BC, died 211 BC); (2) his son P. Cornelius Scipio Africanus ('Scipio Africanus Maior/ the Elder', 236–183 BC), who also fought Hannibal; and (3) P. Cornelius Scipio Aemilianus Africanus Numantinus ('Scipio Africanus Minor/the Younger', 185–129 BC), who destroyed Carthage in the Third Punic War.

39 Polybius 3.46.7–11, trans. I. Scott-Kilvert (1979), op. cit.

40 Polybius 3.46.12, trans. I. Scott-Kilvert (1979), op. cit.

41 Livy 21.32.7, trans. S. Kershaw.

42 Livy 21.33.7.

43 W. C. Mahaney et al., 'Biostratigraphic Evidence Relating to the Age-Old Question of Hannibal's Invasion of Italy, I: History and Geological Reconstruction', *Archaeometry*, vol. 59, no. 1 (February 2017), https://onlinelibrary.wiley.com/doi/full/10.1111/ arcm.12231, accessed 17 June 2018. See also G. de Beer, *Hannibal's March* (London: Sidgwick & Jackson, 1967).

44 Livy 21.35.9, trans. S. Kershaw.

45 The Trebia is a tributary of the Po, which it joins to the west of Placentia. Livy places the battle on the right bank, Polybius more plausibly on the left.

46 He was a Plebeian and a *novus homo*, and had already served as consul in 223 BC; he was famous for his controversial *lex Flaminia* of 232 BC, which dealt with land reform, and the construction of the Circus Flaminius in 221 BC.

47 Polybius 3.80.3.

48 Fabius had been consul in 233 and 228 BC, and censor in 230 BC. 'Cunctator' ('the Delayer'), mentioned later, was not his official cognomen.

49 See Polybius 3.93–4; Livy 22.15–17.

50 For the full account of the battle, see Polybius 3.112–16; Livy 22.47, with discussions by F. Walbank, op. cit., ad. 3.107–17, pp. 435–48.

51 Livy 22.51.9, trans. A. de Selincourt (1965), op. cit.

52 Virgil, *Aeneid* 6.845–6, trans. C. Day Lewis, op. cit.

53 Livy 25.31.9, trans. A. de Selincourt (1965), op. cit.

54 Plutarch, *Marcellus* 21.1, trans. S. Kershaw; Livy 25.40.1–3.

55 Plutarch, *Marcellus* 21.1–2, trans. S. Kershaw.

56 Livy 27.16.7 ff.

57 Pliny, *NH* 34.40.

58 Plutarch, *Marcellus* 21.5, trans. B. Perrin, in Plutarch, *Lives, Volume V: Agesilaus and Pompey. Pelopidas and Marcellus* (Cambridge, MA: Harvard University Press, 1917).

59 Livy 25.40.2, trans. S. Kershaw.

60 Plutarch, *Marcellus* 21.5, trans. Kershaw.

61 Plutarch, *Marcellus* 30, trans. I. Scott-Kilvert, in Plutarch, *Makers of Rome: Nine Lives* (Harmondsworth: Penguin, 1965).

62 Livy 27.49.1, trans. A. de Selincourt (1965), op. cit. The River Metaurus (modern Metauro) flows into the Adriatic near Fano, between Ancona and Rimini. For the battle, see Livy 27.46–9.

63 Horace, *Odes* 4.4.37 ff., trans. N. Rudd, in Horace, *Odes and Epodes*, edited and translated by N. Rudd (Cambridge, MA: Harvard University Press, 2004).

64 See Polybius 14.2–5; Livy 30.3–6.

65 See Polybius 14.8; Livy 30.6–9.

66 Livy 30.20.3, trans. F. G. Moore, in Livy, *History of Rome, Volume VIII: Books 28–30* (Cambridge, MA: Harvard University Press, 1949).

67 Livy 30.20.3, trans. F. G. Moore, op. cit.; cf. Polybius 9.5 and 10.2.

68 Polybius 15.9, trans. I. Scott-Kilvert (1979), op. cit.

69 The phrase never appears in exactly this form. See Plutarch, *Cato the Elder* 27.1: 'δοκεῖ δέ μοι καὶ Καρχηδόνα μὴ εἶναι' ('I think that Karthage should not exist'); Pliny, *NH* 15.20: '*[Cato] clamaret omni senatu Carthaginem delendam*' ('[Cato] shouted to the entire Senate that Carthage ought to be destroyed'); Aurelius Victor, *De Viris Illustribus* 47.8: '*Carthaginem delendam censuit*' ('he thought that Carthage ought to be destroyed'); Florus, *Epitoma de Tito Livio bellorum omnium annorum DCC*, Liber primus, XXXI: '*Cato inexpiabili odio delendam esse Carthaginem . . . pronunciabat*' ('Cato pronounced with implacable hatred that Carthage ought to be destroyed'). See also, C. E. Little, 'The Authenticity and Form of Cato's Saying "Carthago Delenda Est"', *Classical Journal*, vol. 29, no. 6 (1934), pp. 429–35; S. Thürlemann, '*Ceterum censeo Carthaginem esse delendam*', *Gymnasium*, no. 81 (1974), pp. 465–75.

70 Livy 33.47–8.

71 Livy 33.47–9. According to Nepos 23.7.6 it was in 196 BC.

72 Livy 35.14.5–12, trans. S. Kershaw. There are question marks over the story. Livy says he got the story from the annalist (probably) Claudius Quadrigarius, who got it from Acilius (*c.*150 BC), who

wrote a Roman history in Greek. The same story appears in Appian 11.10. But according to Livy 34.59.8, Scipio wasn't a member of this particular embassy.

73 Livy 37.45.15, trans. H. Bettenson, in Livy, *Rome and the Mediterranean: Books XXXI–XLV of The History of Rome from Its Foundation* (Harmondsworth: Penguin, 1976).

74 Nepos 23.10–11; Justin 32.4.

75 According to Livy 49.51 the Romans *were* concerned about Hannibal's presence in Bithynia. See also Nepos 23.12.1–3.

76 Livy 39.51, trans. H. Bettenson, op. cit. Plutarch, *Flamininus* 20.5, quotes Livy pretty well verbatim.

77 Plutarch, *Flamininus* 21.1, trans. B. Perrin, in Plutarch, *Lives, Volume X: Agis and Cleomenes. Tiberius and Gaius Gracchus. Philopoemen and Flamininus* (Cambridge, MA: Harvard University Press, 1921).

78 Juvenal, *Satires* 10.58 ff., trans. P. Green, in Juvenal, *The Sixteen Satires* (Harmondsworth: Penguin, 1967); cf. 8.161, 6.291.

6. Graecia Capta: Resistance in the Greek East – Philip V, Antiochus III and Perseus of Macedon

1 Polybius 1.1.5, trans. W. R. Paton (2010), op. cit.

2 Horace, *Epistles* 2.1.225, trans. S. Kershaw.

3 Strattis fragment (fr.) 28.2 Koch.

4 Plutarch, *Alexander* 51, trans. S. Kershaw.

5 See S. Casson, *Macedonia, Thrace, and Illyria* (Oxford: Oxford University Press, 1926), pp. 157–9; A. P. Dascalakis, *The Hellenism of the Ancient Macedonians* (Thessaloniki: Institute for Balkan Studies, no. 74, 1965), pp. 50–95; N. G. L. Hammond and G. T. Griffith, *A History of Macedonia, II* (Oxford: Clarendon Press, 1979), pp. 46–54.

6 Herodotus 5.22, trans. A. D. Godley, in Herodotus, *The Persian Wars, Volume III: Books 5–7* (Cambridge, MA: Harvard University Press, 1922).

7 Hesiod fr. 7. See M. L. West, *The Hesiodic Catalogue of Women* (Oxford: Clarendon Press, 1985), p. 10.

8 *Die Fragmente der griechischen Historiker* (*Fragments of the Greek Historians, FGrH*) 4 F 74.

9 Pindar frr. 120–1; Bacchylides fr. 20B.

10 Thrasymachus 85 B 2 DK.

11 The Roman proconsul in Macedonia and Greece.

12 Philip's signing of this peace effectively cancelled his earlier alliance with Hannibal.

13 The authenticity of the list of states and rulers allegedly included by Rome in the peace, and its significance for future Roman policy in the Hellenistic world, are controversial.

14 Livy 29.12.14, trans. F. G. Moore, op. cit.

15 Livy doesn't mention a non-aggression clause attested by Polybius 16.34.7.

16 Ptolemy was twelve or thirteen years old at the time.

17 This refers to the sun, not to Ptolemy.

18 *Orientis Graeci Inscriptiones Selectae* (*OGIS*) 90, trans. M. M. Austin, *The Hellenistic World from Alexander to the Roman Conquest: A Selection of Ancient Sources in Translation* (Cambridge: Cambridge University Press, 1981), p. 374. See p. 285 f.

19 *Cf.* Plutarch, *Pyrrhus* 16.5, quoted on p. 69.

20 Plutarch, *Flamininus* 5.4, trans. B. Perrin (1921), op. cit.

21 Livy 32.5, trans. S. Kershaw.

22 Plutarch, *Flamininus* 10.5, trans. B. Perrin (1921), op. cit.

23 Plutarch, *Flamininus* 16.4, trans. S. Kershaw.

24 Livy 34.49.8–11, trans. J. C. Yardley, in Livy, *History of Rome, Volume IX: Books 31–34* (Cambridge, MA: Harvard University Press, 2017).

25 *Sylloge Inscriptionum Graecarum* (*SIG*) III 601.

26 Polybius 21.32, trans. S. Kershaw. Polybius' 'τὴν ἀρχὴν καὶ τὴν δυναστείαν τοῦ δήμου τῶν Ῥωμαίων' must translate the Latin formula '*imperium maisestatemque populi Romani*'.

27 Livy 34.52.

28 Plutarch, *Flamininus* 9.6–7, trans. B. Perrin (1921), op. cit.

29 Plutarch, *Flamininus* 15.1, trans. B. Perrin (1921), op. cit.

30 Plutarch, *Flamininus* 15.2, trans. B. Perrin (1921), op. cit.

31 Plutarch, *Flamininus* 15.3–17.5.

32 He escaped: see p. 111; cf. Livy 37.45.

33 The text of the treaty is reproduced in Polybius 21.42 and Appian 11.39.

34 Livy 39.5.13–16.

35 See M. M. Miles, *Art as Plunder: The Ancient Origins of Debate about Cultural Property* (Cambridge: Cambridge University Press, 2008).

36 See Livy 39.8–18; *CIL* 12.581 = *ILS* 18 = *Inscriptiones Latinae Liberae Rei Publicae (ILLRP)* 511.

37 Strabo 13.2.4, trans. H. L. Jones, in Strabo, *Geography, Volume VI: Books 13–14* (Cambridge, MA: Harvard University Press, 1929).

38 Appian 9./4./19, trans. P. Jones and K. Sidwell, op. cit., p. 21.

39 For the battle, see Polybius 29. 17; Livy 44.36–43; Plutarch, *Aemilius Paullus* 16–23.

40 Pliny, *NH* 34.54.

41 Plutarch, *Aemilius Paullus* 32–4, trans. A. H. Clough, in Plutarch, *Plutarch's Lives*, corrected from the Greek and revised by A. H. Clough (Boston: Little, Brown and Co., 1859).

42 Pausanias 7.16.7–10, trans. W. H. S. Jones, in Pausanias, *Description of Greece, Volume III: Books 6–8.21 (Elis 2, Achaia, Arcadia)* (Cambridge, MA: Harvard University Press, 1933).

43 *De Viris Illustribus* 60, trans. S. Kershaw.

44 Strabo 6.381, trans. J. J. Pollitt, *The Art of Rome c.753 BC–AD 337: Sources and Documents* (Cambridge: Cambridge University Press, 1983), p. 47.

45 Lucius Mummius.

46 Aemilius Paullus.

47 Perseus of Macedon, who traced his descent back to Achilles. Aeacus was Achilles' grandfather.

48 Virgil, *Aeneid* 6.836 ff., trans. C. Day Lewis, op. cit.

49 Pliny, *NH* 15.74. Plutarch tells a similar version of the story in *Cato the Elder* 27.1. See F. J. Meijer, 'Cato's African Figs', *Mnemosyne*, Fourth Series, vol. 37, fasc. 1/2 (1984), pp. 117–24.

50 He was the son of L. Aemilius Paullus, the victor at Pydna.

51 See R. T. Ridley, 'To Be Taken with a Pinch of Salt: The Destruction of Carthage', *Classical Philology*, vol. 81, no. 2 (1986).

52 Homer, *Iliad* 6.448–9, trans. W. R. Paton, in Polybius, *The Histories, Volume VI: Books 28–39* (Cambridge, MA: Harvard University Press, 1922).

53 Polybius 38.21.1, trans. W. R. Paton (1922), op. cit.

54 Horace, *Epistles* 2.1.161 ff., trans. N. Rudd, in Horace and Persius, *Horace: Satires and Epistles. Persius: Satires* (Harmondsworth: Penguin, 1979).

55 Livy 34.4.4, trans. S. Kershaw.

56 Pliny, *NH* 33.150.

57 Juvenal, *Satires* 3, trans. G. G. Ramsay, in Juvenal and Persius, *Juvenal and Persius* (Cambridge, MA: Harvard University Press, 1918).

58 Livy 29.19.12, trans. S. Kershaw.

59 Cicero, *Pro Rabirio Postumo* 26–7.

60 Plutarch, *Aemilius Paullus* 6.5.

61 Quoted by Pliny, *NH* 29.13, trans. P. Jones and K. Sidwell, op. cit., p. 24.

62 Horace, *Epistles* 2.1.156 ff., trans. N. Rudd (1979), op. cit.

7. Viriathus: Iberian Shepherd, Hunter and Warrior

1 Cicero, *On the Manilian Law* 65 (66 BC), trans. P. Jones and K. Sidwell, op. cit., p. 25.

2 Called 'the Elder' to distinguish him from his more famous/notorious son and popular reformer, also called Tiberius Sempronius Gracchus.

3 Appian says it lasted seveteen years (155–139 BC); Livy, Florus, Orosius and Eutropius make it fourteen years; Diodorus makes it eleven; and Velleius Paterculus, Justin and Pompeius Trogus make it ten.

4 Strabo 3.3.6.

5 'Celtiberians' refers to Iberians who had taken on board elements of Celtic culture from the Celtic tribes who had formerly occupied their territory.

6 Polybius 35.1, trans. S. D. Olson, in Polybius, *The Histories, Volume VI: Books 28–39. Fragments*, edited and translated by S. D. Olson,

translated by W. R. Paton, revised by F. W. Walbank and C. Habicht (Cambridge, MA: Harvard University Press, 2012).

7 Appian 6.60, trans. B. McGing, in Appian, *Roman History, Volume I* (Cambridge, MA: Harvard University Press, 1912a).

8 Lucilius 26.701–1; Nonius 186.31.

9 Diodorus Siculus 33.1.1.

10 Diodorus Siculus 33.1.2–3.

11 Diodorus Siculus 33.1.1–3, trans. F. R. Walton, in Diodorus Siculus, *Library of History, Volume XII: Fragments of Books 33–40* (Cambridge, MA: Harvard University Press, 1967).

12 Dio Cassius 22.73.1–4, trans. E. Cary and H. B. Foster, in Dio Cassius, *Roman History, Volume II: Books 12–35* (Cambridge, MA: Harvard University Press, 1914a).

13 Tribola is just to the south of Urso (modern-day Osuna in southern Spain).

14 Appian 6.61.

15 Appian 6.62, trans. B. McGing (1912a), op. cit. Diodorus has a more prosaic version in which Vetilius is just captured and executed: 33.1.3.

16 The location of Mons Veneris is a matter of conjecture: the Sierra de San Vicente, Sierra de San Pedro and Sierra de Gredos are all suggested. See L. Silva, *Viriathus and the Lusitanian Resistance to Rome 155–139 BC* (Barnsley: Pen & Sword Military, 2013), p. 292, n. 32.

17 Diodorus Siculus 33.2.

18 The city of Segobrida is modern Cabeza de Griego, close to Cuenca.

19 Frontinus, *Stratagems* 3.10.6.

20 Frontinus, *Stratagems* 3.11.4.

21 Florus 1.33.15; cf. Orosius 5.4.5.

22 The inhabitants of Segovia.

23 Frontinus, *Stratagems* 4.5.22.

24 Appian 6.65. The cities are not named.

25 Itucca has been identified with Tucci, the later colonia Augusta Gemella Tucci, mentioned by Pliny, *NH* 3.12.

26 *Thorubou barbarikou* (θορύβου βαρβαρικοῦ) in Greek.

27 Appian 6.67, trans. B. McGing (1912a), op. cit.

28 Appian 6.67, trans. B. McGing (1912a), op. cit.

29 Diodorus Siculus 33.7.6, trans. F. R. Walton, op. cit.

30 Diodorus Siculus 33.7.7, trans. F. R. Walton, op. cit.

31 The Guadiana River valley.

32 It is uncertain where these towns are: they might be modern Écija, Gaudix and Porcuna, although Pliny (*NH* 3.12) equates Gemella with Tucci.

33 Appian 6.69.

34 Appian 6.69, trans. B. McGing (1912a), op. cit.

35 Diodorus Siculus 33.1.4.

36 '*Aequis condicionibus*', Livy, *Periochae* 54.

37 Diodorus Siculus 33.7.1, trans. F. R. Walton, op. cit.

38 Diodorus Siculus 33.7.2.

39 Diodorus Siculus 33.7.3, trans. F. R. Walton, op. cit.

40 Appian 6.70, B. McGing (1912a), op. cit.

41 Dio Cassius 22.78.1, trans. E. Cary and H. B. Foster (1914a), op. cit.

42 Appian 6.71, trans. S. Kershaw.

43 Appian 6.72.

44 Diodorus Siculus 33.19.

45 Dio Cassius 22.75.1.

46 According to Appian. Diodorus Siculus (33.21) calls them Audas, Ditalces and Nicorontes, and adds that they came from Urso.

47 Appian 6.74; Diodorus Siculus 33.21.

48 Eutropius, *Breviarium ab Urbe Condita* 4.16.2, trans. J. S. Watson, *Justin, Cornelius Nepos, and Eutropius*, (London: George Bell and Sons, 1886). Appian says that Caepio allowed them to enjoy what they had already received, but referred their extra demands to Rome. See also Diodorus Siculus 33.1.4, 21.1; Livy, *Periochae* 54; Velleius Paterculus 2.1.3; Appian 6.74–5; Orosius, *History Against the Pagans* 5.4.14.

49 Valerius Maximus, *De Factis Dictisque Memorabilibus* 9.4.6, trans. D. R. Shackleton Bailey, in Valerius Maximus, *Memorable Doings and Sayings, Volume II: Books 6–9* (Cambridge, MA: Harvard University Press, 2000).

50 Velleius Paterculus, *Compendium of Roman History* 2.1.3, trans. W. Shipley, in Velleius Paterculus, *Compendium of Roman History. Res Gestae Divi Augusti* (Cambridge, MA: Harvard University Press, 1924).

51 Appian 6.75, trans. B. McGing (1912a), op. cit.

52 Florus 1.33.15, trans. E. S. Forster, in Florus, *Epitome of Roman History* (Cambridge, MA: Harvard University Press, 1929).

8. Jugurtha: The Struggle to Free Africa from Rome

1 Sallust, *Bellum Jugurthinum (BJ)* 4.7, trans. J. C. Rolfe, in Sallust, *The War with Catiline. The War with Jugurtha*, edited by John T. Ramsey, translated by J. C. Rolfe (Cambridge, MA: Harvard University Press, 2013).

2 Sallust, *BJ* 41.2–4, trans. J. C. Rolfe (2013), op. cit.

3 Sallust, *BJ* 5.1–2, trans. S. Kershaw.

4 Sallust, *BJ* 7.4–5, trans. J. C. Rolfe (2013), op. cit.

5 Sallust, *BJ* 7.4–5, trans. S. Kershaw.

6 Sallust, *BJ* 8.2, trans. J. C. Rolfe (2013), op. cit.

7 Sallust, *BJ* 10.6, trans. J. C. Rolfe (2013), op. cit.

8 Livy, *Periochae* 62.

9 No such town is known.

10 Adherbal's speech appears in Sallust, *BJ* 14.

11 Sallust, *BJ* 14.25, trans. J. C. Rolfe (2013), op. cit.

12 In 117 or early 116 BC.

13 Sallust, *BJ* 16.1, trans. S. Kershaw.

14 Sallust, *BJ* 20.1, trans. J. C. Rolfe (2013), op. cit.

15 Sallust, *BJ* 20.2, trans. J. C. Rolfe (2013), op. cit.

16 Livy, *Periochae* 64.

17 Sallust, *BJ* 21.4, trans. J. C. Rolfe (2013), op. cit.

18 Sallust, *BJ* 25.3, trans. J. C. Rolfe (2013), op. cit.

19 Sallust, *BJ* 29.1, trans. J. C. Rolfe (2013), op. cit.

20 Sallust, *BJ* 31.11–13, trans. J. C. Rolfe (2013), op. cit.

21 Sallust, *BJ* 35.10, trans. S. Kershaw.

22 Because of the political upheavals at Rome, these elections were postponed.

23 Sallust, *BJ* 38.1.

24 Location unknown.

25 Chief centurion.

26 Livy 3.28.11.

27 Sallust, *BJ* 40.5, trans. J. C. Rolfe (2013), op. cit.

28 Cicero, *Brutus* 128B.

29 Sallust, *BJ* 43.1. Metellus was acquitted by the Mamilian Commission.

30 Sallust, *BJ* 46.3–4, trans. J. C. Rolfe (2013), op. cit.

31 Sallust, *BJ* 52.1–4, trans. J. C. Rolfe (2013), op. cit.

32 Sallust, *BJ* 54.4, trans. J. C. Rolfe (2013), op. cit.

33 The fighting is described by Sallust, *BJ* 56–60.

34 Sallust, *BJ* 62.9, trans. S. Kershaw.

35 Sallust, *BJ* 66.2, trans. J. C. Rolfe (2013), op. cit.

36 Sallust, *BJ* 82.2.

37 Sallust, *BJ* 85.

38 Sallust, *BJ* 91.7.

39 Sallust, *BJ* 97.4, trans. J. C. Rolfe (2013), op. cit.

40 Sallust, *BJ* 98.6–7, trans. J. C. Rolfe (2013), op. cit.

41 Sallust, *BJ* 101.11, trans. J. C. Rolfe (2013), op. cit.

42 Plutarch, *Sulla* 3.2, trans. B. Perrin, in Plutarch, *Lives, Volume IV: Alcibiades and Coriolanus. Lysander and Sulla* (Cambridge, MA: Harvard University Press, 1916b).

43 Sallust, *BJ* 113.5–7, trans. J. C. Rolfe (2013), op. cit.

44 Plutarch, *Sulla* 3.4, trans. B. Perrin (1916b), op. cit.

45 Livy, *Periochae* 104.

46 The Tullianum.

47 Plutarch, *Marius* 12.2–4, trans. B. Perrin (1920), op. cit. Other accounts say he was strangled: see Eutropius 4.27.6; Orosius 5.15.19.

48 *CIL* 2.3417; *ILS* 840.

49 Sallust, *BJ* 114.4, trans. S. Kershaw.

9. The Cimbri and the Teutones: A Germanic Threat to Italy

1 Tacitus, *Germania* 37, trans. A. J. Church, W. J. Brodribb and L. Cerrato, in Tacitus, *The History of Tacitus* (Cambridge and London: Macmillan, 1864).

2 See Strabo 2.3.6; S. Kershaw, *A Brief History of Atlantis: Plato's Ideal State* (London: Robinson, 2017), pp. 128 ff.

3 Strabo 7.2.1, trans. H. L. Jones, in Strabo, *Geography, Volume III: Books 6–7* (Cambridge, MA: Harvard University Press, 1924).

4 Strabo 7.2.2; cf. Plutarch, *Marius* 11.2–9.

5 Strabo 7.2.3.

6 See B. Cunliffe, *The Extraordinary Voyage of Pytheas the Greek* (London: Allen Lane, 2001).

7 Pliny, *NH* 37.11.

8 Plutarch, *Marius* 11.3.

9 Strabo 5.1.8.

10 Livy, *Periochae* 113.

11 Appian 4.13, trans. B. McGing (1912a), op. cit.

12 *ILS* 4595, 4596, cf. 9377.

13 Florus 38.3.2, trans. E. S. Forster, op. cit.

14 Diodorus Siculus 35.37, trans. F. R. Walton, op. cit.

15 This Brennus, of the Prausi tribe, should not be confused with the sacker of Rome. See p. 23 ff. It is by no means certain that the Delphic gold was actually at Tolosa.

16 Dio Cassius 27.90.1.

17 Strabo 4.1.13.

18 Livy, *Periochae* 67, trans. S. Kershaw.

19 See P. Chrystal, *Roman Military Disasters: Dark Days and Lost Legions* (Barnsley: Pen & Sword Military, 2015).

20 Livy, *Periochae* 68.

21 Florus 3.5.

22 Plutarch, *Marius* 11.1.

23 Plutarch, *Marius* 11.2, 11.8.

24 In practice a century usually comprised eighty men.

25 See Plutarch, *Marius* 13.

26 Florus 3.4–5, trans. E. S. Forster, op. cit.

27 Plutarch, *Marius* 15.5, trans. B. Perrin (1920), op. cit.

28 Plutarch, *Marius* 16.3, trans. B. Perrin (1920), op. cit.

29 Florus 3.9, trans. E. S. Forster, op. cit.

30 Plutarch, *Marius* 19.7, trans. B. Perrin (1920), op. cit.

31 Florus 3.10. For a full description of the battle, see Plutarch, *Marius* 15–22.

32 Florus 3.12.

33 See Plutarch, *Marius* 23–7, for a full account.

34 Plutarch, *Marius* 25.6, trans. B. Perrin (1920), op. cit

35 Plutarch, *Marius* 25.1–2, trans. B. Perrin (1920), op. cit.

36 Valerius Maximus (6.1) says that they wanted to be sent as a gift to the Vestal Virgins and promised to take vows of chastity.

37 Florus 3.16, trans. E. S. Forster, op. cit.

38 Plutarch, *Marius* 27.3–6.

39 Florus 3.18, trans. E. S. Forster, op. cit.

10. The Italian War: Resistance and Rebellion in Italy

1 This is one reason why many allied states did not make as big a fuss as they might have done: their leaders had already achieved Roman citizenship, and so were part of 'the Establishment'.

2 Appian, *Civil Wars* 1.18–20; Plutarch, *Romulus* 27.4–5; Plutarch, *Gaius Gracchus* 10.4–5; Cicero, *De Oratore* 2.40. See also I. Worthington, 'The Death of Scipio Africanus', *Hermes*, vol. 117, no. 2 (1989), pp. 253–6.

3 Cicero, *De Officiis* 3.47 (44 BC), trans. D. Stockton, in *LACTOR 13: From the Gracchi to Sulla: Sources for Roman History, 130-80 BC* (London: London Association of Classical Teachers, 1981).

4 The dating of Saturninus' legislation between his first tribunate of 103 BC and his second in 100 BC is disputed.

5 Plutarch, *Marius* 28.2, trans. B. Perrin (1920), op. cit.

6 Cicero, *De Officiis* 3.47, trans. D. Stockton, op. cit.

7 Cicero, *Pro Balbo* 48 (65 BC), trans. D. Stockton, op. cit.

8 The name appears in the Diodorus Siculus manuscript as Pompaeus.

9 The *praenomen* Gaius wasn't used by the Domitii, so his name should probably read Gnaeus. The man named here could be Gnaeus Domitius Ahenobarbus (consul 96 BC).

10 Diodorus Siculus 37.13.1, trans. F. R. Walton, op. cit. According to Plutarch, *Cato Minor* 2, Pompaedius Silo was on friendly terms with Drusus the Elder, and had visited his house on one occasion.

11 Asconius 67C, trans. D. Stockton, op. cit.

12 Asconius 67C, trans. D. Stockton, op. cit.

13 See Velleius Paterculus 2.14.1–2.

14 Hybrida came from Sucro in northern Spain. He was the first senator to come from Hispania.

15 Florus 2.6.18.

16 Some ancient authors call it the Marsic War, because it involved the Marsi tribe.

17 Diodorus Siculus 37.2.4–7; Strabo 5.241; Velleius Paterculus 2.16.4.

18 Diodorus Siculus 37.2.1, trans. F. R. Walton, op. cit.

19 Plutarch, *Marius* 33.3–6.

20 Appian, *Civil Wars* 1.49.

21 Cicero, *Pro Balbo* 21, trans. D. Stockton, op. cit.

22 Velleius Paterculus 2.16, trans. D. Stockton, op. cit.

23 Appian 2.15.3.

11. Spartacus: The Gladiator who Challenged Rome

1 Karl Marx, letter to Engels dated 27 February 1861: Karl Marx and Friedrich Engels, *Werke* (Berlin, 1955), pp. 30, 160. Marxism has been highly influential in the study of ancient slavery over the last century. For useful resources about Spartacus, follow the links at https://open.conted.ox.ac.uk/series/spartacus, accessed 18 August 2018.

2 B14b Vetter (1953), no. 35. Whether this shows Spartacus himself or a gladiatorial contest in which the fighter's 'stage-name' is Spartacus is unclear, but the admiration for him remains. See M. Beard, *Pompeii: The Life of a Roman Town* (London: Profile Books, 2008), p. 44; A. van Hoof, 'Reading the Spartaks Fresco Without Red Eyes', in S. T. A. M. Mols and E. M. Moorman (eds), *Omni pede stare; saggi architettonici e circumvesuviani in memoriam Jos de Waele* (Studi della Soprintendenza Archeologica di Pompei 9, Naples: Electa, 2005), pp. 251–6.

3 Strabo 14.5.2. NB he says that Delos 'could' (*dynamene*) do this, not that it actually did, but the numbers remain staggering.

4 Slaves were not liable for military service; free peasants were.

5 Appian, *Civil Wars* 1.7, trans. D. Stockton, op. cit.

6 In Greek, *tou Nomadikou genous*, which some scholars suggest might be a corruption of the name of the Maedi tribe from Thrace, who

were allies of Mithridates VI of Pontus, raided Greece and Macedon, and had their lands ravaged by Sulla. It is possible, but not certain, that Spartacus was one of the Maedi, and was captured during those events.

7 *Praotes* in Greek, which might be better translated as 'dignified'.

8 Plutarch, *Crassus* 8.2, trans. R. Warner, in Plutarch, *The Fall of the Roman Republic: Six Lives by Plutarch* (Harmondsworth: Penguin, 1958).

9 See, for example, Herodotus 5.3; Thucydides 2.95–101.

10 Herodotus 5.6.1.

11 See C. Webber and A. McBride, *The Thracians 700 BC–AD 46 (Men-at-Arms)* (Oxford: Osprey Publishing, 2001), p. 7; Z. Archibald, *The Odrysian Kingdom of Thrace: Orpheus Unmasked* (Oxford Monographs on Classical Archaeology, Oxford: Clarendon Press, 1998), p. 100.

12 Plato, *Republic* 4.435e–436a; *Laws* 367e.

13 Polybius 27.12.

14 Strabo 9.2.4; Polyaenus, *Stratagems* 7.43.

15 Polyaenus, *Stratagems* 7.2.6.

16 Tacitus, *Annals* 4.46.1.

17 The *rumpia* was a polearm about 1.5 metres long, with a straight or slightly curved, single-edged iron blade with a triangular cross-section, which could be used for thrusting and/or slashing. See C. Webber and A. McBride, op. cit.

18 Florus 2.8.1, trans. E. S. Forster, op. cit.

19 See, for example, Appian 12.109.

20 Diodorus Siculus 38/39.21, trans. F. R. Walton, op. cit.

21 Appian, *Civil Wars* 1.116.1.

22 Florus 2.8.8, trans. E. S. Forster, op. cit.

23 Plutarch, *Crassus* 8; Appian, *Civil Wars* 1.116.1.

24 Florus 2.8.12. It could be, however, that Florus is just using the term in a generic way to disparage Spartacus.

25 See A. Leibundgut, *Die Römischen Lampen in der Schweiz* (Bern: Francke, 1977); S. Vucetic, 'Roman Sexuality or Roman Sexualities? Looking at Sexual Imagery on Roman Terracotta Mould-made Lamps', *TRAC 2013: Proceedings of the Twenty-Third Annual*

Theoretical Roman Archaeology Conference, London 2013 (Oxford: Oxbow Books, 2014), p. 140.

26 *CIL* IV.4342, 4397, trans. S. Kershaw.

27 *CIL* IV.4345, trans. S. Kershaw.

28 *CIL* IV.4356, trans. S. Kershaw.

29 *CIL* IV 2508, trans. S. Kershaw.

30 Sallust *Histories* 3, fr. 98A, trans. B. D. Shaw, *Spartacus and the Slave Wars: A Brief History with Documents* (Boston and New York: Bedford/St Martin's, 2001).

31 Seneca, *On Clemency* 1.24, trans. J. W. Basore, in Seneca, *Moral Essays, Volume I: De Providentia. De Constantia. De Ira. De Clementia* (Cambridge, MA: Harvard University Press, 1928).

32 Livy 32.26.4–18.

33 Livy 33.36.1–3.

34 Diodorus Siculus 34/35.2.1–24; Photius, *Library* 284–86b.

35 Diodorus Siculus 34/35.2.25–3.11.

36 Diodorus Siculus 34/35.2.11–12, trans. G. Booth (1814) and F. Hoefer (1865) at http://attalus.org/translate/diodorus34.html, accessed 7 January 2019.

37 Diodorus Siculus 34/35.2.16.

38 Strabo 14.38.1.

39 Diodorus Siculus 36.6.1, trans. G. Booth and F. Hoefer, op. cit.

40 Diodorus Siculus, 36.10.2–3, trans. G. Booth and F. Hoefer, op. cit.

41 Diodorus Siculus, 36.11.2, trans. G. Booth and F. Hoefer, op. cit.

42 Plutarch, *Crassus* 8; Varro: Sosipater Charisius 1.133 (ed. H. Keil).

43 The numbers vary slightly in the sources: 84 in Eutropius 6.7.2; 78 in Plutarch, *Crassus* 8; 74 in Livy, *Periochae* 95, and Orosius 5.24; about 70 in Appian, *Civil Wars* 116.1; less than 50 in Cicero, *Ad Atticum* 6.2.8; and 30 or rather more in Florus 2.8.3.

44 Some sources imply that the people under Crixus' command were Germans.

45 Plutarch, *Crassus* 9, trans. B. Perrin, in Plutarch, *Lives, Volume III: Pericles and Fabius Maximus. Nicias and Crassus* (Cambridge, MA: Harvard University Press, 1916a). See also Florus 2.8.4; Orosius 5.24.

46 Appian, *Civil Wars* 1.116

47 Plutarch, *Crassus* 9. Appian, *Civil Wars* 1.116, calls him Ouarinios Glabros; Florus, 2.8.4, calls him Clodius Glabrus.

48 Plutarch, *Crassus* 9; Frontinus, *Strategems* 1.5.21; Appian, *Civil Wars* 1.116; Florus 2.8.4

49 Livy, *Periochae* 95.2, calls him Publius Varenus.

50 Frontinus, *Strategems* 1.5.22; Sallust *Histories* 3, fr. 98A.

51 Plutarch, *Crassus* 9; Appian, *Civil Wars* 1.116

52 Florus 8.3.5.

53 Sallust, *Histories* 3, fr. 98A, trans. B. D. Shaw, op. cit.

54 Orosius 5.24.3, trans. B. D. Shaw, op. cit. Orosius is using the exact technical vocabulary of the Roman arena; cf. Florus 8.3.9.

55 Appian 1.116. We do not know how he obtained this figure.

56 Florus 8.3.6.

57 Appian, *Civil Wars* 1.117, trans. B. D. Shaw, op. cit.; cf. Florus 2.8.10–11.

58 Plutarch, *Crassus* 9.7; Livy, *Periochae* 96.

59 Plutarch, *Cato Minor* 8.

60 Appian, *Civil Wars* 1.117, trans. B. D. Shaw, op. cit.

61 Livy, *Periochae* 96; Florus 8.2.12, Plutarch, *Crassus* 10; Appian, *Civil Wars* 1.117.

62 Plutarch, *Crassus* 10, trans. B. Perrin (1916a), op. cit.; cf. Sallust, *Histories* 4.22; Appian, *Civil Wars* 1.117.

63 Appian, *Civil Wars* 1.118, trans. B. D. Shaw, op. cit.; cf. Orosius 5.24.6; Florus 2.8.12.

64 Sallust, *Histories* 4.28; Cicero, *Verrines* 2.5.5.

65 Plutarch, *Crassus* 10; Florus 2.8.13.

66 Appian, *Civil Wars* 1.119.

67 Frontinus, *Stratagems* 1.5.20.

68 Plutarch, *Crassus* 10, trans. B. Perrin (1916a), op. cit.

69 Sallust, *Histories* 4.32.

70 See Plutarch, *Crassus* 11; Appian, *Civil Wars* 1.119.

71 Plutarch, *Crassus* 11; Sallust, *Histories* 4.34.

72 Frontinus, *Stratagems* 2.4.7, 2.5.34; Livy, *Periochae* 97.1.

73 Plutarch, *Crassus* 11, trans. B. Perrin (1916a), op. cit.

74 Appian, *Civil Wars* 1.120, trans. B. D. Shaw, op. cit.

75 Florus 2.8.13–14.

76 Appian, *Civil Wars* 1.120.

77 Plutarch, *Pompey* 31.2, trans. S. Kershaw.

78 Aulus Gellius, *Attic Nights* 5–6.21; Cicero, *In Pisonem* 24–58; Pliny, *NH* 15.125.

79 Florus 1.47.10.

12. Mithridates VI: The 'Poison King' of Pontus

1 Velleius Paterculus 2.18.1–3, trans. W. Shipley, op. cit.

2 Plutarch, *Moralia* 624A; Athenaeus 10.415e.

3 Pliny, *NH* 7.88.

4 Appian 12.112, trans. B. McGing, in Appian, *Roman History, Volume II* (Cambridge, MA: Harvard University Press, 1912b).

5 Aelian, *De Natura Animalium* 7.46.

6 The Roman Emperor Caligula was credited with this phrase (Suetonius, *Gaius* 20.1). A very similar saying (where 'accept' replaces 'fear') is attributed to Tiberius (Suetonius, *Tiberius* 59).

7 See S. Kershaw (2007), op. cit., pp. 92 ff.

8 Pausanias 3.23.3–5, trans. W. H. S. Jones and H. A. Ormerod, in Pausanias, *Description of Greece, Volume II: Books 3–5 (Laconia, Messenia, Elis 1)* (Cambridge, MA: Harvard University Press, 1926); cf. Appian 12.28.

9 Appian 12.28; Plutarch, *Sulla* 11; Florus 1.40.8; Strabo 10.5.4; Pausanias 3.23.3–5.

10 See Plutarch, *Sulla* 11.5–7; Appian 12.29.

11 See Diodorus Siculus 38.7.1; Plutarch, *Sulla* 12.5–14; Pausanias 9.33.6, 10.21.6.

12 Plutarch, *Moralia* 505A–B, trans. W. C. Helmbold, in Plutarch, *Moralia, Volume VI: Can Virtue Be Taught? On Moral Virtue. On the Control of Anger. On Tranquility of Mind. On Brotherly Love. On Affection for Offspring. Whether Vice Be Sufficient to Cause Unhappiness. Whether the Affections of the Soul are Worse Than Those of the Body. Concerning Talkativeness. On Being a Busybody* (Cambridge, MA: Harvard University Press, 1939); the passage ends with a quotation from Homer, *Odyssey* 11.54.

13 Plutarch, *Sulla* 18.3–4, trans. B. Perrin (1916b), op. cit.

14 For the battle, see, for example, Livy, *Periochae* 82; Strabo 9.414; Plutarch, *Lucullus* 3.6, 11.6; *Sulla* 16–19; Florus 1.40.11; Appian 12.42–5.

15 Livy, *Periochae* 82.

16 Plutarch, *Sulla* 21.4, trans. B. Perrin (1916b), op. cit. Plutarch must have written this just before AD 115. For the battle see, for example, Livy, *Periochae* 82; Frontinus, *Stratagems* 2.3.17, 8.12; Plutarch, *Lucullus* 3.6, 11.6; Plutarch, *Sulla* 20.3–22.7; Florus 1.40.11; Appian 12.49.

17 Appian 12.54.

18 See, for example, Diodorus Siculus 38.8.4; Livy, *Periochae* 83; *FGrH* 252.A3; Velleius Paterculus 2.24.1; Plutarch, *Sulla* 25.1–3; Appian, 12.59–6.

19 See, for example, Sallust, *Histories* 1.27; Livy, *Periochae* 83; *FGrH* 252.A3; Velleius Paterculus 2.23.6; Plutarch, *Lucullus* 4.1; Plutarch, *Sulla* 23.6–24.7, 43.3–4; Florus 1.40.11–12; Appian 12.56–8.

20 See S. Kershaw, *A Guide to Classical Civilization* (London: Robinson, 2010), pp. 268 ff.

21 See Appian 12.65–6.

22 Cicero, *De Lege Manilia* 8, trans. C. D. Yonge, in M. Tullius Cicero, *The Orations of Marcus Tullius Cicero* (London: Henry G. Bohn, 1856).

23 Appian 12.69–70.

24 See, for example, Livy, *Periochae* 93; Plutarch, *Lucullus* 7.6; Appian 12.68–71.

25 See, for example, Cicero, *Academica* 2.1–2; Velleius Paterculus 2.33.1; Plutarch, *Lucullus* 6.1–6, 45.2; Appian 12.68–72.

26 Plutarch, *Lucullus* 11.4, trans. B. Perrin (1914), op. cit.

27 Plutarch, *Lucullus* 15–17.

28 Memnon, *History of Heracleia* 30.1.

29 See, for example, Sallust, *Histories* 4.59–61; Plutarch, *Lucullus* 24.1–7, 46.1; Appian 12.84.

30 See, for example, Sallust, *Histories* 4.64–6, 4.67.15; Frontinus, *Stratagems* 2.1.14, 2.4, 26.5–29.2; Appian 12.85.

31 See Cicero, *De Lege Manilia* 23–4; Plutarch, *Lucullus* 32.1–4.

32 See, for example, Plutarch, *Lucullus* 35.1–2; Plutarch, *Pompey* 39.2; Appian 12.88–9; Dio Cassius 36.12.1–13.2, 42.48.2.

33 His speech *pro Lege Manilia* still survives.

34 Velleius Paterculus, 2.33.4, trans. W. Shipley, op. cit.

35 Plutarch, *Pompey* 31.6, trans. B. Perrin (1917), op. cit.

36 Dio Cassius 36.49.1–2, trans. E. Cary and H. B. Foster, in Dio Cassius, *Roman History, Volume III: Books 36–40* (Cambridge, MA: Harvard University Press, 1914b).

37 Dio Cassius 36.49.8, trans. E. Cary and H. B. Foster (1914b), op. cit.

38 Plutarch, *Pompey* 32.8.

39 See Strabo 12.555; Appian 12.105, 115; Dio Cassius 36.50.3, 49.39.3.

40 Plutarch, *Pompey* 37.1–2, trans. B. Perrin (1917), op. cit.

41 Plutarch, *Pompey* 41.2; Appian 12.107–9; Dio Cassius 37.11.1–4.

42 Plutarch, *Pompey* 41.3, trans. B. Perrin (1917), op. cit.

43 Appian 12.110–12, 12.117; Pausanias 3.23.5; Dio Cassius 37.12.1–14.1.

44 See Pliny, *NH* 25.5–7, 62–3, 65, 127, 29.24; Martial 5.76.1–2; Juvenal, *Satires* 6.660–1, 14.252–3.

45 Appian 12.111, trans. B. McGing (1912b), op. cit.

13. The Parthian Shot: Crassus at Carrhae

1 Cicero, *De Divinatione* 2.22, trans. W. A. Falconer, in Cicero, *On Old Age. On Friendship. On Divination* (Cambridge, MA: Harvard University Press, 1923).

2 Plutarch, *Crassus* 2.2.

3 Plutarch, *Crassus* 16.2, trans. B. Perrin (1916a), op. cit.

4 Catullus 11, written before Crassus' expedition; Horace, *Odes* 2.16, written some decades later.

5 Herodotus 3.106.2.

6 Plutarch, *Crassus* 17.2, trans. B. Perrin (1916a), op. cit.

7 Cicero, *Ad Atticum* 4.13, trans. S. Kershaw.

8 Plutarch, *Crassus* 17.3.

9 Josephus, *Bellum judaicum* (*BJ*) 1.179; Josephus, *Antiquitates judaicae* (*AJ*) 14.105–111.

10 Plutarch, *Crassus* 18.2, trans. B. Perrin (1916a), op. cit.; Dio Cassius 40.16.

11 Plutarch, *Crassus* 18.3, trans. B. Perrin (1916a), op. cit.

12 See Plutarch, *Crassus* 20.1–22.6; Florus 1.46.6–7; Dio Cassius 40.20.1–4; Festus, *Breviarium* 17.1.

13 Plutarch, *Crassus* 21.1, trans. B. Perrin (1916a), op. cit.

14 Plutarch, *Crassus* 21.3.

15 Plutarch, *Crassus* 21.6, trans. B. Perrin (1916a), op. cit.

16 Plutarch, *Crassus* 22.1–3.

17 Plutarch, *Crassus* 22.4, trans. B. Perrin (1916a), op. cit.

18 Plutarch, *Crassus* 23.7, trans. B. Perrin (1916a), op. cit.

19 That is, in the style of the Persian armies who had invaded Greece under Darius I and Xerxes in the fifth century BC.

20 Plutarch, *Crassus* 24.2, trans. B. Perrin (1916a), op. cit.

21 Plutarch, *Crassus* 24.3, trans. B. Perrin (1916a), op. cit.

22 Plutarch, *Crassus* 24.2, trans. B. Perrin (1916a), op. cit.

23 Plutarch, *Crassus* 25.11–12; Dio Cassius 40.21.2–24.3.

24 Plutarch, *Crassus* 27.4, trans. B. Perrin (1916a), op. cit.

25 Our sources do not make it explicit which member of the *gens Coponia* this is.

26 Plutarch, *Crassus* 30.2, trans. B. Perrin (1916a), op. cit.; cf. Dio Cassius 40.26.1.

27 Plutarch, *Crassus* 31.1, trans. B. Perrin (1916a), op. cit.

28 Plutarch, *Crassus* 31.2–5; cf. Dio Cassius 40.26.3–27.2.

29 Dio Cassius 40.27.2.

30 Plutarch, *Crassus* 33.5, trans. S. Kershaw.

31 Euripides, *Medea* 1169–71, trans. B. Perrin (1916a), op. cit.

32 Plutarch, *Crassus* 33.

33 The legionary eagles that Crassus had lost at Carrhae were eventually recovered by Tiberius, in the years before he became Rome's second emperor.

34 See Caesar, *BG* 8.54 f.; Dio Cassius 43.51, 44.46; Suetonius, *Caesar* 44; Plutarch, *Caesar* 58, *Pompey* 56.

14. Vercingetorix: Rebellion in Gaul

1 Livy, *Periochae* 107, says that he wrote 'an account of Caesar's actions against the Gauls, who had revolted almost without exception under Vercingetorix, leader of the Arvernians, [which] contains accounts of difficult sieges of several towns, such as Avaricum of the Bituriges and Gergovia of the Arvernians' (trans. A. C. Schlesinger, in Livy, *History of Rome, Volume XIV: Summaries. Fragments. Julius Obsequens. General Index* (Cambridge, MA: Harvard University Press, 1959). Unfortunately this does not survive, so we do not even have a Roman counter-narrative to that of Caesar.

2 Caesar, *BG* 1.1.

3 Caesar, *BG* 6.1, trans. W. A. McDevitte and W. S. Bohn, in C. Julius Caesar, *Caesar's Gallic War* (1st edn, New York: Harper & Brothers, 1869).

4 Caesar, *BG* 6.13.

5 Caesar, *BG* 6.17.

6 Caesar, *BG* 6.18.

7 Caesar *BG* 6.19, trans. W. A. McDevitte and W. S. Bohn, op. cit.

8 See S. Ghezal, E. Ciesielski, B. Girard et al., 'Embalmed heads of the Celtic Iron Age in the south of France', *Journal of Archaeological Science*, in press, corrected proof (online 7 November 2018), https://www.sciencedirect.com/science/article/pii/S0305440318303194?via%3Dihub, accessed 2 January 2018.

9 Caesar, *BG* 7.3.

10 Caesar, *BG* 7.3, trans. S. Kershaw.

11 Caesar, *BG* 7.3, trans. S. Kershaw.

12 Caesar, *BG* 7.4.

13 Caesar, *BG* 7.4.

14 Caesar, *BG* 7.5.

15 Caesar, *BG* 7.8, trans. H. J. Edwards, in Caesar, *The Gallic War* (Cambridge, MA: Harvard University Press, 1917).

16 Plutarch, *Caesar* 26.3, trans. B. Perrin, in Plutarch, *Lives, Volume VII: Demosthenes and Cicero. Alexander and Caesar* (Cambridge, MA: Harvard University Press, 1919).

17 Caesar, *BG* 7.13.

18 Caesar, *BG* 7.14, trans. H. J. Edwards, op. cit.

19 Caesar, *BG* 7.15, trans. H. J. Edwards, op. cit.

20 Caesar, *BG* 7.20.

21 A small type of catapult.

22 Caesar, *BG* 7.25, trans. H. J. Edwards, op. cit.

23 Caesar, *BG* 7.28.

24 Caesar, *BG* 7.29–30; cf. Dio Cassius 40.34.

25 Dio Cassius 40.35.

26 Caesar, *BG* 7.36, trans. S. Kershaw.

27 Caesar, *BG* 7.36.

28 Caesar, *BG* 7.37, trans. H. J. Edwards, op. cit.

29 Caesar, *BG* 7.38, trans. H. J. Edwards, op. cit.

30 Caesar, *BG* 7.8, trans. H. J. Edwards, op. cit.

31 Dio Cassius 40.36.4, trans. E. Cary and H. B. Foster (1914b), op. cit.

32 Caesar, *BG* 7.66, trans. H. J. Edwards, op. cit.

33 Caesar, *BG* 7.72.

34 Caesar, *BG* 7.73.

35 Caesar, *BG* 7.74.

36 Caesar, *BG* 7.77, trans. S. Kershaw.

37 Dio Cassius 40.40.2–4.

38 Caesar, *BG* 7.75–6.

39 Caesar, *BG* 7.85, trans. H. J. Edwards, op. cit.

40 Caesar, *BG* 7.88.

41 Plutarch, *Caesar* 27.7, trans. B. Perrin (1919), op. cit.

42 Plutarch, *Caesar* 27.9–10, trans. B. Perrin (1919), op. cit.

43 Dio Cassius 40.41.3.

44 T. Mommsen, *Römische Geschichte*, vol. 7 (Leipzig: Reimer & Hirsel, 1854–6).

45 Caesar, *BG* 8.49, trans. H. J. Edwards, op. cit.

15. Cleopatra VII: The Whore Queen of Incestuous Canopus

1 Augustine, *City of God* 3.26.

2 The great Library at Alexandria.

3 B. Chase-Riboud, *Portrait of a Nude Woman as Cleopatra* (New York: William Morrow & Co., 1987).

4 W. W. Tarn, in S. A. Cook, F. E. Adcock and M. P. Charlesworth (eds), *The Cambridge Ancient History: Volume X, the Augustan Empire 44 BC–AD 70* (Cambridge: Cambridge University Press, 1934), p. 111.

5 Musée du Louvre, Paris (E 27113), trans. J. Rowlandson and R. S. Bagnall, *Women and Society in Greek and Roman Egypt: A Sourcebook* (Cambridge: Cambridge University Press, 1998), p. 37.

6 Shakespeare, *Antony and Cleopatra* I.iv.5–7.

7 Plutarch, *Antony* 27.3–4, trans. B. Perrin (1920), op. cit.

8 Plutarch, *Antony* 27.2, trans. A. H. Clough, op. cit.

9 Dio Cassius 42.34.3, trans. S. Kershaw.

10 Dio Cassius 42.34.5, trans. E. Cary and H. B. Foster, in Dio Cassius, *Roman History, Volume IV: Books 41–45* (Cambridge, MA: Harvard University Press, 1916).

11 Plutarch, *Antony* 27.2, trans. S. Kershaw.

12 Galen, *De compositione medicamentorum secundum locos* (XII.403–4 K. G. Kühn, *Medicorum Graecorum Opera*).

13 For example, the silver tetradrachm of Antony and Cleopatra, *c.*37–32 BC, Weill Goudchaux Collection, London. On the reverse is Antony with the legend 'Antonius Imperator for the third time and triumvir'.

14 B. Pascal, *Pensées* (Paris, 1669).

15 For example, the basalt statue of Cleopatra VII, *c.*51–30 BC, in the Rosicrucian Egyptian Museum, San Jose, California (RC 1582). The statue was identified in 1983 as an image of Cleopatra VII by the Dutch Egyptologist Jan Quaegebeur, who compared the profile of the statue with the Greek-style coin portraits of Cleopatra VII.

16 For example, the steatite statue of Cleopatra VII, *c.*51–30 BC, in the Musée du Louvre, Paris (E 13102).

17 For example, the marble statue of Cleopatra VII, *c.*51–30 BC, in the Metropolitan Museum of Art, New York (89.2.660).

18 For example, the black basalt statue of Cleopatra VII, *c.*51–30 BC, in the Hermitage Museum, St Petersburg (3936).

19 Dio Cassius 51.22.3, trans. S. Kershaw.

20 See M. Lefkowitz, op. cit., p. 35 ff., and p. 475, n. 5 here.

21 See, for example, P. J. Jones, *Cleopatra: A Source Book* (Norman: University of Oklahoma Press, 2006), for a selection of material.

22 M. Lefkowitz, loc. cit.

23 For example, Propertius, *Elegies* 3.11.39, quoted on p. 294.

24 The battle was fought on 9 August 48 BC. See Caesar, *Civil War* 3.93–6.

25 Plutarch, *Pompey* 77, trans. S. Kershaw.

26 Caesar, *Civil War* 3.104, trans. J. Gardner, in Julius Caesar, *The Civil War* (Harmondsworth: Penguin, 2004).

27 Cicero, *Ad Atticum* 11.6, trans. E. S. Shuckburgh, in Cicero, *The Letters of Cicero; the whole extant correspondence in chronological order, in four volumes* (London: George Bell and Sons, 1908–9).

28 Plutarch, *Caesar* 49, trans. R. Warner, op. cit.

29 Cicero, *Ad Atticum* 15.15, 13 June 44 BC, trans. S. Kershaw.

30 Cicero, *Letter to Atticus*, 16 April 44 BC, trans. S. Kershaw.

31 Quoted by Cicero, *Philippics* 13.11.24, trans. S. Kershaw.

32 Plutarch, *Antony* 250, trans. I. Scott-Kilvert (1965), op. cit.

33 Plutarch, *Antony* 25.3–4, trans. I. Scott-Kilvert (1965), op. cit.

34 Plutarch, *Antony* 26.1–3, trans. I. Scott-Kilvert (1965), op. cit.

35 Plutarch, *Antony* 28.

36 Plutarch, *Antony* 31.1, trans. S. Kershaw.

37 Propertius, *Elegies* 3.11.39, trans. S. Kershaw.

38 Quoted by Suetonius, *Augustus* 69, trans. S. Kershaw.

39 Plutarch, *Antony* 54.3, trans. S. Kershaw.

40 Augustus, *Res Gestae* 25, trans. A. Lentin, in K. Chisholm and J. Ferguson (eds), *Rome: The Augustan Age* (Oxford: Oxford University Press, 1981).

41 Virgil, *Aeneid* 8.675–713; cf. the more prosaic account by Velleius Paterculus 2.84–7.

42 Horace, *Epodes* 9.11 ff., trans. M. Oakley, in Horace, *The Collected Works*, translated by Lord Dunsany and M. Oakley (London: Dent, 1961). Propertius also speaks of Cleopatra spreading her 'foul mosquito-nets' over Roman landmarks.

43 Plutarch, *Antony* 76–7.

44 Dio Cassius 51.11, trans. I. Scott-Kilvert, in Cassius Dio, *The Roman History: The Reign of Augustus* (London: Penguin, 1987).

45 Plutarch, *Antony* 71.

46 Nicander, *Theriaka* 182 ff., trans. A. S. F. Gow and A. F. Scholfield, in Nicander, *The Poems and Poetical Fragments*, edited with a translation and notes by A. S. F. Gow and A. F. Scholfield (New York: Arno, 1979). Nicander wrote somewhere between 241 and 133 BC.

47 Dio Cassius 51.12–13, trans. I. Scott-Kilvert (1987), op. cit.

48 Plutarch, *Antony* 85.

49 Horace is echoing a sixth-century BC poem by Alcaeus, celebrating the death of a loathed tyrant:

> Now it is fitting to drink and carouse
> With all one's might, for Myrsilus is dead.

50 One of Rome's finest wines.

51 Again Cleopatra is not named: Horace calls her *regina*.

52 That is, Octavian.

53 Horace, *Odes* 1.37.1 ff., trans. J. Michie, in Horace, *The Odes of Horace* (Harmondsworth: Penguin, 1964).

54 Lucan, *Pharsalia* 10.5, trans. S. Kershaw.

55 Dio Cassius 51.15, trans. I. Scott-Kilvert (1987), op. cit.

56 Appian 12.121, trans. B. McGing (1912b), op. cit.

57 Augustus, *Res Gestae* 27, trans. S. Kershaw.

58 *Papyrus Berolinensis* 25.239. See P. Van Minnen, 'An Official Act of Cleopatra (with a Subscription in her Own Hand)', *Ancient Society*, no. 30 (2000), pp.29 –34. *Ginesthoi* is a phonological variant of *ginestho* that was used in the Greek of Cleopatra's day. See S. Teodorsson, *The Phonology of Ptolemaic Koine* (Studia Graeca et Latina Gothoburgensia 36, Lund: Berlingska Boktryckeriet, 1977), pp. 163 ff., 235.

16. Arminius: Bring Me Back My Legions!

1 Augustus, *Res Gestae* 34, trans. A. Lentin, op. cit.

2 Velleius Paterculus 2.89, trans. A. Lentin, op. cit.

3 Augustus, *Res Gestae* 29, trans. S. Kershaw.

4 Augustus, *Res Gestae* 26.

5 Modern Tirol and part of eastern Switzerland, including lands between the north-eastern Alps and the upper Danube.

6 Pliny, *NH* 3.136–8, trans. H. A. Rackham, in Pliny, *Natural History in Ten Volumes, II, Books 3–7* (rev. edn, Cambridge, MA: Harvard University Press, 1949).

7 They lived between the eastern Alps and the Danube, including the valleys of the Rivers Save and Drave, and bordering on the Danube from modern Vienna to Belgrade.

8 Augustus, *Res Gestae* 30, trans. A. Lentin, op. cit.

9 Velleius Paterculus 2.117, trans. W. Shipley, op. cit.

10 Iranians from central Asia who had migrated after around 200 BC over south Russia.

11 Thracians of the Transylvanian upland. See pp. 367–369.

12 Tacitus, *Germania* 1.1–2, trans. M. Hutton and W. Peterson, in Tacitus, *Agricola. Germania. Dialogue on Oratory,* translated by M. Hutton and W. Peterson, revised by R. M. Ogilvie, E. H. Warmington and M. Winterbottom (Cambridge, MA: Harvard University Press, 1914).

13 Tacitus, *Germania* 2.2, 4.1–3, trans. M. Hutton and W. Peterson, op. cit.

14 Caesar, *BG* 6.22, trans. H. J. Edwards, op. cit.

15 Tacitus, *Germania* 7.1–3.

16 Tacitus, *Germania* 11.3–6, trans. M. Hutton and W. Peterson, op. cit.

17 Tacitus, *Germania* 6.2–6, trans. M. Hutton and W. Peterson, op. cit.

18 Tacitus, *Germania* 14.2, trans. M. Hutton and W. Peterson, op. cit.

19 Tacitus, *Germania* 14.2, trans. M. Hutton and W. Peterson, op. cit.

20 Caesar, *BG* 6.23–4; cf. Tacitus, *Germania* 28.1.

21 Caesar, *BG* 6.21; cf. Tacitus, *Germania* 14–15.

22 Tacitus, *Germania* 20.

23 Tacitus, *Germania* 21.3, trans. S. Kershaw.

24 Caesar, *BG* 6.21, trans. H. J. Edwards, op. cit.; cf. Tacitus, *Germania* 19.

25 Tacitus, *Germania* 17.1, trans. M. Hutton and W. Peterson, op. cit.

26 Tacitus, *Germania* 8.1–2.

27 Tacitus, *Germania* 25.

28 Caesar, *BG* 6.21, trans. H. J. Edwards, op. cit.

29 Tacitus, *Germania* 9.3, trans. S. Kershaw.

30 Tacitus, *Germania* 23.1–2, trans. M. Hutton and Peterson, op. cit.

31 Velleius Paterculus 2.117.2.

32 Dio Cassius 59.18.

33 Velleius Paterculus 2.117.4, trans. W. Shipley, op. cit.

34 Velleius Paterculus 2.118.1.

35 Velleius Paterculus 2.118.2, trans. W. Shipley, op. cit.

36 Tacitus, *Germania* 36.1–2, trans. M. Hutton and W. Peterson, op. cit.

37 Velleius Paterculus 2.118.2, trans. W. Shipley, op. cit.

38 Tacitus, *Annals* 1.55.

39 Tacitus, *Annals* 1.60.3.

40 Dio Cassius 59.20.4, trans. E. Cary and H. B. Foster, in Dio Cassius, *Roman History, Volume VII: Books 56–60* (Cambridge, MA: Harvard University Press, 1924).

41 Velleius Paterculus 2.119.2, trans. W. Shipley, op. cit. Tacitus also talks of Arminius' perfidy: *Annals* 1.55.

42 Florus 2.30.37, trans. N. Pollard and J. Berry, *The Complete Roman Legions* (London: Thames & Hudson, 2012); cf. Tacitus, *Annals* 1.60.3.

43 Velleius Paterculus 2.120.6, trans. S. Kershaw.

44 Velleius Paterculus 2.119.5, trans. W. Shipley, op. cit.

45 Tacitus, *Annals* 1.61, trans. C. H. Moore and J. Jackson, in Tacitus, *Histories: Books 4–5. Annals: Books 1–3* (Cambridge, MA: Harvard University Press, 1931).

46 See J. Harnecker, *Arminius, Varus and the Battlefield at Kalkriese: An Introduction to the Archaeological Investigations and Their Results* (Bramsche: Rasch Verlag, 2004).

47 Dio Cassius 56.22.2; Velleius Paterculus 2.120.3.

48 Dio Cassius 56.22.2–4; Velleius Paterculus 2.120.4.

49 Suetonius, *Augustus* 23.2, trans. S. Kershaw.

50 Germanicus' names are complex: his personal name (*praenomen*) is not known, although he was probably named Nero Claudius Drusus after his father, or perhaps Tiberius Claudius Nero after his uncle. He received the honorific title (*agnomen*) Germanicus in 9 BC, when it was posthumously granted to his father for his

victories in Germania. When Tiberius adopted him, he retained Germanicus and took the names Julius and Caesar. So henceforth he was Germanicus Julius Caesar.

51 Tacitus, *Annals* 1.55, trans. Tacitus, *Annals* 1.61, trans. C. H. Moore and J. Jackson, op. cit.

52 Tacitus, *Annals* 1.61, trans. C. H. Moore and J. Jackson, op. cit.

53 See Tacitus, *Annals* 1.58.

54 Tacitus, *Annals* 1.63.

55 Tacitus, *Annals* 1.65.

56 Tacitus, *Annals* 1.68, trans. C. H. Moore and J. Jackson, op. cit.

57 See http://www.livius.org/articles/place/fossa-drusiana/?, accessed 2 August 2018.

58 Tacitus, *Annals* 2.9.

59 Tacitus, *Annals* 2.10.

60 Tacitus, *Annals* 2.14, trans. C. H. Moore and J. Jackson, op. cit.

61 Tacitus, *Annals* 2.14, trans. S. Kershaw.

62 Tacitus, *Annals* 2.21, trans. C. H. Moore and J. Jackson, op. cit.

63 *L'Année Épigraphique (AE)*, no. 508 (1984).

64 See S. Kershaw, *A Brief History of the Roman Empire* (London: Robinson, 2013), p. 75 f.

65 Tacitus, *Annals* 1.41.3; Suetonius, *Gaius* 9.1. The word is a diminutive of *caliga* = a leather hobnailed sandal worn by Roman soldiers. Originally it was used quite sentimentally, and conjured up none of the horrors that it now does. *Caligula* is singular = 'Little Boot', not 'Little Boots'.

66 Tacitus, *Annals* 2.44, trans. S. Kershaw.

67 Tacitus, *Annals* 2.44, trans. S. Kershaw.

68 Tacitus, *Annals* 2.44, trans. S. Kershaw.

69 Tacitus, *Annals* 2.46.

70 Tacitus, *Annals* 2.88, trans. C. H. Moore and J. Jackson, op. cit. For Pyrrhus, see p. 711 f.

71 Tacitus, *Annals* 2.88, trans. C. H. Moore and J. Jackson, op. cit.

72 Tacitus, *Annals* 2.88, trans. C. H. Moore and J. Jackson, op. cit.

17. Boudicca: Queen of the Iceni, Scourge of Rome

1 Caesar, *BG* 5.12–13, trans. A. and P. Wiseman, in K. Chisholm and J. Ferguson, *Rome: The Augustan Age* (Oxford: Oxford University Press, 1981).

2 Strabo 4.5.1–2, trans. J. C. Mann and R. G. Penman (eds), *LACT Literary Sources for Roman Britain* (London: LACT Publications, 1978).

3 Caesar, *BG* 5.12–14, trans. A. and P. Wiseman, op. cit.

4 Claudian, *De Consulatu Stilichonis*, 2.250 ff., trans. C. Mann and R. G. Penman (eds), *LACTOR 11: Literary Sources for Roman Britain* (2nd edn, London: London Association of Classical Teachers, 1985).

5 Strabo 4.5.1–2, trans. J. C. Mann and R. G. Penman (1978), op. cit.

6 Tacitus, *Agricola* 12.3–4, trans. M. Hutton, *Tacitus: Agricola, Germania, Dialogus* (London: Heinemann; Cambridge, MA: Harvard University Press, 1970).

7 Tacitus, *Agricola* 11, trans. M. Hutton, op. cit.

8 Tacitus, *Agricola* 12, trans. M. Hutton, op. cit.

9 Horace, *Odes* 1.35.29–30, trans. S. Kershaw.

10 Horace, *Odes* 4.14.47–8, trans. J. Michie, op. cit.

11 See S. Kershaw (2013), op. cit., pp. 92–8.

12 Caesar gives his account of the British expeditions at *BG* 4.20–5.23.

13 The spelling 'Caractacus' comes from an inferior manuscript of Tacitus; the manuscripts of Dio Cassius call him both Karatakos and Kartakes; his Celtic name was Caradoc.

14 Dio Cassius 60.21.4. Suetonius calls Cunobellinus 'King of the Britons' – in reality he was just the tribal chief of the Catuvellauni. His name means 'Strong as a Dog' in Brittonic. He is Cymbeline in Shakespeare's play of that name.

15 Dio Cassius 60.19.5 ff, trans. J. C. Mann and R. G. Penman (1985), op. cit.

16 *CIL* 6.920 = *ILS* 216 (restored), Capitoline Museum, Rome. Trans. D. R. Dudley, *Urbs Roma: A Sourcebook of Classical Texts on the City and its Monuments* (London: Phaidon, 1967).

17 Tacitus, *Annals* 12.37, trans. J. Jackson, in Tacitus, *Annals: Books 4–6, 11–12* (Cambridge, MA: Harvard University Press, 1937a).

18 Dio Cassius, *Epitome* of Book 61.33.3, trans. E. Cary and H. B. Foster, Dio Cassius, *Roman History, Volume VIII: Books 61–70* (Cambridge, MA: Harvard University Press, 1925).

19 Caesar, *BG* 6.13.

20 Caesar, *BG* 6.14, trans. H. J. Edwards, op. cit.

21 Suetonius, *Nero* 18, trans. S. Kershaw.

22 The spelling Boudicca has been adopted here. Boadicea probably originates from a misprint. Tacitus most likely spelled her name as it is used here. However, there is evidence that the Britons called her Boudica, pronounced 'Bow-DEE-kah', rhyming 'bow' with 'low'. The Greek sources call her Buduika. See K. Jackson, 'Queen Boudicca?', *Britannia*, no. 10 (1979), p. 255; C. D. Williams, *Boudica and Her Stories: Narrative Transformations of a Warrior Queen* (Newark: University of Delaware Press, 2009), pp. 44 ff. The modern 'bodacious' has nothing to do with her name.

23 Ulpian, in Justinian, *Digest* 1.19.1–2, trans. A. Watson, in Justinian, *The Digest of Justinian, Vol. 1* (Philadelphia: University of Pennsylvania Press, 1985).

24 Tacitus, *Annals* 14.31, trans. S. Kershaw.

25 The spelling of the tribal name varies in the ancient sources between Trinobantes and Trinovantes. Philology suggests Trinovantes is closer to the actual form current in Britain.

26 For the arguments against believing that the temple at Colchester was dedicated to Claudius during his lifetime, see D. Fishwick in *Britannia*, no. 3 (1972), pp. 164 ff.

27 Dio Cassius 62.2.1.

28 Tacitus, *Annals* 14.32.

29 Tacitus, *Agricola* 15.2–3, trans. J. C. Mann and R. G. Penman (1985), op. cit.

30 Tacitus, *Annals* 12.31.

31 See the discussion by Kevin K. Carroll in *Britannia*, no. 10 (1979), p. 197 ff.

32 Tacitus, *Annals* 14.31, trans. J. Jackson, *Tacitus, Annals: Books 13–16* (Cambridge, MA: Harvard University Press, 1937b).

33 Dio Cassius 62.2.2–4, trans. J. C. Mann and R. G. Penman (1985), op. cit.

34 Tacitus, *Annals* 14.31, trans. J. Jackson (1937b), op. cit.

35 Tacitus, *Annals* 14.32, says he lost the entire infantry force of his legion.

36 Tacitus, *Annals* 14.32.

37 Tacitus, *Annals* 14.33, trans. J. Jackson (1937b), op. cit.

38 Dio Cassius 62.2.1, trans. J. C. Mann and R. G. Penman (1985), op. cit.

39 Caesar, *BG* 4.33, trans. S. A. Handford, in Julius Caesar, *The Conquest of Gaul*, revised with a new introduction by Jane F. Gardner (London: Penguin, 1982).

40 Otherwise unknown.

41 Juvenal, *Satires* 4.126–7, trans. S. Kershaw.

42 The distinction is not entirely clear. Jordanes also refers to the *biga* and *currus* as being different: it is possible that *biga* = *essedum* and *currus* = *covinnus* (see p. 340). *Currus* is the term that Tacitus uses for British chariots, including that of Boudicca: *Agricola* 12; *Annals* 14.35.

43 Pomponius Mela, *De Chorographia* 3.43, trans. S. Kershaw.

44 Lucan, *Pharsalia* 1.426, trans. S. Kershaw.

45 Silius Italicus, *Punica* 17.416 f., trans. S. Kershaw.

46 Governor from AD 76 to 78.

47 Frontinus, *Stratagems* II.3.18.

48 Jordanes, *Getica* 1.2.14–15, trans. C. C. Mierow, in Jordanes, *The Gothic History of Jordanes* (Princeton: Princeton University Press, 1915).

49 Arrian, *Ars Tactica* 19, trans. P. A. Stadter, in 'The Ars Tactica of Arrian: Tradition and Originality', *Classical Philology*, vol. 73, no. 2 (1978), pp. 117–28.

50 *Roman Republican Coinage* (*RRC*) 448/2a, *RRC* 448/2b.

51 The actual site has not been clearly identified.

52 Tacitus, *Annals* 14.34.

53 Dio Cassius 62.6.3, trans. C. A. Williams, *Roman Homosexuality* (2nd edn, Oxford: Oxford University Press, 2010), p. 154.

54 Tacitus, *Annals* 14.35, trans. J. Jackson (1937b), op. cit.

55 Tacitus, *Annals* 14.37, trans. M. Grant, in *Tacitus: The Annals of Imperial Rome*, translated with an introduction by M. Grant (rev. edn, Penguin: Harmondsworth, 1989). For the full battle narrative, see Tacitus, *Agricola* 15–16, *Annals* 14.29–39; Dio Cassius 62.1–12.

56 Tacitus, *Annals* 14.38–9.

57 See S. Kershaw (2013), op. cit. pp. 118–35.

58 Tacitus, *Histories* 3.45, trans. J. C. Mann and R. G. Penman (1985), op. cit.

59 Tacitus, *Histories* 3.45, trans. J. C. Mann and R. G. Penman (1985), op. cit.

60 Tacitus, *Agricola* 25, trans. S. Kershaw.

61 See Tacitus, *Agricola, passim.*

62 Tacitus, *Agricola* 30, trans. S. Kershaw.

18. Judaea Capta: Revolts in Judaea

1 Pliny, *NH* 13.46, trans. H. A. Rackham (1945), op. cit.

2 Tatian, *Oration to the Greeks* 29.1–2.

3 Tacitus, *Histories* 5.4.1, trans. C. H. Moore and J. Jackson, op. cit.

4 Tacitus, *Histories* 5.5.1–3, trans. C. H. Moore and J. Jackson, op. cit.

5 Josephus, *Against Apion* 1.58, trans. S. Kershaw.

6 Josephus, *Against Apion* 1.71; cf. the prolegomena to *BJ* 3.6.7.

7 See *CIL* 3.86; B. Isaac, 'Orientals and Jews in the *Historia Augusta*: Fourth Century Prejudice and Stereotypes', in I. Gafni, A. Oppenheimer and R. D. Schwartz (eds), *The Jews in the Hellenistic-Roman World: Studies in Memory of Menahem Stern* (Jerusalem: Zalman Shazar Center, 1996), p. 268.

8 Josephus, *AJ* 20.263–4, trans. L. H. Feldman, in Josephus, *Jewish Antiquities, Volume IX: Book 20* (Cambridge, MA: Harvard University Press, 1965); cf. *AJ* 1.7.

9 Paul, Philippians 3.5 (King James version).

10 Acts of Paul 23.6 (King James version).

11 Paul, Galatians 1.13; Paul, Philippians 3.6; Acts 8.1–3.

12 Acts 21.17–28.

13 Acts 21.30–32.

14 Acts 21.33–40.

15 Acts 22.25–27.

16 Matthew 22.21; Mark 12.17; Luke 20.25.

17 Luke 3.14.

18 Governors of Judaea were only known as procurator from AD 44, starting with Cuspius Fadus.

19 Josephus, *De Bello Judaico* 3.7.23, trans. S. Kershaw.

20 See S. Kershaw (2013), op. cit., pp. 118–35.

21 The only substantial surviving account of the siege is Josephus, *De Bello Judaico* 5–6.

22 Josephus, *De Bello Judaico* 7.7.1, trans. H. St J. Thackeray, in Josephus. *The Jewish War, Volume III: Books 5–7* (Cambridge, MA: Harvard University Press, 1928).

23 Josephus, *De Bello Judaico* 7.9.1, trans. H. St J. Thackeray, op. cit.

24 Josephus, *De Bello Judaico* 7.10.1, trans. H. St J. Thackeray, op. cit.

25 Juvenal, *Satires* 6.156 ff., trans. P. Green, in Juvenal, *The Sixteen Satires*, translated with an introduction and notes by P. Green (3rd edn, London: Penguin, 1998).

26 Josephus, *AJ* 20.7.2. He promises to tell his readers what happened to Agrippa and his wife, but there is no further mention of them in his extant works.

27 Sibylline, *Oracle* 4.130–6, trans. A. E. Cooley and M. G. L. Cooley, *Pompeii and Herculaneum: A Sourcebook* (London and New York: Routledge, 2013), p, 56.

28 G. Alföldy, 'Eine Bauinschrift aus dem Colosseum', *ZPE*, no. 109 (1995), pp. 195–226. Not all scholars accept Alföldy's hypothesis, but the funding undoubtedly came from the spoils of war.

29 Suetonius, *Domitian* 12.2, trans. J. C. Rolfe, in Suetonius, *Lives of the Caesars, Volume II: Claudius. Nero. Galba, Otho, and Vitellius. Vespasian. Titus. Domitian. Lives of Illustrious Men: Grammarians and Retoricians. Poets (Terence. Virgil. Horace. Tibullus. Persius. Lucan). Lives of Pliny the Elder and Passienus Crispus* (Loeb Classical Library 38, Cambridge, MA: Harvard University Press, 1914).

30 Suetonius, *Domitian* 15.1; Dio Cassius 67.14.1 f.

31 *Historia Augusta, Hadrian* 14.2.

32 Pausanias 1.5.5, trans. P. Levi, in Pausanias, *Guide to Greece, Volume 1, Central Greece*, translated with an introduction by P. Levi (rev. edn, London: Penguin Classics, 1979).

33 His name appears in several different forms.

34 Jerome, *Against Rufinus* 3.31.

35 Eusebius, *Church History* 4.6.2, trans. K. Lake, in Eusebius, *Ecclesiastical History, Volume I: Books 1–5* (Cambridge, MA: Harvard University Press, 1926).

36 P. Yadin 2 52 = SB VIII 9843, ll. 11–15, trans. S. Kershaw. Text at http://www.papyri.info/ddbdp/sb;8;9843, accessed 22 August 2018. Most of the other letters found at the site were written in Hebrew and Aramaic.

37 Dio Cassius, 69.13.1, trans. E. Cary and H. B. Foster (1925), op. cit.

38 Eusebius, *Church History* 4.6.3, trans. K. Lake, op. cit.

39 Dio Cassius 69.14, trans. E. Carey, op. cit. We do not know how he arrived at these figures.

40 Eusebius, *Church History* 4.6.3.

19. Decebalus: Genocide in Dacia

1 Tacitus, *Histories* 1.2, trans. S. Kershaw.

2 Tacitus, *Germania* 30, trans. A. J. Church, W. J. Brodribb and L. Cerrato, op. cit.

3 Tacitus, *Germania* 31, trans. A. J. Church, W. J. Brodribb and L. Cerrato, op. cit.

4 Martial, *Epigrams* 2.2, trans. S. Kershaw.

5 Suetonius, *Julius Caesar* 44.3.

6 Appian 23; Suetonius, *Augustus* 63.

7 Dio Cassius 67.6.1, trans. E. Cary and H. B. Foster (1925), op. cit.

8 Ovid, *Metamorphoses* 1.717, 4.727.

9 Juvenal, *Satires* 8.201.

10 Valerius Maximus 3.2.12.

11 It could also be wielded with two hands. See M. Schmitz, *The Dacian Threat, 101–106 AD* (Armidale: Caeros, 2005), p. 31.

12 Dio Cassius 68.6.1, trans. E. Cary and H. B. Foster (1925), op. cit.

13 Dio Cassius 68.7.5, trans. E. Cary and H. B. Foster (1925), op. cit.
14 Dio Cassius 68.9.5–6, trans. E. Cary and H. B. Foster (1925), op. cit.
15 Dio Cassius 68.11–12.
16 Dio Cassius 68.14.4, trans. E. Cary and H. B. Foster (1925), op. cit.
17 Dio Cassius 68.15.1.
18 Dio Cassius 68.16.3, trans. E. Cary and H. B. Foster (1925), op. cit.
19 *CIL* 6.960.

20. Parthia, Persia and Palmyra

1 E. Gibbon, *The History of the Decline and Fall of the Roman Empire* (London: Strahan and Cadell, 1776–88), vol. 1, ch. 3.31.
2 Lucian, *How to Write History* 20.
3 Fronto, *Principia Historiae* 13–15, trans. A. R. Birley, 'The Wars and Revolts', in M. van Ackeren (ed.), *A Companion to Marcus Aurelius* (Chichester: Wiley-Blackwell, 2012), p. 219.
4 See S. Kershaw (2013), op. cit., pp. 216 ff.
5 E. Gibbon, op. cit., vol. 1, ch. 1.5.
6 Ulpian, in Justinian, *Digest* 1.5.17; Dio Cassius 78.9.
7 Procopius, *History of the Wars* 3.2.2–3, trans. H. B. Dewing, in Procopius, *History of the Wars, Volume II: Books 3–4 (Vandalic War)* (Cambridge, MA: Harvard University Press, 1916).
8 Zosimus, *New History* 1.29, trans. G. J. Vossius, *History of Count Zosimus, Sometime Advocate and Chancellor of the Roman Empire* (London: Green and Chaplin, 1814).
9 *Ka'ba-i Žardušt (ŠKZ)*, Gk. l. 49.
10 Mas'udi, *Moruj* II.159.
11 See L. Koenen and C. Römer, *Der Kölner Mani-Kodex. Abbildungen und diplomatischer Text* (Bonn: Habelt, 1985).
12 Around 100 kilometres south-west of Mosul in modern Iraq.
13 J. Henrichs and L. Koenen, 'Der Kölner Mani-Kodex', *Zeitschrift fur Papyriologie und Epigraphik*, no. 19 (1975), p. 18 (Greek text), p. 21 (translation).

14 In some sources (for example, Aurelius Victor and Eutropius) there are only two Gordians, with II and III being combined, although the author of *Historia Augusta, The Three Gordians* regards these authorities as 'uninformed'.

15 *Historia Augusta, The Three Gordians* 27.5.

16 V. G. Lukonin, *Kul'tura sasanidskogo Irana* (Moscow: Otcherki po istorii kul'tury, 1969), pp. 55, 164, 166, pl. II, no. 283; R. Ghirshman, 'Châpur Ier, "Roi de rois" sans couronne', *Acta Iranica*, no. 4 (1975), p. 258.

17 *Historia Augusta, The Three Gordians* 26.3, trans. D. Magie, in *The Scriptores Historiae Augustae, Volume II* (Cambridge, MA, and London: Harvard University Press, 1924).

18 *Historia Augusta, The Three Gordians* 26.6–27.3, trans. D. Magie, op. cit.

19 *Historia Augusta, The Three Gordians* 27.6.

20 Some sources implicate Philip the Arab's doctors in deliberately aggravating Timesitheus' condition.

21 *Roman Coins and Their Values* (RCV) III 8941; *Royal Imperial Coinage* (RIC) IV–3 69; *Roman Silver Coins* (RSC) 113.

22 P. Huyse, *Die dreisprachige Inschrift Šābuhrs I. An der Ka'ba-i Žardušt (ŠKZ)*, 2 vols, (London: SOAS, 1999), vol. 1, pp. 26–8.

23 Other interpretations read the image as one of Ardashir I's victories, an early relief of Shapur from before his coronation, and a later image of his defeat of Valerian.

24 *The Inscription of Shapur I at Naqsh-E Rustam in Fars* 4–5, trans. A. Maricq, 'Res Gestae Divi Saporis', *Syria*, no. 35 (1958), pp. 295–360.

25 *The Inscription of Shapur I* 4–5, trans. A. Maricq, op. cit.

26 *The Inscription of Shapur I* 4–5, trans. A. Maricq, op. cit.

27 *The Inscription of Shapur I* 9 ff., trans. A. Maricq, op. cit.

28 Lactantius, *On the Deaths of the Persecutors* 5.2 ff., trans. W. Fletcher and A. Fletcher, in A. Roberts and J. Donaldson (eds), *The Ante-Nicene Fathers, Vol. VII, Fathers of the Third and Fourth Centuries: Lactantius, Venantius, Asterius, Victorinus, Dionysius, Apostolic Teaching and Constitutions, Homily, and Liturgies* (Edinburgh: T. & T. Clark, 1886).

29 *Historia Augusta, The Two Gallieni* 17.1. The quotation is variously attributed to Anaxagoras and to Xenophon.

30 *Historia Augusta, The Two Gallieni* 16.1–17.9, trans. D. Magie, op. cit.

31 *Historia Augusta, The Thirty Tyrants* 30.15, trans. S. Kershaw.

32 *Historia Augusta, The Two Gallieni*, 13.3, trans. D. Magie, op. cit.

33 *Historia Augusta, The Two Gallieni* 13.5, trans. D. Magie, op. cit.

34 *Historia Augusta, The Two Gallieni* 14.4–11.

35 *Historia Augusta, The Two Gallieni* 25.3, trans. D. Magie, op. cit.

36 *Historia Augusta, Claudius* 18.4, trans. S. Kershaw.

37 *Historia Augusta, The Two Gallieni* 13.5. Establishing the actual sequence of events is fraught with difficulty: see, for example, A. Watson, *Aurelian and the Third Century* (London and New York: Routledge, 1999), p. 61.

38 For example, *Historia Augusta, Claudius* 12.5; Eutropius 9.12; Zonaras 12.26. Other sources give seventy-seven days or 'a few months (or days)', and there was at least time for most mints to strike coins.

39 Zosimus, *New History* 1.44.1, trans. G. J. Vossius, op. cit.

40 Zosimus, *New History* 1.44.2, trans. G. J. Vossius, op. cit.

41 Zosimus, *New History* 1.50.4, trans. G. J. Vossius, op. cit.

42 Zosimus, *New History* 1.51.1.

43 Zosimus, *New History* 1.52.3–4.

44 Zosimus, *New History* 1.53.1–3.

45 Zosimus, *New History* 1.54.2–3, trans. G. J. Vossius, op. cit.

46 Zosimus, *New History* 1.55.2, trans. G. J. Vossius, op. cit.

47 *Historia Augusta, Thirty Tyrants* 30.24 ff., trans. S. Kershaw.

48 *Historia Augusta, Probus* 21.4, trans. S. Kershaw.

49 *Historia Augusta, Probus* 19.7, trans. S. Kershaw.

50 See S. Kershaw (2013), op. cit., pp. 291 ff.

51 Tacitus, *Germania* 3.1–2, trans. A. J. Church, W. J. Brodribb and L. Cerrato, op. cit.; cf. Ammianus Marcellinus 26.7.17; M. P. Speidel, *Ancient Germanic Warriors: Warrior Styles from Trajan's Column to Icelandic Sagas* (London and New York: Routledge, 2004), pp. 101 ff.

52 *Comparison of Mosaic and Roman Law* 5.3, trans. N. Lewis and M. Reinhold (eds), *Roman Civilization: Selected Readings, Volume*

II, The Empire (3rd edn, New York: Columbia University Press, 1990), p. 549.

53 See, for example, T. D. Barnes, 'Constantine and the Christians of Persia', *Journal of Roman Studies*, no. 75 (1985), pp. 126–36.

54 See 'Kidarites', *Encyclopædia Iranica*, online edition (2009), http://www.iranicaonline.org/articles/kidarites, accessed 2 September 2018.

55 See, for example, Ammianus Marcellinus 16.9.4, 17.5.1, 19.1.7–2.1.

56 Ammianus Marcellinus 24.6, trans. S. Kershaw.

57 Libanius 28.254–5.

58 Ammianus Marcellinus 25.3.6, trans. S, Kershaw; cf. Libanius 18.269–70; Eutropius, *Breviarium* 10.16.

59 See G. W. Bowersock, *Julian the Apostate* (Cambridge, MA: Harvard University Press, 1978), pp. 123–4.

60 Other interpretations are available: see P. Calmeyer, 'Vom Reisehut zur Kaiserkrone', *AMI*, no. 10 (1977), pp. 168–88; A. S. Shahbazi, 'Ardašir II', *Encyclopædia Iranica*, vol. II (New York: Columbia University, 1987), pp. 380–1.

61 Ammianus Marcellinus 25.5.4, trans. W. Hamilton, op. cit.

62 Ammianus Marcellinus 25.7.13, trans. S. Kershaw.

63 Ammianus Marcellinus 25.10.

64 Ammianus Marcellinus 26.1.3, trans. W. Hamilton, op. cit

65 Ammianus Marcellinus 26.5.4, trans. S. Kershaw.

21. Fritigern: The Gothic Hannibal

1 Ammianus Marcellinus 31.4.9, trans. S. Kershaw.

2 Anon., *On Matters Military* 6.1, trans. G. Halsall, op. cit., p. 46. Written in AD 360s–370s.

3 Ammianus Marcellinus 29.4.1, trans. W. Hamilton, op. cit.

4 Ammianus Marcellinus 26.6.15.

5 See, for example, P. Heather, *The Goths* (Oxford: Blackwell, 1996), pp. 51–93; H. Roued Olsen, 'Reflections on Culture Connections', *LAG*, no. 8 (2007), http://www.academia. edu/1786963/Reflections_on_culture_connections_-_ Examining_connections_between_South_Scandinavia_and_

the_Sintana_de_Mures_Cernjachov_culture_from_AD_270-410_Period_C2_to_D1, accessed 2 September 2018.

6   Cassiodorus lived from AD 490 to *c.*585. His work on the Goths is no longer extant.

7   Quoted in P. Brown, *The Making of Late Antiquity* (Cambridge, MA, and London: Harvard University Press, 1978), p. 123.

8   Lactantius, *On the Deaths of the Persecutors* 4.3, trans. A. Fletcher, in A. Roberts and J. Donaldson (eds), *The Ante-Nicene Fathers Vol. VII, Fathers of the Third and Fourth Centuries: Lactantius, Venantius, Asterius, Victorinus, Dionysius, Apostolic Teaching and Constitutions, Homily, and Liturgies* (Edinburgh: T. & T. Clark, 1886).

9   Themistius, *Oration* 10.135, trans. D. Moncur, in P. J. Heather and J. F. Matthews, *The Goths in the Fourth Century* (Liverpool: Liverpool University Press, 1991), p. 40.

10 Ammianus Marcellinus, 30.6.6, trans. W. Hamilton, op. cit.

11 The Alani, aka Alans, were a bellicose, horse-breeding, nomadic, pastoral people from the steppes to the north-east of the Black Sea.

12 Ambrose, *Expositio evangelii secubdun Lucam* 10.10, trans. S. Kershaw. The Taifals, aka Tayfals (*Taifali, Taifalae* or *Theifali* in Latin), were of Germanic/Sarmatian origin.

13 Virgil, *Georgics* 2.105 f., trans. C. Day Lewis, op. cit.

14 A. Goldsworthy, *The Fall of the West: The Slow Death of the Roman Superpower* (London: Weidenfeld & Nicolson, 2009), p. 261.

15 Ammianus Marcellinus 31.4.5, trans. J. C. Rolfe, in Ammianus Marcellinus, *Ammianus Marcellinus with an English Translation*, vol. 3 (Cambridge, MA: Harvard University Press, 1940).

16 Ammianus Marcellinus 31.5.7, trans. J. C. Rolfe (1940), op. cit.

17 Ammianus Marcellinus 31.10.1, trans. S. Kershaw.

18 Socrates Scholasticus, *Church History* 4.33.

19 For a bibliography relating to the Battle of Adrianople, see http://www.uvm.edu/~bsaylor/rome/adrianople.html, accessed 3 September 2018; see also http://awmc.unc.edu/wordpress/wp-content/uploads/2012/09/13-1_Major_Battle_Sites_of_the_Fourth_Century.pdf, accessed 3 September 2018.

20 Themistius, *Orations* 16.210b–c, trans. P. J. Heather and D.

Moncur, in Themestius, *Politics, Philosophy and Empire in the Fourth Century: Themistius' Select Orations*, translated with commentary by P. J. Heather and D. Moncur (Liverpool: Liverpool University Press, 2001).

21 Themistius, *Orations* 34, trans. R. J. Panella, in Themestius, *The Private Orations of Themistius* (Berkeley: University of California Press, 2000).

22. Alaric the Goth: Sacker of Rome

1 Theodoret, *Church History* 5.17.3.

2 See G. Halsall, *Worlds of Arthur: Facts and Fictions of the Dark Ages* (Oxford: Oxford University Press, 2013), p. 255; cf. https://www.theguardian.com/books/2017/jan/16/mary-beard-arron-banks-eu-ukip-twitter-rome, accessed 17 June 2018.

3 P. J. Heather, op. cit., p. 139.

4 Eusebius, *Life of Constantine* 1.31, trans. S. Moorhead and D. Stuttard, *AD 410: The Year that Shook Rome* (London: British Museum Press, 2010), p. 41.

5 Rufinus, *Historia Eremitica* 9.33, trans. A. Cameron, *The Later Roman Empire: AD 284–430* (London: Fontana, 1993), p. 76.

6 Orosius, *Histories Against the* Pagans 7.35.19, trans. I. W. Raymond, op. cit.

7 Eunapius fr. 62, trans. W. C. Wright, *Lives of the Philosophers and Sophists* (Cambridge, MA: Harvard University Press, 1921); cf. Zosimus, *New History* 6.1–4.

8 Jordanes, *Getica* 29.46, trans. C. C. Mierow, op. cit.

9 Zosimus, *New History* 5.7.5–6, trans. S. Moorhead and D. Stuttard, op. cit., p. 72.

10 Eunapius fr. 897, trans. S. Moorhead and D. Stuttard, op. cit., p. 72.

11 See J. Long, *Claudian's* In Eutropium: *Or, How, When, and Why to Slander a Eunuch* (Chapel Hill and London: University of North Carolina Press, 1996).

12 See M. Kulikowkski, 'Barbarians in Gaul, usurpers in Britain', *Britannia*, no. 31 (2000), pp. 325–45.

13 Gregory of Tours, *Libri Historiarum* (*LH*) 1.9; cf. Orosius, *Histories Against the Pagans* 7.40.3.

14 Orientius, *Commonitorium* 2.184, trans. S. Kershaw.

15 Zosimus, *New History* 5.29.9, trans. S. Kershaw. The quotation comes from Cicero, *Philippics* 12.14.

16 Jerome, *Letter to Principia* 1.121.

17 Zosimus, *New History* 5.40.3, trans. R. T. Ridley, op. cit.

18 Zosimus, *New History* 5.41.7, trans. R. T. Ridley, op. cit.

19 Zosimus, *New History* 5.50.2–3, trans. R. T. Ridley, op. cit.

20 Zosimus, *New History* 5.6.11.

21 AD 240–320.

22 Lactantius, *Divine Institutes* 7.15, trans. N. Lewis and M. Reinhold (eds), op. cit., p. 628.

23 Orosius, *History Against the Pagans* 7.39.

24 Jerome, *Letter to Principia* 13, trans. S. Moorhead and D. Stuttard, op. cit., p. 129 ff.

25 Augustine, *City of God* 1.7 ff., trans. M. Dods in P. Schaff, *The Nicene and Post-Nicene Fathers of the Christian Church, First Series, Vol. 2* (Edinburgh: T. & T. Clark, 1890).

26 Jerome, *Letter to Demetrias* 7, trans. S. Moorhead and D. Stuttard, op. cit., p. 129 ff; the quotation comes from Virgil, *Aeneid* 10.79.

27 Jerome, *In Ezekiel*, III *Praef.*, trans. B. Ward-Perkins, *The Fall of Rome and the End of Civilization* (Oxford: Oxford University Press, 2005), p. 28.

28 Jordanes, *Getica* 30.158, trans. W. S. Davis, *Readings in Ancient History, Illustrative Extracts from the Sources, II, Rome and the West* (Boston, New York and Chicago: Allyn and Bacon, 1913).

29 http://www.merlinburrows.com/found-treasure-tomb-king-alaric-410, accessed 7 September 2018.

23. Attila the Hun: Born to Shake the Nations

1 Jordanes, *Getica* 24.121, trans. S. Kershaw. See pp. 410 ff.

2 Jordanes, *Getica* 24.121–2, trans. C. C. Mierow, op. cit.

3 Ammianus Marcellinus 31.2.2 f., trans. S. Moorhead and D. Stuttard, op. cit., p. 54 f.

4 Ammianus Marcellinus 31.2.7 f., trans. S. Moorhead and D. Stuttard, op. cit.

5 See, for example, Herodotus 4.100.

6 Jordanes, *Getica* 35.180, trans. C. C. Mierow, op. cit.

7 Jordanes, *Getica* 35.182, trans. C. C. Mierow, op. cit.

8 Priscus of Panion fr. 10, trans. S. Mitchell, *A History of the Later Roman Empire AD 284–641: The Transformation of the Ancient World* (Oxford: Blackwell, 2007), p. 105.

9 His third consulship fell in AD 446.

10 Gildas, *De Excidio et Conquestu Britanniae* 1.20, trans. S. Kershaw.

11 The Romans knew him as *Gaisericus* or *Geisericus*; modern works also call him Geiseric or Genseric.

12 Jordanes, *Getica* 35.180, trans. C. C. Mierow, op. cit.

13 Priscus fr. 8, in *Fragmenta Historicorum Graecorum*, trans. J. B. Bury.

14 Priscus fr. 8, in *Fragmenta Historicorum Graecorum*, trans. J. B. Bury.

15 Jordanes, *Getica* 49.254, trans. C. C. Mierow, op. cit.

16 Jordanes, *Getica* 49.254, trans. C. C. Mierow, op. cit.

17 Jordanes, *Getica* 50.261, trans. C. C. Mierow, op. cit.

18 *Weser-Zeitung* (28 July 1900), second morning edition, p. 1, trans. S. Kershaw.

24. Barbarian Warlords: Gaiseric and the Fall of Rome

1 E. Gibbon, op. cit., vol. 1, chapter 10.3.

2 For a translation of the letter, see E. G. Holt, *A Documentary History of Art* (Princeton: Princeton University Press, 1957), p. 251.

3 A. Pope, *An Essay on Criticism* (London: W. Lewis, 1711), ll. 686 ff.

4 J. T. Desaguliers, *Course in Experimental Philosophy* (London: J. Senex, W. Innys and R. Manby, and J. Osborn and T. Longman, 1734), pp. 1–2.

5 W. Cowper, 'On the Burning of Lord Mansfield's Library, Together with his MSS. by the Mob, in the Month of June 1780' (1780).

6 H. Grégoire, *Oeuvres de l'abbé Grégoire* (Nendeln: KTO Press, 1977), vol. 2, pp. 257–78; dated 14 Fructidor An. II (31 August 1794).

7 H. Grégoire, *Mémoires de L'Abbé Grégoire*, edited by J.-M. Leniaud (Paris: Éditions de Santé, 1989), p. 60.

8 Pliny, *NH* 4.99, trans. H. A. Rackham (1949), op. cit.

9 Tacitus, *Germania* 2.3–4, trans. A. J. Church, W. J. Brodribb and L. Cerrato, op. cit.

10 Tacitus, *Germania* 2.5, trans. A. J. Church, W. J. Brodribb and L. Cerrato, op. cit.

11 Tacitus, *Germania* 43.3–4.

12 Ptolemy 2.11.18.

13 *Historia Augusta, Marcus Aurelius Antoninus* 12.13.

14 *Historia Augusta, Marcus Aurelius Antoninus* 14.2, trans. S. Kershaw.

15 *Historia Augusta, Marcus Aurelius Antoninus* 14.6, trans. S. Kershaw.

16 Dio Cassius 72.12.2, trans. S. Kershaw.

17 Dio Cassius 72.12.1–2, trans. E. Cary and H. B. Foster, in Dio Cassius, *Roman History, Volume IX: Books 71–80* (Cambridge, MA: Harvard University Press, 1927).

18 See S. Kershaw (2013), op. cit., pp. 139 ff.

19 Dio Cassius 72.3.1–2.

20 Dio Cassius 77.20.3–4, trans. E. Cary and H. B. Foster (1927), op. cit.

21 See S. Kershaw (2013), op. cit., pp. 168 ff.

22 Zosimus, *New History* 1.48, trans. R. T. Ridley, op. cit.

23 Dexippus fr. 7.

24 Zosimus, *New History* 1.68.1–2, trans. R. T. Ridley, op. cit.

25 Jordanes, *Getica* 2.114, trans. C. C. Mierow, op. cit.

26 Jordanes, *Getica* 2.114, trans. C. C. Mierow, op. cit.

27 See, for example, Zosimus, *New History* 6.3.2; Orosius, *Histories Against the Pagans* 7.40.4.

28 Jerome, *Letter* 123.16, trans. W. H. Fremantle, G. Lewis and W. G. Martley, *Nicene and Post-Nicene Fathers, Second Series, Vol. 6*, edited by Philip Schaff and Henry Wace (Buffalo, NY: Christian Literature Publishing Co., 1893).

29 Hydatius, *Chronicle* 297.16 Lem. 48, trans. R. W. Burgess, in *The Chronicle of Hydatius and the Consularia Constantinopolitana: Two*

Contemporary Accounts of the Final Years of the Roman Empire (Oxford: Oxford University Press, 1993).

30 Hydatius, *Chronicle* 297.17 Lem. 49, trans. R. W. Burgess, op. cit.

31 Olympiodorus fr. 29.1.

32 Hydatius, *Chronicle* 301.1 Lem. 86.

33 Hydatius, *Chronicle* 301.4 Lem. 89, trans. R. W. Burgess, op. cit.

34 Hydatius, *Chronicle* 302.5 Lem. 90; Victor of Vita, *History of the Vandal Persecution* 1.2. The date of the crossing is problematical: see R. W. Mathisen, 'Sigisvult the patrician, Maximinus the Arian and political stratagems in the Western Roman Empire, c.425–507', *Early Medieval Europe*, no. 8 (1999), p. 177, n. 6; M. E. Gil Egea, *África en tiempos de los vándalos: continuidad y mutaciones de las estruturas sociopolíticas romanas* (Alcalá-de-Harenas: Universidad de Alcalá, Servicio de Publicaciones, 1998), pp. 179–81.

35 See Procopius, *History of the Wars* 3.3.30–6.

36 Leo, *Epistula* 12.8, 12.11.

37 Possidius, *Vita Augustini* 28, trans. A. Fellowes, in Possidius, *The Life of Saint Augustine by Possidius Bishop of Calama* (Villakova, PA: Augustinian Press, 1988).

38 Procopius, *History of the Wars* 3.3.35–6, trans. H. B. Dewing, op. cit.

39 John of Antioch fr. 201.4–5, trans. C. D. Gordon, *The Age of Attila: Fifth-century Byzantium and the Barbarians* (Ann Arbor: University of Michigan Press, 1960), pp. 52–3. Procopius, *History of the Wars* 1.4.16–28, has a story that Optila and Thraustila were put up to it because Petronius Maximus' wife had been raped by Valentinian III and may have committed suicide as a result.

40 Hydatius, *Chronicle* 308.31 Lem. 162. There is controversy over the identity of the daughter: other sources say she is Valentinian III's younger daughter, Galla Placidia the Younger.

41 See, for example, Hydatius, *Chronicle* 308.31a.455; Priscus fr. 20; Procopius, *History of the Wars* 1.4.38–9.

42 Procopius, *History of the Wars* 2.9.5, 1.5.4.

43 Malchus, *Chron.* 366, trans. R. C. Blockley, *The Fragmentary Classicising Historians of the Later Roman Empire: Eunapius, Olympiodorus, Priscus and Malchus* (Liverpool: Cairns, 1983).

44 Sidonius, *Carmina 7*.

45 Sidonius, *Carmina 7*.587–598, trans. W. B. Anderson, in Sidonius, *Poems, Letters, Books 1–2*, with an English translation, introduction and notes by W. B. Anderson (Cambridge, MA: Harvard University Press, 1936), p.169.

46 John of Antioch fr. 202, trans. C. D. Gordon, op. cit., p.116.

Epilogue

1 W. C. Sellar and R. J. Yeatman, *1066 and All That: A Memorable History of England, comprising all the parts you can remember, including 103 Good Things, 5 Bad Kings and 2 Genuine Dates* (London: Methuen & Co., 1930).

2 P. Brown, *The World of Late Antiquity, AD 150–750* (New York: Harcourt Brace Jovanovich, 1971).

3 W. Goffart, *Barbarians and Romans AD 418–584: The Techniques of Accommodation* (Princeton: Princeton University Press, 1980), p. 35.

4 R. W. Mathisen and D. Shanzer, *Society and Culture in Late Antique Gaul: Revisiting the Sources* (Aldershot: Ashgate, 2001), p. 1, 2, n. 4.

5 R. W. Mathisen and D. Shanzer (eds) (2011), op. cit., introduction.

6 J. G. Herder, *Outlines of a Philosophy of History*, trans. T. Churchill (London: Johnson, 1800), p. 421.

7 Byron, *Childe Harold's Pilgrimage, Canto IV* (London: John Murray, 1818), stanza CVII.

8 C. P. Cavafy, 'Waiting for the Barbarians', trans. E. Keeley and P. Sherrard, in C. P. Cavafy, *Collected Poems* (Princeton: Princeton University Press, 1975).

Bibliography

Aillagon, J.-J. (ed.), *Rome and the Barbarians: The Birth of a New World* (Milan: Skira, 2008).

Alföldi, A., *Early Rome and the Latins* (Ann Arbor: University of Michigan Press, 1965).

Astin, A. E., *Scipio Aemilianus* (Oxford: Clarendon Press, 1967).

Balsdon, J. P. D. V., *Romans and Aliens* (Chapel Hill: University of North Carolina Press, 1979).

Barrett, A. A. (ed.), *Lives of the Caesars* (Oxford: Blackwell, 2008).

Batty, R., *Rome and the Nomads* (Oxford: Oxford University Press, 2007).

Beckman, M., *The Column of Marcus Aurelius: The Genesis and Meaning of a Roman Imperial Monument* (Chapel Hill: University of North Carolina Press, 2011).

Bellen, H., *Metus Galliern – Metus Punicus. Zum Furchtmotiv in der romischen Republik* (Wiesbaden: F. Steiner, 1985).

Beloch, K. J., *Römische Geschichte bis zum Beginn der punischen Kriege* (Leipzig: W. De Gruyter, 1926).

Bennett, J., *Trajan Optimus Princeps: A Life and Times* (London and New York: Routledge, 1997).

Birley, A. R., *Hadrian, The Restless Emperor* (London: Routledge, 1997).

——, *Marcus Aurelius: A Biography* (2nd edn, London: Routledge, 1987).

——, *Septimius Severus: The African Emperor* (rev. edn, New Haven: Yale University Press, 1988).

Boatwright, M. T., *Hadrian and the City of Rome* (Princeton: Princeton University Press, 1987).

——, *Peoples of the Roman World* (Cambridge: Cambridge University Press, 2012).

Boethius, A., *The Golden House of Nero* (Ann Arbor: University of Michigan Press, 1960).

Bonfante, L. (ed.), *The Barbarians of Ancient Europe: Realities and Interactions* (New York: Cambridge University Press, 2011).

Bowersock, G. W., *Roman Arabia* (Cambridge, MA: Harvard University Press, 1983).

Brauer, G. C., *The Young Emperors, Rome, AD 193–244* (New York: Thomas Y. Crowell, 1967).

Braund, D., *Rome and the Friendly King: The Character of the Client Kingship* (London: Croom Helm, 1984).

Breaugh, M., *The Plebeian Experience: A Discontinuous History of Political Freedom* (New York: Columbia University Press, 2013).

Breeze, D. J., *The Northern Frontiers of Roman Britain* (London: Batsford, 1982).

Broughton, T. R. S., *The Magistrates of the Roman Republic, Vol. 1: 509 BC–100 BC* (Cleveland, Ohio: Case Western Reserve University Press, 1951).

Brown, P., *The Making of Late Antiquity* (Cambridge, MA, and London: Harvard University Press, 1978).

——, *The World of Late Antiquity, AD 150–750* (New York: Harcourt Brace Jovanovich, 1971).

Bryce, T., *The Trojans and Their Neighbours* (London: Routledge, 2006).

Bury, J. B., *The Invasion of Europe by the Barbarians* (London: Macmillan, 1928).

Cameron, A., *The Later Roman Empire: AD 284–430* (London: Fontana, 1993).

Cartledge, P., *The Greeks* (Oxford: Oxford University Press, 1993).

Champion, J., *Pyrrhus of Epirus* (Barnsley: Pen & Sword Military, 2009).

Chisholm, K. and J. Ferguson (eds), *Rome: The Augustan Age* (Oxford: Oxford University Press, 1981).

Christie, N., *The Fall of the Western Roman Empire: An Archaeological and Historical Perspective* (London and New York: Bloomsbury Academic, 2011).

Colledge, M. A. R., *Parthian Art* (Ithaca: Cornell University Press, 1977).

Cornell, T. J., *The Beginnings of Rome: Italy and Rome from the Bronze Age to the Punic Wars (c.1000–264 BC)* (Routledge History of the Ancient World) (London and New York: Routledge, 1995).

Curchin, L. A., *Roman Spain: Conquest and Assimilation* (London: Routledge, 1991).

Curtis, V. S. and S. Stewart (eds), *The Age of the Parthians* (London and New York: I. B. Tauris, 2007).

Dauge, Y. A., 'Le Barbare: Recherches sur la conception romaine de la barbarie et de la civilisation', *Annales, Économies, Sociétés, Civilisations*, vol. 38, no. 4 (1983), pp. 975–7.

De Beer, G., *Hannibal's March* (London: Sidgwick & Jackson, 1967).

Derow, P. S., A. Erskine and J. Crawley, *Rome, Polybius, and the East* (Oxford: Oxford University Press, 2014).

Drinkwater, J. and H. Elton, *Fifth-century Gaul: A Crisis of Identity?* (Cambridge: Cambridge University Press, 1992).

Dudley, D. and G. Webster, *The Roman Conquest of Britain* (London: Batsford, 1965).

Duggan, A., *He Died Old: Mithradates Eupator King of Pontus* (London: Faber & Faber, 1958).

Eck, W., 'The Bar Kokhba Revolt: The Roman Point of View', *Journal of Roman Studies*, no. 28, (1999), pp. 76–89.

Errington, R. M., *History of the Hellenistic World* (Malden and Oxford: Blackwell, 2008).

Esmonde-Cleary, A. S., *The Ending of Roman Britain* (London: Routledge, 1991).

Gardner, A., *An Archaeology of Identity: Soldiers & Society in Late Roman Britain* (Walnut Creek: Left Coast Press, 2007).

Garipzanov, I. H., P. J. Geary and P. Urbanczyk, *Franks, Northmen, and Slavs: Identities and State Formation in Early Medieval Europe* (Turnhout: Brepols, 2008).

Garnsey, P. and C. Humphress, *The Evolution of the Late Antique World* (Cambridge: Orchard Academic, 2001).

Garoufalias, P., *Pyrrhus, King of Epirus* (London: Stacey International, 1979).

Gibbon, E., *The History of the Decline and Fall of the Roman Empire* (London: Strahan & Cadell, 1776–88).

Glazer, N. and P. Moynihan (eds), *Ethnicity: Theory and Experience* (Cambridge, MA: Harvard University Press, 1975).

Goffart, W., *Barbarians and Romans AD 418–585: The Techniques of Accommodation* (Princeton: Princeton University Press, 1980).

Goldsworthy, A., *The Fall of the West: The Death of the Roman Superpower* (London: Weidenfeld & Nicolson, 2009).

Goodman, M., *Rome and Jerusalem: The Clash of Ancient Civilizations* (London: Allen Lane, 2007).

Gruen, E. S., *Culture and National Identity in Republican Rome* (London: Duckworth, 1993).

——, *Diaspora: Jews Amidst Greeks and Romans* (Cambridge, MA: Harvard University Press, 2002).

——, *The Hellenistic World and the Coming of Rome* (Berkeley, Los Angeles and London: University of California Press, 1984).

Hall, E., *Inventing the Barbarian: Greek Self-Determination Through Tragedy* (Oxford: Oxford University Press, 1989).

Hall, J. M., *Ethnic Identity in Greek Antiquity* (Cambridge: Cambridge University Press, 1997).

——, *Hellenicity: Between Ethnicity and Culture* (Chicago: University of Chicago Press, 2002).

Halsall, G., *Barbarian Migrations and the Roman West, 376–568* (Cambridge: Cambridge University Press, 2009).

——, *Worlds of Arthur: Facts & Fictions of the Dark Ages* (Oxford: Oxford University Press, 2013).

Hammond, N. G. L., *Epirus: The Geography, the Ancient Remains, the History and Topography of Epirus and Adjacent Areas* (Oxford: Clarendon Press, 1967).

Harnecker, J., *Arminius, Varus and the Battlefield at Kalkriese: An Introduction to the Archaeological Investigations and Their Results* (Bramsche: Rasch Verlag, 2004).

Harrel, S., *The Nisibis War: The Defence of the Roman East AD 337–363* (Barnsley: Pen & Sword Military, 2016).

Harrison, T. (ed.), *Greeks and Barbarians* (Edinburgh: Edinburgh University Press, 2002).

Hartog, F., *The Mirror of Herodotus: The Representation of the Other in the Writing of History* (Berkeley: University of California Press, 1988).

Haynes, H., *Tacitus on Imperial Rome: The History of Make-Believe* (Berkeley and Los Angeles: University of California Press, 2003).

Heather, P. J., *The Fall of Rome: A New History* (London: Macmillan, 2005).

——, *The Goths* (Oxford: Blackwell, 1996).

Heather, P. J. and J. F. Matthews, *The Goths in the Fourth Century* (Liverpool: Liverpool University Press, 1991).

Hoddinott, R. F., *The Thracians* (Ancient Peoples & Places, 98) (London: Thames & Hudson, 1981).

Horsfall, N., *The Culture of the Roman Plebs* (London: Duckworth, 2003).

Hughes, I., *Stilicho: The Vandal Who Saved Rome* (Barnsley: Pen & Sword Military, 2010).

Hunink, V., *Oh Happy Place! Pompeii in 1000 Graffiti*, selected, translated and annotated by V. Hunink (Sant'Oreste: Apeiron, 2014).

Johnstone, A. C., *The Sons of Remus: Identity in Roman Gaul and Spain* (Cambridge, MA, and London: Harvard University Press, 2017).

Jones, A. H. M., *Constantine and the Conversion of Europe* (London: Macmillan, 1948).

——, *The Later Roman Empire: A Social, Administrative and Economic Survey* (Oxford: Basil Blackwell, 1964).

Jones, B. W., *The Emperor Titus* (London: Croom Helm, 1984).

Jones, T., *Barbarians: An Alternative History* (London: BBC Books, 2006).

Katz, S., *The Jews in the Visigothic and Frankish Kingdoms of Spain and Gaul* (Cambridge, MA: Mediaeval Academy of America, 1937).

Keay, S. J., *Roman Spain* (London: British Museum Publications, 1988).

Kelly, C., *The End of Empire: Attila the Hun and the Fall of Rome* (New York and London: Norton, 2009).

Kershaw, S. P., *A Brief Guide to Classical Civilization* (London: Robinson, 2010).

——, *A Brief Guide to the Greek Myths* (London: Robinson, 2007).

——, *A Brief History of the Roman Empire* (London: Robinson, 2013).

Kneppe, A., *Metus temporum: zur Bedeutung von Angst in Politik und Gesellschaft der römischen Kaiserzeit des 1. und 2. Jhdts. n. Chr.* (Stuttgart: Steiner, 1994).

Kulikowski, M., *Rome's Gothic Wars: From the Third Century to Alaric* (Cambridge: Cambridge University Press, 2007).

Lane, J., *The Siege of Masada* (Brisbane: InHouse Publishing, 2015).

Lefkovitz, M., *Not Out of Africa. How Afrocentrism Became an Excuse to Teach Myth as History* (New York: New Republic and Basic Books, 1996).

Lenski, N. E., *Failure of Empire: Valens and the Roman State in the Fourth Century AD* (Berkeley and Los Angeles: University of California Press, 2002).

Lepper, F. A., *Trajan's Parthian War* (Oxford: Oxford University Press, 1948).

Lepper, F. and S. Frere, *Trajan's Column: A New Edition of the Cichorius Plates* (Gloucester: Alan Sutton, 1988).

Lévêque, P., *Pyrrhos* (Bibliothèque des Écoles françaises d'Athènes et de Rome, Fascicule 185) (Paris: E. de Boccard, 1957).

Levick, B., *Claudius* (New Haven: Yale University Press, 1990).

——, *Vespasian* (London and New York: Routledge, 1999).

Long, J., *Claudian's In Eutropium: Or, How, When, and Why to Slander a Eunuch* (Chapel Hill and London: University of North Carolina Press, 1996).

MacMullen, R., *Corruption and the Decline of Rome* (New Haven and London: Yale University Press, 1988).

Maenchen-Helfen, O., *The World of the Huns: Studies in Their History and Culture* (Berkeley: University of California Press, 1973).

Mathisen, R. W. and D. Shanzer (eds), *Romans, Barbarians, and the Transformation of the Roman World* (Farnham: Ashgate, 2011).

Mattern, S. P., *Rome and the Enemy: Imperial Strategy in the Principate* (Berkeley: University of California Press, 1999).

Matthews, J., *Western Aristocracies and Imperial Court AD 364–425* (Oxford: Clarendon Press, 1975).

Matyszak, P., *The Enemies of Rome: From Hannibal to Attila the Hun* (London: Thames & Hudson, 2004).

Mayor, A., *The Poison King: The Life and Legend of Mithradates, Rome's Deadliest Enemy* (Princeton: Princeton University Press, 2010).

McGing, B. C., *The Foreign Policy of Mithridates VI Eupator King of Pontus* (Leiden: E. J. Brill, 1986).

Meijer, F., *Emperors Don't Die in Bed* (London and New York: Routledge, 2004).

Meijer, F. J., 'Cato's African Figs', *Mnemosyne,* Fourth Series, vol. 37, nos 1/2 (1984), pp. 117–24.

Mellor, R., *The Roman Historians* (New York: Routledge, 1999).

Merrills, A. H. (ed.), *Vandals, Romans and Berbers: New Perspectives on Late Antique North Africa* (Aldershot and Burlington: Ashgate, 2004).

Merrills, A. H. and R. Miles, *The Vandals* (Chichester: Wiley-Blackwell, 2014).

Mildenberg, L., *The Coinage of the Bar Kokhba War* (Aarau-Frankfort am Main: Verlag Sauerländer, 1984).

Millar, F., *The Roman Near East, 31 BC–AD 337* (Cambridge, MA. and London: Harvard University Press, 1993).

Miller, M., 'Persians in the Greek Imagination', *Mediterranean Archaeology,* nos 19/20 (2006), pp. 109–23.

Mitchell, L., *Panhellenism and the Barbarian in Archaic and Classical Greece* (Swansea: Classical Press of Wales, 2007).

Mitchell, S., *A History of the Later Roman Empire AD 284–641: The Transformation of the Ancient World* (Oxford: Blackwell, 2007).

Moorhead, S. and D. Stuttard, *AD 410: The Year that Shook Rome* (London: British Museum Press, 2010).

Mouritsen, H., *Plebs and Politics in the Late Roman Republic* (Cambridge: Cambridge University Press, 2001).

Murdoch, A., *Rome's Greatest Defeat: Massacre in the Teutoburg Forest* (Stroud: History Press, 2006).

Netzer, E., 'The Rebels' Archives at Masada', *Israel Exploration Journal,* vol. 54, no. 2 (2004), pp. 218–29.

Peddie, J., *Invasion: The Roman Conquest of Britain* (New York: St Martin's Press, 1987).

Price, S. R. F., *Rituals and Power: The Roman Imperial Cult in Asia Minor* (Cambridge: Cambridge University Press, 1984).

Raaflaub, K. A., *Social Struggles in Archaic Rome: New Perspectives on the Conflict of the Orders* (2nd edn, Oxford: Blackwell, 2004).

Richardson, J. S., *Hispaniae: Spain and the Development of Roman Imperialism, 218–82 BC* (Cambridge: Cambridge University Press, 1986).

——, *The Romans in Spain (A History of Spain)* (Oxford and Cambridge, MA: Blackwell, 1996).

Richmond, I. A., 'The Roman Siege-Works of Masada, Israel', *Journal of Roman Studies*, no. 52 (1962), pp. 142–55.

Ross Holloway, R., *The Archaeology of Early Rome and Latium* (London and New York: Routledge, 1994).

Rossi, L., *Trajan's Column and the Dacian Wars*, trans. J. M. C. Toynbee (London: Thames & Hudson, 1971).

Rousseau, P. (ed.), *A Companion to Late Antiquity* (Oxford: Wiley-Blackwell, 2009).

Said, E., *Orientalism* (New York: Pantheon, 1978).

Sampson, G. C., *The Crisis of Rome: The Jugurthine Wars and the Rise of Marius* (Barnsley: Pen & Sword Military, 2010).

Schäfer, P., *A History of the Jews in Antiquity* (London and New York: Routledge, 1995).

——, *Judaeophobia: Attitudes towards the Jews in the Ancient World* (Cambridge, MA, and London: Harvard University Press, 1997).

Schäfer, P. (ed.), *The Bar Kokhba War Reconsidered: New Perspectives on the Second Jewish Revolt Against Rome (Texts and Studies in Ancient Judaism)* (Tübingen: Mohr Siebeck, 2003).

Shahîd, I., *Rome and the Arabs: A Prolegomenon to the Study of Byzantium and the Arabs* (Dumbarton Oaks: Harvard University Press, 1984).

Shaw, B. D., *Rulers, Nomads and Christians in Roman North Africa* (Aldershot and Brookfield: Variorum, 1995).

Sherwin-White, A. N., *Racial Prejudice in Imperial Rome* (The Gray Memorial Lectures, 1965–6) (Cambridge: University Press, 1967).

——, *Roman Foreign Policy in the East 168 BC to AD 1* (London: Duckworth, 1984).

Silva, L., *Viriathus and the Lusitanian Resistance to Rome 155–139 BC* (Barnsley: Pen & Sword Military, 2013).

Smallwood, E. M., *The Jews under Roman Rule: From Pompey to Diocletian* (Leiden: E. J. Brill, 1976).

Snowden, F. M., *Before Color Prejudice: The Ancient View of Blacks* (Cambridge, MA: Harvard University Press, 1983).

——, 'Misconceptions about African Blacks in the Ancient Mediterranean World: Specialists and Afrocentrists', *Arion: A Journal of Humanities and the Classics*, Third Series, vol. 4, no. 3 (Winter 1997), pp. 28–50.

Southern, P., *Empress Zenobia: Palmyra's Rebel Queen* (London and New York: Continuum, 2008).

Speidel, M. P., *Ancient Germanic Warriors: Warrior Styles from Trajan's Column to Icelandic Sagas* (London and New York: Routledge, 2004).

Swain, S., *Hellenism and Empire: Language, Classicism and Power in the Greek World, AD 50–250* (Oxford: Clarendon Press, 1996).

Thompson, E. A., *The Early Germans* (Oxford: Clarendon Press, 1965).

——, *The Huns*, revised and edited by P. Heather (Oxford: Wiley-Blackwell, 1999).

Thompson, L. A., *Romans and Blacks* (Norman: University of Oklahoma Press, 1989).

Vogt, J., *Ancient Slavery and the Ideal of Man*, trans. Thomas Wiedemann (Cambridge, MA: Harvard University Press, 1975).

Walbank, F. W., *A Historical Commentary on Polybius: Vol. 1, Commentary on Books I–VI* (Oxford: Oxford University Press, 1970).

——, *A Historical Commentary on Polybius: Vol. II, Commentary on Books VII–XVIII* (Oxford: Oxford University Press, 1967).

——, *A Historical Commentary on Polybius: Vol. III, Commentary on Books XIX–XL* (Oxford: Oxford University Press, 1979).

Wallace-Hadrill, J. M., *The Barbarian West, 400–1000* (London: Hutchinson, 1952).

Ward-Perkins, B., *The Fall of Rome and the End of Civilization* (Oxford: Oxford University Press, 2005).

Wiedemann, T. E. J., 'Barbarian', in *The Oxford Classical Dictionary*, edited by Simon Hornblower, Antony Spawforth and Esther Eidinow (4th ed, Oxford: Oxford University Press, 2012).

Wiegels, R. and W. Woesler (eds), *Arminius und die Varusschlacht: Geschichte, Mythos, Literatur* (Paderborn: Schöningh, 2003).

Woolf, G., *Tales of the Barbarians: Ethnography and Empire in the Roman West* (Blackwell Bristol Lectures on Greece, Rome and the Classical Tradition (Chichester and Malden: Wiley-Blackwell, 2011).

Yadin, Y., *Bar-Kokhba: The Rediscovery of the Legendary Hero of the Last Jewish Revolt against Imperial Rome* (London: Weidenfeld & Nicolson, 1971).

Index

INDEX

Bocchus, King of Mauretania 169, 170, 171, 172–3, 174
Boii 265
Boiorix 180, 185
Bomilcar 164, 165, 168, 169
Bonifacius 440, 459, 460–1, 461–2
Bostra 390
Boudicca 336, 337–8, 342–3
Bracari 153
Brennus 23–4, 28–9, 32, 34, 35–6
Brigantes 333, 344, 345
Britain 263, 327–46, 365, 404–6, 423, 425, 440, 456
Brixia (Brescia) 446
Bruttii 62
Brutus, Lucius Iunius 19
Burebistas 368
Burgundiones 394, 455
Buteo, Marcus Fabius 96
Butheric 417
Byzacena 463
Byzantine Empire 468

Cabeira, Battle of 233
Cadmean victories 70, 102
Cadmus 70
Cadurci 264
Caecilius, Gaius 322
Caecina Severus, Aulus 319
Caecus, Appius Claudius 71
Caedicius, Lucius 317
Caepio, Quintus Servilius 149, 151, 152, 153, 154–5, 180–1, 181
Caesar, Julius 235, 244, 257, 279, 281, 285, 308, 310, 311, 368
  assassination of 290
  in Britain 263, 327–8, 331–2, 334–5, 340–1
  and Cleopatra VII 285, 289–90, 292, 298, 300
  Gallic campaigns 259–77, 306
Caesar, Lucius Julius 197
Caesar, Lucius Pomponius Germanicus 322
Caesarion 290, 294, 295, 300
Calcedonii 345, 365
Calgacus 345–6
Calidius, Quintus 231
Caligula, Gaius Caesar, Emperor 323, 331, 332, 349, 350
Callaici 152
camels 233, 250
Camillus, Marcus Furius 32–3, 34, 35, 36, 50, 51, 56, 57, 58
Camulodunum (Colchester) 332, 336, 337–8
Canidius, Publius 301
Cannae, Battle of 101, 102, 118
Canuleius, Gaius 50
Capito, Gaius Ateius 245

Cappadocia 224, 225, 226, 230, 385
Capsa (Gafsa) 171
Caracalla, Emperor 378–9, 454
Caratacus 332, 333–4, 344
Carbo, Gnaeus Papirius 178
Carians xxxiii
Carnutes 263
Carpetania 151–2
Carrhae 253, 387
Carrhae, Battle of 254–5, 304, 375
Cartagena 105, 136
Carthage, Carthaginians 73, 74, 75, 76, 85–102, 104–13, 130–1, 132, 462
Cartimandua, queen of the Brigantes 333, 343–4
Carus, Emperor 395
Cassander of Macedon 65
Cassiodorus, Magnus Aurelius 406–7
Cassius, Gaius Avidius 377
Cassius Longinus, Gaius 249, 250–1, 254, 257
Catalaunian Fields, Battle of the 446
Cato the Elder 109, 126, 130–1, 132, 134, 243
Catulus, Gaius Lutatius 92
Catulus, Quintus Lutatius 184
Catus, Decianus 336
Catuvellauni 332
Caudex, Appius Claudius 91
Caudinus, Lucius Cornelius Lentulus 78, 81
Cave of Letters, Judaea 363
Celtiberians 94, 137, 145, 155, 181
Celtillus 263
Celts 24, 260, 306
  see also Gaul, Gauls
Cenabum (Orléans) 263, 265, 445
censuses 78
Cerialis, Quintus Petillius 338, 344–5
Chaeronea, Battle of 228–9
Chalcedon, Battle of 232
chariots 339–41
Chariovalda 320
Chase-Riboud, Barbara 280–1
Chatti 319, 322, 365–7
Chauci 321
Cherusci 314, 319, 320, 321, 322, 323, 367
children, Roman 47, 50
Christian persecutions 360, 385, 400, 461
Cicero 9–10, 89, 135, 189, 192, 198, 201, 232, 235–6, 289, 290, 426
Cilicia 225, 234, 236, 385
Cimbri 175–81, 183–4, 185, 274, 306
Cimmerian Bosphorus 177
Cineas 68, 71, 74
Cirta 162, 163, 169
Cisalpine Gaul 259, 264
Classicanus, Gaius Julius Alpinus 343
Claudian 329, 418, 420, 422, 423

INDEX

INDEX